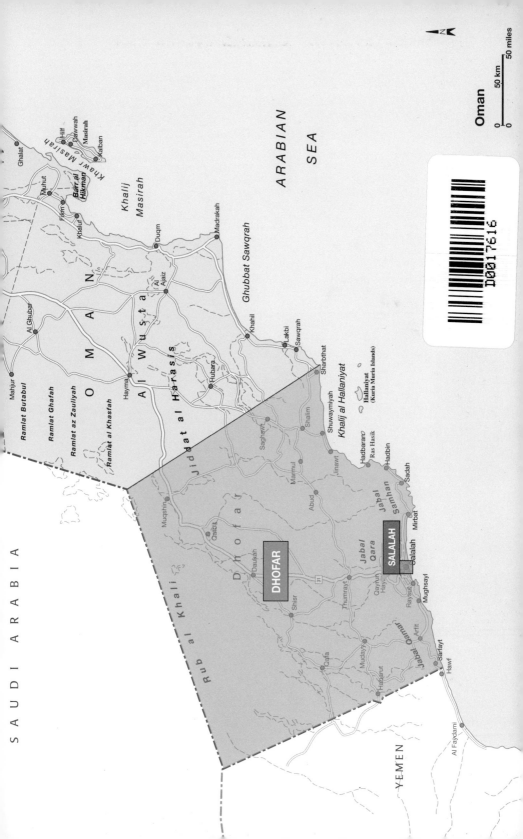

INSIGHT ⊙ GUIDES

OMAN AND THE UAE

www.insightguides.com/Oman

⊙ Walking Eye App

Your Insight Guide now includes a free app and eBook, dedicated to your chosen destination, all included for the same great price as before. They are available to download from the free Walking Eye container app in the App Store and Google Play. Simply download the Walking Eye container app to access the eBook and app dedicated to your purchased book. The app features an up-to-date A to Z of travel tips, information on shops, activities and destination highlights, as well as hotel, restaurant and bar listings. See below for more information and how to download.

MULTIPLE DESTINATIONS AVAILABLE

Now that you've bought this book you can download the accompanying destination app and eBook for free. Inside the Walking Eye container app, you'll also find a whole range of other Insight Guides destination apps and eBooks, all available for purchase.

DEDICATED SEARCH OPTIONS

Use the different sections to browse the places of interest by category or region, or simply use the 'Around me' function to find places of interest nearby. You can then save your selected restaurants, bars and activities to your Favourites or share them with friends using email, Twitter and Facebook.

Contents

FREQUENTLY UPDATED LISTINGS

Restaurants, bars and hotels change all the time. To ensure you get the most out of your guide, the app features all of our favourites, as well as the latest openings, and is updated regularly. Simply update your app when you receive a notification to access the most current listings available.

Shopping in Oman still revolves around the traditional souks that can be found in every town in the country — most famously at Mutrah in Muscat, Salalah and Nizwa, which serve as showcases of traditional Omani craftsmanship and produce ranging from antique khanjars and Bedu jewellery to halwa, rose-water and frankincense. Muscat also boasts a number of modern malls, although these are rare elsewhere in the country.

TRAVEL TIPS & DESTINATION OVERVIEWS

The app also includes a complete A to Z of handy travel tips on everything from visa regulations to local etiquette. Plus, you'll find destination overviews on shopping, sport, local events, health, children's activities and more.

HOW TO DOWNLOAD THE WALKING EYE

Available on purchase of this guide only.
1. Visit our website: www.insightguides.com/walkingeye
2. Download the Walking Eye container app to your smartphone (this will give you access to both the destination app and the eBook)
3. Select the scanning module in the Walking Eye container app
4. Scan the QR code on this page — you will be asked to enter a verification word from the book as proof of purchase
5. Download your free destination app* and eBook for travel information on the go

* Other destination apps and eBooks are available for purchase separately or are free with the purchase of the Insight Guide book

THE BEST OF OMAN AND THE UAE: TOP ATTRACTIONS

From ultra-modern cities to time-warped mudbrick mountain villages, here are some of the top attractions that Oman and the UAE have to offer.

△ **Old Dubai.** Wander through the endless souks, traditional houses and wind towers of old Dubai, lined up along either side of the bustling Creek, still busy with old-fashioned wooden dhows. See page 195.

△ **Salalah.** A world away from the rest of Oman, Salalah is at its most memorable during the annual *khareef* (monsoon), when the surrounding mountains turn a verdant green. See page 163.

▽ **Burj al Arab.** The modern Gulf's most iconic landmark, the sail-shaped Burj al Arab rises majestically above the coast of southern Dubai – stunning by day, and even more spectacular after dark. See page 208.

△ **Sheikh Zayed Grand Mosque.** Abu Dhabi's most dramatic sight: a huge snow-white mosque, topped by dozens of domes and soaring minarets, and opulently decorated inside with vast carpets and chandeliers. See page 187.

△ **Sharjah Museums and Galleries.** Self-styled "cultural capital" of the UAE, Sharjah boasts an excellent array of museums and galleries, covering everything from Arabic calligraphy to antique aeroplanes. See page 213.

△ **Musandam Peninsula.** The mountains of Arabia at their most dramatic, as the red-rock Hajar mountains go tumbling down into the sea, creating a spectacular sequence of sheer cliffs and steep-sided *khawr*s. See page 173.

▷ **Jabrin Fort.** The finest of Oman's 500-odd forts, with beautifully restored interiors offering a tantalising glimpse into the life of the country's former rulers. See page 146.

◁ **Mutrah Souk, Muscat.** The biggest and most absorbing souk in the region, stuffed full of tiny shops selling all manner of traditional produce from honey to frankincense. See page 122.

▽ **Nizwa and the Western Hajar.** Oman's most historic city, with a magnificent fort and atmospheric souks tucked away in the lee of the craggy Western Hajar mountains. See page 141.

△ **Sharqiya Sands.** Magnificent stretch of untamed desert, with huge wind-blown dunes dotted with occasional hardy shrubs and trees or even hardier Bedu. See page 155.

THE BEST OF OMAN AND THE UAE: EDITOR'S CHOICE

Watch locals bargaining over goats in Nizwa, hike around Jabal Shams's spectacular Balcony Walk, or recline on the beach in Dubai sipping cocktails in the shade of a five-star palace – just a few of the region's hugely varied attractions.

Sheikh Zayed Grand Mosque.

TOP TRADITIONAL ATTRACTIONS

Friday Market, Nizwa. Colourful weekly market in historic Nizwa, with hundreds of robed locals haggling over goats, cows and other livestock. See page 143.

Sultan Qaboos Grand Mosque, Muscat. Vast modern mosque in contemporary Islamic style, with richly decorated interiors. See page 126.

Dhow Wharfage, Dubai. Hundreds of superb old wooden dhows moor up along the Creek, with cargo piled high on the adjacent waterfront. See page 202.

Women's Souk, Ibra. Lively traditional women-only souk, particularly popular amongst colourfully attired local Bedu ladies. See page 157.

At the animal market, Nizwa.

BEST SOUKS AND SHOPPING

Al Husn Souk, Salalah. Fragrant souk in old Salalah, particularly famous for its superb array of local frankincense. See page 164.

East Souk, Nizwa. Atmospheric cluster of neatly restored traditional souk buildings. See page 143.

Al Arsa Souk, Sharjah. Quaint little souk in the heart of Sharjah's Heritage Quarter, with narrow alleyways lined with quirky shops. See page 215.

Gold and Spice Souks, Dubai. Dubai's two most colourful souks, with shop windows full of gold and sacks loaded full of herbs and spices. See pages 200 and 202.

Ibn Battuta Mall, Dubai. Weird and wonderful modern mall with extravagant decor themed after the travels of Ibn Battuta. See page 210.

Central Market Souk, Abu Dhabi. A stunning, postmodern souk designed by Norman Foster, opened in 2014. See page 185.

At Dubai's Spice Souk.

BEST MOUNTAIN EXPERIENCES

Wadi Bani Awf. Oman's classic off-road drive, descending from the heights of the Hajar mountains down the precipitous Wadi Bani Awf. See page 144.

Al Hoota Cave. Walk into the depths of this vast cave, strung with stalactites, in the depths of the Western Hajar mountains. See page 144.

The Balcony Walk. The most spectacular hike in the region, running around the edge of a vast natural bowl below the towering Jabal Shams. See page 145.

Snake Gorge. Hop over boulders and wade through pools on one of Oman's classic adventure hikes. See page 144.

Jabal Akhdar. Marvellous mountain plateau, dotted with a string of traditional villages sitting high above the great natural chasm of Wadi Al Ayn. See page 141.

Tawi Atayr and Taiq Sinkhole. A pair of vast, cavernous sinkholes in the uplands of the remote Dhofar mountains. See page 166.

Beehive tombs, Bat.

BEST CULTURAL ATTRACTIONS

Dubai Museum, Dubai. In the historic old Al Fahidi Fort, and offering an excellent overview of local history, culture and commerce. See page 197.

Jumeirah Mosque Tour, Dubai. The only mosque in the city open to non-Muslims, with informative tours hosted by local Emirati guides. See page 207.

Sharjah Museum of Islamic Civilisation. Superb modern museum highlighting Islamic contributions to science, art and architecture. See page 216.

Al Fahidi Historical Neighbourhood, Dubai. Wonderful old Iranian quarter (formerly known as Bastakiya), stuffed with fine old mansions topped with dozens of wind towers. See page 198.

Royal Opera House, Muscat. Oman's premier venue for music and performing arts. See page 125.

Bait al Zubair, Muscat. Absorbing museum covering the traditional arts and crafts of Oman. See page 121.

Bronze Age Tombs, Bat and Al Ayn. Enigmatic clusters of beautifully preserved beehive tombs, dotted across the mountainous fringes of the Western Hajar. See page 147.

Sheikh Zayed Grand Mosque, Abu Dhabi. Monumental modern mosque, whose cluster of snow-white domes and soaring minarets rise high above southern Abu Dhabi. See page 187.

Saadiyat Cultural District, Abu Dhabi. The city's shining new home to five outstanding museums, including the much-anticipated Louvre Abu Dhabi. See page 187.

COAST, BEACHES AND DESERT

Diving and snorkelling in Musandam. The best diving and snorkelling in the region, amidst some of Oman's finest natural scenery. See page 242.

Boat trip through Khawr Sham. Traditional dhows make daily tours of the stunning fjord, with pods of playful dolphins for company en route. See page 175.

Turtle-watching at Ras al Jinz. Dozens of green turtles heave themselves up onto this beach nightly to lay their eggs. See page 154.

Dune-bashing in the Sharqiya Sands. Roll, bump and bounce across the sweeping dunes. See page 156.

Sur. Historic Omani port, and home to the only boatyard in the country still making traditional dhows by hand. See page 152.

Fujairah. Miles of fine golden-sand beaches, backed by the rugged Hajar mountains and offering the UAE's best snorkelling and diving. See page 227.

On a dhow cruise along the Khawr Sham, Oman.

A camel on the beach in Ajman.

ARABIA THEN AND NOW

Contrasting but complementary, Oman and
the UAE offer fascinating insights into
Arabia's past, present and possible future.

*Mutrah Corniche at night,
Muscat.*

Two of the Middle East's most absorbing destinations, Oman and the UAE offer a fascinating window into Arabia's traditional past and an exhilarating glimpse of its dynamic urban future. Images of the region are a kaleidoscopic jumble of contrasting sights, ranging from futuristic skyscrapers and super-sized shopping malls through to rustic mudbrick forts and old-fashioned wooden dhows, often within a few miles of one another.

The histories of the two countries are closely interwoven. Until recently, life in both revolved around a string of vibrant and cosmopolitan coastal ports – Muscat, Dubai, Sharjah, Sur, to name just a few – while inland, tribes of hardy Bedu eked a meagre living out of the deserts and mountains of the interior.

*Football fans at Al Rashid stadium,
Dubai.*

The discovery of oil in the 1960s changed all that, bringing modest prosperity to Oman, unimaginable wealth to Abu Dhabi, and providing the funds to help kickstart Dubai's dramatic growth. The contrasts between the two countries are now perhaps more obvious than their shared historical roots. Parts of the UAE (Dubai especially) have thrown themselves headlong into the modern world, embracing business and tourism with kamikaze gusto. Oman, by contrast, has taken a much more circumspect approach to Western values, modernising by slow and careful degrees.

For the visitor, the two countries offer contrasting but interestingly complementary experiences. The modern UAE is largely contemporary in appearance (although fascinating pockets of history remain), and many of the country's headline attractions – the ultra-modern cityscapes of Dubai in particular – are very much of our time.

By contrast, much of Oman's appeal is entirely natural: from the unforgettably dramatic Hajar mountains through to vast swathes of uninhabited desert and unspoilt beaches frequented by nesting turtles, with dolphins splashing in the waters offshore. Oman is also particularly rich in reminders of Arabia's past, with hundreds of venerable old forts, watchtowers and traditional mudbrick villages scattered across the country, nestled amidst date plantations and watered by traditional *falaj* irrigation channels.

Trekking up Wadi Halfayn in the Jabal Al Akhdar mountains, Oman.

LAND AND ENVIRONMENTS

From vast sand dunes to rugged mountains and palm-fringed coast, Oman and the UAE boast a surprisingly varied range of landscapes.

The common perception of the Arabian peninsula as a vast expanse of empty desert doesn't do justice to the natural variety of the UAE and, especially, Oman, and the range of landscapes and environments can come as something of a surprise to first-time visitors – the sight of the verdant mountains of Dhofar during the annual *khareef* (monsoon), for instance, could hardly be further from the desert stereotype, while the craggy Hajar mountains and the often verdant coastlines of Oman, swathed in endless date plantations, also challenge received opinions.

The range of natural landscapes in turn support a surprisingly wide array of flora and fauna, ranging from the hardy frankincense trees of the Dhofar mountains through to the African birdlife found along the coast, and a range of elusive mammals including the Arabian oryx and the Arabian leopard, often talked about, but very rarely seen. The coastal waters, too, are rich in marine life, including pods of frolicking dolphins in Musandam, Muscat and elsewhere, through to the whales and thousands of turtles which continue to frequent the southern coast of Oman.

Sharqiya Sands dunes.

The deserts

Much of the interior of the UAE and Oman is desert, although this single word covers a multitude of subtly varying landscapes. The sandy deserts which are synonymous with the Arabian peninsula in the imagination of many can be found here, although they cover only a relatively small portion of the country. The magnificent dunes of the Sharqiya Sands – known to geographers as an erg (or "sand sea", derived from the Arabic *arq*) – are the most notable example, while extensive dunes

can also be found around Al Ain and in the northern UAE around Ras al Khaimah. To experience the region's finest dune formations, however, you'll have to visit the remote Rub al Khali (Empty Quarter) in the far southwest of Oman. Many of the interior deserts, however, are stony rather than sandy (technically a "hamada" or "reg"): bare, windswept plains covered in a mix of gravel and rock, supporting scant, hardy vegetation.

Coastal deserts also ring the seaboard of much of southern Oman, comprising a variety of sand, gravel and *sabkha* (salt-flats) landscapes, backed by cliff and rock formations sometimes moulded into surreal shapes by the combined effects of wind, sand and sea.

The mountains

Mountains cover only a relatively small part of the UAE and Oman, but provide many of the region's most stunning landscapes. The principal range is the mighty Hajar, which runs parallel to the coast down the east side of the peninsula, starting in Musandam, running south through Fujairah before re-entering Oman and running down past Muscat almost to the southeasternmost tip of the country – major peaks (running north to south) include Jabal Harim in Musandam (2,087 metres/6,487ft), Jabal Hafeet (1,249 metres/4,098ft) above Al Ain in the UAE, and Jabal Shams near Nizwa, the highest peak in either country (3,005 metres/9,859ft).

The name Hajar (meaning "stone") could hardly be more appropriate, given the mountains' lack of tree cover or any other surface vegetation, with vast slabs of rock laid bare, exposing millions of years of geological activity with textbook clarity. Most of the range is made up of various types of limestone, including older grey and yellow formations through to outcrops of so-called geological "exotics" – pale, whitish "islands" of younger

Sunset at Rub al Khali, Empty Quarter.

OMAN'S GEOLOGY

Oman is one of the world's most rewarding geological destinations, the Hajar mountains particularly. Much of Oman's spectacular mountain scenery derives from its location at the southeastern corner of the Arabian continental plate where it meets the Eurasian oceanic plate. As the Red Sea grows wider, Oman is being pushed slowly north and forced underneath the Eurasian plate, a massive tectonic shunt which has created the long mountainous chain of the Hajar. The various rock strata exposed on the towering cliff faces of Wadi Bani Kharus in Oman are particularly famous, showing formations spanning over 500 million years, from the Cretaceous period to the Late Proterozoic era.

Most of the rocks which now make up the Hajar mountains were actually formed underwater – as can be seen from the incongruous submarine fossils which dot the summit of Jabal Harim in Musandam. As the Arabian plate was forced beneath the Eurasian, large swathes of submarine rock were pushed up on top of the mainland. These include Oman's ophiolites: rocks formed in the oceanic crust which have been lifted above water – of particular interest to geologists as they reveal processes normally buried kilometres beneath the sea. They also provide Oman with the low, crumbling red-rock mountains which you can see along the Sumail Gap, around the Rustaq Loop and in many parts of the Eastern Hajar.

limestone, such as Jabal Misht and Jabal Khawr, respectively north and south of Al Ayn in Oman. Wadis are a characteristic feature of the Hajar, which boasts many spectacular examples, ranging from the broad wadis Sumail and Jizzi which cross the range from the coast to the interior, through to sheer-sided, needle-thin gorges such as Wadi Bimah (Snake Gorge).

In the far south of Oman lie the almost equally spectacular Dhofar mountains, encircling the city of Salalah on the coast – particularly striking during the annual *khareef*, when rain and mist descend on the heights, turning them a verdant green and creating rushing rivers and waterfalls amidst the usually parched landscape.

Human geography

The human geography of the region has been largely moulded by its physical contours. Not surprisingly, the densest population areas have grown up around the coastal areas in both Oman and the UAE, while the barren interior was (and still largely is) relatively unpopulated – the Al Ain/Buraimi conurbation straddling the border between the two countries is still the only really substantial inland city in the region, and inland towns are mainly restricted to oasis areas such as Al Ain and Liwa, or those with particular strategic military or mercantile significance, such as Nizwa and Ibra. Population levels around the coast have always been much higher, with towns developing around convenient creeks or natural harbours in places like Dubai, Sharjah, Ajman, Muscat and Sur.

Settlement into the region came from two major directions: a first wave of Arabs (known as Qahtani or Yamani – literally "Yemeni") from the Ma'rib region in what is now Yemen, and a second wave of Arabs (known as Adnani or Nizari) from the Nejd, in what is now central Saudi Arabia. Arabs of Adnani stock largely make up the current indigenous population of the UAE, while Oman is split between Adnani- and Qahtani-descended tribes. Tensions between the two ethnic groups have coloured Omani history right up until the early 20th century, and remain an important marker of cultural identity, while physical evidence of the contrasting origins of the two groups can still be seen.

In addition, large migrations by sea from Persia resulted in extensive settlements down the Batinah coast in Oman since antiquity, whilst much more recent influxes of Iranian and Indian settlers in the UAE, and a deluge of expats across the region, has had a further dramatic effect on the human topography of the region.

The divide between coast and interior still persists in many ways – the coast remains far more cosmopolitan, liberal and multicultural, as it always has been, while the interior remains relatively conservative.

A friendly face in Oman.

Wildlife

Despite its largely arid and inhospitable environment, the UAE and, particularly, Oman support an unexpectedly wide range of animal life – scientific surveys have discovered no fewer than 200 species of mammal, reptile and bird even amidst the waterless dunes of the Sharqiya Sands. The rugged Hajar mountains are where you'll find many of the region's most distinctive species, including the shaggy tahr and the legendary Arabian leopard, while inland, the desert plains are home to the majestic Arabian oryx and occasional herds of gazelle. Coastal lagoons and salt-flats support sizeable populations of migratory birds, while the offshore waters are rich in sea life, including exceptional numbers of turtles, dolphins and whales.

Around 75 species of mammal can be found in the region, although almost all are rare and seldom seen in the wild. Perhaps the most famous is the Arabian leopard, while the deserts of southern Oman support populations of various small and medium-sized antelopes. Of these, the best known is the Arabian oryx (or white oryx; *Oryx leucoryx*; in Arabic, *al maha*). This has become one of the iconic animals of Oman – and, indeed, of other countries around the Gulf: one hypothesis suggests that the oryx is in fact the mythical unicorn itself, given that its two long horns can easily merge into one when the animal is seen in profile. Living in herds of around 10 to 15 animals, the remarkably strong and hardy oryx is perfectly adapted to desert life, and capable of going without water for months, surviving entirely on moisture contained in foliage. Other resident antelopes include the Arabian gazelle (or mountain gazelle; *Gazella gazella*) and the less common reem gazelle (or sand gazelle; *Gazella subgutturosa marica*).

> *Arabian oryx and other rare mammals can be seen at the Dubai Desert Conservation Reserve (www.ddcr.org), between Dubai and Al Ain, either by visiting on a day trip from Dubai or staying at the luxurious Al Maha Desert Resort, within the reserve itself.*

The rare Arabian tahr (*Arabitragus jayakari*) is a mix of antelope and goat, with thick curved horns and a dense woolly fleece. It's now extremely rare in the wild, clinging to a few remote spots in the mountains. The Nubian ibex (*Capra ibex nubiana*) is another rare goat-antelope – males sport particularly impressive curved horns, reaching up to a metre in length. Other mammals (all similarly rare) include canine species such as the Arabian wolf, striped hyena and Blanford's fox, and small felines such as the caracal, Gordon's wild cat (or sandcat) and the prettily named but surprisingly ferocious honey badger. Rodents include the colourful Indian-crested porcupine and the small hyrax.

Birdlife is also plentiful in the region, thanks to its location on migratory routes between Europe, Asia and Africa, attracting a wide range of visiting birds, some of which also breed here – of the nearly 500 species of bird recorded in Oman, only 85 are actually permanent residents. Mountains, coast and desert all have their characteristic avian residents. Dhofar and southern Oman are particularly rich in birdlife (see page 160). Elsewhere, large numbers of migratory aquatic birds frequent the coastal lagoons and creeks, including herons, sandpipers, plovers and

An Arabian oryx.

flamingos, which can be seen even close to central Dubai itself at the Ras al Khor bird sanctuary, as well as in many other locations around the region. Common birds of prey include the majestic Egyptian vulture, often seen surfing the thermals above the Hajar mountains. For further information about the birds of Oman, visit www.birdsoman.com, run by local experts Hanne and Jens Eriksen.

Oman's extensive coastline and relatively unspoilt marine environment also play host to an outstanding array of marine life, including numerous dolphins (spinner dolphins being the most frequently sighted, while common, bottlenose and humpback dolphins can also be found) and no fewer than 20 species of cetaceans including blue, humpback, sperm and Bryde's whales, as well as false killer whales, killer whales and whale sharks. Four of the seven main species of marine turtle also nest in Oman (green, olive ridley, hawksbill and loggerhead).

Environmental issues

The environment of the region is under increasing threat, in the UAE especially. Although the UAE has finally lost its inglorious title as the country with the largest per capita environmental footprint in the world

been estimated that the Burj Khalifa requires cooling energy equivalent to that provided by 10,000 tonnes of melting ice per day, while Ski Dubai keeps its snow frozen in the middle of the desert at a similarly vast energy cost. Dubai and Abu Dhabi's innumerable skyscrapers are also particularly energy-inefficient, while the cost of greening large swathes of desert in Abu Dhabi emirate (a particular passion of the late Sheikh Zayed) similarly consumes vast quantities of water, as do the myriad golf courses and swimming pools around the country. Possible environmental

A pair of Egyptian vultures.

and is increasingly more aware of the need to conserve resources, it still ranks high on the list of most environmentally wasteful countries on the planet. The need for year-round air-conditioning and the lack of natural water supplies (drinking water has to be created using extremely energy-intensive desalination techniques) are both partly to blame, as is the country's car-centred culture (featuring, typically, huge, petrol-hungry 4x4s) and scant public transport. The fact that utilities like water and electricity are so heavily subsidised as to be virtually free to UAE nationals hardly encourages conservation of resources either.

Major landmarks and other attractions also burn up a prodigious amount of fuel: it's

problems associated with the construction of the vast Palm Jumeirah in Dubai have been widely publicised, while preliminary work on the Palm Jabal Ali involved burying an entire national marine park under the island's foundations. Ironically, despite its still considerable oil reserves, Dubai now actually consumes more energy than it produces. Thankfully it has now started setting green economy targets, and wants 5 percent of its energy to come from solar power by 2020.

Ironically, it is Abu Dhabi which has for once out-thought its neighbour, headlined by the new Masdar project, a low-rise, carbon-neutral development which will eventually serve as home to some 50,000 people (see page 97).

DECISIVE DATES

c.5000–3000 BC
Evidence of coastal and inland settlements.

c.3000 BC
Magan, an area roughly corresponding with the UAE and northern Oman, supplies the city states of southern Mesopotamia with a range of raw materials, including copper.

c.2500–2000 BC
Umm an Nar period, characterised by elaborate tombs, far-reaching trade networks and sophisticated crafts.

c.2000 BC–1st millennium BC
Arab tribes arrive from southwest and central Arabia. They find coastal communities and inland wadis inhabited by people of Persian origin.

1300–300 BC
The Iron Age; development of the *falaj* system.

563 BC
Cyrus the Great from Persia conquers Oman, founding the Achaemenid dynasty.

300 BC
The region is part of a trade network involving the whole of the Arabian peninsula, while

Petroglyphs carved into rock, Musandam.

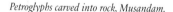

frankincense is exported from southern Oman to Greece and Rome.

1st century AD
The *Periplus of the Erythraean Sea*, a description of trade around the coast of the Indian Ocean, designates Oman as Persian.

AD 226–640
The Sassanid period. Persian seamen control sea trade.

630
Islam is brought to Oman.

751
Oman elects its first Imam, Julanda bin Mas'ud.

8th–9th centuries
Arab seafaring and trading are at their height, with voyages as far as China.

10th century
Sohar in Oman is a hub of maritime trade.

14th century
Hormuz, an island off modern-day Iran, controls the mouth of the Gulf.

16th century
The Portuguese dominate trade in the Gulf and the

Overlooking Nizwa mosque.

Indian Ocean, capturing Muscat in 1507.

1624–1738
Ya'ruba dynasty rules Oman.

1646
Commercial treaty is signed between Oman's Imam and the British East India Company.

1650
Imam Sultan bin Saif expels the Portuguese.

1718–28
Civil war in Oman.

1730s
Saif bin Sultan II of Oman invites the Persians to help him secure his bid to be Imam.

1742
The Persians take control of Muscat.

1747
Ahmed bin Said drives the Persians from Oman and establishes the Al bu Said dynasty.

Painting of Sheikh Zayed at the Al Ain Palace Museum, Abu Dhabi.

1761
Abu Dhabi is founded.

1820
A British campaign to quash Qawasim "pirates" culminates in the razing of Ras al Khaimah and other Qawasim ports, including Sharjah, Umm al Qaiwain, Ajman and Lingah. British involvement in the Emirates begins.

1830s
The pearl trade is at its height.

1833
Dubai's Bani Yas sets up its own principality, ruled by the Al Maktoum family.

1853
In return for ceasing hostilities at sea, the British guarantee to protect the Trucial States from external attack.

1892
The Exclusive Agreement is signed with Britain, preventing the rulers of the Trucial Coast from forming agreements with any other foreign government.

1930s
The pearl industry declines following the arrival of the Japanese cultured pearl.

1932
Imperial Airways (later British Airways) begins air service to Sharjah.

1936–52
The rulers of the Trucial States sign oil concessions with the Iraq Petroleum Company.

1951
A causeway is built linking Abu Dhabi to the mainland.

1952
Saudis occupy part of Buraimi, but are eventually (1955) driven out.

1954–9
Imamate rebellion under Ghalib ibn Ali in Oman.

1959
Oil is discovered in Abu Dhabi.

1962–75
Dhofar Rebellion in Oman.

1967
Oman produces oil in commercial quantities.

1970
Accession of Sultan Qaboos bin Said in Oman.

1971
Britain withdraws from the Gulf. The United Arab Emirates is inaugurated on 2 December.

1973
Oman's first airport, Seeb International, opens.

1980
Iran–Iraq War.

1990
Iraq invades Kuwait. Gulf War ensues.

1991
Oman's Majlis Ash Shura, a consultative council with 59 elected members, is inaugurated.

1995
Oman celebrates Sultan Qaboos's silver jubilee.

2004
Death of Sheikh Zayed bin Sultan Al Nahyan, president of the UAE.

2008
Credit crunch hits the Middle East. Dubai is nearly bankrupt.

2010
Opening of Burj Khalifa, the world's tallest building.

2011
"Arab Spring" sweeps through Middle East. Clashes in Oman leave several protesters dead.

2015
Both Oman and the UAE continue to crack down on freedom of expression, harassing critics of government and pro-reform activists.

A mural of Sultan Qaboos, Muscat.

ARCHAEOLOGY

Recent archaeological explorations of Oman and the
UAE have revealed a rich and varied ancient history.

If there is a general perception that the south-east corner of the Arabian peninsula has, until recent times, been relatively isolated, nothing could be further from the truth. From as early as 5000 BC, the area played an important part in the development of the ancient civilisations of the Middle East.

There are practically no historical documents originating from the UAE and Oman prior to the Islamic period, though there are references to the region by neighbouring peoples and trading partners from as early as c.2330 BC. Unfortunately these are few and far between, so the historical framework used by archaeologists is based primarily on the results of excavations.

Prehistoric prelude (5000–3000 BC)

Many of the earliest archaeological sites lie along the shores of the Arabian Gulf and the Gulf of Oman. Until about 16,000 years ago, when sea levels began to rise, the area now occupied by the Gulf would have formed a river valley extending as far as the Strait of Hormuz. The shoreline of the Gulf of Oman would have been distant from its present location and 100–150 metres (330–490ft) lower than the present-day mean sea level. When the sea level began to rise it attained something like its present level about 8,000 years ago, creating a variety of coastal landscapes. These varied marine habitats afforded a glut of easily obtained food such as shellfish, fish, turtle and dugong. Mangroves attracted birdlife which could be hunted, and adjacent inland areas supported gazelle and, later on, grazing for sheep, goats and cattle.

The archaeological remains left by these early communities are distinguished by large accumulations of shells that were collected for food and then discarded. Excavation of "shell

Sumhuram archaeological site.

middens" at Ras al Hamra near Qurm has revealed the ground plan of small groups of circular buildings, indicated by stone foundations or arrangements of post-holes. Other finds show that the inhabitants were adept at making stone tools and shell artefacts, including personal jewellery and large shell hooks. Such items were often found amongst burials, which form large cemeteries and hint at the social complexity of the fishing communities.

On the Gulf Coast similar shell middens are found along the margins of former lagoons, for example at Umm al Qaiwain and the Hamriyah area of Sharjah. Some of the Gulf Coast middens have also provided evidence of contact with southern Iraq from 5000–4000 BC, in particular a type of pottery called Ubaid, named after a site in southern Iraq. The pottery was clearly imported at this early date, though whether directly or indirectly has not been confirmed. However, similar finds on the island of Dalma (Abu Dhabi) suggest that the inhabitants were already accomplished sailors by this time.

Coastal midden sites were occupied up to and beyond 3000 BC. Prior to this it is probable that the arid conditions of Arabia today were not so harsh and that open grassland was available. Many of the stone tools, including finely crafted arrowheads, found in desert areas probably date from 5000–3000 BC and represent inland hunting and herding communities contemporary with the coastal communities.

The Hafeet period (3000–2500 BC)

From around 3000 BC there is evidence of renewed contact between the region and southern Mesopotamia. In the late 4th millennium BC there are references in Mesopotamian texts to a place named Dilmun (now Bahrain), and towards the end of the 3rd millennium, c. 2330 BC Dilmun is mentioned along with Magan and Meluhha.

Between them, these three places supplied the city-states of southern Mesopotamia with a range of raw materials and exotic goods, including timber, stone and, above all, copper. On the basis of the abundance of copper deposits, and archaeological evidence that they were being exploited as early as the 3rd millennium BC, Magan, sometimes referred to in texts as "the Copper Mountain of Magan", is thought to be the area of southeast Arabia which loosely corresponds with the present-day UAE and Oman. Meluhha is generally identified as the Indus Valley.

Renewed contacts with Mesopotamia from the end of the 4th millennium are an indication of Magan's developing trading relations with surrounding countries, as described some 700 years later in Mesopotamian texts. Evidence includes pottery imported from Mesopotamia found in tombs.

These tombs are of a type unique to the UAE and Oman at this time, when they became a conspicuous feature of the landscape – large stone cairns, often placed in clearly visible groups along the ridges or summit of a mountain to form a dramatic skyline. Tombs of this type were first excavated at Jabal Hafeet near Al Ain and are often called "Hafeet tombs". Others have a characteristic beehive shape and are

consequently called "beehive tombs". Both the Hafeet and beehive tombs date from the end of the 4th millennium to c. 2500 BC.

These tombs indicate the probable distribution of settlement, and there is evidence that a farming, oasis-based economy had been introduced by this time. Excavations at the important site of Hili 8, near Al Ain, have shown that by 3000 BC agriculture was established, with wheat, barley and dates being cultivated. Crops and the herding of sheep, goats and cattle, introduced at an earlier date, as shown by some of the coastal midden sites, led to settlement in

Ancient burial chamber in the archaeological grounds at Hili, near Al Ain.

inland areas where there was sufficient water for irrigation. A settlement pattern similar to that of more recent times began to emerge, and from 2500 BC there is a clear picture of what these early settlements were like.

Umm an Nar period (2500–2000 BC)

The era from 2500–2000 BC is referred to as the Umm an Nar period, named after the small island near Abu Dhabi where excavations by Danish archaeologists first produced evidence for this period. During this time a new type of tomb was introduced. Circular and averaging about 9 metres (30ft) in diameter, it stands above ground and has a smooth exterior wall built of finely worked masonry. Some of the tombs on the island of Umm an Nar also had relief carvings on the outer wall, depicting wild animals such as gazelles and snakes, as well as domesticated animals like cattle. There are also depictions of camels, which were probably domesticated by this time.

Excavation has shown that the tombs were used for multiple burials with a range of grave goods, including pottery (some imported from Mesopotamia, Iran or the Indus), stone vessels, bronze weapons, shell rings and shell and stone beads. The most spectacular Umm an Nar tomb

excavated so far is displayed in Hili Archaeological Park, near Al Ain(see page 190). It has carvings on the outer wall of humans as well as animals.

The excavations at Hili 8, near Hili Archaeological Park, show that settlements from this period included large defensive towers. It is probable that similar towers were also built from the beginning of the 3rd millennium, and thus represent an established local tradition. The towers were probably surrounded by smaller buildings made from mudbricks and date palm wood. At Hili, Bat and Wadi Bahla towers are distributed over a large area. They

Bat Tombs, Oman.

COPPER MINING

Ancient Magan was an important supplier of stone and copper. Sites in Oman such as Maysar, in the Wadi Samad area near Nizwa, have produced clear evidence for the mining, processing and export of copper on a large scale during the 3rd millennium BC, including anvil and crushing stones, a smelting oven and copper beads and rings, chisels, knives and axes. It has been estimated that up to 4,000 tonnes of copper were produced in the region in the Umm an Nar period.

Small-scale copper mining continued in northern Oman through to the late Middle Ages and beyond. However, by the late 19th century foreign competition (principally copper sheeting imported from Bombay)

had extinguished the local mining industry.

Both stone and copper are still readily obtained in the UAE and Oman, and though oil and natural gas have dominated the economy for decades, recent attempts to reduce dependence on oil in Oman have seen a regeneration of the copper-mining industry. In 1983 a mine at Lasail, in Wadi al Jizzi near Sohar, was reworked for the first time since antiquity, and new deposits have since been found in Yanqul, north of Ibri, inland at Hatta, and on the Batinah Coast at Shinas. There are now a number of large-scale copper mines around Sohar, producing vast quantities of copper along with small quantities of gold and silver.

probably defined and defended the area of habitation and cultivation.

From the beginning of the 3rd millennium local pottery had been produced, and during the Umm an Nar period pottery and other craft industries flourished. Distinctive stone vessels

Umm an Nar tombs were crowded affairs. One of the tombs at Hili is thought to have remained in use for up to two centuries, and to store the remains of several hundred people.

Recent excavations suggest that many of the 3rd-millennium settlements continued to be occupied during the 2nd millennium. However, there are radical changes in the architecture of tombs and the range of pottery and other objects produced.

Wadi Suq period (2000–1300 BC)

At the beginning of the 2nd millennium at least two types of tomb are characteristic. The first is circular, 3–4 metres (10–13ft) in diameter, with a central, below-ground, stone-lined burial chamber. Such tombs were first excavated in

A 5,000-year-old stone tomb at Al Ayn, Oman.

were manufactured and widely distributed, not only locally, but also to places in southern Iraq, Bahrain, Iran and the Indus. Likewise, imported items continued to arrive in southeast Arabia, and the resulting distribution of exported and imported goods reflects the network of trading relations described in the Mesopotamian texts of the later 3rd millennium.

At the end of the 3rd millennium Magan ceased to be mentioned in Mesopotamian texts and Dilmun appears to have had a monopoly over the supply of goods to Mesopotamia. However, the range of exports remained much the same, with a large demand for copper, and since Dilmun had no copper sources of its own Magan probably remained the main supplier.

Wadi Suq, at the east end of Wadi Jizzi between Buraimi and Sohar in Oman. Subsequently Wadi Suq was adopted to describe the period from around 2000 to c.1300 BC.

The second type of tomb characteristic of the early Wadi Suq period was first recorded at Shimmel, near Ras al Khaimah. The Shimmel-type tombs are rectangular, a few metres wide but several metres long, and stand above ground.

Imported items continue to show ongoing trading links with surrounding countries, and coastal settlements, particularly Ras al Jinz near Ras al Hadd in Oman, which appears to have flourished during the Umm an Nar and Wadi Suq periods, provide evidence for the highly developed maritime trade of this period.

The Iron Age (c.1300–300 BC)

The Iron Age saw an increase in the number and variety of settlements, which may have been due to the development of the *falaj* system of irrigation. Coastal middens continued to be occupied, villages evolved along the courses of wadis in mountainous areas, and there is evidence of larger villages of mudbrick houses, as excavated at Rumeilah and Hili 2 near Al Ain. There is also evidence of fortified hilltop settlements, such as at Lizq in Wadi Samad, Oman.

As in previous periods, changes are evident in the pottery and soft-stone vessels manufactured.

continuously occupied for 700 years, from the end of the Iron Age onwards. Excavations have recovered amphorae from Rhodes, alabaster vessels from the Yemen, and other imported goods. The town had a necropolis of monumental tombs, while traces of a fort, graves with sacrificed camels and horses have also been found. There is even evidence that the town was minting its own coinage.

Contemporary with this phase of occupation (the first centuries AD) is Ad Door near Umm al Qaiwain, which was probably the port for inland Mileiha. Coins of the type minted at Mileiha have been found there, as well as similar graves with

The post-Iron Age site of Ed Dur.

The discovery of distinctive vessels in neighbouring countries such as Bahrain indicates that maritime trade had become an important part of the regional economy.

The post-Iron Age period

From *c.* 300 BC, the UAE and Oman formed part of a trade network that involved the whole of the Arabian peninsula and linked the countries of the Mediterranean with those of the Indian Ocean. Dhofar became important for the supply of frankincense, and by the 1st century AD maritime trade was conducted around the entire Arabian peninsula.

One of the main sites of the period is Mileiha, south of Dhaid, which appears to have been

Wadis (the Arabic word for "valleys") are a common feature of the landscape of the UAE and Oman. Many served for millennia as important trade and migratory routes, offering relatively safe passage through otherwise perilous mountain ranges.

sacrificed camels, pottery from the eastern Mediterranean, and items from neighbouring parts of Arabia, Iraq and Iran.

In Wadi Samad there is evidence of occupation of the same date as Mileiha and Ed Dur, and a wide range of items, some similar to finds at Mileiha and Ed Dur, have been excavated.

Dhow-building in Sur, Oman.

MARITIME HERITAGE

The UAE and Oman share an illustrious seafaring
history. As early as the 8th century, trade vessels
from the Gulf were sailing all the way to China.

The Arabian peninsula is often associated
in the minds of outsiders with its desert
interior and hardy tribes of wandering
Bedu. In fact, much of the history, commerce
and culture of the UAE and Oman has actually
been played out around its coast, where a string
of lively and surprisingly cosmopolitan trading
towns grew up, establishing far-reaching connections with Persia, India, Africa and even as
far away as China. Textiles, horses, spices and
slaves were all widely traded, while the lucrative
frankincense route bought enormous wealth
to the ports of Dhofar. In more recent times
oil has largely taken the place of more picturesque goods, while the smuggling of arms,
cigarettes, gold and diamonds to Iran and India
has also played a surprisingly important role
in the economies of places like Dubai and the
Musandam peninsula.

Maritime matters continue to play a crucial
role in the contemporary life of the region, as
witnessed by the huge modern container and
tanker ports of Muscat, Sur, Sohar, Salalah,
Fujairah and Dubai. Colourful reminders of
earlier times can also be seen, most notably
at the intriguing dhow wharfages in Dubai
and Sharjah.

The pattern of trade

The Arabian peninsula stands between the
Indian Ocean and the Mediterranean, flanked
by two long seas, the Arabian Gulf (or Persian
Gulf) and the Red Sea, both of which have
historically served as channels down which
goods have travelled from the Indian Ocean
to the centres of civilisation in the Near East
and Mediterranean.

With the coming of Islam in the 7th century AD, both the Gulf and Red Sea were

An Arab passenger boat in the 13th century.

crucial to the eastern trade of the Islamic
world. But it is perhaps the Gulf which has
the more glorious commercial history of the
two, and Oman commands the Strait of Hormuz, which join it to the Indian Ocean. As
the centuries wore on, many commodities
were passed on to Europe, first through the
medium of Genoa and then Venice.

But not all the Indian Ocean trade was long-
distance. Much of it was within the Indian
Ocean itself. Over the millennia, this trading
activity brought about a tremendous mixing of
peoples around the coasts of the entire ocean
and a lot of cultural as well as commercial
exchange. The coves at Muscat and Mutrah, and
the beach at Sohar, have witnessed the comings

and goings of Mesopotamians, Persians, Arabs, Indians, Africans, Greeks, Jews, Turks, Italians, Portuguese and northern Europeans.

The antiquity of the sea route

By the time of the Greek and Roman empires, trade from Ethiopia, southwest Arabia and India into the Near East and Mediterranean was in full swing, much of it by camel caravan along the land routes of the Arabian peninsula. Gradually this trade transferred from the land routes to the Red Sea, as seafarers from Egypt, with Mediterranean ships, began

trade between Sri Lanka and the Gulf, to the detriment of the Red Sea. It was this tradition that the Arabs took over after the spread of Islam in the 7th century. The first named Arab to make the voyage to China was an Omani in AD 750.

The exploits of early Arabian sailors inspired the legendary stories of Sindbad the Sailor – claimed by Omanis to have been a native of the town of Sohar.

An illustration from the Arabian Nights tale, 'The Story of Sindbad the Sailor'.

to master the monsoon routes. By c.100 BC these interlopers had discovered that in their strongly built, square-rigged ships they could sail direct from Aden to India using the southwest monsoon, something which the Indian Ocean ships with their stitched construction were too fragile to do.

A vigorous trade developed, with merchants reaching India and China, and paying for luxury goods with Roman coin. This eventually caused a serious drain of precious metals in the Roman Empire, leading to devaluation and a slump in trade in the 3rd century BC.

When the sea trade revived, during Sassanid rule of Persia in the 5th century, it was in the hands of Persian seamen. They controlled

Medieval ships

The average Arabian seaman in pre-modern times spent his days and nights exposed to the elements, in conditions of hardship and hard work. First of all, he would have made a voyage in a smallish vessel, the planks of which were not nailed but stitched together, a mode of ship-building that came as a constant surprise to Europeans and Arabs from the Mediterranean, such as Marco Polo and the North African explorer Ibn Battuta who had first-hand experience of them.

Hull planks were stitched together edge-to-edge with coconut twine, and the ribs were fitted later – the exact opposite of European boats. Gaps were caulked with a mixture of coir and fish oil. Except in larger vessels even a partial deck or a cabin was a luxury. Ships were still pointed at both ends, and used steering oars, one on each side. The square sail had evolved into something more triangular, enabling ships to sail close to the wind, though not to tack in a modern sense.

The boat was essentially a cargo-carrying tub which needed constant maintenance. Crew and passengers accommodated themselves as best they could on top of the cargo, and ablutions were carried out in a precarious box slung out over the side of the boat. The main advan-

merchants and even contribute to the decline of a port. The rewards of a single successful voyage were correspondingly prodigious: a merchant could make his fortune for life. They would set out from the Omani coast in late November or early December and make the round trip to China in 18 months, returning with the end of the northeast monsoon in April or May. Ships sailing to India and East Africa also made use of the northeast monsoon season. The breezes of the southwest monsoon in April to May were handy on the return from East Africa, blowing the ships back to the Omani coast.

European Trading Galleons in Muttrah's Harbour, an oil painting attributed to the Dutch painter Jan Peeters (1642–80).

tage of such a craft was that it was flexible in heavy surf, and therefore less likely than more robustly built ships to be smashed while coming inshore. These fragile craft could be quite large, some carrying up to 400 men.

At the height of Gulf trade, in the 9th century, Gulf and Omani seamen were sailing all the way to China in such ships, and there was a huge colony of Arab merchants at Canton. By sailing all the way like this Arab merchants could cut out the middleman and make massive profits.

Gulf merchants' tales of the 8th–10th centuries describe hair-raising shipwrecks and adventures, and enormous mercantile risks. The loss of a single cargo could ruin a group of

By the 13th century the stern rudder was invented, but not the tiller: it was operated by a system of ropes, which allowed the rudder to be unshipped easily when the boat was beached.

By now Arab merchants were no longer sailing direct to China. Instead, the Chinese were sailing to the Malabar Coast and the Palk Strait between Ceylon and India, where goods were transhipped to Indian and Arab vessels. By the 13th century large junks could be seen in Malabar ports, and the 14th century saw the extraordinary Ming Voyages, when the Chinese in fleets of vast junks sailed around the shores of the Indian Ocean, reaching East Africa and the Omani coast at Dhofar.

These voyages stopped abruptly in the 1430s and the Chinese left the Indian ports. By the time of the European discovery of the East in 1498 their voyages were a distant memory.

The great ports

Medieval merchants set out from the great Islamic port of Basra on the Shatt al Arab in Iraq. But the large ships required to make the China run could not anchor off Basra, and so ports further down the Gulf became important points of trans-shipment – first Siraf in Persia, and then Sohar on the Omani coast.

abundance... There are wonderful markets all along the coast. Houses are high and built of teak wood and mudbricks, and there is a canal of fresh water."

Eventually Qais Island supplanted Siraf and Sohar, and by the 14th century Qais was ousted by the island of Hormuz. With its satellite ports at Qalhat in eastern Oman and Julfar near present-day Ras al Khaimah, Hormuz completely controlled the mouth of the Gulf. By the early 1500s Muscat, with its natural harbour, had supplanted Sohar and Qalhat on the Omani coast.

Portuguese carracks.

For wonderful insights into the techniques of traditional Arabian dhow building and life at sea aboard one such boat, read Tim Severin's *The Sindbad Voyage.*

Sohar flourished. It was at the point where trade from Aden and East Africa met the trade coming and going to India and China. Sohar was, as the 10th-century Arab geographer Muqaddasi observed, "the hallway to China, the storehouse of the East and Iraq, and the stay of the Yemen... There is no city bigger than this on the China Sea. It is a populous and beautiful spot, where wealth and fruits are in

Cargoes combined high-value commodities with bulk goods, because all ships need ballast. From Iraq these bulk goods were mainly dates, while the Arabian ports of the Gulf and Oman supplied dates, leather and dried fish. From East Africa the bulk goods were timber; from India, rice, dried foods, teak and other shipbuilding timber; and from China, copper cash, other metals and sugar.

But the glamour and profit were in the high-value goods, whose worth increased with every merchant and port they passed through. Oman and the Arabian shore of the Gulf provided horses, frankincense and pearls. From India and Ceylon came gemstones, glass, ironware, swords, cotton cloth, spices and aromatics such as sandalwood and incense. China's silk, porcelain, lacquerwork, metalwork and other manufactures were in big demand. In exchange,

> The arrival of Portuguese ships in the Gulf introduced profound changes to Arab shipbuilding, including nailed instead of stitched construction, square sterns and tiller-operated rudders – although shipbuilding continued to be carried out in the time-honoured way, entirely by eye.

Vasco da Gama's voyage around the Cape of Good Hope in 1498 changed the face of seafaring in the Gulf.

the Islamic lands sent glassware, carpets, muslin, brocade, perfumes, incense, weapons and armour – but also money.

Perhaps the most valuable raw commodities came from East Africa: gold, slaves, ivory, rhino horn and leopard skins. Of all the seafaring Arabs, it was the Omanis who dominated the rich East African trade, introducing its hugely prized products into the economies of the Islamic Near East.

Portuguese power

It was into East Africa, in 1498, that the first Western threat to local control of maritime trade since Greco-Roman times arrived: the Portuguese. Under Vasco da Gama the Portuguese rounded the Cape of Good Hope into the Indian Ocean in 1498, and proceeded to dominate the international trade of the Gulf and Indian Ocean for over a century. Portuguese trade was a royal monopoly carried forward by gunpowder and force of arms, and the small Portuguese fleets had an impact on the people of the Indian Ocean shores out of all proportion to their numbers. They came in search of Indian spices and the spice islands of Indonesia, and of other luxury goods which the Venetian monopoly had made so costly in Europe. Their greatest colonial visionary, Affonso d'Albuquerque, quickly realised the strategic importance of Aden, Hormuz and Malacca in the trade.

Hormuz, whose inhabitants were a mixture of Arabs and Persians, commanded the Musandam Strait, and in spite of being a waterless island had grown immensely wealthy by raising customs dues on all cargoes passing up the Gulf.

The Portuguese took Hormuz after their capture of Muscat in 1507. While they diverted some of the trade from the Far East around the Cape of Good Hope, they profited from the rest by levying customs dues on the Gulf route just as the Hormuzis had done before them. They built a line of forts along the Omani, African and Indian coasts and farther east, with Goa as their capital. Muscat, Sohar and Hormuz were key to their control of the Gulf. The twin Portuguese forts dominating Muscat's old harbour were built at this time.

The Omani Empire

The Portuguese saw off Ottoman Turkish attacks in the 16th century, but others were to come early in the 17th century from Persia, Holland, England and Oman. Unlike the Portuguese, the other European nations arrived as merchant companies wishing to trade in peace.

During the 1630s and 1640s a renascent Omani Imamate succeeded in ejecting the Portuguese from Muscat and their coastal forts. The Omanis captured Portuguese ships, and went on to establish a maritime empire. Their ships and seamen, who often included European renegades, were an equal match for those of the Portuguese, English, Dutch and French. By the end of the 17th century they had also taken control of a stretch of the East African coast down to Zanzibar and Mombasa, expelling the Portuguese. Oman became a power on parts of the Persian coast, and even at times up the Gulf as far as Bahrain.

In the mid-18th century Oman fell victim to civil war and a revived Persia under Nadir Shah, who took Muscat in 1742. But after 1744 the reunited Omanis drove out the Persians. Omani fortunes began to revive again, just as a rival sea power, the Qawasim of Sharjah and Ras al Khaimah, rose up in the southern Gulf.

between London and the Company's growing possessions in India. When Napoleon's occupation of Egypt in 1798 blocked the Red Sea route one British response was to enter into treaty relations with the Omani Sultan in Muscat, a move which inevitably placed them in opposition to the Qawasim. At the same time, the British blamed the Qawasim for the piracy that then plagued the Gulf and led a series of seaborne campaigns against the so-called "Pirate Coast". These climaxed in 1820 in the destruction of the Qasimi fleets and the first of the Maritime Truces.

A fanciful depiction of a pirate raid.

The Qasimi "pirates", 1722–1820

The Qawasim of Ras al Khaimah seized Lingah on the Persian shore following the death of Nadir Shah in 1747. The rise of their ports at Sharjah and at Ras al Khaimah, which had replaced ancient Julfar just to the north, was remarkably rapid and brought them into conflict with Omani maritime ambitions.

By 1780 the Qawasim were firmly established on the Persian side of the southern Gulf too. Very soon they began to threaten Muscat's control of the trade from India and East Africa into the Gulf.

By now the British East India Company was set to become involved. The Gulf was becoming increasingly vital to communications

British officials almost certainly exaggerated the Qawasim's involvement in piracy, but their campaign against them was determined. In 1806 the British attacked Ras al Khaimah. In 1809 Ras al Khaimah, Lingah, Luft and Shinas were burnt and ships destroyed, and Ras al Khaimah was bombarded again in 1816. Finally, between 1819 and 1820, a large naval and military operation was mounted which razed Ras al Khaimah. Its ships were destroyed, along with those of Sharjah, Umm al Qaiwain, Ajman, Lingah and other Qasimi ports.

The maritime peace, 1820–53

It was only after this expedition that maritime peace became a real prospect, and

Britain's continuous and official involvement began in what are now the Emirates. The destruction of Qasimi ports and ships was followed by a "General Treaty of Peace with the Arab Tribes" in 1820. Britain's primary aim was to pacify the seas and so secure its route to India.

The decline of the Qawasim was hastened by the growth of Abu Dhabi and Dubai as competitors on the pearl banks. Abu Dhabi had emerged only in the late 18th century and its sheikh had signed the General Treaty of Peace in 1820. Dubai too was included, but Dubai's

In 1835, the rulers of Sharjah, Dubai, Ajman and Abu Dhabi signed an inviolable truce under British pressure, outlawing acts of war at sea during the pearling season. Made year-round for 10 years in 1843, it became the Perpetual Treaty in 1853.

Perpetual peace

With the Perpetual Treaty of Peace of 1853, the rulers of the Gulf Coast agreed to cease hostilities at sea, and in return the British undertook to protect them against external attack. The British were determined not to become

Pearl divers selling seashells to the passengers of passing ships near Muscat in 1955.

real emergence as the chief trading port on the southern Gulf was due to the migration there in 1833 of the Al bu Falasah, a clan of the Bani Yas from Abu Dhabi. Its leading family, Al Maktoum, set about turning themselves into the merchant princes of the Gulf Coast, a position they have held ever since.

One long-term result of the peace was an expanding pearl trade. An ancient Gulf industry, pearling was recorded by Greek and Roman writers and probably traces its origin to the late Stone Age. Pearls are not found in abundance in Omani waters outside the Gulf, but the shallow southern Gulf off the Trucial Coast was rich in pearl oysters and the warm sea shallow enough to make diving feasible.

PEARLING

Up until the 20th century, the UAE's great natural resource was not oil, but pearls, gathered from the sea in conditions of extreme hardship and considerable danger. Diving took place in the hot summer months and boats were out at sea for up to four months at a time. The men would dive on empty stomachs (to avoid getting cramp) to depths of over 20 metres (65ft) and were vulnerable to attacks by jellyfish and sharks. By the turn of the 20th century there were about 1,200 pearling boats based in ports along the UAE coast, manned by some 22,000 men – a very considerable proportion of the population at that time.

involved in disputes on land. However, as the 1860s wore into the 1870s, the line between peace at sea and peace on land became more and more difficult to discern.

By then the Gulf's importance as a channel for imperial communications had greatly increased. In 1862 the British started a fortnightly steamer service from Bombay to Muscat and some of the Gulf ports. Equally significantly, in 1864 they laid the first submarine telegraph cable in the Gulf, running from Karachi to Bushire and Fao via the Musandam peninsula in Oman.

Oman's decline

British support to Muscat continued throughout the 19th century and into the 20th. Sultan Said (ruled 1807–56) maintained a fleet of warships and merchantmen which included European ships, and even sent one of them to New York and London in 1840 and 1842.

By the time he died in 1856 the Omani maritime realm extended once again from enclaves on the Persian coast to large stretches of the East African coast. Although hampered by Britain's anti-slaving policy, Sultan Said developed the economy of Zanzibar, which

Life on Dubai's Creek before the bridges were built across it.

THE LAST DHOWS

The coast of the UAE and Oman was once lined with dozens of dhow-building yards, turning out hundreds of boats a year for local fishermen and traders, and providing a vital element in the region's economic life. In recent years, however, the advent of modern boat-building techniques and production lines has inevitably caused this most traditional and labour-intensive of Arabian industries to decline, almost to the point of extinction, and the high cost of commissioning a new wooden dhow means that local fishermen now generally prefer more modern, albeit more functional, vessels.

Sur is now home to the last surviving traditional boatyard in Oman (see page 153), although dhow-building yards can be seen in the UAE at Dubai, Ajman, Umm al Qaiwain and Ras al Khaimah (albeit in significantly reduced circumstances compared to times past). All these places continue to produce traditional wooden dhows following time-honoured designs, meticulously crafted by hand using only the simplest of tools and offering a living link with the artisanal traditions of centuries past. Despite the boatyards' apparently bleak future, one potential lifeline has emerged in recent years with the increasing popularity of traditional dhow cruises amongst visiting tourists, meaning that the ancient traditions of Arabian boat-building may yet survive a little longer into the 21st century.

became almost a second Omani capital. After his death, the Omani Empire was split between his two sons, Thuwaini and Majid, into Oman and Zanzibar.

This split was economically damaging to Oman. Other blows to its maritime prosperity followed in quick succession. Steamships were bad enough, but the Suez Canal was opened in 1869, making the Red Sea much more important than the Gulf. In addition, the British had set about suppressing the slave and arms trades, which were lucrative sources of income for merchants and rulers in Muscat, Sur and Dubai.

The boat-building yard in Sur, the last traditional boatyard in Oman.

Oman then began a long period of economic decline which lasted right up until the 1960s, and its role in the international sea trade of the Indian Ocean all but vanished.

Great power rivalry

After 1869, rivalry among the Great Powers began to threaten Britain's position in the Gulf. The Ottomans occupied Al Hasa and Qatar in 1871, and claimed eight Trucial Coast settlements, and in 1887 a resurgent Persia took over some Qasimi territory on the Persian shore. This prompted Britain to obtain from the sheikhs of the Trucial Coast a written assurance not to correspond or agree with any other government, or to allow agents of other governments to reside in their territories.

By the early 1890s both France and Germany were trying to establish a presence in the region. In March 1892, therefore, Britain developed the 1887 assurance into an Exclusive Agreement, the basis of her relations with the Trucial States until 1971. Nonetheless, in the 1890s Russia also joined the race to seek a foothold in the Gulf.

By the end of World War I all these threats had evaporated, and Britain found itself in a position of unprecedented power in the Gulf.

20th-century developments

The first two-thirds of the 20th century were a period of long, slow decline for Oman, reflected in the steady dip in prosperity of its coastal ports – Britain's ongoing attempts to stamp out the lucrative trade in smuggled arms was particularly keenly felt. Sultan Qaboos's accession to the throne in 1970 marked a period of dramatic change and modernisation. A string of huge new modern ports were constructed at Muscat, Salalah, Sur and Sohar, both for trade and as conduits for the country's new oil exports, while more informal maritime trading networks were also established – the smuggling run between Khasab and Iran was particularly lucrative.

Smuggling also played a crucial role in the burgeoning economy of Dubai, while the country's visionary leader Sheikh Rashid commissioned vast new docks at Port Rashid and Jabal Ali, as well as a new dry dock facility – which proved particularly lucrative during the Iran–Iraq War thanks to the number of tankers damaged in the conflict which limped here for repairs. The vast port at Fujairah, the world's third-largest oil-refuelling port after Rotterdam and Singapore, was another major development.

Vestiges of the region's seafaring past survive even so, most obviously in the dhow-wharfages of Dubai and Sharjah, and in the various dhow-building yards scattered around the coast – while the region's traditional old boats have found a new lease of life as pleasure craft for tourists and locals, offering a living link between the Gulf's historic seafaring past and burgeoning economic present.

Oman's emblem of two crossed swords with a Khanjar and belt on the Palace gates, Muscat.

OMAN'S GREAT DYNASTIES

The Ya'ruba dynasty succeeded in uniting Oman and
turning it into a place of learning and elegance.
The Al bu Said turned it into an imperial power.

The history of Oman from 1624 to the present is the story of two great dynasties:
the Ya'ruba (1624–1738) and the Al Bu
Said (1742 to the present), whose leaders have
succeeded – with varying degrees of success
– in forging the disparate tribes and regions
of Oman into a single unified country. These
two dynasties have provided Oman with some
of the most charismatic figures in its long
and often turbulent history, leaders who succeeded in facing off against the Persians and
Portuguese, whilst also establishing Oman as a
major naval power with dominions as far away
as East Africa and Pakistan.

Before the Ya'rubas

Most of the history of Oman before the coming
of the Ya'rubas is one of conflict and fragmen-
tation between rival Arab tribes and Persian
settlers – even the coming of Islam in 630 AD
failed to bring stability, as the Omanis and
their "heretical" Ibadi creed became the target
for repeated punitive attacks by the Caliphs in
Damascus or Baghdad.

*Oman's current Sultan Qaboos belongs to the Al bu Said
dynasty, in power since 1747.*

The origins of the Omani ruling dynasties
can perhaps be traced back to the election, in
751 AD, of the country's first Imam. Elected by
popular choice, the Imam served as the spiritual
head of Oman's Ibadi community and enjoyed
an often considerable measure of temporal
authority as well, although much of the country continued to be divided along tribal lines
and controlled by local governors and warlords
from the string of forts which could be found
dotted across the country.

Twenty-six imams ruled, mainly from Nizwa,
between 751 and 1154, at which point they
were replaced by the kings *(maliks)* of the
Nabhan dynasty, based in their gigantic fort in

Bahla, from where they exercised control over
much of the country. Little is known of the
350-odd years of Nabhani rule, which continued until the early 1500s and the arrival of the
Portuguese, who occupied the coast and put a
temporary end to Omani sovereignty.

The Ya'ruba dynasty

According to Omani chroniclers the first Imam
of the Ya'ruba dynasty, Nasir bin Murshid, made
the "sun of salvation" shine on the long-afflicted
people of Oman. His reputation rested on uni-
fying the country and capturing Sur and Quri-
yat from the Portuguese and weakening their
hold on the Omani coast.

On Nasir's death in 1649 his cousin Sultan bin Saif was elected Imam and succeeded in ousting the Portuguese from Muscat, where they had been entrenched since the arrival of Affonso d'Albuquerque in 1507. He continued the unification of the country and built the great round fort at Nizwa (see page 141). At this time Oman had considerable sea power, which was used to attack the Portuguese in East Africa.

Sultan's son Bil'arub succeeded him in 1688, although the new Imam's brother, Saif bin Sultan, eventually became stronger, was elected Imam and succeeded his brother. During his

A portrait of Sayyid Said bin Sultan Al bu Said.

reign the Omanis succeeded in considerably weakening Portuguese power in East Africa, where they had been strong since 1503. When Saif died in 1711 his son Sultan bin Saif II became Imam and was another strong ruler.

The unification of the country under these five rulers led to commercial prosperity, the encouragement of learning, and buildings of strength, beauty and elegance such as the magnificent castle at Jabrin, built by Bil'arub. The first trading agreements without the British were made during the Ya'ruba period, in 1646 and 1659.

On Sultan's death in 1718, the unity which Oman had known for nearly a century came to an end and civil war ensued. Fighting over

the succession led to tribal animosity, and the whole of Oman became embroiled in desultory warfare between the two traditional factions of the Ghafiri and the Hinawi. In the late 1730s Saif bin Sultan II – one of the rival claimants to the Imamate, the other being Muhanna bin Sultan – invited the Persians under Nadir Shah to intervene on his behalf, a decision he came to regret as the Persians refused to give up their conquest.

The two rival Imams had died by 1745 and no Ya'rubi claimant came forward. Meanwhile Ahmed bin Said, who held the fort at Sohar, continued to fight the Persians, becoming both a hero and the elected Imam. In 1747 he succeeded in driving the Persians out.

> By the time of his death in 1711, Saif bin Sultan is said to have owned 28 ships, 700 male slaves, and a third of all the date palms in Oman.

The Al bu Said

Thus began the Al bu Said dynasty, which continues to rule Oman to the present day.

Ahmed himself was a man of outstanding courage, vigour, enterprise, generosity and personality. These qualities were sorely needed at the time. At home he was a good administrator of a fairly strong centralised government and he had a liberal reputation. He had in his retinue scholars, Islamic judges and notables. His bodyguard consisted of some 1,000 freemen, 1,000 Zanzibaris and 100 Nubian slaves. Abroad he led an expedition against the Persians at the request of the people of Basrah in southern Iraq, and the Mogul emperor Sha Alam sent an embassy to make a treaty to assist Ahmed against his enemies and to establish in Muscat a resident mission in what came to be known as the "Nabob's house".

Ahmed died in 1783 and his grandson Hamad became the de facto ruler, though his father, Said, had been elected Imam. On Hamad's death in 1788, Sultan – another son of Imam Ahmed bin Said – took the reins of government, though Said remained nominally Imam. Sultan was brave and of noble countenance, and both the British and the French, whose interests were in conflict in the east as well as in Europe, treated him and addressed him as if he were the Imam. He was, however, killed at Lingeh in southern Persia in 1804 by the Qawasim of Ras al Khaimah, who were at war with the Omanis over trade.

Said bin Sultan, often known as "Said the Great", succeeded his father, Sultan, and reigned for 52 years until 1856. Although some of the nobles who held the great castles were often in rebellion and there were incursions by the Wahhabis from what is now Saudi Arabia, his internal authority was in no real doubt. Europeans who met him were impressed by his commanding figure, his courtly, dignified and affable manner and his kindness both to his own people and to foreign visitors.

Said's influence in the Arabian seas was considerable. Like his father he sought to control the trade passing through the Strait of Hormuz, and to this end he retained control of places on the north of the Gulf which had been acquired by Sultan. These were Hormuz, Qishm and Henjam islands together with Gwadar on the coast of Makran, which remained a part of Oman until 1958, and Chahbar.

It was, however, in Africa that he made his deepest impression, and from 1829 his heart and main interests lay there. This was to have profound results later for the sultanate. He sought alliances with local queens in Madagascar and Mozambique and controlled the main Arab settlements on the east coast of Africa, making Zanzibar his second capital and transferring the Omani state archives there. He was very much the "Sailor Sayyid" and had 20 ships of his own for private trade – which he delighted in commanding himself – and paid

Many European travellers have left accounts of him, and Burton, Speke, Livingstone, Grant and Stanley all had good reason to thank the Al bu Said rulers of Zanzibar for assistance in their African explorations. He had 36 children, but a problem arose between two of his sons after his death in 1856 on a voyage to Zanzibar. Thuwaini in Muscat claimed the whole Sultanate but Majid in Zanzibar also claimed it.

The matter was referred to Lord Canning, the Viceroy and Governor-General of India – though the Sultanate had always been regarded as an independent state. With British pragma-

Feisal bin Turki.

much attention to the Omani navy. Britain and Oman had been in treaty alliance since 1800, but Said also negotiated a Treaty of Amity and Commerce with the USA in 1834.

He gave fresh life to interests in East Africa, particularly by introducing cloves as a cash crop in Zanzibar and establishing rice plantations.

tism Lord Canning decided that Majid should rule Zanzibar and pay 40,000 crowns a year to the ruler in Muscat to adjust the inequality in the inheritance, as Zanzibar was at this time by far the richer part. From then on the two parts remained separate, though governed by members of the same family until 1964, when Zanzibar was incorporated into Tanzania.

Thereafter the fortunes of Oman as a maritime power declined, accelerated by the introduction of steamers by the British India Steam Navigation Company in 1862. This put the Omanis at a disadvantage since their ships ceased to be competitive in the carrying trade.

Thuwaini was killed by his son Salim in 1866. A struggle for control of the Sultanate ensued between Azzan bin Qais, based in Rustaq, who headed the tribes of the interior, and Turki, who had been governor of Sohar and was another son of Said bin Sultan. Turki won the day in a battle in Wadi Dhank in 1870 and was recognised by the British. This event has present-day significance, as the Basic Law of the State issued in 1996 specifies that the Sultan of Oman "shall be a male descendant of Sayyid Turki bin Said bin Sultan", who is also "a legitimate son of Omani Muslim parents."

Turki was Sultan until 1888, although he had to cope with rivalries. He was then succeeded by his son, Feisal, who took over at the age of 23 and ruled until his death in 1913. Taimur bin Feisal followed him until 1932, when he abdicated in favour of his son Said bin Taimur.

During these reigns the interior of the country was not always at one with the Sultans and their jurisdiction on the coast. The strong sheikhs of the Harth tribe in the Sharqiyah posed a particular problem, and the very name of the country, Muscat and Oman, reflected this dichotomy.

In 1913 the tribes of the interior elected Salim bin Rashid al Kaharusi as Imam. Eventually

Oman's flag: white represents peace and prosperity, red the struggle to liberate and unify Oman, and green Islam.

IMAM VS SULTAN

Oman's history has developed around two contrasting traditions: the Imamate and the Sultanate. The country's first leaders, the Imams, were traditionally regarded as religious figureheads (although they also often wielded considerable temporal power as well). Imams were chosen by the people according to their personal qualities rather than their social origins, and could be deposed if they were deemed to be acting in an unsatisfactory manner – an early and unusual example of traditional Arabian democracy in action.

The emergence of the Ya'ruba and later Al bu Said dynasties complicated this original picture, with leadership becoming hereditary and absolute, rather than popular and democratic. Many of the early Ya'ruba rulers took the title of Imam, although by the beginning of the Al bu Said dynasty the post had become increasingly irrelevant, and by the beginning of the 19th century had fallen into disuse.

Over a century passed without an Imam until 1913, when the tribes of the interior unexpectedly elected a new Imam to serve as a figurehead for their cause. Things came to a head during the 1950s, when Imam Ghalib of Nizwa led the popular uprising known as the Jabal War against Sultan Said bin Taimur. The rebellion was eventually suppressed, however, and Ghalib was forced into exile, where he died in 2009.

accommodation was reached with an agreement – sometimes called (erroneously) the "Treaty of Seeb" – under which Taimur bin Feisal agreed not to interfere in the affairs of the interior, not to impose taxation in excess of 5 percent and to allow the tribes of the interior to enter Muscat and the coastal towns in safety and freedom. This administrative *modus vivendi* – although in a sense it re-emphasised the historical differences between coast and interior – worked satisfactorily until 1954, when the Imam Mohammed bin Abdulla al Kharusi died and the new Imam Ghalib, with his brother Talib,

husbandry which had become ingrained after many years of hardship, even when oil revenues began to accrue to Oman after 1967.

In 1967 a local rebellion of the Dhofar Liberation Front in the south of the country grew into something more serious, when it received support from the Marxist People's Democratic Republic of Yemen. The intentions of the main revolutionary body were made clear in their name: "The People's Front for the Liberation of Oman and the Arabian Gulf". The situation reached such a point that Said was displaced by his son Qaboos on 23 July 1970.

Military bands at the Omani National Day celebrations, Muscat.

tried to establish central Oman as a separate principality. This matter was not settled on the ground until 1959, and even then the problem was of such a proportion that the "Question of Oman" came up every year at the General Assembly of the United Nations until 1971.

Sultan Said bin Taimur took over a country which was still in debt, the economic situation exacerbated by the general depression of the late 1920s and early 1930s. By his own sustained and patient efforts he largely restored the situation. His stewardship ensured that when Sultan Qaboos took over in 1970 the state's finances were in a relatively flourishing state. A man of great charm and ability, Said was unable to abandon the habits of economy and careful

The reign of Sultan Qaboos

Sultan Qaboos, the 12th member of the Al bu Said dynasty, was 30 on his accession, and he proclaimed his faith in the future by announcing that his country would be known as "The Sultanate of Oman" instead of "Muscat and Oman". He also said in his first speech that under a new flag people would no longer distinguish between the coast and the interior and the southern province of Dhofar. Oman was to be a single country. The auguries were, however, not auspicious. Sultan Said had made no effort to seek international recognition, though his country was and had always been regarded as independent. He remained happy under the penumbra of the British, making it easier for the Imam Ghalib to establish relations with a number of Arab states, leading to "Imamate Offices" in Cairo, Damascus, Riyadh and Beirut.

Apart from the Omanis in rebellion in Dhofar, there were many other Omanis in opposition to Sultan Said, and young men, despairing about the limited educational facilities offered by the only three schools in the country, had sought education abroad – especially in Egypt and the Soviet Union. Thus at home the young Sultan found a country severely affected by the brain drain as well as lacking the infrastructure and services of a modern state. Abroad he had yet to acquire new friends. Only Britain and India were represented diplomatically in Muscat, each with a Consul-General.

There was a shortage of Omanis with the training to bring Oman into the modern world. But the Sultan and the Omanis themselves were undaunted, and with the help of Britain and others began the process. Ministers were appointed, and the governments structured to enable Oman to become a modern state using the gradually increasing oil revenues. The objects were to establish internal peace and security; to frustrate attacks inspired from abroad; to attract back talented but disaffected Omanis; and to gain international recognition.

Early in Sultan Qaboos's reign, Oman also revived its interest in East Africa and many Zanzibaris and Kenyans of Omani origin were welcomed to Oman, and subsequently played important roles in its continuing development.

Goodwill missions were despatched to Arab countries, and in 1971 applications were lodged to join the Arab League and the UN. That both were successful shows that the international community accepted that genuine change had taken place, and the "Question of Oman" was removed from the agenda of the UN.

However, the main challenge to Oman's future in 1971 lay in Dhofar. Although Sultan Qaboos had offered a general amnesty immediately on his accession, the initial effect on the rebels was minimal. Between 1972 and 1975, however, the military balance began to shift in the Sultan's favour, especially as the "hearts and minds" campaign began to carry conviction, and rebels were able to see for themselves that a new era had indeed begun. The growing physical signs of development brought an increasing

number of rebels over to the government side. Thus, as a result of a hard military campaign – fought with the help of Britain, Iran and Jordan in particular – combined with civil measures, the Sultan was able, on 1 December 1975, to announce the end of the war.

The Omani renaissance

Following the resolution of the Dhofar conflict, Sultan Qaboos was able to focus entirely on the massive challenge of developing his moribund country. At the time of Qaboos's accession in 1970, Oman had become an inward-looking

Taimur bin Feisal.

backwater that lagged centuries behind the modern world. There were only three schools in the whole country (in Muscat, Mutrah and Salalah), no newspapers, radio or television, no civil service and only one hospital (with just 23 beds). The average Omani life expectancy was just 47. Muscat still closed its gates at night and, apart from the road to the little airport at Bait al Falaj, there were only two graded roads in the whole country – from Muscat to Sohar and from Muscat to Fahud.

One of the Sultan's first acts was to encourage general education, and schools in makeshift tents were immediately opened in many places. From this small beginning the Omani educational system has reached standards unimaginable earlier. At its apex is the Sultan Qaboos University, which opened to students in 1986.

Dramatic changes in public health also ensued – so much so that it is no longer complaints common to the Third World that are of most concern to Omani doctors, but illnesses of the First World, such as heart disease and cancer. The average life expectancy continues to rise and is now around 75 years for people born in 2012. There are 65 hospitals, 975 private clinics, and some 7,000 registered doctors all over the country.

in 2012 to 9 percent by 2020, lessening the country's clear vulnerability to a decline in oil prices. When the barrel price dropped to record lows in 2015, after years of surpluses, Oman had to run a fiscal deficit of OR600 million, hoping prices would eventually rise. Key to revenue diversification are the vast new industrial zones which have sprung up around the country, centred on the massive ports at Sohar, Sur and Salalah (plus, in the future, Duqm).

Politically, progress has been slower. Oman remains an absolute monarchy, with an unusually high concentration of power in the hands

Omani schoolboys. Most wear the traditional embroidered Omani cap, the kummah.

Sultan Qaboos's achievement in building Oman into a modern state is also illustrated by the many beautiful buildings which have been erected – mosques, government offices, palaces and private houses. Many are based on traditional buildings, which the government has done much to restore all over the country.

Modern Oman at home and abroad

Economically, modern Oman operates through a series of five-year plans with the emphasis on diversifying the economy and moving away from an over-reliance on steadily dwindling oil reserves – with the stated aim of reducing oil's contribution to GDP from around 40 percent

of Sultan Qaboos, even compared to neighbouring states such as the UAE (where power tends to be shared more equally amongst members of the ruling families). Moves towards some form of popular representation have been made, albeit tentatively. In 1981 a State Consultative Council, the Majlis ad Dawla, was established, with 55 members directly appointed by the Sultan. Ten years later came the establishment of the larger Majlis ash Shura, with 83 members elected by popular vote – although it has no legislative powers, serving in a purely advisory role, with all final decisions still being made by Sultan Qaboos and his advisers.

The role of women is also evolving. The first women members of the Majlis ad Dawla were appointed by the Sultan in 2000, while women were finally given the vote in 2003. There are now more women than men in higher education, while they also make up around a third of the country's civil service and constitute a third of employees in the banking sector. Women are also eligible to stand for election to the Majlis ash Shura.

Oman plays an increasingly important role in regional and international affairs thanks to its geographical location on the Indian Ocean and the south side of the Strait of Hormuz, which gives it a strategic importance beyond its size and wealth. For this as well as historical reasons the Omani armed forces have benefited from a large proportion of the Omani budget.

In foreign affairs there has been an extraordinary change since 1970. After admission to the Arab League and United Nations, Omani foreign policy – which was very much that of the Sultan personally – was to reinforce its age-long connections with India and Pakistan and to develop relations with other Arab and neighbouring and friendly states, notably with the moderate states of Egypt and Jordan.

Omani schoolgirls. Until the 1960s girls received no official education.

THE SUCCESSION QUESTION

One of the major questions hanging over Oman at present is the question of who will eventually succeed the ageing Sultan Qaboos; the Sultan remains childless, while his autocratic ruling style (in which he holds most of the principal offices of government himself) means that no strong personalities have yet emerged to take over. Qaboos has declined to name a successor, saying that (under Omani tradition) it will be up to the royal family to decide – although he has also added that if a unanimous decision cannot be reached, he has written the name of his preferred candidate on two pieces of paper which are kept locked in safes in Muscat and Salalah.

Oman's foreign policy has been empirical and pragmatic and is based on good neighbourliness, non-alignment and the encouragement of co-operation between the Gulf states and particularly those of the GCC (Gulf Co-operation Council). Oman's pragmatic policies often appeared in the past to run counter to the political wisdom of the day, but have been subsequently applauded as far-sighted.

The Arab Spring and after

Early 2011 ushered in a wave of tumultuous events – the so-called "Arab Spring" – which saw regimes toppled in Tunisia, Egypt, Yemen and Libya, and widespread clashes in Bahrain, Syria and elsewhere. Even in normally tranquil

Oman repercussions were felt, with a series of nationwide protests, including clashes with police during which several demonstrators were killed. The demonstrations were uniquely Omani, however, in that without exception all the protestors pledged their unswerving loyalty to Sultan Qaboos, focusing on more local problems like ministerial nepotism and corruption, low wages and a lack of jobs. Qaboos, in return, responded by immediately by sacking 12 ministers, raising the minimum wage and promising to create 50,000 new jobs. Most interestingly, he also hinted at the possibility of the Majlis

1,000 people in 2012) means that increasing numbers of young, educated Omanis are entering the workforce without jobs to go to, despite the government's best efforts to diversify the economy and create new industry and employment in places like Sohar, Sur and Salalah. Resentment against the number of expat workers taking jobs in the country was also a feature of the Arab Spring protests, and is unlikely to go away. And, finally, the troublesome question of who will eventually succeed Sultan Qaboos is beginning to cast an increasingly long shadow over the country's future (see box).

Grace Busaidiyah, the first woman elected to the 83-member Majlis Al Shura.

Sultan Qaboos addresses the opening session of the Council of Oman in Muscat in 2011.

ash Shura being given real legislative powers, which would be the first move towards genuine democracy in Oman.

That said, in 2012, six people received prison sentences of up to 18 months and many more were arrested for criticising the government over promised reforms which were never carried out. Although Sultan Qaboos pardoned some 30 online activists and protesters a year later, authorities still harass those who voice any dissent or call for reforms. In 2015, an eminent pro-reform blogger was sentenced to three years in prison on charges of 'undermining the prestige of the state'.

There are other significant challenges. The country's burgeoning birth rate (32 births per

Despite these potential pitfalls, much has been achieved. A recent study by the United Nations Development Programme rated Oman as the "most improved" country over the past 45 years out of the 135 it surveyed, highlighting the lightning speed of progress since 1970 and the general harmony which has been created in a state once riven with faction. And meanwhile the Omanis themselves retain the courtesy and charm for which they are renowned, still justifying the words of the 19th-century traveller J.S. Buckingham: "The people seemed to me to be the cleanest, neatest, best dressed, and most gentlemanly… and inspired a feeling of confidence, goodwill and respect."

THE UAE FROM RAGS TO RICHES

How the discovery of oil and an urgent need for
security persuaded seven of the Trucial sheikhdoms
to put aside local rivalries and form a federation.

After more than a quarter of a century of existence, the United Arab Emirates has proved to be the Arab world's most successful attempt at unity, despite widespread scepticism at its formation in 1971. Attempts by Egypt under Gamal Abdel Nasser and later by Libya under Muammar Gaddafi to merge with other states were short-lived, and the squabbles surrounding such moves made the emotive concept of the "Arab nation" something of a laughing stock among commentators outside the region. The UAE was one of the most unlikely bids for unity, but has shown itself to be the exception to the rule.

Old roots

The well-known rags-to-riches story of the Gulf states of Arabia created by the oil boom of the 1970s and 1980s caused many commentators to look upon the peoples of the region as upstarts. The UAE is quite new as a state – and its inhabitants are rather proud to be nouveaux riches – but these once largely maritime peoples can trace their roots back to prehistoric times. Excavations at Umm an Nar (now in the shadow of an oil refinery), an island off Abu Dhabi, and elsewhere show that in these early times the Gulf Arabs were under two influences – those of Mesopotamia and of the Indus civilisation in India.

The coastal dwellers were the first to deal with European travellers, but inland the Bedu (see page 69) continued their timeless nomadic existence or settled in places where they could grow a few crops, such as dates, or graze small numbers of livestock. The Bedu in particular achieved their sense of belonging not in terms of the districts or fixed borders within which they conducted their spartan lives but through their tribal allegiances to a local sheikh. Long

An aerial view of Abu Dhabi town, 1962.

before the rise of Islam in the 7th century, the land that is now the UAE and the other Gulf states – Kuwait, Bahrain, Qatar, Saudi Arabia and Oman – had a tightly structured Arab society that was divided into tribes, sub-tribes and clans.

Key tribes

The Bani Yas were one such powerful federation of clans, wandering great distances in search of grazing for their camels and then returning to their date gardens around the Liwa oases on the edge of the Empty Quarter.

As long as anyone can remember, the leader of the Bani Yas has always come from the sheikhs of the Al bu Falasah sub-tribe. One of them, called Nahyan, was the ancestor of the present ruling family of Abu Dhabi. As pearls became increasingly popular in India and then among European women in the 19th century, the Bani Yas gravitated towards the rich pearl banks of the Trucial Coast.

The town of Abu Dhabi was founded as early as 1761 after a good supply of water had been found there. A settlement grew down the coast in Dubai as a dependency of Abu Dhabi until 1833, when a faction of Bani Yas left Abu Dhabi and took control of Dubai, proclaiming their independence. The descendants of Maktoum bin Buti, leader of the breakaway, continue to rule the city to this day.

The pearl boom collapsed in the 1930s with the arrival of the Japanese cultured pearl. The ensuing depression caused some pearl boatmen to burn their boats in desperation for fuel. But the search for a new source of energy had begun.

Oil concessions

Between 1936 and 1952 the rulers of the seven Trucial States signed oil concession agreements with the Iraq Petroleum Company, an international consortium. But oil exploration only really began in earnest after World War II.

Abu Dhabi in 1954.

Dubai's commercial pizzazz and liberal values are nothing new. When the city unveiled its new airport in 1960 it was the first in the Gulf to have its own duty-free shop.

By 1900 the pearling industry was enjoying such a boom that not enough men could be found to man the 1,200 boats engaged in the trade. Control passed irrevocably to the sheikhs who ruled the coastal areas, and this power was further reinforced when the British made it clear they were only interested in the coastal areas and effectively endorsed only their rulers.

The decline of the British Empire after the war, especially the granting of independence to India in 1947, helped to speed up changes in the Gulf. The British presence in the region was to linger a few more years. With British help the Trucial Oman Scouts (a defence force) was set up in 1951, while the following year a Trucial States Council was formed to bring a kind of unity to the coastal region through twice-yearly discussions on common problems and interests. The rulers of what became the United Arab Emirates had not met all together since 1905.

The British withdraw

The big bombshell came when Britain's cash-strapped Labour government decided that big savings must be made in defence. In February 1967 the prime minister, Harold Wilson, announced that Britain's military presence east of Suez was to be scrapped by the end of 1971. It spelt the end of British protection in the Gulf and was in breach of written agreements between Britain and the Trucial States, as well as the unwritten Arab law of trust and friendship. The British decision led directly to the formation of the UAE and speeded the process of modernisation in the region, which had already been accelerated by the discovery of massive oil deposits. But the emirates were ill-prepared for sudden independence and had few qualified people, particularly in the spheres of defence and foreign affairs, which the British had long taken care of.

The UAE is formed

Shortly after the British decision to withdraw from the Gulf, the rulers of Abu Dhabi and Dubai announced that they would form a federation and reached an agreement over offshore oil rights. The speed of their action helped to settle frontiers, even though the UAE is now a patchwork of subdivisions making up the seven emirates that form the federation – a process that had never been formalised before because of the changing tribal allegiances.

Abu Dhabi, well aware by 1970 that it was the richest oil emirate, was especially anxious to reach an overall agreement on a federation and clearly demarcated borders because of the mounting importance of oil revenues and the oil rights that would be granted once land divisions had been agreed. From the outset it

adopted a policy aimed at finding a middle ground between any opposing views. Sheikh Zayed bin Sultan Al Nahyan, Abu Dhabi's ruler, repeatedly said that the resources of Abu Dhabi – which in a few years were to carry the emirate's income to the highest in the world – were "at the service of all the emirates".

Dubai and Abu Dhabi invited the other Trucial States – Sharjah, Ajman, Umm al Qaiwain, Ras al Khaimah and Fujairah – to join them in the federation, together with Qatar and Bahrain. There was clearly a strong mutual desire for security, modified by a wish for a degree of

The Ruler's Palace, Abu Dhabi, also in 1954.

THE MAGNIFICENT SEVEN

The formation of the UAE presented considerable constitutional problems, as the leaders of the seven formerly independent statelets attempted to merge their territories into one, while preserving a measure of self-determination. The system adopted was a federal one, not unlike that in the USA. Each emirate gives a percentage of its income to the central government budget, which in return takes responsibility for foreign affairs, security and defence and other national issues. Individual emirates retain a considerable level of internal autonomy and legislative power, however – which explains why the law is so different in conservative Sharjah compared to that in liberal Dubai, just 16km

(10 miles) down the road. In addition, each emirate continues to have its own ruler. Tensions inevitably arise. Dubai's close links with Iran, for example, have been a source of concern when Abu Dhabi has wished to align itself with US policy.

Despite the seven emirates' large measure of individual autonomy, a clear pecking order applies. The ruler of Abu Dhabi, the largest and wealthiest of the emirates, is also automatically the UAE president and head of state, while the ruler of Dubai, the second-largest, serves by default as the UAE's prime minister and head of government – proving that while all seven emirates are equal, some are more equal than others.

The UAE boasts 7 percent of the world's proven oil reserves (with roughly 93 percent in Abu Dhabi, 5 percent in Dubai and 2 percent in Sharjah); these are estimated to last just about 90 years at current production rates.

independence in each emirate, as the departure of the British drew near.

By June 1971, Bahrain had decided it was secure enough on its own and announced in August it would not join the federation, while

the region. The possibility of a threat from the Soviet Union (particularly after its invasion of Afghanistan) always existed in the minds of the Gulf leaders and of the Western politicians whose countries depended on the Gulf's oil.

The volatility of the region was underlined by the Iran–Iraq War, which broke out in 1980, as well as the Arab-Israeli conflict. With the strategic giants of the Gulf – Iran and Iraq – busy fighting each other, the six oil-rich Gulf monarchies (Saudi Arabia, Kuwait, the UAE, Bahrain, Qatar and Oman) seized the chance to set up their own organisation – the Arabian

Bustling Dubai creek.

Qatar followed suit less than three weeks later. Six of the remaining sheikhdoms had reached agreement on a federal constitution by July, and the UAE formally came into being on 2 December. In Ras al Khaimah, Ruler Sheikh Saqr bin Mohammed al Qasimi – hoping that he would find oil on Qatar's scale – held out for another two months before swallowing his pride at the prospect of massive largesse from Abu Dhabi and joined the federation too. Sheikh Zayed of Abu Dhabi became President of the Federation, with Sheikh Rashid bin Saeed Al Maktoum, ruler of Dubai, as vice-president and prime minister.

Security was a major motive for forming the UAE, and such concern was justified in view of the massive oil deposits later discovered in

Gulf Co-operation Council – modelled on the lines of the European Economic Community (now EU), and which formally came into being in 1981.

Diversification and development

Meanwhile, massive changes were taking place in the emirates themselves, each of which was pursuing its own route towards development and economic security. Abu Dhabi, the largest and wealthiest of the seven statelets, followed a cautious path towards modernity under the leadership of the canny Sheikh Zayed, its vast oil reserves freeing it from the need either to diversify or to develop its economy, given that the massive flow of petro-dollars into the city guaranteed every citizen (and their descendants) a very comfortable income for life.

Dubai found itself in a rather different position, given that its oil reserves were only ever a fraction of Abu Dhabi's. Initial revenues had already been invested by the far-sighted Sheikh Rashid into a string of infrastructure projects, including two huge new ports, an airport and the iconic World Trade Centre, laying down the economic basis for the city's subsequent dramatic rise.

Money was even tighter (and oil revenues smaller) in neighbouring Sharjah, which was also plagued with political instability. The emirate's entire banking system collapsed with debts of over US$500 million in 1989 and had to be bailed out by a Saudi consortium. Saudi influence remains strong in Sharjah to this day, accounting for the local adoption of a particularly conservative version of traditional Shariah law.

Meanwhile, the relatively small, unpopulated and oil-less emirates of Ajman, Umm Al Qaiwain, Ras al Khaimah (RAK) and Fujairah struggled along as best they could, helped out with grants from central government in Abu Dhabi, while the creation of large new industrial works in RAK and a vast new oil-exporting port in Fujairah also provided further economic stimulus – as did the new Habshan–Fujairah oil pipeline, opened in 2012.

Nineties and noughties

It was during the 1990s that the UAE really began to capture the world's attention, mainly thanks to a spectacular new series of developments in Dubai instigated by Sheikh Mohammed, the third son of Sheikh Rashid and the driving force behind the emirate's development from the mid-1980s onwards. It was Sheikh Mohammed who commissioned the famous Burj al Arab hotel (1999) and founded Emirates Airlines, which between them have probably done more to establish the UAE in the world's consciousness than any other projects before or since. A further flurry of record-breaking mega-developments were swiftly inaugurated, including the Palm Jumeirah (the world's largest artificial island), Burj Khalifa (the world's tallest building) and the vast Dubailand, intended to become the planet's largest theme park and leisure attraction. Following the economic crisis of 2008, work on Dubailand was stalled for several years, but it resumed in 2013 and is now expected to open by 2020.

Dubai's basic aim in all of this was to become a leading global centre for tourism, transport and business – aiming to dominate the region's economy. Not to be outdone, Abu Dhabi soon hit back with its own string of eye-catching developments, including the Emirates Palace Hotel, Sheikh Zayed Grand Mosque and huge new Saadiyat Island complex which will come complete with five outstanding museums, including Louvre Abu Dhabi (inaugurated in 2015) and Guggenheim museum (opening in 2017), aiming to promote itself as a more cultured alternative to its brash neighbour.

A helicopter view of the Palm Jumeirah in Dubai.

Then, in 2008, just as it seemed the boom would never end, the UAE (Dubai in particular) was brought crashing back down to earth as the result of the global credit crunch. The real-estate market collapsed, investment fled, and Dubai, which had previously been announcing the launch of record-breaking new developments on an almost daily basis, found itself suddenly teetering on the edge of bankruptcy. Abu Dhabi eventually came to the rescue with a massive bail-out package, although many of the city's mega-projects were cancelled or put on hold, and now only a few of the projects have been revived.

Abu Dhabi, protected by its oil revenues, remained relatively unaffected by the crunch, and even began to climb out of Dubai's lengthening shadow thanks to headline events including the purchase of Manchester City football club by Sheikh Mansour (a son of Sheikh Zayed) and the staging, in 2009, of the first Abu Dhabi F1 Grand Prix. The spectacular new Sheikh Zayed Grand Mosque (2007) has also drawn increasing numbers of visitors to the emirate.

Overall, the credit crunch may have signalled the end of the UAE's rock 'n' roll years, although reports of Dubai's demise have been greatly exaggerated, and the city is now beginning to face the future with renewed optimism, getting ready to host the World Expo 2020. With the theme 'Connecting Minds, Creating the Future', the 438-hectare purpose-built expo site is set to be another jaw-dropping project. The exhibition will run well into 2021, when the UEA will celebrate its 50th jubilee. Abu Dhabi, meanwhile, continues to establish itself as a genuine rival to its more glamorous neighbour, while elsewhere in the Emirates more modest industrial and tourist development continues apace. The political union between the seven emirates continues to provide a model of rela-

Extraordinary views from the Burj Khalifa observation deck.

NAMING RIGHTS

As Dubai teetered on the edge of bankruptcy in 2008, rumour abounded as to what price Abu Dhabi would extract in return for bailing out their profligate neighbour; handing over Dubai's Emirates Airlines was mentioned, along with ownership of the Palm islands or other choice local real estate. In the end, Dubai wasn't obliged to relinquish any commercial crown jewels in return for the loan, but it did make one symbolic concession, renaming the new Burj Dubai skyscraper as the Burj Khalifa in honour of Abu Dhabi's ruler, Sheikh Khalifa bin Zayed Al Nahyan – meaning that the name of a rival ruler adorns the loftiest building in the city.

tive political harmony and stability in an often dysfunctional region. The country escaped the widespread protests and uprisings of the Arab Spring in early 2011 almost entirely unscathed (and in stark contrast to nearby Bahrain), although Emirati pro-democracy activists also pressed for reforms. The authorities continue to suppress any dissenting voices – online criticism of the government was even made illegal in 2012. In recent years, the country has been condemned for human rights violations by the European Parliament, Human Rights Watch and Amnesty International. Yet, the economic progress of the country, which is just over four decades old, and which many observers thought would not last even five years, is undeniable.

Father of the UAE

Legendary leader of Abu Dhabi and first president of the UAE, Sheikh Zayed oversaw the country's transformation from impoverished Arabian backwater to today's stable and affluent state.

Governor of Al Ain, ruler of Abu Dhabi and – from its creation in 1971 until his death in November 2004 – first president of the United Arab Emirates: the charismatic figure of Sheikh Zayed bin Sultan Al Nahyan towers over the modern history of the region. A man of great charisma, intelligence and legendary generosity, it was Sheikh Zayed who oversaw Abu Dhabi's astonishing transformation from impoverished desert backwater to oil-rich super-state, as well as establishing the lasting integrity and sovereignty of the UAE in the face of considerable odds.

Born in 1918 in Al Ain, where he grew up and of which he subsequently became governor, Sheikh Zayed never lost his love for his birthplace. The explorer Wilfred Thesiger met him in the 1940s and described him in his classic book *Arabian Sands* as "a powerfully built man of about 30 with a brown beard. He had a strong intelligent face, with steady observant eyes, and his manner was quiet but masterful. He was dressed very simply, in a beige coloured shirt of Omani cloth and a waistcoat which he wore unbuttoned... He wore a dagger and car-tridge belt; his rifle lay on the sand beside him.

"He had a great reputation among the Bedu," Thesiger went on. "They liked him for his easy informal ways and his friendliness, and they respected his force of character, his shrewdness and his physical strength. They said admiringly, 'Zayed is a Bedu. He knows about camels, can ride like one of us, can shoot and knows how to fight.' "

In old age Zayed's hands were still callused from the days when he used to dig, move stones and plant trees while working on restoration of the ancient *falaj* system of canals needed to irrigate the date groves of the Buraimi oasis near Al Ain.

It was in 1966 that his brother Shakhbut, who had ruled the emirate since 1928, was deposed, and Zayed replaced him. The first oil exports had begun only four years before, and two years later the British government was to announce its withdrawal from the Gulf, so that Abu Dhabi and the

other Trucial States were free to manage their own affairs.

The new ruler quickly set about using the new oil revenues to transform Abu Dhabi itself, as well as joining forces with Sheikh Rashid of Dubai in laying the foundations of a new federal state (of which they subsequently became president and vice-president respectively).

President Zayed showed particular skill in achieving lasting harmony between the tradition-ally rival interests of the UAE's seven emirates, each with its own ruler – particularly in the face of a chorus of sceptical observers who claimed that

Sheikh Zayed bin Sultan Al Nahyan, the leading light in the transformation of the UAE and father of the current ruler, Sheikh Khalifa bin Zayed Al Nahyan.

the federation would never work. There is no doubt that Abu Dhabi's soaring wealth helped. Zayed was always quick to help the poorer emirates financially and to spend money on vast public works through-out the country, including a welfare state that is second to none worldwide.

Sheikh Zayed is still revered throughout the UAE, and his portrait remains a common sight in public places, while his tomb, in the magnificent Sheikh Zayed Grand Mosque (see page 187) in Abu Dhabi, continues to draw a steady stream of visitors pay-ing their respects. Zayed National Museum, due to open in 2016 on the Saadiyat Island in Abu Dhabi, will surely be another hit.

EXPLORERS

Oman and the UAE lie on the rim of the Empty Quarter, a vast wilderness of dunes impenetrable to any but a few Bedu until as late as the 1930s.

Arabia has attracted some of the world's best-known explorers, from Charles Montague Doughty to Richard Burton. Names associated with Oman and the UAE in particular include Ibn Battuta, Marco Polo, the 18th-century Danish explorer Carsten Niebuhr, whom William Gifford Palgrave called "the intelligence and courage that first opened Arabia to Europe" and, in the 20th century, Bertram Thomas and Wilfred Thesiger. There were British political agents and Western officials in the employ of the sheikhs who by the very nature of the territory – tribal and inaccessible – were often the first foreigners to set foot in a place.

Wilfred Thesiger

The explorer most fondly remembered in Oman and the UAE today is undoubtedly Wilfred Thesiger (1910–2003), whose two great crossings of the Rub al Khali (Empty Quarter) are documented in his book *Arabian Sands*. Thesiger seized the opportunity to cross the Great Sands when he was offered a job in the region by the Anti-Locust Research Centre. To make himself less conspicuous in hostile country he pretended to be a Bedu from Syria, a disguise that could explain his strange looks and accent. His disguise was generally successful, and often only his closest Bedu companions knew the truth. The one thing that gave him away, they said, were his unusually large feet. They advised him never to leave footprints in the sand.

Crossing the Empty Quarter, an area of harsh extremes.

Another famous visitor to the region was Marco Polo (1254–1234). He visited Dhofar – "a great and noble and fine city" and then sailed up the Omani coast to Qualhat.

Wilfred Thesiger in Bedu dress. Thesiger's success as an explorer was a direct result of his ability to adopt the manners, dress, language and culture of the lands through which he was travelling.

A camel train crossing the sands. Camels – aptly named "ships of the desert" – were crucial to any journey through the Arabian interior, and the loss of an expedition's camels could prove not only inconvenient, but potentially fatal.

THE FIRST TO CROSS THE SANDS

Though Wilfred Thesiger's crossings of the Rub al Khali are probably the most famous, the first Western person to cross the sands was Bertram Thomas in 1931, who trekked from Salalah to Doha in 55 days.

Thomas's book about his journey, *Arabia Felix*, describes the sands as "a vast ocean of billowing sands, here tilted into sudden frowning heights, and there falling into gentle valleys… without a scrap of verdure in view. Dunes of all sizes… with the exquisite roundness of a girl's breasts, rise tier upon tier like a mighty mountain system." He also talked of the "roaring of the sands" which, he said, resembled a ship's foghorn.

Thomas was in Oman as Financial Adviser and Wazir to the Sultan, a post he took up in 1924 after serving as Political Officer in Iraq. Through his position he gained the respect of unpredictable tribal leaders who usually scorned, even murdered, infidels.

This proved invaluable on his journey through the Sands. Thomas claimed the Rub al Khali "obsesses every white man whose life is cast in Arabia".

he 11th-century North frican explorer Ibn attuta visited southeast rabia when he was just 1. His original six-onth Haj extended to a 4-year trip taking him s far as China.

When Percy Cox, British Agent in Muscat from 1899–1904, visited Tanuf, he was told that no rain had fallen since the last British agent had taken photographs there 25 years before. The sheikh demanded compensation for the crops that had perished as a result.

A woman passes before a typical wrought-iron gate in Ras al Hadd.

A Nizwa local.

DAILY LIFE

In spite of the massive changes that have taken place in Oman and the UAE, everyday life remains rooted in traditional values.

Contemporary life in the UAE and Oman is an intriguing blend of the traditional and the modern. Despite both countries' often outwardly contemporary appearance, old-fashioned attitudes still run deep, and social life continues to follow long-established patterns, despite the 21st-century veneer. Starbucks may have replaced the traditional coffee shop, while camels have given way to Toyota four-wheel-drives, but many of the region's immemorial attitudes and cultural norms remain largely unchanged. The oligarchical political traditions and the entrenched position of the ruling sheikhly families; the careful observance of Islamic religious practices; the role of the sexes and the conduct of family life; taboos regarding food, drink and forms of public behaviour, and so on – all these remain intact. Even in liberal and relatively permissive cities such as Dubai, visiting tourists and expats have found themselves falling foul of the authorities as a result of behaviour which would be considered unexceptional in the West, but which is considered offensive – and even illegal – in the Gulf.

An Omani family shopping in Muscat.

Cautious signs of change are afoot. The increasing emancipation of women, who now play an increasingly important role in the business and political life of both countries, is one such development, as are the growing demands for more democratic and representative institutions in Oman and the UAE (although the authorities in both countries continue to crack down on all pro-reform activists).

In addition, burgeoning contact with foreign countries is also creating an increasingly cosmopolitan populace, with growing numbers of Emirati and Omani men marrying foreign women (although instances of local women marrying foreigners remain largely unknown).

Despite modest adjustments, however, traditional values remains firmly entrenched. Tribal identity is still an important marker of one's place in society, in Oman particularly, signifying one's geographical and cultural origins, and perhaps one's status in society as well. Pride in one's country and culture remains strong too, again especially in Oman, where nationals take great pleasure in the gigantic leaps their country has taken over recent decades and in the achievements of its venerated ruler Sultan Qaboos.

Family life and the home

The family and family home remain the core of Emirati and Omani life. Families are typically large (Oman in particular now has a rocketing birth rate – 32 births per 1,000 peo-

> It is customary for guests to remove shoes when entering an Omani or Emirati home – a measure originally adopted for hygiene reasons when streets were dustier than they are today, but now simply a matter of politeness.

ple in 2012, compared to some 11 births per 1,000 in Europe – and an increasingly youthful population – 10 children in one family is not uncommon). Extended families generally co-habit under the same roof, including elderly relatives who are unable to live alone, as well as young married couples, who will typically live in the house of the groom's parents until they are able to afford a home of their own. Western concepts of bachelor living or temporary residence in rented apartments are largely unknown. What's more, according to Shariah law, which is the legal base in the UAE and Oman, living together as an unmarried couple and being in a homosexual relationship are both crimes.

The traditional Emirati or Omani home remains something of a castle. Despite their modern appearance, houses in both the UAE and Oman continue to preserve a decidedly traditional layout, standing quite separate from one another on individual plots of lands, and often surrounded by high enclosing walls – a modern throwback to former times, when houses and settlements were typically heavily walled and fortified against possible attack and shielded from the public gaze to protect the privacy of those (women particularly) within.

Food is a key ingredient of any social gathering at home. Coffee or tea is always offered as a symbol of hospitality, as are dates and sweetmeats. Following meals, the incense burner is filled and passed around, so that guests can fan scented smoke onto their faces. These ceremonies signify the end of the occasion.

Daily life and the social round

Daily life for Omani and Emirati men and women still revolves around the traditional rhythms of religious life: the five daily calls to prayer and the annual religious festivals punctuate the passing year (see page 83).

Social life is also organised, to a large extent, according to traditional patterns. Omani and Emirati men and women often socialise separately – again, following an age-old traditional pattern whereby men and women would gather in separate parts of the house to exchange news and gossip. The pattern persists to this day, whether in the traditional setting of an Omani souk, with men hanging out at the local coffee shop, or in

An Omani mother with her baby.

> Many nationals still follow traditional sports such as falconry and camel racing, although modern sports – particularly football – are popular, and televised broadcasts of major football matches from the Gulf and Europe regularly attract crowds.

the modern malls of Dubai and Abu Dhabi, where groups of Emirati men can commonly be seen socialising over coffee in Starbucks or Costa while their wives cruise the shops looking for clothes.

Whatever its setting, social life in the Gulf retains much of its traditional courtliness and decorum, exemplified by the elaborate round of salutations and extended handshakes which can be observed whenever two nationals meet one another; close friends and relatives of the same sex may also touch or kiss cheeks or (a particularly distinctive local custom) noses. Such pleasantries typically open with the traditional *salaam aleikum* ("Peace be upon you"), followed by the response *wa aleikum a'salaam* ("And peace upon you also"), followed by a long exchange of enquiries and responses concerning one's health, one's news, the health of one's wife, children, cous-

not true of men. In the UAE, increasing numbers of marriages between Emiratis and foreign women have prompted the government to offer significant cash incentives to encourage marriages between Emirati couples. Islam allows a Muslim man to have up to four wives, provided he can support all of them. In fact, most Emirati and Omani men have only one, although a man may take a second if the first is unable to bear him children. Dowries are typically provided by the groom to the bride's family as a guarantee against possible future divorce or the death of the husband,

A bride displays her hennaed hands, decorated the night before her wedding.

ins, and so on which can go on for a considerable amount of time. Invocations to God are also a characteristic feature of such exchanges (and of Emirati and Omani conversation in general) – *insh'allah* ("God willing") and *al hamdu'lillah* ("Thanks be to God") are perhaps the two most common expressions in the local language.

Marriage, education and work

The large majority of young men and women still have an arranged marriage with a partner from a suitable family known to her own family. Often a girl will marry a first cousin or man from the same tribe. Muslim women always marry a Muslim, although the same is

THE COFFEE CEREMONY

Every visitor to a UAE or Omani home will be offered coffee or tea. The traditional Gulf coffee – *kahwa* – is made from green coffee beans, is very strong and sometimes flavoured with cardamom or saffron. Poured from a distinctive coffee pot, it is served in tiny cups without handles, which are refilled several times until a guest "wobbles" the cup from side to side, indicating sufficiency. Three cups is considered the polite number to drink, indicating pleasure at the coffee, but not drinking to excess. The social custom of drinking coffee is also important in business.

offering a measure of financial security to the bride-to-be.

Weddings are typically large and elaborate affairs, spreading over three days or so, with vast quantities of food, music and other entertainment and guests sporting their finest traditional dress (complete with *khanjars* and

> A newborn baby's eyes are lined with kohl to cleanse them from infection and to help protect against the Evil Eye.

up the children. The gender divide is steadily dissolving, however. Emirati and Omani women now make up an increasingly large proportion of those in higher education in the region, generally equal to, or greater than, men at many colleges and universities, while increasing numbers of women now work in government and business. Despite this increasing sexual emancipation, women are still poorly represented in the higher echelons of the countries' ministries and corporations – although again this is something that is equally true of many other "developed" countries around the world.

Gathering outside a mosque in Muscat.

Wearing a traditional face covering or burqa.

possibly rifles in Oman, see page 67). As with many other social events, men and women tend to congregate separately for much of the wedding until the bride and groom finally join together at the end of the festivities. On the evening before her wedding the bride will hold her henna night *(laylat al henna)*, when she will be massaged with perfumed oil and decorated with henna. For this she wears a traditional gold-embroidered green dress and elaborate gold jewellery, often part of her wedding gift.

The roles of the sexes within the family after marriage follow the usual traditional gender patterns, with men going out to work and financing the home, while the wives and other women of the family run the house and bring

Business in the UAE and Oman continues to be based more on personal relationships and mutual trust than legal contracts and corporate formalities, giving business a notably social touch – Western notions of timekeeping may, however, be somewhat lacking.

National dress

All over the Gulf region, one of the most striking features for the visitor is the very noticeable national dress of both men and women – in Oman national dress is mandatory for anyone working in the public services, while most Emiratis in the UAE also wear it as a matter of course. National dress is an *important* marker of national and cultural identity, and virtually all nationals take great pride in their scrupulous personal appearance – and tend to look askance at scruffy Westerners in T-shirts and shorts, which they regard as tantamount to walking around in one's underwear (not to mention skimpy and tight clothing, which can often cause offence, even if most locals are too polite to say anything).

In both countries, the standard apparel is a *dishdasha* (also known as a *thawb* or *kandura*), a loose, ankle-length robe, usually white (although other colours, particularly in Oman, can often be seen). A small tassel *(furakha)* hanging from the neck is a typical feature of the Omani *dishdasha*, traditionally doused in scent or perfumed with frankincense. On formal occasions, men (particularly those of higher social rank) sometimes wear an over-garment, a gauzy black or brown robe *(bisht)* edged in woven gold thread.

In the UAE, the standard item of headwear is the *ghutra*, a loose piece of cotton held in place by black ropes *(iqal)* which formerly doubled as ropes for tethering camels at night. In Oman, men wear either more voluminous and colourful turbans or, more commonly, the *ubiquitous* "Omani cap" *(kummah)*, a richly embroidered cotton headpiece said to have been introduced from the Omani dominions in Zanzibar in the 19th century and now an important symbol of national identity. On special occasions, Omani men may also be seen wearing the traditional *khanjar* (silver dagger) tucked into their waistbands, with perhaps, in particularly traditional settings (amongst the Bedu, especially), a rifle as well.

Women cover their heads and bodies with a voluminous black overdress *(abbaya)*, under which is worn a black headscarf *(shayla)* to cover the hair. The *abbaya* itself, despite its functional blackness, may often be elaborately embroidered, and edged with beads and sequins. The *abbaya* often hides brightly coloured dresses which are long-sleeved with very elaborately embroidered necklines and wrist-to-elbow decoration, sometimes embellished with crystal beading and sequins. Wealthier women may wear designer clothes under their *abbaya*.

The traditional Bedu face mask *(burqa* – not to be confused with the voluminous tent-like garment sported by women in Afghanistan and often known by the same name) is

becoming increasingly rare, although it may still be seen in remoter parts of the UAE and Oman. The Gulf *burqa* is a light and simple structure covering the face, with a thin strip across the forehead and over the nose, leaving the eyes and cheek areas free. The mask stops under the nose, covering the top lip but leaving the chin free. It is made from black cotton, the front covered with a gold, purple or red dye with a bluish sheen. There are several designs, and women may wear a gold one for special occasions. The mask is worn by many married women, though not by all women in public.

A mosque at Job's Tomb, Dhofar, Oman.

Instead the headdress may be drawn across the face as a veil. To wear the *burqa* or not is a matter of personal choice, and can be dependent on the situation.

The way of death

In Islam mourning is not an important part of death. The deceased will be washed and anointed with perfumed oils and then wrapped in a white cloth and borne on a simple bier to the cemetery. The body is always buried (on its side facing Mecca), and if possible burial should take place on the day of death. Forty days after death, the close relatives of the deceased will hold a feast to mark the ascent to heaven, believed to occur after this 40-day period.

A Bedu man kneels on top of a sand dune in the desert.

THE BEDU

The life of the Bedu used to be one of thirst
and hunger, and of great journeys to find
water. The lack of such hardships today is
testing the strength of their culture.

The Bedu of Oman and the Emirates are
among the oldest tribal peoples in the
world. Tracing their ancestry from a mythical hero called Kahtan in the Yemen, these southern Arabian tribesmen are sometimes referred to
as the "Pure Arabs". Kahtan has been identified
with Yoktan, listed in the Old Testament as a
descendant of Shem, a son of Noah, making these
tribes of older, purer Arab stock than the younger
northern tribes that trace their ancestry from
Ishmael. Of these southern tribes the Bait Kathir
and Rashid are the most famous, having been
Wilfred Thesiger's companions on his exploration of the Empty Quarter in the second half of
the 1940s. Other tribes in the region include the
Harasis, Al Wahibah, Ajman and Jenuba.

For modern Westerners concepts of tribal
descent and purity of blood lines may appear
somewhat irrelevant. In Arabia, family ties and
tribal identity are the building blocks of society,
modern as well as traditional. A citizen of any
Arabian Gulf state is identified by a personal
name, then as the child of a father and grandfather, and then by their clan and tribal name.

This sense of being from a line of descent,
of belonging to a family grouping that extends
through a clan and a tribe to a wider society is
fundamental to Bedu life and is probably the
single most important influence within the
relatively young states of the Arabian peninsula.

Bedu is the Arabic word for nomadic
tribespeople. The singular, Badawi, is little
known in the West, so Bedu is used in this
book. The more common Western version,
Bedouin, is a double plural which does not
exist in Arabic.

Bedu women traditionally wear the burqa.

Adapt or die

The Bedu evolved as nomadic herdsmen, living off the products of their animals, drinking
their milk, weaving their hair, making leather
from their skins and eating their flesh. Their
lifestyle was the supreme adaptation of man to
the hostile environment of some of the hottest,
driest areas on earth. The land is too sterile for
them to stay long in any one place. The vegetation is too thin and grows too slowly. Instead
the Bedu learnt to move, following the limited
rains, grazing their animals on small patches of
grass wherever they could be found. It was not
an easy life, but it was survival. T.E. Lawrence
wrote that "the Bedouin ways were hard even
for those brought up in them", that they were "a

death in life". If one asks the Bedu today what life was like in the old days, their tales are of constant thirst and hunger, of great journeys to bring water from wells or to look for areas that had received some rain.

Whenever one thinks of the Bedu one imagines them with their camels and their goat-hair tents. The *bait sharar* ("house of hair") is synonymous with the Bedu. The reality is slightly different. There are tribes who have never lived in tents and those who have traditionally only used tents during winter when a shelter from the cold, wind and occasional

metal bedsteads upended and joined together to form small cabins.

The kindness of strangers

Hospitality is an essential part of Bedu life. In a land where people are few and far between and there is little to sustain life, hospitality was formerly a crucial means of exchanging news and information regarding latest tribal conflicts, the movements of friendly and hostile tribes, sources of possible grazing and areas in which rain had recently fallen – a kind of bush telegraph, with news passing by word of mouth often with

Camels are a vital commodity of Bedu life.

rain has been a necessity. In Oman it is only the tribes of the Empty Quarter, the Bait Kathir and Rashid that have used tents. Previously the tribes of the stony plains, where trees are more plentiful, built their camps around the shade of these natural shelters, often covering them with blankets or cloth to improve them. Other tribes, especially on the coast, used palm fronds to build easily assembled and dismantled shelters called *barasti*. These are still a common sight around the Sharqiya Sands in Oman and along the coasts of the Arabian Gulf. More recently the Bedu have started to use metal grilles to form temporary shelters. These are common among the Bedu on the Jiddat al Harasis in Oman, where they resemble

remarkable speed across the vast distances. In the past any traveller seeing a tent would travel towards it, hopeful of receiving a friendly welcome, although also wary of the possibility that the inhabitants might belong to a rival tribe which whom relations were strained, or even with whom a state of open warfare existed. Thesiger's *Arabian Sands* offers several memorable descriptions of such chance meetings in the desert and the hope of meeting with friends mixed with the fear of being shot at, or worse.

Assuming no hostile relations existed, visitors would exchange for their news and in return would be greeted with tea and coffee and be invited to share a meal. Visitors knew that they would not only receive food and shelter, but also the protection of their host for the duration of their stay and for another three days after – this being the time it takes for all traces of his host's food to pass through his body. The code tying the host to his guest is called the bond of salt. Even if a visitor carried only the salt of his host in his stomach, he could call on his protection.

Camels, a crucial commodity

Up until the adoption of motor vehicles, the entire lifestyle of the Bedu relied on the camel. It was the beast of burden by which they moved their tents and possessions as well as the mode

at all. If need be, the camel can show incredible stamina. H.R.P. Dickson, a British political agent in Kuwait between 1929 and 1936, and author of *The Arab of the Desert*, reported how one Bedu sheikh, in about 1925, rode a camel between Riyadh and Nasriyah, in Iraq, in eight days, covering a distance of about 1,287km (800 miles). On Wilfred Thesiger's first crossing of the Empty Quarter in the winter of 1946–7, his party travelled for two weeks across the sands without finding a well where it could water its animals.

All camels in the Middle East and Arabia are domesticated, and the work of herding, breed-

A Bedu boy in Nizwa.

The accoutrements of modern life have come to the Bedu, too.

Passers-by are welcomed by a set exchange of greetings and the asking of news, to which the reply is always that there is no news, or only good news.

of personal transport. The camel is still a source of milk, meat and wool. The wool, prized for its strength and warmth, is used to make cloaks and equipment such as udder bags, as well as the detailing on the tent curtain.

Under hot summer conditions the Bedu try to water their camels every day or two days, but in winter the period can be weekly or, if the grazing is good, the herds will not be watered

ing and milking them is traditionally the task of men. Each camel will be branded with the mark, called a *wasm*, of its owner and tribe, on its neck, shoulder or hindquarters. However, even a man with over 100 animals will commonly know his own camels individually and will usually have given names to each of them.

Camels are kept by the Bedu primarily as a source of milk. Thus the majority of animals are female. The Bedu will rarely kill an adult camel, unless it is obviously sick and dying. However, they will slaughter the occasional calf, especially a male. The only time that adult camels are normally killed for food is in order to feast a large number of guests such as for a marriage or to honour a visiting sheikh.

The traditional Bedu diet consists primarily of camel milk drunk cold or hot or boiled with bread (a mix called *threat* by the Bait Kathir in Oman), or cooked with rice. Meat is an occasional luxury and more often than not is goat's meat bought in the market. Along the coasts fresh and salted fish is an important staple for people and animals, and sun-dried sardines are a traditional supplementary feed for camels.

The role of Bedu women

Whatever the impression of women in Muslim society in general, Bedu women enjoy a great

of their honour. A Bedu male would not tolerate any person harming his sister's reputation, verbally or otherwise, and until his sister is married he will act as a surrogate husband. Even after her marriage he is responsible for the protection of her honour (more so than her husband) as her reputation is that of his family's, thus her honour is his honour.

Similarly young girls are their brothers' closest confidantes and are encouraged to contribute to their brothers' comfort and public image. Sisters will sew and weave their brothers' clothes and camel trappings, as well as cook

A Bedu guide and his son build a fire to make a coffee.

deal of freedom and play an important role in desert society. In such a harsh environment, and with the heavy demands of a nomadic existence, it would be impossible for the family to survive without the women taking their share of responsibility. What segregation exists is not a reflection of lack of status. Women's separation from strangers and the use of veils is due more to a sense of modesty and the protective concern of the menfolk – a custom more akin to a code of chivalry than a regime of repression.

As children, brothers and sisters are taught to have a special sense of closeness. A young boy is encouraged to see himself as his sister's protector, to bring presents to his female siblings. He is their chaperone in public and champion

their favourite foods for them. From a very early age a girl takes an active part in the daily work of the family. She will herd the sheep or goats if they have any, and an unmarried teenage girl will typically be left to pasture one of the family's camel herds. Where families have no sons, the daughters will often be found herding all the animals and entertaining guests, as well as driving the family vehicles.

Changing times

For all their colourful history and traditions, the huge upheavals in Oman and the UAE over recent decades have largely destroyed traditional Bedu culture. The mass production of motor vehicles has irrevocably altered their formerly camel-centred way of life, as has the emergence of sovereign nation states over whose borders they were formerly wont to wander. Most of all, the growing wealth of the region has offered them the chance finally to escape the hardships and grinding poverty of former generations.

Not surprisingly, many Bedu have migrated to the towns and cities in search of work and education, becoming subsumed into the settled population at large. In the UAE, traditional Bedu life has now almost entirely disappeared, although some of its traditions linger on in remote corners of the country such as the Liwa oasis in Abu Dhabi emirate. In Oman, the Bedu still survive in considerable numbers, particularly around the Sharqiya Sands, although former privations have been eased by the drilling of reliable wells, the provision of mobile medical centres, and regular deliveries by truck of water and animal feed. Mobile phones, too, have put an end to the traditional spreading of news by word of mouth, although the elaborate hospitality and old-fashioned salutations survive, even though the society and culture which created them has now gone for ever.

Old men at a Bedu encampment.

WEAVING

Weaving, almost entirely in the hands of women, is one of the oldest crafts of the Arabian peninsula, and the earliest illustration of the ground loom used by the Bedu is in an Egyptian fresco dating back to over 2000 BC.

Women spin using a stick with a cross-head whorl and hook before dyeing the wool and then re-spinning the material, producing a double strand of yarn. In the past, natural dyes from plants were used; modern synthetic dyes give access to brighter and more varied colours. Most decorative motifs are geometric, but the repertoire also includes stylised representations of familiar objects and animals. The patterns are repeated to the edge of the piece.

The tent curtain, the largest decorated piece of textile made by the Bedu, is usually in black and white. The white is commonly cotton yarn but can be white camel hair. A narrow pattern, it runs the length of the textile and uses symbols and designs, including geometric representations of household objects. Designed to run from the back wall to the front, it is made extra long so that it can be extended into the open space at the entrance of the tent, creating a private space for the women. The curtain is hung with the good side facing into the men's half of the tent. Traditional Bedu textiles can still sometimes be found in the souks around the Sharqiya Sands in Oman, particularly in Sinaw and Ibra.

ALL THAT GLISTERS - JEWELLERY

Jewellery performs much more than a decorative purpose among the Bedu of the Middle East – it can be a talisman or even the family safe deposit.

Visit any gold souk or handicraft market in the UAE or Oman and you'll see examples of the region's traditional silver jewellery – chunky rectangular bracelets or anklets and distinctively heavy necklaces, often decorated with a rustic selection of antique coins, miniature silver boxes and other ornaments.

Such traditional jewellery is no longer manufactured or worn today (except by a few Bedu in Oman), although prized antique pieces of antique Omani silver jewellery can change hands for considerable sums. Women would formerly have made up their own necklaces, adding coins, amulets and pendants either received as gifts, earned through the sale of produce, or found and kept for their magical powers. A woman's jewellery is technically her own, but she often also acts as the family bank, a custom dating from the days of raiding when women were immune from robbery. Even today, silver and gold provide a more trusted way of hoarding wealth than putting money into a bank.

Buy brooches and other silver jewellery at a market.

Traditional Omani silver hirz. The thick chain is decorated with Austrian Maria Theresa Thaler coins (the standard currency of the Gulf up until the 20th century) while the central casket would probably have held a fragment of text from the Qur'an, designed to ward off the evil eye and other maleficent influences.

Protective properties

A woman's wealth, worn as necklaces, bracelets, anklets and decorated veils, is much more than a financial reserve. Silver amulets, boxes and cylinders contain fragments of Qur'anic verse to protect the wearer against accidents, snake bites and scorpion stings. In Oman large round silver pendants called *sumt*, believed to contain an imprisoned *djinn* (demon), are popular.

An ornately attired Omani woman from Salalah, her hands and wrist laden with traditional Bedu jewellery.

A large selection of gold is available in the souks of Dubai.

THE RUSH FOR GOLD

Silver was originally the main metal used in Arabian jewellery – only people of importance could afford gold. All that has changed over the past 50 years, and it's now gold, rather than silver, which is the precious metal of choice for all strata of society.

The region's love affair with gold is plain to see in the glittering gold souks which can be found in most cities – those in Dubai and at Mutrah Souk in Muscat are particularly spectacular, and rank amongst the cheapest places in the world to buy the precious metal. Gold ornaments, produced mainly by expat Asian craftsmen, range from suave modern European designs through to huge and wildly extravagant Arabian-style pieces, although jewellery everywhere is still sold by weight – the quality of the design and workmanship isn't usually factored into the price.

Gold remains an essential component of the bride's price. Most brides expect to receive a full complement of gold jewellery – headdress, rings, necklaces and bracelets. Often this will be specially commissioned.

...ld necklace, Omani Heritage Museum. The use of gold – as ...own in this finely worked necklace – was traditionally ...nited to the upper echelons of Arabian society, typically worn ...ly by the ruling family and other elites.

A traditional Arabic coffee pot.

Foreign workers walk past Dubai's Burj Khalifa.

THE EXPATRIATES

Expats from all over the world call the UAE and
Oman home, bringing a host of international
influences to the region's society and culture.

The majority of people living in the UAE and Oman today are not local Emirati or Omani Arabs, but foreign expats – a quirk of human geography that has made this part of the Gulf one of the most ethnically diverse on the planet. Less than 15 percent of the inhabitants of the UAE are Emirati (and well under 10 percent in Dubai). The situation is less dramatic in Oman, although even there a considerable slice of the country's inhabitants are now foreign. The 2014 census revealed that of the total population of slightly over 4 million, more than 43 percent are expats, mainly from the Indian subcontinent.

Foreigners have settled around the coast of the UAE and Oman for centuries, although the massive expat influx dates from the 1960s and 1970s when the two fledgling countries – sitting on considerable oil reserves but without the sufficient native populations or technical expertise to develop their industry and infrastructure – flung open their doors, recruiting Western experts to build and run the new oil installations, financial institutions and other businesses, and subcontinental labourers to provide the manpower to achieve the dream.

The presence of huge numbers of outsiders is now an inescapable fact of life in the UAE and Oman, giving the region its unique cultural flavour, with Emiratis, Omanis, expat Arabs, Iranians, Indians, Pakistani, Bangladeshi, Filipinas, Africans and assorted Europeans coexisting, albeit obliquely, within the same space – the vast numbers of immigrants from India and Pakistan are particularly striking, and wandering through the streets of Bur Dubai in Dubai or Ruwi in Muscat, for instance, you often have to pinch yourself to remember exactly where you are. For all its laudable multicultural credentials, however, the presence of such large

Dune-bashing, a favourite with expats.

numbers of expats continues to raise some decidedly thorny questions about the identity of the two countries themselves, their cultural past, contemporary identity and possible future.

Who are the expats?

The range of expats in the Gulf is enormous – Dubai alone is home to nationals from over 200 countries, making it one of the most truly cosmopolitan and multicultural cities on the planet. The majority (nearly 60 percent of the total number of expats in the UAE, and over 70 percent in Oman) hail from the subcontinent. India provides the biggest numbers, with a disproportionate number coming from the southern state of Kerala, while numerous Pakistanis and Bangladeshis can also be found, along with smaller numbers of Sri Lankans and Nepalese. Other Arabs and Iranians make up around 20 percent in the UAE, while other nationalities (including Westerners) account for a final 8 percent. Dubai, easily the most ethnically diverse of the Emirates, is also home to a huge Filipina population, many of whom work as waitresses and cleaners in the city's tourist and leisure sectors, and also boasts a sizeable Iranian population who have played an important role in the development of the city since the early 20th century.

Expats they all might be, but a distinct pecking order generally applies (with notable excep-

Historic roots

Foreigners are nothing new in Oman and the UAE, and have been arriving for many centuries in the guise of merchants, mercenaries or

The UAE is perhaps unique amongst former European colonies and dependencies – not only did they not want the British to leave, they even offered to pay to keep UK armed forces on their soil following independence in 1971.

Conspicuous wealth, the Gold Souk, Dubai.

tions). At the top of the scale come the Western technocrats and professionals who supply the UAE (and, to a lesser extent, Oman) with much of the contemporary know-how required to run the place. Expat Arabs can also be found throughout the region, including significant numbers of Lebanese, Egyptians and Syrians, while at the bottom of the heap are the legions of Indian and Pakistani labourers, taxi drivers and shopkeepers.

The various ethnic strands tend to coexist, but not communicate, each nationality and socio-economic group keeping to its own circles. This is particularly the case in the UAE, where Western expats and Indian labourers alike might go years without having any serious interaction with their Emirati hosts.

even slaves. Historically, the region enjoys particularly close links with Iran. Much of the history of coastal Oman was shaped by its contacts with Persia, and Persian settlers occupied parts of the country in antiquity, as well as periodically seizing control of parts of the coast. Dubai and Iran have also enjoyed particularly close links in more recent times. The arrival of large numbers of Iranian merchants in the city in the early 20th century played a major role in establishing it as one of the southern Gulf's most important trading entrepôts, and the elaborate wind-towered houses they built can still be seen in the wonderful Al Fahidi Historical Neighbourhood – while the wind-tower itself has (somewhat ironically) been adopted as an important marker of national identity by the Emiratis, despite its foreign origins.

Links with Britain also run deep, dating back to the 19th century, when the location of both the UAE and Oman on shipping routes to India forced the British to take an active interest in the region. The role of British military and other advisers was a crucial factor in the so-called Omani renaissance which followed the accession of Sultan Qaboos to the throne in 1970, while the UK's post-independence influence on the UAE – formerly the British protectorate known as the Trucial States – has also been considerable.

Other strong foreign links have also added their contribution to the region's multicultural make-up. The existence of the Omani enclave of Gwadur (in what is now the Pakistani province of Baluchistan) since the late 18th century resulted in the arrival of large numbers of Baluchis in the country, where their ancestors continue to live to this day. India itself was another importance source of trade throughout the 19th and 20th centuries, thanks to a mixture of geographical proximity and the influence of the British. The Indian rupee served as the main currency of both Oman and the UAE until modern times, and many Emiratis and Omanis spent time in the subcontinent, Bombay especially. In return, Indian traders began increasingly to settle in the region, in Muscat, Abu Dhabi and (especially) Dubai, establishing powerful trading empires, some of which survive to this day.

Executive perks

Life in the Gulf for Westerners has often been portrayed as some kind of expatriate nirvana: a heady combination of endless sunshine, superlative leisure facilities, a tax-free salary and the opportunity to enjoy a lifestyle which would never be possible back home – not to mention the region's generally liberal attitude to Western evils ranging from alcohol to (in Dubai, particularly) endemic prostitution. All of this is at least partly true, although the flipside of the package are the terms under which Westerners in the region – the UAE, in particular – are allowed to enjoy such benefits. Residence in the country is permitted only so long as you hold a job with approved sponsors, with a visa renewable at three-yearly intervals and no guarantees about the future, even if you buy property in the country.

All of this gives Western expat life in the region its peculiarly transient flavour. The potential nightmare underlying the dream was made brutally clear during the 2008–9 credit crunch, when thousands of Western expats lost their jobs. Stories of Europeans fleeing Dubai in the wake of the real-estate crash and abandoning their cars at the airport for fear of being arrested and thrown into prison for defaulting on loans have become the stuff of urban legend. According to a report in *The Times* in 2009, over 3,000 cars were found left at Dubai's international airport by Westerners fleeing the country.

Working on the expat tan, Dubai.

CITIZENSHIP

The issue of citizenship – or the lack of it – is a particularly vexed subject in the region. UAE citizenship, along with the considerable financial privileges it brings, is jealously guarded, and only a tiny handful of foreigners have succeeded in obtaining it. Many people who have lived all their lives in the UAE continue to carry the nationality of their parents' home country, even if they might never even have visited it, and thus have no legal right of stay in the country which is their de facto home. Obtaining Omani citizenship is only slightly less difficult, even if you were born in the country, and usually requires a minimum of 20 years' residence.

Labour rights and wrongs

Whatever the occasional travails of the region's Western expats, however, they pale into insignificance compared to the plight of the region's subcontinental expats, who have flocked to the region in search of jobs and wages which are unavailable to them at home. Particularly exploited are the hundreds of thousands of construction workers who have provided the muscle and manpower which has helped create the gleaming modern skylines of Dubai and elsewhere. Most are brought to the region by employment agencies in their home countries, often paying their first year's salary for the privilege. Many arrive in the region and find themselves virtual prisoners, their passports confiscated and their wages kept systematically in arrears in order to keep them in order, and confined to squalid labour camps on the margins of the cities which they have helped build. Working conditions are little better, with labourers forced to toil through the blistering heat of the midday Gulf sun often in dangerous working conditions with little or no health and safety – construction-site fatalities occur with depressing frequency.

There is a huge expat workforce in the UAE.

JASHANMAL'S INFLUENCE

A particularly revealing example of the early influence of Indian expats is provided by the story of Mohan Jashanmal, whose Jashanmal bookstores can still be seen in the UAE. His first store opened in Abu Dhabi in 1964 and became a particular favourite of Sheikh Zayed, who visited regularly. Zayed was especially fascinated by Jashanmal's imported pictures of the Empire State Building, UN Headquarters and other foreign sights, saying that Abu Dhabi would soon be able to boast similar landmarks of its own – a bold but prescient claim, given that Abu Dhabi at that time was little more than a cluster of mudbrick houses and dirt-track roads.

Other human rights abuses are also common. Expat housemaids (mainly Filipina) have also been subjected to abuse in the privacy of their employer's home, while human-trafficking and forced prostitution is another major concern, in parts of the UAE at least.

Expats, Emiratis and Omanis

The arrival of vast numbers of foreigners has, of course, had a massive impact on the lives of the people in whose countries they have landed, and although racial tensions have been remarkably absent so far, signs of changing attitudes can clearly be seen.

The virtual deluge of foreigners in the UAE has had its inevitable effect. Native Emiratis, who to begin with were happy to see foreigners arrive to help develop their country, increasingly feel virtual strangers in their own land – particularly given native Emiratis' customary isolation from

> *A side-effect of the flood of largely male expats into the UAE is the country's gender imbalance, with men outnumbering women by over two to one. In Dubai males form 75 percent of the population, making it one of the world's most sexually lopsided cities.*

take well-paid but undemanding jobs in various government ministries and other state organisations (Emiratis comprise 60 percent of the public sector workforce). More than 99 percent of employees in private companies remain expat to this day. The opportunity is there to boost the numbers of employed nationals with the much-anticipated Dubai World Expo 2020.

The situation in Oman is somewhat different, and relations in Oman between natives and expats are generally closer and more harmonious than those in the UAE – a reflection of the lower overall number of foreign workers, and of the

Abu Dhabi's Marina Mall.

the expat workforce at large. Resentment at the insensitive behaviour of foreign residents (not to mention visiting tourists) has become an increasing bone of contention, added to the impending sense that their own indigenous culture is being systematically swamped by foreign influences. The government, in turn, has become increasingly concerned at the lack of involvement by native Emiratis in the economic life of the country, launching a sustained programme of "Emiratisation" aimed at increasing the involvement of local people in private enterprise, and developing the skills of the population at large – although the initiative has had relatively little impact to date, most Emiratis preferring either to live on their considerable state handouts or to

Omanis' generally lower income levels (although, as in the UAE, the government has introduced an "Omanisation" policy designed to boost the number of nationals working for private companies; currently around 10 percent of private sector workers are Omani). Tensions persist even so, and the taking of jobs by expats was a major bone of contention amongst protestors during the demonstrations in early 2011 that marked the Omani phase of the Arab Spring – even though many of the allegedly stolen jobs were ones which Omanis themselves were unwilling or unqualified to take on. As the Omani population hit the 4 million mark in 2014, the government announced its desire to reduce the expat population to 33 percent in order to step up Omanisation.

Sultan Qaboos Grand Mosque, the only mosque in Oman that is open to non-Muslims.

ISLAM IN SOUTHEAST ARABIA

Islam shapes the principles of government as well as private lives, while in Oman a particular brand of Islam, Ibadism, has played a crucial role in the country's history.

Islam remains fundamental to the Gulf. Modern as it might seem, life in the UAE and Oman still revolves around traditional daily and annual religious rhythms, ranging from the five daily prayers that mark the passing of each 24-hour period through to the great festivals which punctuate the year. The dominant form of the religion nowadays in the UAE is the mainstream Sunni version of Islam. The majority of Omanis, however, continue to profess the ancient Ibadi faith, with its uniquely democratic traditions.

Islam, meaning "submission", permeates all aspects of the believer's public and private lives, laying down rules for everyday conduct and social relationships. Distinctions between religion, morality, legal affairs and politics do not exist, for they are judged to be subsumed under God's indivisible law. The faithful express their belief without self-consciousness wherever they happen to be, whether at home, in the street or in the mosque.

A minaret, Bahla, Oman.

The coming of Islam

Islam was revealed to the Prophet Mohammed, a native of Mecca in western Arabia, in a series of revelations beginning in AD 610 and continuing until his death in AD 632. Muslims believe that God vouchsafed these utterances, of which the Qur'an is held to be a verbatim record, as the final and perfected revelation of Islam.

Islam, as the religion of Allah, is believed to have existed unchanged for all time, and to have been the religion of the patriarch Abraham. Subsequent prophets, such as Moses and Jesus, are revered but regarded as not having been in complete possession of the divine Message. Muslims do not believe that Allah is distinct from the God of the Bible and the Torah.

Oman was one of the first countries to embrace Islam, in AD 630 – part of the early spread of the new religion within Arabia during the lifetime of the Prophet Mohammed. The Prophet sent emissaries from Medina, as he did to all the tribes and settlements of Arabia, calling them to Islam. The one he sent to Oman was the general 'Amr bin al-'As, later in the 640s to be the Muslim conqueror of Egypt.

Though 'Amr targeted the flourishing Persian port and capital of Sohar on the Omani coast it was the Arab tribal ruling family, the Julanda, and not the Persian governor, who accepted his message. For the Arabs the call to Islam was the call to eject the ruling Persian colonisers of Oman out of the Batinah coastal plain of Oman.

Following the death of Mohammed in 632 a period of turbulence engulfed the new Islamic world. A series of rebellions broke out against Abu Bakr, the new caliph in Medina, leading to the so-called Ridda Wars, or Wars of Apostasy. Oman was at the forefront of the rebellion, although this was probably less to do with religious than political reasons, with the powerful Azd tribe attempting to reassert their autonomy. According to tradition, Abu Bakr despatched a large force which clashed with the

The dome of the Sultan Qaboos Mosque in Muscat.

Omanis at the Battle of Dibba, resulting in the annihilation of the rebels – the large graveyard near the modern town of Dibba is said to contain the remains of those killed in the fighting.

Ibadism and Imams

Islam would thereafter remain unchallenged as the dominant faith in Oman, although the region's independent-minded and rebellious tribes adopted an unusual brand of the religion that would subsequently characterise the country's religious and political life right up to the present day. Many Omanis began to travel to the great Muslim foundation at Basra. Here they were drawn into the political and ideological conflicts which nearly succeeded in

bringing down the Umayyad Caliphate, creating enormous disorder in the early Islamic state and producing the rebel Khawarij or "Outsiders" movement.

Travellers returning to Oman over the next two centuries introduced Khawarij ideas to Oman, where they developed into the form of the religion known as Ibadism which is still practised by the majority of Omanis right up to the present. In common with other movements which would today be called fundamentalist, the aim of the Ibadis was to restore the pure Islamic state according to the teaching of the Prophet, before it had been corrupted by the third Caliph 'Uthman. Though there were several other centres of Ibadism in early Islam, notably in Yemen and Hadhramaut, today Oman is the only place where it still has a significant number of followers.

True Ibadism is distinguished from orthodox Sunni Islam at the political level in two ways. First, the hereditary principle is anathema. Ibadis believe their ruler should be chosen by an electoral college of good and learned men and proposed to the community. This Imam can be drawn from any family, for the first condition an aspiring Imam must fulfil is that of piety and learning. Second, Ibadis do not believe it is necessary to have an Imam at all times. During periods of political upheaval the Imamate can lapse and go into a state of secrecy, abeyance or latency known as *kitman*. This has occurred in Oman's history, sometimes for centuries.

Of all doctrines of sovereignty, this is a rather minimal one and one likely to appeal to a tribal mentality. In common with other Muslim attempts to reflect the rule of God upon earth, the ideal of the good ruler included the condition that allegiance to him should be withdrawn if, when God's law was transgressed, he showed no sign of repentance. There was no standing army under central command to enforce sovereignty, and no elaborate bodyguard: militias were raised by the Imam calling up tribal levies.

This kind of consultative system works well when everyone is in agreement, but immediately falls apart when they are not. Only rarely, therefore, has the Imamate succeeded in genuinely uniting the tribes of inner Oman. More usually the Imamate has been the political prize sought by rival tribal groupings.

While the Imamate sometimes succeeded in harnessing and harmonising tribalism, it never eradicated it: the Imam was simply a kind of supra-tribal leader, his office modelled on that of a tribal chief.

Sunni Islam on the coast

Not all Omanis are Ibadis, however. A sizeable number subscribe to the Sunni creed of Islam, along with virtually all the population of the UAE (apart from a few Shi'ites of Iranian descent). Established on the cosmopolitan coast, Sunni Islam was traditionally

shorts by men. Other emirates subscribe to a much more liberal interpretation of Islamic law, although a number of Westerners have been caught out as a result of public demonstrations of affection which would pass unnoticed in the West but which can carry a prison sentence for lewd behaviour in the UAE.

> *A Muslim male may take up to four wives, assuming he can support them all – although in practice few take more than one.*

Muslim man praying, Dubai.

more liberal and outward-looking than the Ibadi creed of the interior, and religious freedoms remain carefully protected to this day – you'll find Hindu temples and Christian churches in Dubai, alongside the innumerable mosques.

Differences between the various Emirates persist, even so. The best known is the conservative emirate of Sharjah which, as a result of strong Saudi influence, now follows a strict form of the traditional Islamic Shariah law code. Sharjah law has now banned alcohol and enacted strict "decency laws" which make it a criminal offence for two unmarried people of opposite sexes to be alone together – as well as banning the wearing of jewellery or skimpy

Islam in daily life

The central tenets of the religion, known as the Five Pillars of Islam, form the basis of the faith as practised by all its adherents. The first of the Five Pillars is the declaration of faith (*shahada*), which involves saying the words "There is no god but Allah, and Mohammed is the messenger of Allah". Other pillars include praying five times daily, paying the alms tax (*zakat*), fasting during the holy month of Ramadan and (if one's means allow), making the pilgrimage to Mecca (the Hajj) once in one's lifetime.

Islam permeates many levels of local life in terms of how people (women especially) dress and dietary taboos (with both pork and

Religious invocations form a staple part of Gulf Arabic – hardly a sentence passes in most conversations without the traditional insh'allah ("God willing") or al hamdu'lillah ("Thanks be to God").

(adhan), with the soulful noise of muezzin summoning the faithful resounding from minarets across the country – Arabia's most instantly recognisable aural signature, and one that can be heard in remote mountain villages and modern shopping malls alike. In former times this would have been a person calling from the tower or roof of a mosque; nowadays pre-recorded messages relayed through loudspeakers are the norm. The call to prayer itself is a précis of Islamic beliefs, rather like the *shahada*, usually centred on multiple renditions of the words *Allahu*

alcohol being forbidden), as well as providing the region with many of its most characteristic Arabic expressions and idioms.

For the visitor, the most obvious sign of Islamic life are the daily calls to prayer

A prayer-book sign on the road from Quiryat, Oman.

THE EVIL EYE AND OTHER MAGICAL BELIEFS

As in many countries across the Muslim world, the concept of the Evil Eye *(ayn al hasud)* is still very much alive and well in the UAE and Oman – the idea that an envious or hostile person can cause you bad luck or harm by a simple look or turn of speech. The concept of the Eye goes back into the depths of antiquity, and is also backed by the authority of the Qur'an, which warns against it.

There are believed to be many different ways of warding off the eye, while most traditional Arabian jewellery (see page 74) features protective amulets or small boxes in which pieces of Quranic text were kept to protect the wearer. The usual formula for

avoiding appearing to give the Eye is to say *masha allah*, meaning "God has willed it", rather than expressing direct praise or admiration, which might be construed as envy.

The Evil Eye is just one of many quasi-religious magical beliefs which have taken root in the Gulf. In Oman, in particular, there is also a widespread fear of jinns, powerful supernatural beings who can take possession of those unfortunate enough to offend them, causing misery, pain and even death. The jinns of the Bahla area are particularly notorious, credited with a variety of actions ranging from turning milk sour to carrying off entire mosques in the middle of the night.

Akbar ("God is Great"), usually sung with a rising flourish.

Muslims are expected to pray five times daily at fixed times. The prayers *(salah)* are known, in order, as *fajr* (dawn), *dhuhr* (noon), *asr* (late afternoon), *maghrib* (just after sunset) and *isha'a* (between sunset and midnight). Muslims will attempt to reach a mosque in time for prayers; failing this, they will simply pray wherever they happen to be at the time, usually kneeling on a small prayer rug. The important thing is not the location, but the fact that the worshipper is in a state of ritual purity both mentally and physi-

expected to purify mind and body and reaffirm their relationship with God. During Ramadan, Muslims are required to fast from dawn to dusk, while music and dancing is also frowned upon.

The breaking of the fast at dusk, known as *iftar*, is the highlight of the day, often with lavish amounts of food and drink being consumed to compensate for the day's efforts (ironically, it is said that many people actually gain weight during Ramadan). Special "*iftar* tents" are erected in many places, from village squares to five-star hotels, with sumptuous Arabian buffets. Things get even more colourful

Shoes must be removed before prayer.

cally – ritual pre-prayer ablutions *(wudhu)* are particularly important, and all mosques come equipped with washrooms. The stimulating tours of Jumeirah Mosque in Dubai (see page 207) offer interesting insight into prayer rituals.

Annual festivals

Supplementing the daily round of prayer are the great annual festivals celebrated by Muslims across the world, which are conscientiously observed in both the UAE and Oman.

Pre-eminent amongst Islamic festivals is the month-long Ramadan, celebrated during the lunar month of Ramadan (exact dates vary from year to year). Ramadan is a time of fasting and religious reflection during which Muslims are

and busy during Eid Al Fitr, the day marking the end of Ramadan.

The region's second major festival is Eid Al Adha, the "Festival of the Sacrifice". Falling around 70 days after the end of Ramadan, this celebrates the willingness of Abraham (or Ibrahim, as he is known to Muslims) to sacrifice his son Ismail at the command of God (although having proved his obedience, he was permitted to sacrifice a ram instead). Large numbers of animals are slaughtered and the meat divided amongst the poor during the festival, making for a rather grisly sight in parts of the region, Oman especially, where huge numbers of carcasses can often be seen literally piled up by the roadside.

FOOD AND DRINK

The UAE and Oman provide an eclectic crucible of Arabian, Indian and European culinary traditions.

The Gulf stands at something of a culinary crossroads, midway between the classic Middle Eastern cuisines of the Levant to the west and the spicier cooking of the Indian subcontinent to the east, with a dash of Iranian and European influences thrown in for good measure. Both Indian and Middle Eastern cuisines are both well represented throughout the region, as are a range of other global cooking styles, although traditional Emirati and Omani remain considerably more elusive.

Ingredients and influences

Given its largely hostile climate, food production in the UAE and Oman has traditionally been limited, with nutrition usually at subsistence levels and based around readily available foodstuffs like dates and fish. Fish was particularly important around the coast (and was also dried and sent up into the mountains both for human and animal consumption), while inland there was a heavy reliance on the ubiquitous date – an unusually rich, concentrated and durable source of food which was perfectly suited to the nomadic Bedu lifestyle, supplemented by simple flatbreads cooked over campfires and considerable quantities of coffee. Roasted meat – wild oryx and other animals – was eaten when available, although it was usually something of an uncommon luxury, and the hunting of such animals remained a difficult and highly prized skill amongst the Bedu, at least until the advent of 4x4s and semi-automatic machine-guns. Camels were also occasionally slaughtered and eaten on important occasions (camel remains a popular food in Dhofar to this day). Bananas, papayas, mangoes and citrus fruits were also cultivated, while the cooler heights of the Jebel Akhdar produced a supply of temperate produce – peaches, pears, grapes, apples and

Cooking on an open-air grill at a restaurant in Salalah, Oman.

pomegranates, along with a wide range of vegetables and the area's famous rosewater. Such foodstuffs remained scant, however, and by and large the region had neither the wealth nor the natural produce to allow the development of a classical cuisine like that of North India, Iran or the Turkish Ottomans.

External influences brought to the coast by merchant dhows or overland by trading caravan introduced new outside elements: spices from India became an established feature in Gulf cooking, while dishes were adopted from the cuisines of other countries around the Gulf, Iran, the subcontinent and, of course, the Arab lands around the Mediterranean to the west.

Traditional regional cooking

Traditional Gulf cuisine is poorly represented in restaurants, although a few establishments are doing their best to revive local culinary traditions, such as the Bin Ateeq chain in Oman along with places like Kargeen and Ubhar in Muscat and the Khan Murjan Restaurant in Dubai.

Regional Emirati and Omani cuisine provides an interesting, lightly spiced blend of Indian and Arabian cooking traditions, most of them centred on biryani-style baked rice and meat concoctions – local offshoots of the better-known Indian biryani or Iranian *polo*.

Tea and dates are traditionally consumed after breaking the fast during Ramadan.

> The Dubai Friday brunch is a city institution, particularly popular amongst the city's European expat set. Many restaurants lay on all-you-can-eat (and sometimes drink) deals. It usually kicks off around midday, and can last for the remainder of the afternoon.

Local variants include dishes like *fouga* (a kind of Emirati-style chicken biryani) and *goboli* (rice cooked with lamb, spices, onions and raisins). Other similar biryani-style dishes you may encounter (particularly in Oman) include the Afghan-style *kabuli* (or *qabooli*), the Saudi *kabsa* (also known as *maqboos* or *machbus*) and the Yemeni *mandi*. In theory, each of these regional variants has its own distinct character and style of preparation, although it's difficult to generalise.

Other old-fashioned recipes include *harees laham* (lamb with wheat in cow ghee); *shuwa* (slow-roasted meat cooked in a clay oven, like the classic Yemeni *mandi*); *mashuai* (whole spit-roasted kingfish served with lemon rice); and *marak* (traditional vegetable curry), although these rarely make their way onto restaurant menus.

Chicken (*dijaj*) remains the staple ingredient in most biryanis, kebabs and curries, although various other types of meat are also available going under the name *laham* (literally "meat"), which usually means beef or lamb, but might also conceivably mean goat or (in Salalah) camel.

There's lots of top-quality fish available along the Omani coast, although to see it done justice you'll have to shell out for a meal at one of Muscat's upmarket seafood restaurants – or go to Dubai, which is where a lot of the catch ends up. The local kingfish (*kenadh*), shark (*qersh al samak*) and lobster (*sharkha*) are particularly good, as is the ubiquitous *hammour* (grouper), a versatile white fish which can be found on menus across the region.

Middle Eastern cuisine

Mainstream Middle Eastern cuisine – often referred to as "Lebanese" (although "Levantine" might be a more accurate description) – is widely found throughout both the UAE and Oman. Many of the most typical dishes originated in the countries of the Levant, around the eastern end of Mediterranean, during the Ottoman period.

The classic Middle Eastern meal always opens with a selection of meze – small dishes, shared amongst a group of diners, rather like Spanish tapas. Many of these have established themselves in mainstream world cuisine – bowls of olives, along with hummus, falafel and tabouleh. Others remains less well known outside the region, including classics such as *fattoush* (a type of salad with toasted bread), *kibbeh* (deep-fried lamb balls mixed with cracked wheat), *fatayer* (triangular pastries filled with cheese or spinach), as well as dips such as *foul madamas* and *baba ghanouj* (made from fava beans and eggplant respectively, blended with lemon juice, oil, chilli and garlic).

Grilled meats, or kebabs, form the basis of more substantial dishes. Easily the most common form of Arabian food is the ubiquitous shwarma – spit-roasted chicken and/or beef carved off and served wrapped in bread with salads – the Gulf version of the doner kebab (also served laid out on a piece of bread on a plate with chips and salad – the so-called "shwarma plate"). You'll never go far in the Gulf without seeing a local shwarma café, with dripping haunches of meat enveloped in clouds of temptingly flavoursome smoke. Other common dishes include the Lebanese *shish taouk* (chicken kebabs served with garlic sauce) and Turkish-style kofte kebabs. Most kebabs are served with Arabian-style flatbread *(khubz)* and a bowl of hummus and accompanying salad.

Lebanese food can be found across the region, from humble cafés in backwater Oman and the UAE through to glitzy establishments in Abu Dhabi and Dubai – more upscale places often double as impromptu party venues, with live music and the ubiquitous belly-dancer, often not getting going until past 11pm, and then cracking on until the small hours.

Kibbeh are lamb balls in a bulgar shell.

Lebanese manakish, a kind of pizza.

DATES

Dates provide the region with its most distinctive culinary experience – and a living link with the region's harsh history. Dates underpinned the traditional nomadic lifestyle of the desert interior, providing a concentrated, transportable and long-lasting source of nutrition which was perfectly adapted for the nomadic lifestyle of the region's Bedu – even today, local Muslims still traditionally break their daytime Ramadan fast by eating a single date as night falls.

Dates have remarkable nutritional qualities, offering an excellent source of protein, vitamins and minerals. Their high sugar content (up to 80 percent) protects them against bacterial decay and makes them extremely durable – dried dates can last for years, making them perfectly adapted to survive in the heat of the Gulf, even without refrigeration. They can also be pressed for their juice or used to make wines and syrups. In earlier times, boiling date syrup, poured onto the heads of attackers, was even used as a military weapon. They were also the region's most important export before the discovery of oil.

Numerous different varieties of date are grown all over the Gulf, ranging dramatically in size and colour, from dark brown to pale, almost honey-coloured varieties – the best are treasured and savoured by local connoisseurs, like fine wines in France.

Subcontinental spices

Indian food, in one form or another, forms the mainstay of modern Gulf cuisine – a result of both long-standing historic links between the two regions and the presence of huge numbers of subcontinental expats in the region. In the major cities, upmarket restaurants offer superb renditions of classic North Indian dishes, on a par with anything you'll find in the West (or, indeed, in India itself) – Indego by Vineet and Nina's in Dubai offer particularly good and innovative contemporary Indian cooking, while the much-loved Mumtaz Mahal in

Local produce at a Muscat vegetable market.

Muscat can't be beaten for traditional classics in a relaxed atmosphere. For a true taste of Gulf-style Indian food, nothing beats a visit to one of the downmarket – but often surprisingly excellent – Indian and Pakistani cafés which cram the streets of Bur Dubai in Dubai or Ruwi in Muscat, offering a wide range of dishes stretching from classic North Indian Punjabi and Mughlai dishes through to feisty South Indian *masala dosas*, *uttapam* and *thalis*.

Elsewhere, a kind of low-grade pseudo-Indian style of cooking remains the staple of down-at-heel cafés across both the UAE and, especially, Oman, featuring ubiquitous biryanis and other Indian- or Pakistani-style chicken or mutton curries – although these bear little relation to the

food served up in the West, or, indeed, in the subcontinent itself.

International influences

Many of the cities of the modern Gulf now boast surprisingly exalted culinary credentials. Dubai, in particular, has established itself as the Middle East's major culinary hotspot, attracting celebrity chefs ranging from Pierre Gagnaire, Giorgio Locatelli and the late Santi Santamaria to Sanjay Kapoor and Vineet Bhatia, India's first-ever Michelin-starred chef. Abu Dhabi and Muscat also boast a fair roster of top chefs, mainly based at the restaurants of top-end hotels such as the Emirates Palace in Abu Dhabi and the Al Bustan, Shangri-La and Grand Hyatt hotels in Muscat.

Thai and Chinese restaurants have also made considerable inroads into the local dining scene in the major cities, although the style of Chinese cuisine served up in many places is a hybridised Indo-Sino style of cuisine, with rather more spice than is authentic. Dubai is also particularly good for Iranian food (evidence of the city's long-standing links with that country), featuring hearty *chelo* kebabs and *polos* (Iranian-style biryanis, traditional featuring slow-cooked meats leavened with saffron and barberries). Moroccan food can also be found throughout the main cities of the region, with signature dishes including the classic spicy *harira* soup, *pastilla* (pigeon pie) and various tagines and couscous dishes.

Fast-food outlets have made inevitable inroads into the region, and branches of McDonald's, Subway, Domino's Pizza and suchlike are now pretty much everywhere. For a more rewarding take on local fast food, look out for branches of the Lebanese Zaatar w Zeit chain, with outlets across Dubai and Abu Dhabi, offering fast-food Lebanese-style cuisine, including the classic Lebanese *manakish* (a kind of Middle Eastern-style pizza served with thyme, yoghurt and cheese).

Desserts

No traditional meal in Oman would be complete without a portion of halwa, the rather sickly dessert which has become something of a national dish, and which can be seen piled up in china bowls and plastic tubs in shops and souks across the country. Halwa is made in a wide range of different styles, across Europe, the Middle East and Asia. Omani halwa is wheat-based, which gives it a quite different taste and texture to the nut-based halwas found in Eastern Europe, Greece and Turkey, made from a mix of semolina, ghee (clarified butter), sugar and rosewater, flavoured with cardamom and almonds and slow-boiled over a wood fire.

Umm Ali, a sweet Arabian-style bread pudding, is another favourite dessert, while you might also come across *lokhemat* – deep-fried balls of flour flavoured with cardamom and served with lime and cardamom syrup.

Drinks and shisha

Coffee remains central to life in the UAE and Oman – not just a drink, but a kind of social adhesive which oils the wheels of traditional hospitality, performed according to the traditional coffee ceremony etiquette. Itinerant coffee-pourers can still often be seen patrolling the lobbies of upmarket hotels, government ministries and other public spaces, dispensing drinks from ornate copper pots, usually with a tray of dates to hand as well. The drink itself is notably different from that consumed in the West, served without milk and sugar but flavoured with spices including cardamom and/or cloves – intense, aromatic and slightly bitter, and traditionally drunk from tiny handle-less cups, like oversized thimbles. More mainstream Western coffee houses such as Starbucks, Costa and many other chains have also now established themselves throughout the region, proving popular with an eclectic mixture of expats and locals – an engagingly contemporary update of the traditional coffee house.

Tea *(shay)* is also universally popular, although not of particularly high quality – the classic Lipton's teabag is ubiquitous, although you may hit upon a local Indian café serving up the classic subcontinental *masala chai*, sweet and heavily spiced. Fruit juices are also widely available, usually particularly good in Lebanese establishments, as are all the usual global fizzy drinks. You may also come across the traditional *laban*, a type of sour buttermilk.

Alcohol is widely available across the region (in Dubai and Abu Dhabi particularly), although punitive taxes keep prices high and local laws mean that establishments are usually only found in top-end hotels – independent pubs and licensed restaurants remain a rarity. Most establishments model themselves on ersatz English pubs, complete with faux-British wood-panelled decor and with a stereotypical range of international tipples.

There's also a tempting selection of more stylish bars in Dubai, Abu Dhabi and Muscat, however, often offering superb beachside locations or high-rise settings, and with an upmarket selection of cocktails and shots aimed firmly at the expat and tourist party set.

The traditional meal concludes with shisha: Arabian-style tobacco smoked in one of the distinctive waterpipes (hookah, *narghil* or "hubbly-bubbly") which can be found across the Middle East. Shisha cafés are enormously popular in the UAE (although surprisingly rare in Oman), while many restaurants also serve shisha, although

A Nizwa couple in Pizza Hut; western chains are popular.

> The Arabic word for coffee, *qahwah*, is thought to be the origin of the English word "coffee", via the Turkish *kahve* and the Italian *caffè* – although *qahwah* may derive from Kaffa, in Ethiopia, an original home of the coffee shrub.

the UAE's smoking ban means that it can now only be served in outdoor venues or in separate smoking areas. Most shisha cafés will have at least 10 types of shisha to choose from (often more), including unflavoured blends alongside various fruit-scented concoctions such as apple, lemon and grape – much gentler on the throat and infinitely more aromatic than Western cigarettes.

A sunset view of Sheikh Zayed Road in Dubai.

ARCHITECTURE

From traditional mudbrick forts and palm-thatch
huts to futuristic steel-and-glass high-rises, the UAE
and Oman present a kaleidoscopic array of Arabian
architecture past and present.

Oman and the UAE between them offer a fascinating range of architecture both ancient and modern, from the time-warped mudbrick forts and mountain villages of the Omani interior to the ultra-modern skyscrapers of Abu Dhabi and Dubai – a striking physical symbol of the whirlwind changes which have swept through the region in recent decades. The traditional architecture of Oman is as fine as anything in the Islamic world, with a staggering collection of majestic castles dotting the country's mountains, coast and desert, along with innumerable watchtowers, walled towns and villages, and intricately engineered *falaj* systems – a marvellous compendium of local building traditions, making exemplary use of the very simplest building materials. The more forward-looking cities of the UAE, meanwhile, are rapidly transforming themselves into showpieces of modern architecture at its most extravagant and inventive, attracting a string of top international architects and boasting a range of iconic contemporary landmarks, including Dubai's celebrated Burj al Arab and Burj Khalifa, the world's tallest building.

A wind tower at Al Bateen dhow harbour, Abu Dhabi.

> Looking forward, the region's finest architectural creation will undoubtedly be the Saddiyat Island development in Abu Dhabi, with major landmarks by top architects including Norman Foster, Frank Gehry, Jean Nouvel, Tadao Ando and Zaha Hadid.

Traditional materials

Traditional buildings in Oman and the UAE often give the marvellous impression of having grown organically out of the landscapes in which they sit, their ochre-coloured walls blending seamlessly with the surrounding mountains or desert, so that it is sometimes difficult to know where nature ends and building begins, with forts moulded around the contours of the rocks on which they sit and mudbrick villages rising out of the earth from which they were created.

Much of this sense of connection between building and landscape derives from the ingenious use of locally available materials: mudbrick, coral, mountain rock, palm-thatch, mangrove wood – but little (if anything) imported or foreign. The simplest form of traditional building in the region is the *barasti* hut, fashioned from nothing but trimmed palm branches and leaves tied together to form impromptu shelters – impermanent but surprisingly effective in providing a modicum of shade, while the permeable palm-frond "walls" allowed breezes to blow through, taking advantage of whatever breezes were available. These were the types of dwelling which most Emiratis and Omanis of the coastal regions lived in right up to the 1950s and 1960s, and replicas can be seen in various museums and forts around the region.

Larger buildings were generally fashioned from mudbrick. Mudbrick (or adobe, from

using layers of pounded gypsum, while walls were strengthened by the insertion of mangrove poles bound with rope.

More elaborate structures, whether mudbrick, stone or a mixture of both, were often faced with *sarooj*, a type of mortar-cum-plaster. *Sarooj* was made from a mixture of mud and limestone burnt together at extremely high temperatures for up to a week. The resultant ash was then mixed with water (again, sometimes with the addition of a fermenting agent) and the paste used to bind bricks and stone, and to provide the smooth and shiny plaster finish

Inside Nakhal Castle on Oman's Batinah Coast.

the Arabic *al tob*, meaning "mud") was made from alluvial clay, containing fine particles of grit and silt, mixed with chopped straw to strengthen the resultant bricks. A fermenting agent, such as sugar-cane syrup, was also sometimes added. The resulting mixture was then left to "cure" for four or five days before being moulded into bricks.

Stone was also often used, often in combination with mudbrick: either slabs of locally quarried rock in the mountains or coral-stone *(fesht)* along the coast – look closely at the walls of many of the region's lowland forts and traditional buildings and you can still make out the delicate outlines of submarine sponges and other corals. Stones were cemented together

which can still be seen on the walls of many Omani forts today.

Imported materials were only rarely used – roofs and doors of Indian teak and other hardwoods can sometimes be found, although most timbers used are locally sourced mangrove poles, used not only to strengthen walls but also to form roofs, usually with a layer of palm leaves laid on top.

Houses and forts

Fine old traditional houses can be seen across the region, many of them now restored as museums (such as the Heritage House in Dubai, Bait al Naboodah in Sharjah and Bait al Zubair in Muscat) – although it's worth remembering that these elaborate mansions are far from typical of the living arrangements enjoyed by the former population at large, most of whom lived in simple, ephemeral *barasti* palm-thatch huts until quite recent times.

Traditional houses follow a fairly standard pattern, arranged around a central courtyard (*housh*), sometimes with a verandah (*liwan*), providing a space where inhabitants could cook, play, take the air and graze a few animals in complete privacy; some courtyards even boast a well and perhaps a couple of trees. Exterior walls are usually plain and largely windowless in order to protect the privacy of those within. Rooms usually include a *majlis* (meeting room) in which the family would have received guests and exchanged news (some larger houses have two separate *majlis* for men and women), along with assorted bedrooms, kitchens and storerooms. In the UAE, most large houses also boast one or more wind towers. The overall effect of most traditional houses is often understated, verging on the austere, although the overall plainness is often relieved by richly carved details including lavish wooden doors and screens, or by geometrical floral designs framing windows, doorways and arches, made from gypsum coloured with powdered charcoal.

Traditional local architecture was remarkably well adapted for its environment (unlike today's modernistic high-rises). Walls were built thick and windows kept small to exclude the scorching heat outside, while both coral and adobe helped to preserve the coolness of the interiors thanks to their excellent natural insulating properties. Houses were also built close to one another, partly for security, and also to provide shade in the narrow alleyways between.

The innumerable forts of the region follow a similar pattern in terms of their overall construction and internal living arrangements, though obviously they tend to be much larger in size, and boast additional defensive features (see page 127).

Contemporary Islamic architecture

Despite the advent of concrete and steel, many of the region's modern buildings still follow traditional patterns. The layout of the modern Emirati and Omani villa, for instance,

retains the slightly embattled appearance of an old-fashioned traditional dwelling, usually enclosed in high walls to protect the privacy of those within and standing proudly apart from its neighbours. Religious architecture too remains virtually unchanged, with all mosques in the region following decidedly old-fashioned designs, such as the landmark Jumeirah Mosque in Dubai of 1978 (essentially a replica of a medieval Egyptian Fatimid mosque) or the Grand Mosque in nearby Bur Dubai, rebuilt in 1990 along decidedly traditional lines. Many modern buildings in the UAE also continue to

Looking through Al Alam Palace gates, Old Muscat.

MASDAR CITY

Oddly, it's Abu Dhabi, the most petrol-centred of the Emirates, which has taken the first steps towards addressing environmental concerns with its vast new Masdar City development (www.masdar.ae), close to the international airport. Masdar is intended to house around 50,000 people and become the world's first zero-carbon, zero-waste city, relying entirely on renewable energy. Cars will be banned inside the city, while a perimeter wall will exclude hot desert winds, and narrow shaded streets inside will funnel cool breezes across the city. The whole development is due for completion in 2020–5, but parts have already opened to visitors.

sport emblematic wind towers, even if they no longer have any practical function.

More original reworkings of traditional regional architecture can also be seen. Perhaps the most inventive is the flamboyant Al Alam Palace in Muscat, with its multicoloured, pseudo-Islamic tilework, stone-carving and pointed arches given a colourful contemporary makeover, or the same city's vast Sultan Qaboos Grand Mosque, a slightly minimalist reworking of the traditional Grand Mosque, or even the spectacular new Royal Opera House Muscat, another fine example of Omani mod-

Many modern Dubai buildings are designed in traditional Emirati style.

ern architecture. The even more extravagant Sheikh Zayed Grand Mosque in Abu Dhabi follows a similar theme, with a range of international Islamic influences going into its eclectic design. The jewel in the crown is arguably the new souk in Abu Dhabi designed by Norman Foster, which successfully blends elements of traditional Arabian architecture with stylish contemporary decor.

Also notable are the many striking examples of faux-Arabian kitsch which have begun mushrooming across the region. Dubai has shown a particular fondness for the style – unoriginal and even rather cheesy, although the sheer extravagance with which some

examples have been carried through compels reluctant admiration, as in the vast Madinat Jumeirah complex, with its hundreds of sand-coloured wind towers, or the opulently decorated interiors of the atmospheric Souk Khan Murjan – both of which present contemporary Islamic designs with a touch of Hollywood, or perhaps Disney. The landmark Emirates Palace in Abu Dhabi is another good example, the extravagant interiors being particularly fine.

Futuristic architecture in the UAE

Modern architecture has flourished in the Gulf, and the speed at which places like Dubai and Abu Dhabi have grown has resulted in one of the most spectacular building booms of modern times – at one point in the mid-noughties it was estimated that, astonishingly, a quarter of all the world's construction cranes could be found in Dubai alone. The exploding real-estate market, ready supplies of apparently limitless finance and widespread availability of large plots of unused land all conspired to turn Dubai, in particular, into an enormous building site, further heated by a general absence of the sort of zoning rules, planning permissions and conservation issues which so often haunt major new constructions in the West (and in striking contrast to Oman, where governmental restrictions have ensured that cities across the country have preserved their traditional low-rise, white-washed outline – the absence of high-rise buildings in Muscat is particularly striking).

The wide open desert spaces of Dubai and Abu Dhabi thus provided a kind of tabula rasa on which architects could doodle – and then see their doodles take shape with lightning speed. The results are inevitably mixed. Some of the modern architecture in the Gulf is spectacularly ugly, some is notable as much for its sheer quirkiness as for its ultimate success, although the region also boasts a clutch of undoubted modernist masterpieces, as well as some superb urban architectural ensembles, such as the teetering high-rises of Sheikh Zayed Road in Dubai or the shiny mass of glass-fronted high-rises looming above Abu Dhabi's corniche.

Dubai is a veritable encyclopaedia of contemporary design ranging from the good through to the bad, the mad and the downright ugly.

Some of Dubai's most memorable buildings are decidedly quirky in inspiration: the strange Dusit Thani hotel, for example, inspired by the traditional Thai *wai* greeting, with hands placed together in welcome (although it actually looks more like an enormous upside-down tuning fork), or the landmark Etisalat Building, topped by what looks like a vast golf ball (a design now copied in other Etisalat buildings in Dubai, Abu Dhabi and elsewhere).

Many of the city's finest buildings pay oblique homage to the emirate's former maritime traditions, with various sail-shaped architectural motifs, exemplified by the celebrated clubhouse of the Dubai Creek Golf Club (1993), a fascinating sculptural creation whose instantly recognisable outline is inspired by the triangular shapes of the traditional *lateen* sail. The sail motif is invoked again in the superb National Bank of Dubai (designed by Carlos Ott, 1998), its towering Creekside facade comprising a single enormous "sail" surrounded by highly reflective aluminium cladding, mirroring boats on the waters below. Best of all, however, is the superlative Burj al Arab (Tom Wright, 1999), whose land-facing side provides Dubai with its largest and most magnificent architectural sail, memorably illuminated at night. The newest addition to this list will be Zaha Hadid's Opera House in Dubai, due in 2016.

Although most of the region's finest modernist icons can currently be found in Dubai, Abu Dhabi has gone to great lengths to catch up with its chic neighbour. With attractions scheduled to open from later in 2015 onwards, the city's new Cultural District on Saadiyat Island will host a cluster of five museums all housed in stupendously modern buildings designed by world-famous architects.

High-rise cities and environmental concerns

Dubai is now the tallest city in the world, outstripping traditional skyscraper hotspots like New York and Hong Kong, with 28 of the world's 200 tallest buildings (compared to 13 in New York and 11 in Hong Kong), while Abu Dhabi, too, is looking increasingly to the clouds, with a current total of four buildings in the top 200. Pride of place goes to the jaw-dropping Burj Khalifa, far and away the world's tallest man-made structure, while other landmarks include the twin Emirates Towers (formerly the tallest buildings in the Middle East) and the soaring JW Marriott Marquis hotel (the tallest hotel in the world).

> *The publicity and marketing potential of landmark buildings was recognised early by Dubai ruler Sheikh Mohammed, who commissioned the Burj al Arab to provide Dubai with an international icon to rival the Eiffel Tower or Statue of Liberty.*

The wind tower provides courtyard cooling at the Institute of Science and Technology in Masdar City.

Impressive though they undoubtedly are, the massed high-rises of Dubai are, as environmentalists often point out, remarkably badly suited to the Gulf. The vast quantities of glass, steel and aluminium cladding in which such buildings are characteristically wrapped act as enormous heat-traps, sucking up sunlight from the fierce desert sky and tending to overheat constantly – with the resultant need for endless air-conditioning to cool them back down again. The need for similarly energy-intensive elevators and pumping systems to move people, water and other necessities up and down such huge structures is another environmental burden.

THE ARTS

From superbly crafted traditional artefacts through to cutting-edge contemporary visual arts, Oman and the UAE offer a rich variety of artistic traditions.

The modern countries and city-states of the Gulf are often derided for their rampant materialism and general lack of culture, but traditional arts and culture do survive, along with some innovative contemporary art galleries.

The region's various artisanal traditions are particularly notable, such as its striking jewellery (see page 74). Most are now in danger of extinction, although superb traditional antiques can still be found in shops and souks throughout the country. Oman is particularly rich in handicrafts, ranging from quaintly rustic Bahla pottery through to fabulously intricate metalwork including traditional silver *khanjars* (daggers), chunky Bedu jewellery and *mukkabbah* (the round airtight containers which were formerly used to store volatile items like frankincense). Traditional Bedu textiles can also sometimes be found in the souks around the Sharqiya Sands, featuring colourful abstract geometrical designs somewhat reminiscent of India.

The region also boasts its own unique roster of performing arts. The writing and reading of poetry remains a popular pastime, commemorating the old Arabian traditions of oral recitation which date back to the Quran and beyond. Poetry recitals are held regularly in the UAE, although these are largely inaccessible to outsiders, while traditional folk music and dancing is also popular. Major poetry recitals and concerts are often broadcast on TV.

Artist being interviewed during the Art Dubai festival.

Men performing a traditional dance at the Heritage Village in Shindaga, Dubai.

Top-quality carpets and kilims from Iran and other major rug-producing centres in Central Asia are widely available across the Gulf, particularly in Dubai and Sharjah – often at bargain prices.

The Majlis Gallery.

MODERN ART IN DUBAI AND THE UAE

Dubai might not be the most culturally cutting-edge city in the world, but in one area at least it has established itself as an unlikely crucible of contemporary creativity: the visual arts. The city is now a veritable hothouse of Arabian fine arts, providing a major international showcase for the work of leading artists from across the Middle East. Much of the credit goes to the string of innovative galleries established in the insalubrious industrial suburb of Al Quoz, off Sheikh Zayed Road near Dubai Marina, by expatriate entrepreneurs from Syria, Iran and Egypt drawn to the area's low rents and spacious warehouses, and seeing a potential market in Dubai.

These now serve (along with other galleries such as the long-established Majlis Gallery in the Al Fahidi Historical Neighbourhood, formerly known as Bastakiya, see page 198, and another cluster of more upmarket venues in The Gate building) as a major showcase of contemporary Arabian art, backed up by two major arts festivals: the huge Art Dubai festival at Dubai Marina (four days in mid-March; www.artdubai.ae) and the more left-field SIKKA Art Fair (formerly known as the Bastakiya Art Fair; one week in mid-March).

Other cities in the UAE also boast a burgeoning visual arts scene. The Sharjah Art Gallery hosts regular exhibitions of new work, while the Sharjah Biennial (two months in alternate years; www.sharjahbiennial.org), is now a major fixture on the international contemporary art calendar. The arrival of the new Louvre and Guggenheim museum in Abu Dhabi is likely to further accelerate the country's rise to international artistic prominence.

Traditional Arabian calligraphy.

...ver khanjar ...emonial dagger) ...n the Al Ain ...tional Museum. ...anjars were an ...ntial item of ...litional Bedu dress ...until recent times, ...l are still often worn ...festive occasions.

...ditional pots on show at Jabrin Castle.

The Crown Prince of Dubai and Godolphin trainer Saeed bin Suroor with horse Prince Bishop after winning the Dubai World Cup in March 2015.

SPORTS AND OUTDOOR ACTIVITIES

From traditional camel racing to Formula 1 Grand Prix, the UAE and Oman offer a wealth of spectator sports alongside myriad adventure activities and other outdoor diversions.

Sport in the Gulf is booming – a combination of the region's perfect Mediterranean winter climate, the natural sporting passions of its inhabitants, and the conscious decision of its rulers to use sporting events as a way of boosting the region's international profile. Qatar's successful bid for the 2020 FIFA World Cup is the most eye-catching example to date, although this bid has now been tainted by the FIFA corruption scandal. The UAE has also secured hosting rights to an increasing number of top global sporting events, including the season-ending F1 Grand Prix in Abu Dhabi and the DP World Tour Championship golf tournament in Dubai, as well as a host of leading tennis, rugby, running and other tournaments (while the Abu Dhabi takeover of English football club Manchester City – and subsequent multi-million-pound spending spree – has also generated enormous publicity overseas).

While the UAE (Dubai in particular) boasts the lion's share of organised sporting events, Oman comes into its own for adventure activities and other outdoor diversions, including superlative diving, wonderful mountain hiking and a range of wilderness activities including wadi- and dune-bashing, canyoning, caving and climbing – an energetic way of exploring the country's memorable landscapes.

Horse racing

Arabia has been famous for its horses since antiquity, and every thoroughbred racehorse competing in the world today can trace its lineage back to three Arab stallions – the Godolphin and Darley Arabian and the Byerley Turk – that were taken to Britain more than three centuries ago to improve the speed and stamina of the domestic breed. Not surprisingly then,

Daniel Ricciardo completing his final practice ahead of the Abu Dhabi Formula One Grand Prix at Yas Marina Circuit in 2014.

modern horse racing has now taken firm root in the region, particularly in Dubai, thanks to the efforts of the equine-loving Sheikh Mohammed and his brothers, who now count themselves amongst the world's most successful racehorse owners through their prestigious Godolphin stable.

Evidence of the seriousness with which Dubai takes its racing can be seen in the spectacular new Meydan Racecourse (www.meydan. ae). The racing season is held during the cooler winter months from November to March, culminating in the prestigious Dubai World Cup, the world's richest horse race, with prize money of a cool US$10 million. Race meets are also a major feature on the city's social calendar, attracting a lively crowd of Emiratis and expats, although no betting is allowed.

Meydan is not the only racecourse in the UAE, however, and there are also more low-key tracks at Jabal Ali (in the far south of Dubai), at Abu Dhabi and Sharjah. Details of forthcoming meetings can be found at www.emiratesracing.com.

Golf

Golf is burgeoning in the Gulf – much to the despair of environmentalists, who see the region's ever-expanding number of lush 18-hole courses, with their water-guzzling greens and fairways, as one of the prime examples of a local ecological disaster-in-the-making. Green politics aside, the region offers superb opportunities either to play or to watch top international pros in action.

Dubai, once again, takes centre stage, hosting the region's two leading tournaments. The Dubai Desert Classic (www.dubaidesertclassic. com), held at the Emirates Golf Club in Dubai Marina during February/March, is the region's oldest major golfing event, first held in 1993 and now established as a leading fixture on

Dubai Creek Golf Club.

KINGS OF THE TURF

Few horse-racing stories over recent decades have been as eye-catching as the rise of Dubai's Maktoum family to become one of the world's leading owners – and now breeders – of racehorses, driven by Dubai ruler Sheikh Mohammed and his brothers Hamdan and Ahmed. It was while studying at Cambridge in England in the 1960s that Sheikh Mohammed first became attracted to the atmosphere of the nearby Newmarket racecourse, and within 10 years he and his brothers all had horses in training there. Their first big win came when Hamdan's horse Touching Wood won the 1982 St Leger at Doncaster, while Hamdan followed up this success with 1989 and 1994 Derby winners Nashwan and Erhaab.

Following these triumphs, the Maktoum brothers established the remarkably successful Godolphin Racing Stables, whose various global triumphs have included the remarkable hat-trick recorded by the Lammtarra, a son of the Derby winner Nijinsky. He only ran three times as a three-year-old, but achieved the historic treble of the Derby at Epsom, the King George VI and Queen Elizabeth Stakes at Ascot, and then the Prix de l'Arc de Triomphe at Longchamp. Today, the family has more than 1,500 racehorses in training in Dubai, Europe and North America, along with vast property interests in thoroughbred stud farms in England, Ireland and the USA – an investment of US$2.4 billion.

the PGA European Tour. Past winners feature a virtual who's who of golfing greats, including Ernie Els, Tiger Woods, Colin Montgomerie, Seve Ballesteros and Stephen Gallacher.

Newer but even more prestigious is the DP World Tour Championship (www.europeantour.com; four days in November/December). First held in 2009, this is one of the world's richest golfing events. The championship forms the grand finale to the season-long European Tour, with the tour's 60 top players battling it out for US$8 million in prize money at the spectacular new Greg Norman-designed "Earth" course in

com). There's also a growing number of courses in Abu Dhabi and elsewhere in the region.

Motorsports

Not surprisingly given the Emirati and Omani obsession with big cars and all things petrol-driven, motorsports have proved a big hit in the region. The leading event is the season-ending Formula 1 Abu Dhabi Grand Prix, held at Yas Island in mid-November (www.yasmarinacircuit.com). The race was first staged in 2009, when it was won by Red Bull's Sebastian Vettel, who repeated his victory at the dramatic 2010 race

Robotic jockeys control camels during Al Marmoom Heritage Festival at the Al Marmoom Camel Racetrack.

Dubailand. Lee Westwood won the inaugural event in 2009, while Henrik Stenson won the last two tournaments (2013–4).

If you want to play yourself, Dubai has a superb selection of golf courses open to visitors (although green fees can be spectacularly high), including Dubai Creek Golf & Yacht Club and the Emirates Golf Club (www.dubaigolf.com), the nearby Montgomerie at Emirates Hills (www.themontgomerie.com), the Four Seasons' Al Badia course at Dubai Festival City (www.albadiagolfclub.ae), the Arabian Ranches' desert course in Dubailand (www.arabianranchesgolfdubai.com), the Els Club in Dubai Sports City in Dubailand (www.elsclubdubai.com), and the Jumeirah Golf Estates in Dubai Marina (www.jumeirahgolfestates.

and again in 2013. It was Lewis Hamilton who triumphed in 2011 and 2014.

In Dubai, the state-of-the-art track at the Dubai Autodrome (www.dubaiautodrome.com) in Dubailand hosts various other international events through the year, as well as offering visitors the chance to try their hand at karting, have a go at driving a F1-style single-seater car, or to take their own vehicles for a spin around the track. More challenging terrain is on offer during the Abu Dhabi Desert Challenge (www.abudhabidesertchallenge.com), a FIA-sanctioned car and motorbike rally, held in March/April in the deserts around Abu Dhabi.

On the water, one round of the UIM Class One World Offshore powerboat championships (www.class-1.com) is held in Dubai in late October/early November.

Other sports

Other traditionally European sports have also found an unlikely but surprisingly successful home in Dubai. The Dubai Duty Free Tennis Championships (late Feb/early March; www.dubaidutyfreetennischampionships.com) is an established fixture on the men's and women's singles circuit, attracting most of the world's top players – past winners have included Venus Wiliams, Justine Henin, Agnieszka Radwańska, Simona Halep, Andy Roddick, Rafael Nadal, Novak Djokovic (who has won four times) and Roger Federer, who has won the men's event seven times, including the latest one in 2015.

Even more popular is the annual Dubai Rugby Sevens tournament (www.dubairugby7s.com). Part of the IRB Sevens World Series, this is one of the highlights of the international rugby sevens calendar, featuring all the best international teams, with recent winners including South Africa, Fiji, Samoa and England. The tournament also provides an excuse for some of the city's most raucous expat partying. Matches are played at the purpose-built The Sevens stadium, on the edge of the city next to the road to Al Ain.

Cricket, too, has found a home in Dubai, helped along by the city's large population of cricket-mad subcontinental expats. Matches are held at the 25,000-seater cricket stadium at the Dubai Sports City (www.dsc.ae) in Dubailand, which hosts occasional one-day and Twenty20 internationals between leading teams – England, Australia, South Africa and Pakistan have all played here over the past few years.

Endurance sports can also be found. The leading event is, again, held in Dubai, whose Dubai Marathon (www.dubaimarathon.org) has been running (as it were) since 2006. Held in mid-January, the race starts and finishes in the Dubai Marina, with runners heading all the way up the coastal Jumeirah Road, and then turning around and running all the way back down again. Further up the road, the RAK Half Marathon (www.rakmarathon.org), held in February, is another leading event, again attracting leading competitors from around the world – Kenya's Mary Keitany set a new world record here in 2011, which remains unbeaten to this day. She also won in 2012 and 2015.

Over the border, the Tour of Oman (www.tourofoman.om) cycling race, first held in 2010, attracts a strong field of international riders and is held over six days in February at various locations around Muscat and the Western Hajar.

At 2015's 24 Hours Dubai Race.

SPORTS STARS IN DUBAI

As well as hosting an ever-expanding number of sporting events, Dubai has also lured increasing numbers of international sporting celebrities to the city. In 2002 the government offered David Beckham a free villa on the Palm Jumeirah island, after which a number of other international footballers bought properties on the island.

Not that it's all footballers. Roger Federer trains regularly in Dubai, while various top golfers – including Ernie Els, Colin Montgomerie and Greg Norman – have been involved in designing golf courses in the city.

Traditional sports

Despite the onslaught of Western-style sports around the region, a few resolutely traditional pastimes persist. The most popular is undoubtedly camel racing. Racing camels are taken no less seriously than their equine counterparts, with the finest racers changing hands for over US$100,000. There are racetracks throughout the UAE and

Racing camels can reach speeds of 60kmph (37mph), and peak at the age of around three or four. They are nurtured on a diet of honey, ghee, barley, alfalfa, eggs and dates – along with secret concoctions devised by their trainers.

Oman. Meetings are usually held early in the morning during the cooler winter months – an entertaining sight as the camels' owners charge alongside the racetrack in trucks, exhorting their beasts to ever greater efforts. Until recently small boys, often trafficked from Pakistan or India, were employed as jockeys. Pressure from human rights organisations eventually led to the banning of this practice in both the UAE and Oman. The UAE, along with Qatar, pioneered the development of "robot" jockeys that simulate the weight and actions of young riders.

An even more antiquated sporting event is bull-butting, which can still be seen at various locations including Fujairah and along the Batinah Coast of Oman at Sohar, Seeb and other places. Traditional dhow racing is staged in Abu Dhabi and at the Al Gaffal Traditional Dhow Race in Dubai Marina in May – the only chance you'll get in the region to see traditional wooden boats under their distinctive triangular lateen sails.

Diving and watersports

The UAE and, particularly, Oman offer some superlative diving, with fine, and often surprisingly unspoilt underwater landscapes and a stunning array of marine life – while the relative lack of visitors means that dive sites remain refreshingly uncrowded. There's a well-developed network of dive schools across the country, often run by European expats, offering a wide range of diving, as well as the usual PADI courses. Muscat itself boasts a considerable number of operators, with whom you can arrange trips to the wonderful Dayminiyat Islands, as well as to other locations closer to the capital. At the northern end of the country, Musandam is popularly claimed to have the country's best diving amidst the spectacular coastal scenery around the remote town of Kumzar, home to a superb range of marine life including hammerhead and leopard whale sharks, mink whales, manta, eagle rays and turtles, as well as numerous species of smaller tropical fish. There are also excellent

underwater possibilities at the opposite end of the country in Dhofar, particularly around Mirbat. The presence of cold currents produced by the annual *khareef* (monsoon) create unique underwater environments here, including a mix of corals and kelp.

Diving opportunities in the UAE are mainly clustered around the east coast emirate of Fujairah – a couple of local operators, plus outfits in Dubai, can arrange trips.

Dubai is the top venue for watersports, with activities most easily arranged via one of the hotels in the Dubai Marina. All the marina

Walking up Wadi Shab, Oman.

beach hotels (apart from the Ritz-Carlton) have their own watersports centre, offering a wide range of activities including windsurfing, sailing, kayaking, water-skiing, wakeboarding and parasailing (but not jet-skiing, which the authorities have banned). Local operators include Sky & Sea Adventure (www.watersportsdubai.com), who can be found at the Hilton Jumeirah Resort.

Trekking

The mountains of Oman are trekking country par excellence, with dramatic paths threading their way across the windswept heights of some of the country's most spectacular ridges, or winding through sheer-sided wadis and canyons. The government has established an

Falconry

Hawking is an old and much-loved pastime in the Gulf. Falconers pay huge sums of money for the very best birds and pamper them accordingly.

Falconry is a source of great passion in the Gulf. The sport grew out of the traditional lifestyle of the Bedu, who used falcons for hunting. During

Falconry is an enduringly popular pastime.

winter, on the edge of any major town, it is common to see members of the local falconry club exercising and training their birds in the cool of the evening.

The main source of falcons in the Emirates is the livestock market in Sharjah, where dealers import birds from Iran and Pakistan. Aged between six months and three years, a bird can be worth anything between US$240 and US$32,000. Females are preferred over males as they are on average one-third larger.

Although it is illegal to trade in wild birds, they are favoured over more docile captive-bred falcons, which were thought to lack the natural hunting instinct. Happily, captive-bred falcons are now becoming more popular. By contrast, mature wild birds are hard to train but are exceptional hunters. These attract more experienced falconers.

Catching birds

The best time to capture a bird is on its first autumn migration as it passes over the desert on its way south. These immature wild birds are relatively easy to train, but already have a well-developed hunting instinct.

The saker, from the Arabic *saqr*, is the most popular bird on account of its size, toughness and versatility. Known for its intelligent hunting tactics, it predicts the movements of its prey and uses the landscape to hide its attacks.

Smaller and more fragile than the saker is the peregrine falcon *(shahin)*. Built for speed, it is designed to kill on the wing and is vulnerable on the ground. Difficult to keep in captivity, peregrines have become rare and valuable. The lanner, or *shahin wakri*, is a small falcon, like the peregrine, but with the qualities of the saker. Gyrfalcons have also appeared in Arabia in recent years. Mostly captive-bred, they are exotics, not desert falcons, adapted to live in the Arctic, and prized for their size (twice that of a peregrine) and good looks.

Hawking today

The hawking season is very short, from October to January and coinciding with the autumn migration of the game birds, mostly houbara. The traditional falcon species are also migratory and cannot stand the desert summer. It was once common for falconers to release their birds at the end of each hunting season.

Now owners hang on to favourite or valuable birds throughout the year, keeping them in luxurious air-conditioned cages, while veterinary care is provided by dedicated falcon hospitals in Abu Dhabi and Dubai.

Falcons have also discovered an unexpected but important new role in the UAE's modern cities, being used to scare away the flocks of pigeons which are wont to perch on high-rise buildings and cover them with droppings – an effective alternative to unsightly netting or anti-roosting spikes.

Falconry displays are sometimes arranged by local tour operators or hotels (particularly desert camps). You can also visit the falcon hospital in Abu Dhabi – see www.falconhospital.com for details.

extensive network of (usually well-marked) hiking trails around the country, particularly in the Western Hajar. The areas around Jabal Shams and Jabal Akhdar are particularly rewarding, criss-crossed with numerous spectacular high-altitude treks, often following the routes of old donkey trails through remote traditional villages en route. Wadi walks are another popular excursion, such as the beautiful walk up Wadi Shab or the more challenging trek into Snake Gorge (Wadi Bimah) off Wadi Bani Awf – an exhilarating scramble up the gorge, clambering over boulders and wading (or occasionally swimming) through rock pools.

Despite the usually benign conditions, trekking in Oman should not be attempted lightly. It's imperative to carry sufficient water and also to keep a close eye on the weather. Conditions can change with spectacular suddenness during rain, particularly in wadis, many of which are prone to potentially fatal flash-flooding. It pays to go with an experienced guide or tour company such as the Muscat Diving and Adventure Centre (www.holiday-in-oman.com), Oman's leading adventure-tour operator.

> Oman's most spectacular short trek is the marvellous hike, known as the "Balcony Walk", around Wadi Nakhr, the so-called Grand Canyon of Oman.

Adventure sports and activities

The UAE offers numerous opportunities to take to the air. For hot-air ballooning over the UAE desert contact Balloon Adventures in Dubai (www.ballooning.ae). For the ultimate views of Dubai, book yourself in for a helicopter tour, offering jaw-dropping views of the city's burgeoning skyline – as well as perfect views of super-sized constructions like the Palm Jumeirah and World archipelago which simply can't be seen properly from the ground. A number of tour operators offer helicopter tours – Aerogulf (based at the international airport; www.aerogulfservices.com) is one of the best established. Tours don't come cheap, as you'd expect, with prices at around US$200 for a 15-minute flight.

For an even more memorable adrenalin rush, SkyDive Dubai (www.skydivedubai.ae) offers a range of skydiving programmes catering to both first-time jumpers and experienced divers. Jumps take place in the spectacular skies above southern Dubai and the Palm Jumeirah, currently costing Dhs1999 for a tandem jump. For the next best thing to jumping out of a plane, check out iFly Dubai indoor skydiving centre (www.iflyme.com) at Mirdif City Centre, just east of the airport, with virtual flying inside a powerful vertical wind tunnel.

Once again, Oman is the place to head to for remote wilderness adventures. Off-road driving is a perennial favourite, either wadi-bashing through the Hajar mountains or

A 4x4 entering Wadi Tawi along the coast of Oman.

dune-bashing across the Sharqiya Sands (see page 149). Other desert activities are offered by camps around Wahibah, including quad-biking, sand-skiing and more low-key activities like horse and camel riding and desert hikes. Back in the mountains, there's plenty of scope of experienced rock-climbers to take to the craggy cliffs of the Hajar, while a trio of via ferratas, in Snake Gorge, Wadi Nakhr and Bandar Khayran, offer the chance to climb the heights without specialised skills or equipment. Caving is another possibility for those with the requisite experience, and suitably equipped cavers can also explore the country's remarkable though still largely unexplored subterranean wonders.

Sunset near Sohar.

Villas in Nizwa.

Camels in Dhofar.

Oman

0	50 km
0	50 miles

OMAN

A detailed guide to the entire country, with principal
sites clearly cross-referenced by number to the maps.

*Omani man at Nizwa
animal market.*

Compared with other countries around the Arabian
Gulf, Oman is a refreshing paradox: a country that
has succeeded in embracing the modern world
whilst also holding fast to its traditional cultural roots –
economically prosperous, politically stable, but also rich in
reminders of times past. For the visitor, Oman is the only
country in the region that is both accessible and authentic:
safe, welcoming and easy to explore, but offering a rich and
satisfying taste of traditional Arabia at its most memorable.

Oman is a relatively compact country by Middle Eastern or Asian
standards – roughly the size of Italy, and with most
of the population clustered along the coast. The starting point for most visitors is the low-key capital of
Muscat, a sprawling modern metropolis which preserves some absorbing reminders of times past in the
old-fashioned districts of Mutrah and Old Muscat.
Inland lie the craggy heights of the Western Hajar
mountains, centred on the historic capital of Nizwa
and covered in a fascinating patchwork of majestic
forts and mudbrick villages. East of here, the mountains roll down to the sleepy Batinah Coast, with
endless fishing villages and further forts huddled
amidst dense swathes of date palms. South of Muscat, Sharqiya province offers a varied array of idyllic coastal scenery dotted with turtle beaches, while

*A wooden door at Khasab Castle,
Musandam.*

inland stretch the dramatic wadis of the Eastern Hajar mountains and
the magnificent dunes of the Wahibah Desert.

At the far northern end of the country (and separated from the rest of
Oman by a swathe of UAE territory), the Musandam peninsula shows
the country at its most scenically spectacular, with huge red-rock mountains plunging down into a tangle of sheer-sided fjords and sea cliffs,
best explored by boat amidst pods of cavorting dolphins. At the opposite
end of the country, the southern province of Dhofar is different again,
visited by the annual *khareef* (monsoon) which turns the region a misty
green each year from June to September, creating impromptu rock pools
and waterfalls amidst the beautiful Dhofar mountains which encircle the
historic city of Salalah – and offering a memorable conclusion to one of
Arabia's most scenically spectacular and culturally absorbing countries.

An ornate doorway in the Sultan Qaboos Grand Mosque.

MUSCAT

Oman's low-key capital has been transformed over the past five decades, but retains a pleasantly relaxed atmosphere, as well as many reminders of its long and cosmopolitan history.

O man's understated capital, Muscat, provides a pleasant mix of traditional and modern. The city has boomed dramatically since the accession of Sultan Qaboos in 1970, transforming from a modest cluster of small, self-contained towns and villages into the sprawling modern metropolis you see today. This is now undoubtedly the heart of the nation, home to a quarter of the country's population (and five times the size of the next largest city, Seeb), the seat of government and the nation's commercial powerhouse.

Despite this, **Muscat ❶** (Masqat) retains much of its old-fashioned charm, particularly around the historic old enclaves of Mutrah and Old Muscat, and compared to other major cities around the Gulf, the whole place remains resolutely low-key. There are no skyscrapers, and most of the large office blocks and ministries adhere to the traditional Gulf Arab style of architecture, in keeping with the Muscat Municipality's book of acceptable architectural designs, meaning that pitched roofs are forbidden, and that new buildings must be either white or sand-coloured. And presiding over it all is the image of Sultan Qaboos himself. Every shop and office has a picture of the Sultan hanging in its reception.

Bait al Zubair Museum.

Although Muscat's foundation dates from the 1st century, the town didn't really get going until the 14th and 15th centuries, following the decline of Sohar. In the 16th century Muscat had the ambiguous honour of attracting the Portuguese, who occupied the city and used it as their main base in the country – and where they remained until ousted by the Omanis in 1650. The city subsequently played a leading role in national affairs, while the decision of Sultan Hamad bin Said to move

Main Attractions
Al Mirani and Al Jalali forts
Al Alam Palace
Bait al Zubair
Mutrah Souk
Bandar al Jissah
Sultan's Armed Forces
Museum
Qurm Beach
Royal Opera House
Sultan Qaboos Grand
Mosque

Al Mirani Fort, in Old Muscat, was built by the Portuguese.

his court here in 1784 (where it has largely stayed ever since) effectively established it as the pre-eminent city in Oman.

Muscat can be a disorienting place at first sight. The capital was originally just two small and quite separate towns: Muscat proper – the area now known as **Old Muscat** – and the mercantile centre of Mutrah down the road. These two have now been utterly swallowed up by the surrounding suburbs, although they preserve their own distinct characters and still feel largely separate from the rest of the modern city, which stretches from the bustling central business district of Ruwi through a string of suburbs west to the international airport and beyond.

Old Muscat

Towards the southern end of the city, now rather lost within the city's ever-expanding suburban sprawl, stands the original settlement of Muscat, usually referred to as "Old Muscat", with a neat huddle of buildings ancient and modern clustered

around a rocky horseshoe bay. A pair of hoary old Portuguese forts (1587–8) stand proudly on either side of the bay: **Al Mirani** Ⓐ to the west and **Al Jalali** Ⓑ opposite. Both are quite unlike the traditional Omani fort – each essentially just a narrow building perched on top of a sheer-sided rock outcrop. Neither fort is open to the public, and Al Jalali is completely off-limits, although you can get a good view of it from across the harbour. Look out too for the names of various ships on the cliffs ringing the east side of the bay, painted onto the rocks by the crews of visiting vessels – like a kind of maritime visitors' book. The young Horatio Nelson is said to have scrambled up the rocks here during a visit to Muscat in the 1770s, despite his fear of heights.

Nestled between the two forts lies the striking **Al Alam Palace** (Flag Palace) Ⓒ, one of the six official royal residences of Sultan Qaboos, built in 1972 in striking contemporary Islamic style, with towering columns in blue and gold. It's not open

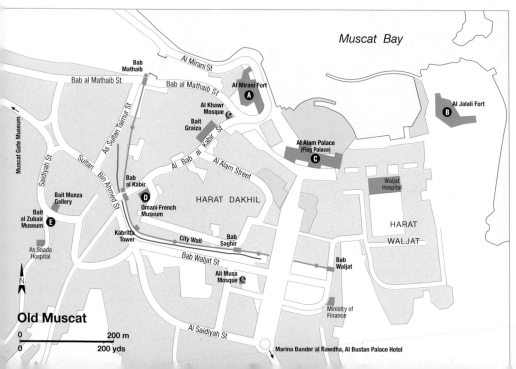

Old Muscat

to the public, although you can walk right up to the main gates for a good view of the facade. Close by stands the new **National Museum**, opened in 2015. This major new attraction showcases 6,000 years of Omani heritage and history in numerous themed galleries covering the country's land, people, maritime history, arms and armour, religion and so on.

From here, it is a 10-minute walk west to **Bab al Kabir** (Kabir Gate), the main gate in the old city walls. Just inside Bab al Kabir stands the renovated 18th-century Bait Fransa, the residence of French consuls until 1920 and which now houses the **Omani-French Museum** ⓓ (Sat–Wed 9am–1pm and 4–8pm). Built by Ghaliah bint Salim, a niece of Sultan Said bin Sultan, the house was presented to Paul Ottavi, the first French consul in Oman, to serve as the French Consulate by Sultan Feisal bin Turki al Said in 1894 and now hosts various exhibits relating to the history of the French in Oman.

South of Bab al Kabir lies Muscat's most interesting museum, the

Bait al Zubair ⓔ (tel: 2473 6688; www.baitalzubairmuseum.com; Sat–Thu 9.30am–6pm). Occupying three airy traditional houses set around a garden, the museum displays an excellent selection of weapons, jewellery, costumes, household items and old photographs, while the grounds contain a re-creation of a typical Omani village, complete with *falaj* system. Next door to the museum is the **Bait Muzna Art Gallery** (tel: 2473 9204; www. baitmuznagallery.com; Sat–Thu 9.30am–7pm; free), a former royal home that has been turned into a gallery showcasing modern works by international artists.

Northwest of the Bait al Zubair, one of the old city gateways, now spanning the main road to Mutrah, has been converted into the **Muscat Gate Museum** (Sat–Thu 9.30am–1.30pm, 5–7pm; free), with detailed displays covering the history of Oman and Muscat – although not much in the way of actual exhibits.

Mutrah

The winding waterfront Corniche from Old Muscat to Mutrah is

Al Jalali Fort, Old Muscat.

around 2km (1 mile), passing another old Portuguese stronghold along the way – **Mutrah Fort** (not open to the public) – balanced precariously atop a slender rock outcrop high above the sea.

To the west of the fort is the **Ghalya's Museum of Modern Art** (tel: 2471 1640; www.ghalyasmuseum. com; Sat–Thu 9.30am–6pm). Opened in 2011, the Old House exhibition features typical Omani houses from 1950 to 1975, showcasing life in the country in times when people lived without electricity or tap water. The museum also includes a modern art gallery with works by Omani and international artists.

Mutrah itself is the old commercial heart of the city, busier and considerably more built up than Old Muscat, and arranged around an attractive sweeping corniche with the huge gantries and quays of the Sultan Qaboos Port opposite. The district remains a lively hub of old-fashioned mercantile activity, most of it concentrated in the sprawling **Mutrah Souk** ❻, easily the most

popular tourist attraction in Muscat – perhaps in the whole country. Though modern – concrete shops replaced the original palm structures in the 1970s – the souk remains one of the most authentic in Arabia, its alleyways laced with the smell of frankincense and sandalwood, offering a memorable glimpse of Oman's past. It is easy to get lost if you head off the main street through the souk, although this is a large part of the fun, and you're never more than a couple of minutes' walk from the main thoroughfares. West of the main section of the souk, it is also worth exploring the dazzling **Gold Souk**, reachable from slightly further west down the Corniche.

Continuing along the Corniche past the souk brings you to **Lawatiya** quarter, home to a Shi'ite merchant sect of the same name who originated from Hyderabad. Further along, at the junction with Fish Roundabout, is the **Bait al Baranda** ❼ (Verandah House; http://baitalbaranda.mm.gov. om; Sat–Thu 9am–1pm and 4–6pm), an attractively restored old Muscati

Sporting Oman's national colours.

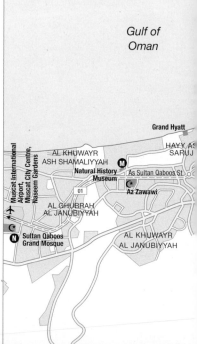

mansion which now houses a modest museum devoted to the history of the city. Just past here is Muscat's lively **fish market**, particularly busy early in the morning when the new catch arrives on the slab and the city's restaurateurs descend to make their daily purchases.

South of Old Muscat and Mutrah

South of Old Muscat, the road winds down the coast amidst craggy ridges and areas of attractively landscaped parkland. About 4km (2.5 miles) down the road, the suburb of Haramil is home to the **Marina Bander ar Rawdah** 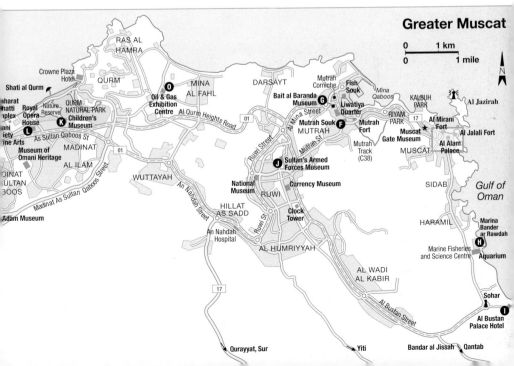 (www.marinaoman.net), from where many of the city's deepwater fishing charters and dolphin-watching trips depart. The once disppointing **Aquarium and Marine Science & Fisheries Centre** (Sun–Thu 8am–2.30pm, Fri 4–6pm; free) is undergoing renovation.

Further south you reach the roundabout at the entrance to Al Bustan Palace Hotel. The fine old wooden dhow, now marooned in

the centre of the roundabout, is the famous *Sohar*, on which British adventurer Tim Severin and his Omani crew sailed from Muscat to Canton in China in 1982 – a fascinating story recounted in Severin's *The Sindbad Voyage*. The boat itself was made in Sur rather than Sohar, despite its name.

Turn left here to reach the spectacular **Al Bustan Palace Hotel** 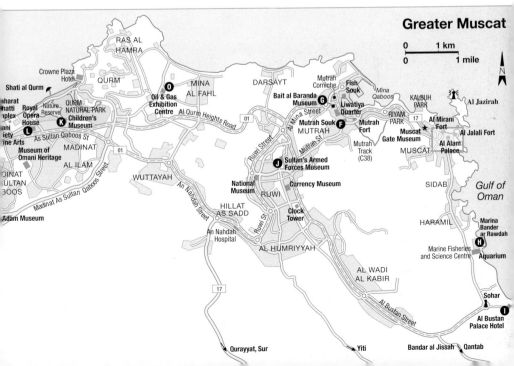, completed in 1985, and comprehensively renovated in 2008. Formerly the top hotel in Oman (and one of the most opulent in the entire Gulf), the hotel has been somewhat upstaged by more recent openings in the city and elsewhere, but remains one of Muscat's nicest places to stay.

Some 5km (3 miles) further south down the coast lies **Bandar al Jissah**, a beautiful bay ringed with rocky cliffs and a much-photographed "rock arch" which features on many boat tours of the capital. The formerly unspoilt beach has now been taken over by the vast **Shangri-La Barr al Jissah Resort** (www.shangri-la.com/muscat/barraljissahresort), comprising

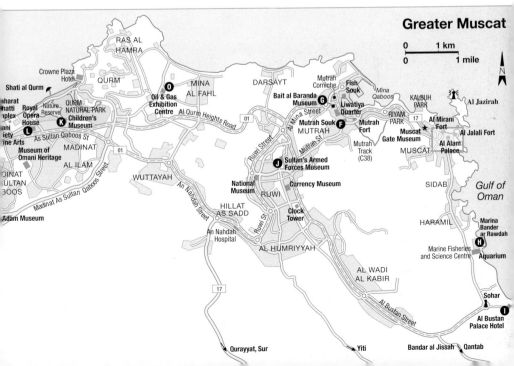

three Arabian-styled hotels, including the super-luxurious Al Husn, spread out along a kilometre of coastline. Despite the hotel, turtles continue to nest on the beach from November to March, although you'll need to stay at or eat in the hotel to gain access. More laid-back and inexpensive views of the bay can be had from the nearby **Oman Dive Centre** (http://omandivecentre.com), which has a good beachside restaurant from which to survey the waves.

Ruwi

A couple of kilometres inland from Mutrah and Old Muscat lies **Ruwi**, now the city's main business and commercial district, with a string of large-scale banks, airline offices lined up along the central Markaz Mutrah al Tijari Street. Nearby, the imposing old Bait al Falaj Fort is home to the **Sultan's Armed Forces Museum ●** (tel: 2431 2646; www.safmuseum.gov.om; Sun–Thu 8am–1.30pm, Sat 9am–noon and 3–6pm) – much more interesting than it might sound, with wide-ranging

exhibits on Omani history backed up with impressive displays of weaponry ranging from antique swords to modern mortars.

A five-minute walk south of the museum down A'Noor Street brings you to **Ruwi Roundabout**, at the southwest corner of the district. This is Muscat with a decidedly subcontinental flavour, home to many expat Indians and Pakistanis and crammed with cheap curry houses. It is one of the liveliest places in the city, especially after dark and particularly along **Souk Ruwi Street**, crammed with dozens of brightly illuminated shops selling gold, textiles and electronics.

Qurm to Ghubrah

West from Ruwi stretches modern Muscat, a rather formless expanse of identikit low-rise, whitewashed suburbs stretching all the way to the international airport. **Qurm**, also west of Ruwi, is one of the city's main shopping areas (and a good place to browse for handicrafts), with a dozen or so small-scale malls

Entrance of Al Alam Palace. Though listed as one of the Sultan's homes, the palace is generally used only for formal affairs.

clustered around Qurm Rounda-bout on the main Sultan Qaboos Road.

North of Qurm proper you'll find **Shati al Qurm** (Qurm Beach), a long swathe of golden sand which runs west from here for several miles, passing many of the city's most upmarket hotels en route. The beach is open to the public throughout, although you'll probably only feel comfortable sunbathing in the areas by the InterContinental and Hyatt hotels. South of the beach stretches the well-kept Qurum Natural Park, a popular family destination, beyond which lies the fun **Children's Museum**  (Sat–Wed 9am–1pm), with hands-on educational displays – a guaranteed hit with children, and fun for grown-ups too.

West of the museum, the Shati Al-Qurm district boasts the majestic **Royal Opera House** (tel: 2440 3300; www.rohmuscat.org.om; daily tours 8.30–10.30am). Opened in 2011, this impressive modern building looks equally stunning day and night and inside and out. It is surrounded by enjoyable gardens and the Opera Galleria shopping centre, with numerous cafés and restaurants.

On the far side of Qurm, the suburb of Khuwayr is the city's main government and diplomatic enclave, with dozens of impressively large ministry buildings lined up alongside the main highway. Nearby on the seafront lies the chintzy **Grand Hyatt Hotel**, one of Muscat's most extravagant buildings, its exterior designed to resemble a Yemeni castle and its interior rivalling that of Al Bustan Palace for pseudo-Arabian opulence. Khuwair is also where you'll find the city's modest **Natural History Museum** (Sat–Wed 9.30am–1.30pm and 5–7pm, Thu 5–7pm), offering a good overview of the country's various regions and their associated flora and fauna, including various stuffed animals and pickled snakes. The complete skeleton of a sperm whale sits in state in the adjacent Whale Hall.

Still further west, the suburb of **Ghubrah** is home to the majestic

The Sohar at the Al Bustan Paloeeh Hotel.

BOAT TRIPS

A number of tour operators around Muscat run enjoyable boat trips along the coast around Bandar al Jissah, offering breezy views of the city's craggy coastline, and usually including a trip through the landmark rock arch which lies just off the beach. Trips include daytime dolphin-spotting excursions (with an excellent chance of seeing either spinner or bottlenose dolphins), while if you are lucky you might glimpse one of the whale sharks or humpback whales which occasionally visit the coast; Sidab Sea Tours' glass-bottomed boat trips (www.sidabseatours.com) offer a good view of what goes on beneath the waves. Many operators also offer popular sunset cruises (usually lasting a couple of hours, with departures at around 4.30pm) – a beautiful way of seeing the sun dip over the coastal mountains.

Sultan Qaboos Grand Mosque (www.sultanqaboosgrandmosque.com; open to non-Muslims, but no children under 12; Sat–Thu 8–11am; free). Opened in 2001, this is one of the largest and most spectacular mosques in the Gulf, constructed in a minimalist modern Islamic style and dressed in vast quantities of white and red-brown marble. Inside, there is room for an estimated 20,000 worshippers in the two prayer halls and surrounding courtyard, with towering minarets at each corner. Compared to the rather chaste exterior, the interior of the main prayer hall is a riot of opulence. The carpet on the floor is the world's second-largest (it took 400 female weavers from the Iranian province of Khorasan four years to make, measures over 60 metres/196ft square and weighs 21 tonnes). The huge Swarovski crystal chandelier in the centre of the hall is a staggering 14 metres (46ft) tall and was often claimed to be the largest in the world until the construction of an even bigger chandelier in Qatar in 2010.

This is also the only mosque in Oman open to non-Muslims; visitors are required to dress conservatively (no shorts or bare arms), while women will be given a scarf with which to cover their hair. Unfortunately, the mosque's popularity and limited opening times for non-Muslims mean that it tends to get overrun with tourists. Arrive early in the day for maximum tranquillity.

West of the city, next to the Muscat airport is the **Oil & Gas Exhibition Centre** (tel: 2467 7834; www.pdo.co.om; Fri–Wed 7am–noon, 1–4pm, Thu 7am–noon; free) with informative displays on everything you always wanted to know about oil extraction. The neighbouring **Planetarium** organises space shows and star-gazing parties (tel: 2467 5542; www.pdo.co.om; one-hour shows in English every Wed; free). Further west, beyond the airport, the **Centre for Omani Dress** has an interesting collection of Omani garments (tel: 9891 9809; www.centreforomanidress.com; Mon and Wed 9.30am–12.30pm).

Qurm Beach.

Towering Strengths

Oman's remarkable wealth of forts and watchtowers provides a memorable reminder of the country's turbulent past.

Wherever you are in Oman, you'll never be far from some kind of traditional fortified building. There are an estimated 500 forts (*qala* or *hisn*) in the country, as well as innumerable watchtowers, fortified houses *(surs)*, walled towns and villages, and other reminders of the country's turbulent and unsettled past.

Virtually every town in Oman has some kind of fort, all of which were formerly of crucial strategic importance, given that whoever controlled the local fort was usually able to command the surrounding region as well. Some forts served simply as military strongholds; others doubled as the residence of the local *wali* (governor), containing elaborate living quarters including *majlis*, bedrooms, kitchens and so on. Many combine both residential and military functions (Nizwa is a particularly good example, with its mighty round tower next to extensive residential quarters), serving both as the home base of the resident militia and seat of local government. In many cases the *majlis* in the nearest particular fort served as a kind of informal parliament for the town or village it protected – a place in which visitors were received and matters of local importance discussed. Forts also served as a refuge for local inhabitants in the event of attack.

Architectural features

Many of the country's forts exemplify Arabian military architecture at its most ingenious, with distinctive local features including slits down which boiling oil or date juice could be poured on the heads of assailants, secret passages, winding and disorienting passages to slow and confuse attackers, and other features (again, the great round tower at Nizwa is a particularly fine example). Many forts also possess their own dedicated *falaj* issuing directly into the fort, offering a guaranteed water supply in the event of a siege.

The vast forts at Bahla and Rustaq are the two largest and most physically impressive in the country (both have been renovated in recent years), while those at Nizwa and Nakhal are also impressive. The finest castle interiors are to be found at the magical fort of Jabrin and in the lovely Bait Na'aman in Barka, whose beautifully decorated interiors offer a compelling insight into life in old Oman.

Watchtowers are another characteristic feature of the Omani landscape. Generally, forts protected the towns and populated areas while watchtowers were used to guard inland trade routes and water supplies. At the sight of invaders, warning shots would be fired to alert people nearby. Other watchtowers were built close to forts for obvious reasons. The highest concentrations of watchtowers are along the main mountain passes such as Wadi Sumail and Wadi Jizzi. Elsewhere, necklaces of watchtowers can be seen atop the hills surrounding major settlements (at Ibra for example – one of the very few large towns in Oman without a fort).

By the time of the accession of Sultan Qaboos in 1970 many of the country's forts and other traditional buildings had fallen into advanced stages of dilapidation. Ongoing restoration efforts are attempting to save as much of Oman's heritage as possible – a huge project which has now succeeded in bringing many of the majestic fortifications back to life, although significant numbers of other sites – such as the spectacular fort at Jalan Bani Bu Ali – are steadily crumbling into dust.

Nizwa Fort.

Sohar moon and mosque.

SOHAR AND THE BATINAH COAST

The flat and fertile Batinah Coast north of Muscat leads to Sohar, once the most important trading centre in the Arabian peninsula. Today the region is famous mainly for its dates.

North of Muscat stretches the Al Batinah region, a narrow coastal plain bounded by the sea on one side and the Hajar mountains on the other. This is one of the most fertile regions in the country, covered in innumerable date plantations, while fishing is another important source of employment, with endless lines of boats pulled up on the beaches which dot the coast. This was formerly the wealthiest and most cosmopolitan part of the country, centred on the great port of Sohar, one of the major trading emporiums of its day. Things are a lot quieter now, although a great sequence of forts still stands guard over the region, commemorating its former economic and strategic importance.

Getting around the Batinah is straightforward, thanks to the fast (if dull) dual-carriageway coastal highway which runs from Muscat via Seeb, Barka and Sohara and on to the UAE border, a total distance of 270km (168 miles). Unfortunately, the highway runs a couple of kilometres inland, out of sight of the sea, although smaller local roads can get you down to the coastal beaches. Inland, another major road runs to Rustaq, as the heart of the so-called Rustaq Loop, a rewarding inland detour in the shadow of the Western Hajar, via some of the

country's finest forts, and with a number of exhilarating off-road routes to explore on the way.

From Muscat to Al Sawadi

Heading north out of the capital, the coastal highway passes **Muscat International Airport** before reaching **Seeb ②**, the first major settlement along the Batinah Coast (although technically it forms part of the Muscat Capital Area). This is one of the most personable towns in Oman, centred on the lively Wadi al Bahais

Taking cover.

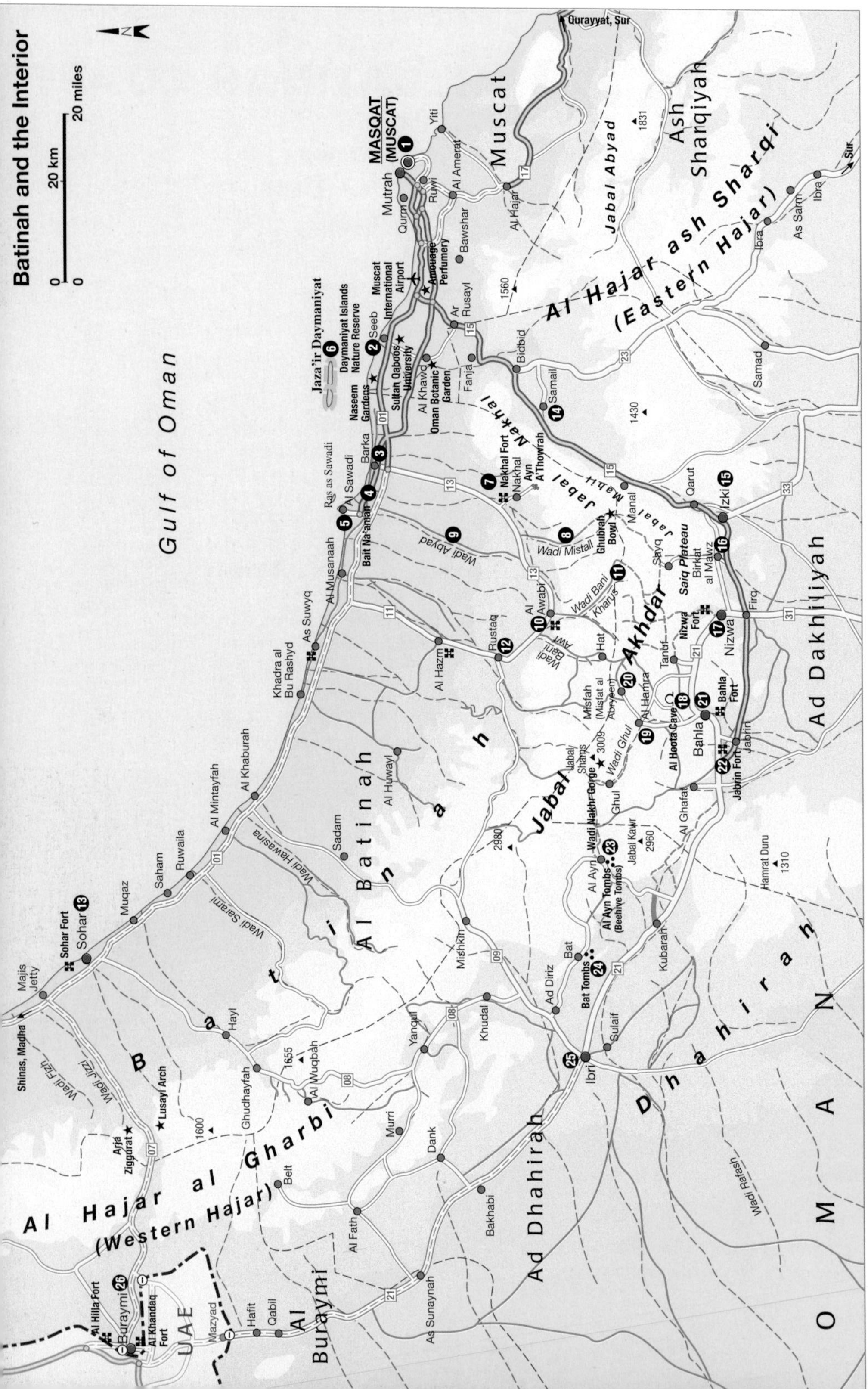

Batinah and the Interior

N

20 km
20 miles
0
0

Gulf of Oman

Qurayyat, Sur

MASQAT (MUSCAT) 1
Mutrah
Ruwi
Al Amerat
Yiti
Qurm
Bawshar
Al Hajar
Muscat

Muscat International Airport
Amouage Perfumery
Ar Rusayl
15
Fanja
Bidbid
Samail
23
1560
Jabal Abyad
1831

Ash Sharqi

Al Hajar ash Sharqi
(Eastern Hajar)

As Sarm
Ibra
Ibra
Sur
Samad
1430

Jaza'ir Daymaniyat 6
Daymaniyat Islands Nature Reserve
Naseem Gardens
Sultan Qaboos University
Oman Botanic Garden
Al Khawd

Ras as Sawadi
Al Sawadi
Barka 3
Bait Na'aman 4
Al Musanaah
5
As Suwyq
Khadra al Bu Rashyd
Al Huwayl
Al Hazm
11
Al Mintayfah
Al Khaburah
Ruwalla
Saham
Muqaz

Nakhal Fort
Nakhal 7
Ayn A'Thowrah
13
9
Wadi Mistall
Jabal Nakhal
Ghubrah Bowl
8
Jabal Shams 3009

Wadi Abyad

Rustaq
Awabi 10
12
Wadi Bani Awf
Wadi Bani Kharus
11
Hat
Jabal Akhdar
Manal
15
Qarut
33
Izki 15
16
Saiq Plateau
Birkit al Mawz
Firq
31
Nizwa Fort 17
Nizwa

Tanuf
20
Al Hamra
19
Al Hoota Cave 18
Bahla 21
Bahla Fort
Jabrin 22
Jabrin Fort

Ghul
Wadi Ghul
2980
2960
Al Ghafat
Kubarah
Hamrat Duru 1310

Mistfah (Misfat al A'Abryeen)
Wadi Nakhr Gorge 24

Al Ayn
Jabal Kawr 2960
23

Al Ayn Tombs (Beehive Tombs) 23

Bat
Ad Diriz
Bat Tombs 24
Sulaif
Ibri 25
21

Khudal
Yanqul
08
Murri
Dank
Belt
Al Fath
Bakhabi
As Sunaynah
21
Wadi Rafash
Wadi Sarami
Wadi Hawasina

Al Batinah

Jabal Akhdar

Ad Dakhiliyah

Ad Dhahirah

Dhahirah

O M A N

Sohar Fort 13
Sohar
Majis Jetty
Shinas, Madha
Wadi Fizh
07
Aqir Ziggurat
Lusayl Arch
1600
1655
Ghudhayfah
Al Wuqbah
08
Mishkim
Sadam
09
Al Hajar al Gharbi
(Western Hajar)

B a t i n a h

Al Khandaq Fort
Buraymi 26
Al Hilla Fort
UAE
Hafit
Qabil
Wazyad
Al Buraymi

Street which loops through the centre, flanked with a colourful selection of shops selling gold, perfumes, textiles, furniture and so on. There is also an extensive, breezy corniche, always busy after dark, beyond which lies the town's harbour, with dozens of boats moored up within a curling breakwater. Seeb harbour will soon become home to the new **Omani Aquarium** (completion expected late 2015, early 2016).

The nearby **Sultan Qaboos University**, opened in 1986, has some 15,000 students, of whom around 50 percent are women, a remarkable achievement considering that just four decades or so ago, schooling for girls was officially forbidden.

South of the university, the area around Al Khawd is seeing the development of the **Oman Botanic Garden**, which will be the largest botanic garden on the Arabian Peninsula when completed.

Barka ❸ (40km/25 miles from Seeb) is the next town of significance on the coast and the springboard for the Rustaq Loop (see page 132).

The imposing **Barka Fort** (Sun–Thu 8am–2pm; free), dating from the early Ya'ruba period, lies 400 metres/yds west of the main crossroads in town. The former *wali*'s quarters have been furnished as they might have appeared a century ago, while there are fine views down the coast from the terrace above.

About 5km (3 miles) beyond Barka down the main coastal highway (and then 2km/1 mile down a side road on the right) is the even more atmospheric **Bait Na'aman ❹** (Sun–Thu 8.30am–2.30pm), a fortified house dating from the 1690s, which formerly served as one of the country residences of the ruling Imams. The interior is particularly interesting, beautifully restored and with a wealth of furnishings and artefacts which give a powerful sense of what life was like here back in former times.

Like Fujairah in the UAE, the Batinah is known for its bullfights. Barka is one of various towns along the coast (along with Seeb, Sohar and Musannah) to host fights, which take place every

An art vendor in Seeb Souk.

An Amouage boutique.

SCENTS OF PLACE

Just outside Seeb next to the Nizwa highway, the Amouage showroom and factory (www.amouage.com) welcomes visitors interested in learning more about Oman's most luxurious scent and the various traditional products with which it is made. Founded in 1983 by a member of the royal family, the Amouage factory now produces a range of scents for men and women featuring an array of traditional local ingredients, including high-quality silver frankincense and myrrh from Salalah and roses from Jabal Akhdar – a sumptuous olfactory memory of the varied fragrances of Oman. As you would probably expect, however, Amouage products don't come cheap: the signature "Gold" perfume will set you back around £215 (US$335) for a 100ml bottle.

Friday in winter starting around 4pm. The rules are simple – the referee pairs animals, roughly based on equal height and weight, which are then led out and set against one another to the cheers of the exclusively male crowd. When one bull takes a tumble in the dust the other is declared victor (see page 229). Most contests last less than five minutes, but should the fight turn vicious, a rope secured to a front leg of each animal allows their owners to keep control.

Al Sawadi ❺ is a large fishing community 9km (5 miles) along a turn-off from the "prancing horses monument" on the coastal highway. The tarmac stops at the end of a long beach where you will find the low-key Al Sawadi Beach Resort (www.alsawadi-beach.om), a good base for diving trips out to the nearby Daymaniyat Islands (Jaza'ir Daymaniyat). Just offshore lie the rocky Sawadi Islands; boat trips out to them can be arranged with fishermen on the beach, whilst you can walk to the one nearest the shore at low tide.

Further out to sea, 16km (10 miles) off the coast, is the **Daymaniyat**

Islands Nature Reserve ❻, comprising nine limestone islets. Between April and September, thousands of migratory birds nest on the islands, including the rare sooty falcon. Large numbers of hawksbill and green turtles also nest in the sandy inlets protected by rocky overhangs. Diving and snorkelling trips to the islands can be arranged through the dive centre at the Al Sawadi Beach Resort, as well as via several dive operators in Muscat. A permit is required to land.

The Rustaq Loop

Rising majestically inland from the coast are the craggy heights of the **Hajar mountains**. Highway 13 cuts inland from Barka, travelling via the grandiose forts of Nakhal, Rustaq and Al Hazm before rejoining the coastal highway – a fine day trip popularly known as the Rustaq Loop. Forts apart, there is also fine mountain scenery along the way, while side tracks into adjacent wadis offer some of Oman's finest off-road driving. The Rustaq Loop can easily be visited from Seeb, Al Sawadi or even Muscat.

*A decorated room in
Nakhal Fort.*

Highway 13 turns off the main roundabout at Barkha, from where it is a 30-minute drive inland to reach the superb **Nakhal Fort ❼** (Sat–Thu 9am–4pm, Fri 9–11am), crowning a spur at the head of the wadi coming down out of the mountains. The fort's foundations are believed to pre-date Islam, though it was remodelled in the 9th, 16th, 19th and 20th centuries and now stands as an awesome tribute to the skills of ancient Omani stonemasons, soaring to a height of 30 metres (98ft). The fort was entirely self-contained, with well-water and storage rooms for stockpiling in event of a siege. The *wali* lived on the mezzanine level in winter and on the breezy upper terrace during the hot summer months. His *majlis* is lined with hand-woven carpets and rifles decorate the walls. The women's *majlis* is spread with carpets and cushions while a master bedroom contains a quaint four-poster bed. A sweeping panorama can be enjoyed from the top of the fort.

The main road through Nakhal continues 2.5km (2 miles) to the **Ayn A'Thowrah hot springs**, a shady oasis with a stream running under the date palms. The water here is warm enough to poach an egg. Locals picnic around the hot spring on Friday.

Some 15km (9 miles) further along Highway 13 past Nakhal, a side road heads off south of the highway into **Wadi Mistall ❽**, a dramatic narrow gorge which opens out soon afterwards into the Ghubrah Bowl, a huge, flat gravel plain, ringed by the mountains of the **Jabal Nakhal** and **Jabal Akhdar**. On the far side of the bowl, a rough track climbs vertiginously up to the tiny village of Wekan, one of Oman's most spectacularly located mountain villages, sitting athwart the routes of some of the country's finest hiking trails.

A further 3km (2 miles) along Highway 13, the village of A'Subaikha is the starting point for another fine off-road trip, this one into the pretty **Wadi Abyad ❾** (White Wadi), set between low red-rock hills and dotted with palm trees and rock pools. The water in some of the pools often turns a distinctive milky white due to the high concentrations of dissolved calcium it contains. This is one of Oman's

FACT

The Batinah region is said to derive its name from an Arabic root meaning "to be hidden" – and from out at sea the tawny-coloured Hajar mountains glowering over the narrow coastal plain do indeed conceal it from sight.

Bait Na'aman, near Barka.

These pots for sale near Sohar are traditionally used for storing dates.

Wekan has an incredible location.

more challenging wadis to drive since there's no actual track, and parts of the wadi often flood – just pick your way across the loose gravel, trying not to get bogged down en route.

A further 35km (22 miles) on from Nakhal, the town of **Al Awabi** is home to yet another fort (Sun–Thu 8am–2pm; free), which was recently extensively renovated. The pretty little structure is built in a mixture of stone and mudbrick with a small plain mosque standing in front. The main tower is an interesting study in traditional Omani plumbing arrangements, with no fewer than three hole-in-the-floor toilets, all carefully designed so that waste products would fall outside the castle walls and (potentially) onto the heads of the villagers outside.

Directly behind Awabi Fort, a narrow fissure in the mountains marks the start of the spectacular **Wadi Bani Kharus** ⑪, now easily accessible thanks to the construction of a new black-top road stretching all the way to the end of the wadi. A sequence of seven villages lines the floor of the wadi, with old-fashioned mudbrick houses and

date plantations squeezed in below the towering cliffs. The wadi is also of particular interest to geologists, with layers of sedimentary and mineral strata spanning over 500 million years, from the Cretaceous period to the Late Proterozoic era, exposed with textbook clarity in the cliffs above.

A few kilometres west of Awabi you pass the end of the spectacular track which descends from the mountains via **Wadi Bani Awf** (see page 144).

Another 10km (6 miles) or so from here is the town of **Rustaq** ⑫, historically one of the most important in the interior, though the sprawling modern town is largely featureless and preserves disappointingly little of its history, with the exception of its mighty fort, the second-largest in the country after Bahla, which has recently reopened after extensive renovation (Sat–Thu 9am–4pm, Fri 8am–11pm, 2–4pm). A fort has stood on the site for more than 1,000 years, built over the site of a spring which gushes around its base. It is thought to have been founded by the Persians in the pre-Islamic period and subsequently became the first capital

of the Ya'ruba dynasty under the Imam Nasir bin Murshid (died 1649). The fort was rebuilt under Imam Saif bin Sultan (died 1711), who was responsible for a massive building programme all over the interior. Saif bin Sultan also repaired the *falaj* and planted more than 30,000 date palms around Rustaq. He is buried in the western corner of the Wind Tower. The first Imam of the Al bu Said dynasty, Ahmed bin Said (died 1783), also ruled from Rustaq, where he exercised control over the interior and coast. This broke down under his sons Said and Sultan, who split the Imamate, with Said based in Rustaq, and Sultan, the more powerful of the two brothers, ruling from Muscat.

It is a further 20km (12-mile) drive to **Al Hazm**, a modest village dominated by another recently restored huge fort (Sat–Thu 9am–4pm, Fri 8am–11pm, 2–4pm). With lots of charmingly lit-up passageways and secret tunnels where a torch will come in handy, it is a great fun to explore. The three-storey limestone and wood structure with two cylindrical towers was built in 1708 by the Imam Sultan bin Saif II, who moved here from Rustaq – an inscription on the right of two decorated wooden gates identifies him as the builder.

Sohar

The approach to **Sohar** ⓭, the capital of the Batinah, is marked by a huge arch across the highway: a road to the right off the "date palm roundabout" cuts through a new business district to the old centre on the sea. Sohar is a pleasant town with clean streets lined with white houses and tropical gardens. At one time it was one of the most important trading centres on the Arabian peninsula: "Its traders and commerce cannot be enumerated. It is the most developed town in Oman," wrote Ibn Hawqal in *The Oriental Geography*, a 10th-century manual of the region. Sohar's fortunes have recently revived, thanks to the development of a major new port, an aluminium smelter, factories and oil refineries.

Archaeological excavations date the city to the 3rd millennium BC when copper was mined in Wadi Jizzi. The city rose to prominence following the

A basket of fresh dates in Rustaq.

STORY OF THE DATE

A staple food of the Bedu, a symbol of hospitality to strangers, the traditional break to the Ramadan fast, an essential ingredient at weddings, circumcisions and feasts – the date is revered throughout the Arab and Islamic world.

In the 19th century dates were Oman's biggest export, with India and the US its chief markets. Ships would leave Oman laden with dates and return with rice, coffee, sugar, spices, cloth, china, gunpowder and paper.

Today, though date production is no longer essential to the economy, its potential is being reconsidered as part of ongoing efforts to wean the country away from oil. There are some 10 million date palms, occupying around 54 percent of cultivable land, and annual production is estimated at over 300,000 tonnes.

The luxurious Sohar Beach Hotel.

Sohar fish market

The seaport was absorbed into the Persian kingdom of Hormuz in the 14th century, but following capture by Portugal in 1507 its fortunes began to ebb. For the next hundred years, Portugal maintained a trade blockade which slowly choked the commercial life out of Sohar. Even after the Portuguese left Oman in the mid-16th century, the city's fate was sealed by internecine disputes. As a result, shipping from India and East Africa discharged in Sur and Aden, and many local merchants and sea captains moved elsewhere.

The most dramatic sight in town is the whitewashed, recently renovated **Sohar Fort** (Sat–Thu 9am–4pm, Fri 8–11am) at the eastern end of the corniche in the so-called "old town" – although the original souk was demolished in the 1990s and replaced with the current modern suburban villas. The original building, believed to date from the early 14th century, is said to have been so large that it took 1,000 men to defend it – though it surrendered to Albuquerque without a single

decline of the frankincense trade in Dhofar and the weakening power of the Caliphate in Baghdad, reaching its zenith in the 10th century. The city was destroyed and most of its inhabitants slain by the Buyids of Baghdad in 971. Nonetheless, a description as late as the 12th century mentions 12,000 houses elaborately constructed of brick and teak and of traders from a dozen different countries rubbing shoulders in its sprawling souks.

cannon being fired. A Portuguese miniature shows the fort with six towers and surrounded by palm groves, but today only a single tower rises from its courtyard.

Sohar fort is the last resting place of Sayyid Thuwaini bin Said bin Sultan Al bu Said, one of two sons of the great Sultan Said bin Sultan under whom Oman regained prominence in the 19th century. On the demise of Sultan Said, Thuwaini became ruler of Oman and a colony on the Makran Coast of what is now Pakistan, while his brother was awarded Zanzibar and Omani possessions in East Africa. Sultan Thuwaini ruled for only a decade. In 1866 he was shot by his son while asleep in the fort during preparations for a military expedition to recapture Buraimi Oasis.

Almost next door to the fort stands the large **Sultan Qaboos Mosque**, with its eye-catching gold dome. A five-minute walk inland is the town's **handicrafts souk**, occupying a walled enclosure decorated with miniature watchtowers. On sale here are baskets, pottery, textiles, leatherwork, silverwork, natural medicines and traditional Omani sweets.

Heading north along the corniche brings you to the town's striking modern **fish market**, designed in the shape of a traditional dhow. A couple of kilometres further north you will find the Sohar Beach Hotel (www.soharbeach.com) and a spacious swathe of public **beach**, with wide, mud-coloured sands scattered with seashells. Next to the beach lies an attractively shady park arranged around a large lake.

Three roads continue from Sohar. The coastal highway continues north to the border of the UAE at **Khatmat Milahah**. Route 07 cuts off for **Al Buraimi** and another crossing point into the UAE. The journey along a tarmac road takes around two hours up through Wadi Jizzi, passing some of Oman's wildest and most dramatic mountain scenery en route, with jagged rock summits rising to either side of the road. Finally, Highway 08 travels inland to **Yanqul** and then joins up with route 9 to **Ibri**, offering a convenient shortcut up into the Western Hajar.

TIP

If you're travelling from Sohar up to Buraimi, note that the Oman border control is actually in Wadi Jizzi, about 40km (25 miles) before you reach Buraimi. If heading on to the UAE, you will be stamped out of Oman here. If you're returning from Buraimi to Sohar, make sure you don't have your visa cancelled by mistake.

The iconic figure of Sindbad.

SINDBAD AND SOHAR

Inhabitants of Sohar like to claim that their city was the birthplace of the legendary Sindbad the Sailor, hero of the *1,001 Nights* and innumerable subsequent films and cartoons – even if there is disappointingly little concrete evidence to back the claim. According to the *1,001 Nights* themselves, Sindbad was a merchant hailing from Baghdad who set out on a series of seven voyages, surviving shipwreck and assorted incredible dangers on each one before finally making his way back to Baghdad laden with fabulous riches. In fact, Sindbad is clearly a symbolic rather than a historical figure, and his adventures derive from a long tradition of maritime yarns, tall tales and other folklore collected over the centuries by roving Arab seafarers – including, quite possibly, sailors from Oman itself.

NIZWA AND THE INTERIOR

Historically the power base of the Imamate, the Interior is a rich and rewarding region to visit, with a string of majestic forts and magnificent mountain scenery.

The area of Oman historically known as the Interior refers to the region lying beyond the Hajar mountains where, from fortified strongholds, the Imams contested the authority of the sultan in Muscat. Hence the name "Muscat and Oman" which was used to describe the country prior to 1970 – Muscat being the capital enclave and Oman what an Australian might call the Outback. The Interior is the kernel of traditional Oman. The new towns growing up along Highway 15 may create an illusion of the present but only a few steps off the road lie ancient villages.

The Interior is largely made up of the provinces of Ad Dakhiliyah and Ad Dhahirah. Ibri, the regional capital, and Buraimi are the main towns in Ad Dhahirah, a sparsely populated area largely covered in waterless gravel desert (though rich in oil and gas) which sees hardly any tourists. Ad Dakhiliyah, by contrast, is the most visited part of Oman, home to three of the country's most famous forts – Nizwa, Bahla and Jabrin – and some of its finest scenery.

The Samail Gap to Nizwa

Wadi Samail, a natural break between the Western and Eastern Hajar mountains, has been the artery between the coast and the Interior for centuries.

The broad dry valley was the obvious course for the motorway from Muscat to Nizwa, providing 166km (103 miles) of relaxed driving.

The first of the many settlements along the Gap is **Fanja** (35km/22 miles from Muscat). Typically, the new town lies along the road, while the old walled village (accessible via a right-hand turn after the bridge) sits in an easily defensible position atop a large rocky hill; it is a pretty huddle of largely derelict mudbrick houses and a single watchtower,

Main Attractions

Al Hoota Cave
Wadi Bani Awf
Al Hamra
Jabal Shams
Wadi Nakhr
Misfah
Bahla Fort
Jabrin Fort
Al Ayn Tombs

The ruined village of Tanuf.

At a viewpoint on Jabal Akhdar.

commanding magnificent views over the pass below.

Further along the highway is a turn to **Bidbid,** whose quaint little restored fort (not open to the public) used to guard the junction of the old trade routes from Muscat, Nizwa and Sur. These now meet at a new flyover crossing the northern Sharqiya to Sur.

The town of **Samail**  ends its name to the pass. Modern Samail is a surprisingly large and sprawling affair. The actual wadi runs around 4km (2.5 miles) east of the highway, slightly away from the new town and in complete contrast to it: an extraordinarily lush little valley full of date palms hemmed in below low-lying rocky hills. The wadi's former strategic importance is borne out by the remarkable number of fortifications that dot the area, including a long line of watchtowers on the ridges above the wadi and the neatly restored Samail Fort itself (around 3km/2 miles down the wadi from modern Samail, although it is not open to the public).

Further up the highway some 103km (64km) from Muscat lies

the venerable town of **Izki** ⓯. Once again, the disorienting modern town sprawls for a considerable distance along the highway, with the old town tucked away a few kilometres distant (most easily found if you take the back road to Birkat al Mauz). Here you'll find the collapsing remains of an impressive old stone fort and the small walled town next door overlooking the broad swathe of Wadi Halfayn. Izki is also home to the Falaj al Malki, said to be the oldest in the country and one of five Omani *falaj* now protected as a Unesco World Heritage Site.

Birkat al Mawz ⓰ (Pool of Bananas) is another of the area's traditional oasis villages, with a dense patchwork of plantations clustered around the inevitable *falaj* and fort – in this case the Unesco World Heritage-listed Falaj al Khatmeen and the impressive restored Bait al Ridaydha (not open to the public).

Birkat al Mawz is also the turn-off for the **Saiq Plateau,** lying at an altitude of roughly 2,000 metres (6,562ft) beneath the summit of

Jabal Akhdar (Green Mountain). The plateau offers an invigorating escape from the lowland heat. The summer temperature does not exceed 30°C (86°F) and nights are pleasantly cool (in winter, the temperature drops as low as –5°C/23°F). Spring, when the orchards are covered by a canopy of peach, apricot, apple, pear, plum, almond and walnut blossom, is an enchanting time to visit. Indigenous olives, myrtles and pomegranates as well as ancient juniper trees are abundant. In May, the rose-picking season, the air is filled with the scent of the tiny pink Jabal Akhdar roses.

Access to the plateau is via a wide modern tarmac road, an easy drive, although only 4x4 vehicles are allowed up; you'll be turned back at the police checkpoint if you're not in a suitable vehicle. The plateau's main settlement is the surprisingly large town of **Saih Katenah**, where you'll find petrol, shops and the attractive Jabal Akhdar Hotel, a good base from which to explore the area. Behind Saih Katenah, the plateau falls away spectacularly, with kilometre-high cliffs dropping sheer into the dramatic Wadi al Ayn below. A series of time-warped traditional villages – **Al Aqr**, **Al Ayn** and **A'Sherageh** – are perched perilously around the rim of the cliffs, with old mudbrick houses surrounded by rose gardens and strips of agricultural terracing carved neatly out of the mountainside: a picture-perfect slice of traditional Oman, and with marvellous views over the surrounding mountains.

Nizwa

Route 15 ends at the historic town of **Nizwa** ⓱, long-time capital of the Interior and for many years also the seat of the ruling Imam – right up until the 1950s the town had a reputation for religious fanaticism and a general suspicion of outsiders – Wilfred Thesiger, passing through the area in the late 1940s, was advised to avoid the town on pain of possible arrest and imprisonment. Ironically, in the few decades since Thesiger's aborted visit the town has reinvented itself as

A woman picking cultivated roses

THE ROSE HARVEST

The roses of Jabal Akhdar (the damask rose, *Rosa Damascena*) are highly prized, not only for their intrinsic beauty – most apparent during the months of April and May, when flowers bloom in gardens across the plateau, turning entire villages a delicate shade of pale pink – but also as a valuable source of local income.

The area's roses are particularly sought after thanks to their use as an ingredient in the region's highly prized rose water, generally considered the finest in the country, and with demand consistently outstripping supply. Roses (introduced to Jabal Akhdar by early Persian settlers) flourish in the mountains' temperate climate – Al Aqr is a particularly notable centre of production, packed with dozens of small rose gardens.

Rose petals are harvested in May, still following largely traditional methods. The petals are first carefully plucked (usually done during the cool early morning to help preserve their delicate aroma) and then boiled in an oven. The resultant rose-scented steam is drawn off, allowed to condense, and then filtered to produce rose water. This has various uses, being drunk with tea or coffee as well as serving as an essential ingredient in the production of traditional Omani halwa. Rose water rubbed into the scalp is also said to relieve headaches.

TIP

Most shops in Nizwa souk open for business around 8am but close between 10am and 11am and don't reopen until around 5pm in the afternoon – don't expect to get much shopping done in the middle of the day, when the entire town can be eerily quiet.

one the most touristed and foreigner-friendly destinations in the country.

The heart of the town itself is essentially unchanged, although extensive restoration works during the 1990s have given it a thorough scrub and polish, making it look much neater and cleaner than it probably ever did previously. The basics remain the same, however, with the huge round tower of the town's majestic fort and grand Sultan Qaboos Mosque rising out of the centre, surrounded by a neat ochre huddle of old-fashioned souks.

First point of call for most visitors is Nizwa's splendid **fort** (Sat–Thu 9am–4pm, Fri 9–11am), raised over a period of 12 years by Imam Sultan bin Saif in the late 17th century. According to one source it was financed by spoils from Ras al Khaimah, while a second theory claims it was financed by an Omani attack on the tiny Portuguese colony of Diu on the Malabar Coast of India. Whichever is correct, Nizwa's importance in the long struggle between Muscat and the Interior is reflected in its fort, built here to serve

Nizwa Fort.

as a residence and administrative centre for the Imams.

Big rather than aesthetically pleasing, it consists of a massive circular tower with foundations sunk 30 metres (98ft) deep to withstand vibrations from mortar fire. Several of more than 400 gun emplacements still have cannons *in situ*, one of them inscribed with the name of the Imam Sultan bin Saif and another a gift from the city of Boston to the first Omani ambassador to the US. A narrow staircase leading up to the tower is kinked at each level, leading to a false door with gun emplacements and apertures in the ceiling to pour boiling oil onto any invader who managed to penetrate this deep inside the fort.

The easy climb opens into the drum of the tower with 120 positions for askars to stand guard on the parapets. The top – 40 metres (130ft) above the souk – commands a panoramic view of the landmark brown-domed mosque next to the fort, the maze of flat-topped houses and the belt of palms surrounding Nizwa like a cordon sanitaire. To the northeast, Jabal

Akhdar is angled menacingly against the sky, with its tallest peak, Jabal Shams (3,009 metres/9,872ft), the highest point in eastern Arabia, usually swathed in cloud.

Southwest of the fort stretch the various buildings making up Nizwa's celebrated **souk**. The area around the fort is dedicated mainly to tourist souvenirs and handicrafts, providing a showcase for Nizwa's celebrated craftsmanship, including its fine silver jewellery and *khanjars*, as well as copperware and leatherwork.

Heading east from the fort, the small **East Souk** (open in the morning) is the most atmospheric in Nizwa, and the only one to have escaped restoration. It looks incongruously ramshackle now compared to the surrounding buildings, but provides a much clearer idea of what Nizwa formerly looked like, with tiny shops clustered beneath crumbling mudbrick arches and a makeshift corrugated-iron roof propped up on weathered old wooden beams.

At the eastern end of the East Souk lies a much-photographed miniature square usually stacked full of quaint displays of **Bahla pottery** (see page 145); you can also see a short section of the old **city walls** here. South of here lie the more functional food and wholesale souks, with different areas devoted to fish, meat, fruit, vegetables and dates.

Immediately south of here, the open-air Goat Market is home to Nizwa's famous **Friday Market** where hundreds of traditionally attired locals come to trade goats, cows and other livestock – a lively, smelly and quintessentially Omani spectacle. The market starts at around 7–8am and finishes at around 11am in time for Friday prayers.

Around Nizwa

Exiting Nizwa, Route 21 passes the turn-off to the ruined town of **Tanuf**. This was one of a number of places in the area bombed by the British during the 1950s Jabal War, thanks to its connections with the rebel warlord Suleiman bin Himyar, self-styled "King of the Je Akhdar". The rather melancholy fragments of the old

TIP

Thursday is the best day to stay overnight in Nizwa, allowing you the chance to rise early to see the famous livestock market in full swing near the fort.

A four wheel drive makes it across a wadi river in the Western Hajar Mountains.

The pomegranate season.

Villas in Al Hamra.

mudbrick town still stand, largely ruined apart from a single small mosque. Behind the old village, the dramatic fissure in the mountains is **Wadi Tanuf**, the source of the famous Tanuf water, one of Oman's leading mineral waters, which is bottled nearby and sold nationwide.

A couple of kilometres further along Highway 21 a turn-off heads to **Al Hoota Cave** ⑱ (www.alhootacave. com; Sat–Thu 9am–1pm and 2–6pm, Fri 9am–noon and 2–6pm). Oman is peppered with sinkholes and caverns, but this is the only one which is currently accessible to those without specialised potholing skills and equipment. The cave extends for some 5km (3 miles) in total, of which almost 1km is accessible – an impressively large cavern dotted with clumps of stalactites and stalagmites, plus an underground lake. A small train transports passengers from the visitors' centre to the mouth of the cave.

Continuing north along the road past Al Hoota Cave brings you to the start of the spectacular descent of the Western Hajar through **Wadi Bani Awf** (or Auf), generally reckoned to be the most memorable off-road drive in the country. The scenery is dramatic throughout, while the track is likely to jangle the nerves of even experienced wadi-bashers.

The route starts at the sweeping viewpoint of **Sharaf al Alamayn** at the crest of the Western Hajar, with views across the entire range and towards the coast below. From here, a rough track descends sharply down the escarpment leading down to the famously remote village of **Balad Sayt**, hidden away in the folds of the mountainside, with a pretty little cluster of mudbrick houses standing about a sequence of tiny terraced fields. Below Balad Sayt lies Wadi Bimah, or **Snake Gorge**, as it is popularly known, a tiny fissure running between sheer high walls. This is an increasingly popular destination for adventure trips, with extreme hiking into the gorge, jumping and climbing over boulders and wading – or even swimming – through rock pools, although the whole place should be avoided if there is any hint

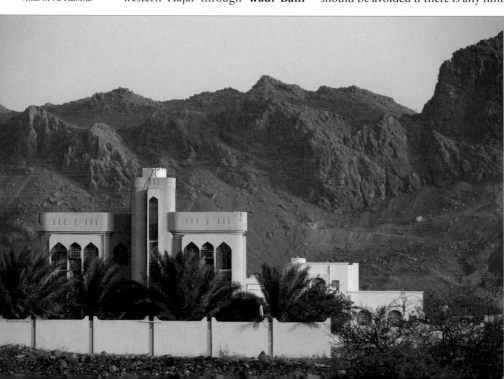

of rain. People have drowned here in flash floods, during which the gorge can flood with frightening speed. Past here the track finally levels off, eventually joining up with Highway 13 near Al Awabi (see page 134).

Alternatively, heading east from Al Hoota brings you shortly afterwards to **Al Hamra** ⑲, one of the most impressive traditional towns in Oman, with streets of grand, although steadily disintegrating, three- and four-storey mudbrick houses arranged around dozens of streets and winding alleyways which roll down the hillside to the extensive date plantation and *falaj* below – although unusually for a town of this size, Al Hamra has no fort or town wall. A couple of the old houses on the main street have now been turned into museums, including the **Bait al Safah** (daily 9am–5.30pm; closed June–Aug), an attractively restored old house renovated with artefacts and traditional furnishings, and the more rustic Bait al Jabal (daily 9am–5pm), whose time-warped interior is filled with assorted dusty local antiques and artefacts.

Beyond Al Hamra, a road heads through Wadi Ghul before gradually climbing towards the summit of **Jabal Shams** (Sun Mountain), Oman's highest peak; the latter part of the road is unsurfaced and requires a 4x4. The summit is closed, but a track leads out onto the plateau which affords a spectacular view of **Wadi Nakhr**, popularly known as Oman's Grand Canyon, with its almost vertical, 1000-metre (3,280ft) drop to the wadi below. The memorable trek around the edge of the canyon, known as the **Balcony Walk**, takes about four hours including the return journey.

Accessible via a steep road from Al Hamra, **Misfah** (or Misfat al Abryeen) ⑳ is one of the country's prettiest villages, with a fascinating tangle of mudbrick houses and an idyllic *falaj*, from where steps lead down to a tiny mosque, offering spectacular views over the surrounding hills.

Bahla and Jabrin

The small town of **Bahla** ㉑, 40km (25 miles) west of Nizwa, is utterly

A coffee pot – a traditional symbol of hospitality all over the Middle East.

Bahla.

Jabal Shams.

dominated by its vast fort, the largest in Oman. The Nabahina rulers of Oman from the 12th to the 17th century raised the fort on pre-Islamic foundations and also built the 12km (7.5 miles) of mudbrick town walls, large sections of which can still be seen today. Despite its dilapidated condition, the **Bahla Fort** (Sat–Thu 9am–4pm, Fri 8–11pm) became a Unesco World Heritage site in 1987. Soon after that it closed for a lengthy restoration and reopened 25 years later. You can explore the labyrinth of corridors on your own but we warned there is little signage.

The town is also known for its pottery, with workshops scattered around the area behind the souk. The Aladawi family pottery workshop welcomes visitors and offers you the chance to see pots being made, and the chance to buy them at prices significantly below what you'll pay elsewhere.

Another 10km (6 miles) west lies the marvellous **Jabrin Fort** ㉒ (Sat–Thu 9am–4pm, Fri 9–11am), probably the most interesting in the country. Jabrin served not only as a fort but also as a retreat for the Imams and seat of learning for students of Islamic jurisprudence, medicine and astrology. Certainly its location, set back from the mountains on an open gravel plain, does not suggest that its creator, Imam Bil'arub bin Sultan al Ya'ruba (who died here in 1692 and is buried in a crypt below the fort), felt under threat of attack.

Built in 1671, the three-storey rectangular building has 4-metre (13ft) thick stone walls with north–south towers. In the high-ceilinged rooms with Moghul-style arches are traces of what must have been a sumptuously decorated palace, tastefully restored in 1983. Swirling Islamic inscriptions in the plaster walls are cut as delicately as hand-embroidered lace, rosettes cover the pine-carved ceilings, while astrological designs in what is called the Sun and Moon Room have no parallel in Oman. In contrast to the splendour are the small, plain cells used by students off the third-storey courtyard. Go up a

final flight of steps to the top of the fort for a view of the *jabal* quivering in the heat haze.

Northwest to Ibri

West of Jabrin, Route 21 continues to Ibri, pulling gradually out of the Western Hajar and into the gravel plains beyond. Around halfway to Ibri, a signed turn-off to Amla leads to the village of Al Ayn, home to a remarkable cluster of **Bronze Age beehive tombs** ㉓ (now Unesco-listed), dramatically situated along a ridgetop against the craggy back-drop of Jabal Misht behind.

Even more extensive Bronze Age relics can be found a short drive beyond Al Ayn at the **Bat Tombs** ㉔. The hills around the village of Bat are littered with dozens of tombs, towers and other unidentified structures – a few have been carefully restored, although most are in an advanced stage of collapse.

Ibri ㉕, 36km (22 miles) further down Highway 21, is the heart of the Dhahirah, the northwest shoulder of Oman wedged between the Western Hajar and the Empty Quarter. Historically the town has a pronounced reputation for religious conservatism and tribal belligerence, as noted by Thesiger in *Arabian Sands*, who steered well clear of the place. Modern tourists are likely to receive a warmer welcome, although most still tend to avoid the town, despite the attractively restored old fort (Sun–Thu 8am–2pm; free) in the town centre, next to an attractive little covered souk and surrounded by the atmospheric remains of various fine old mudbrick mansions in various states of collapse.

Also worth a visit is the atmospheric fortified village of **Sulaif**, just east of Ibri. The village was deserted by its inhabitants when the *falaj* dried up some 40 years ago, but the local guardian will show you around the rabbit warren of tiny alleyways, roofless houses, mosques and other mudbrick structures, all of which are gradually returning to dust, before leading you up to the watchtower at the top of the rock outcrop on which the entire village is built.

Decorated tomb, Jabrin Castle.

The battlements of Jabrin Fort.

Demonstrating the traditional craft of basket weaving.

The dramatic Bat Tombs.

The drive up from Ibri skirts the edge of the Empty Quarter, and sand spits across the highway. The **Dhahirah** is barren except for scattered "bag trees", so called because their thorny branches trap wind-blown plastic bags. Nearing Buraimi the road swings close to the rocky outcrop of Jabal Hafeet in Abu Dhabi Emirate.

Note that approaching Buraimi from Ibri, you travel via the UAE, exiting Oman at the border post at Mazyad and then re-entering at the Hili border post in Al Ain (see page 188).

Buraimi

For centuries **Buraimi** ㉖ was an important gateway between the Gulf, Oman and Saudi Arabia. The area has been repeatedly occupied by militia from Saudi Arabia, most recently in 1952 when the Saudis, supported by the American ARAMCO oil company, claimed the oasis for themselves and sent troops to occupy it. They stayed there for three years until, diplomacy having failed, they were driven out by the British-led Trucial Oman Scouts. Not until

1975 were negotiated borderlines finally accepted.

Next to the main roundabout in town stands the **Buraimi souk** and recently restored **Al Hilla Fort** (Sun–Thu 8am–2pm; free). This is actually more of a residential complex rather than a proper fort, with relatively low walls and no towers. Inside there are two courtyards, the first large and largely empty apart from a small mosque, the second dotted with a number of unusually fine residential buildings, decorated with elaborate wooden doors and stone ornamentation.

From Al Hilla, walk down a small side road to the elegantly restored **Al Khandaq Fort** (Sat–Wed 8am–6pm, Thu–Fri 8am–1pm and 4–6pm; free). Built by the Al bu Shamis, a division of the local Na'im tribe, in about 1780, it was strengthened between 1808 and 1813 by Mutlaq al Mutairi, the leader of the occupying Saudis. The fort is surrounded by a deep (though now dry) moat and with elaborately crenellated battlements. There are no displays, but the dramatic architecture and a little imagination make a visit enjoyable.

Wadi-bashing

Head out into the region's mountains and deserts for an exhilarating off-road drive.

The major cities and towns of Oman and the UAE are linked by asphalt highways, but to explore fully what the region's landscape has to offer, visitors should find themselves a seat in a 4x4 and hit the dirt and the dunes.

Wadi-bashing, as off-road driving in the mountains is popularly known (or dune-bashing in the desert), is both a means to an end and an end in itself: not only will it get you from inhabited point A to isolated point B, but you'll have a lot of fun on the way.

Bouncing along a boulder-strewn wadi is like flying through bad turbulence with the "fasten seatbelt" sign on. Those who are not strapped in can become unwilling headbangers. But they usually emerge from the experience unscathed with the exuberance of children after their first spin on funfair dodgem cars.

Off-road driving should not be attempted in ordinary saloon cars. The all-terrain traction provided by four-wheel-drive vehicles is essential. It's also safer if more than one vehicle takes to the wilds at a time: that way, one can tow the other out of trouble if the need arises.

Planning and expertise

The person behind the wheel needs the handling skills of a rally driver, which is why if you're a first-time wadi-basher it's a good idea to have someone else do the work. While 4x4s can be rented, less worrisome off-road tours with experienced drivers are provided by hotels and specialist tour companies.

But even those who are most adept at judging the conditions can get stuck. A little forethought can prevent major problems, and the experienced wadi-basher hopes for the best but prepares for the worst. A long rope, shovel, tyre jack and base are musts. A small ladder or large sheet of tarpaulin can be placed under the wheels for traction. Extra fuel, a spare wheel and tyre pressure gauge are also important features of a successful trip.

Wadi- and dune-bashing depend on tyre pressure as much as skill – lower pressure for driving through sand and desert, and higher for mountain driving. When stuck in soft sand, reducing the tyre pressure and reversing over your own tracks may allow your vehicle to be driven, instead of towed, out of trouble.

To avoid getting stuck, don't change gear in soft sand, as the vehicle will lose the momentum needed to pull it through. If engines are over-revved at the first sign of trouble, the wheels dig further into the sand.

When ascending and descending sandy slopes, the wheels should be kept straight and the most vertical route taken. Attempting to cross a slope diagonally is an invitation for disaster. When going down a slope, the vehicle should be in low gear with the engine instead of the brakes used to slow it down. That way, it is less likely that the front wheels will become stuck and that the rear end will swing around, precipitating a roll.

Wadi-bashing is a great means by which to appreciate the raw beauty of the desert and mountains. It can be done year-round, but it is important to keep a close eye on the weather, especially if there's even a hint of rain in the air. Flash-floods can occur with frightening suddenness, and drownings are not unknown

Wadi-bashing is fun and exhilarating.

A traditional Omani coffee pot.

SUR, THE EAST AND THE WAHIBAH DESERT

This region offers a beautiful coastline, the characterful old shipbuilding city of Sur and the dunescapes of the Sharqiya Sands, making an excellent three- or four-day excursion from Muscat.

outheast of Muscat stretches **Al Sharqiyah** (The East) province, one of Oman's most diverse and colourful regions. Scenically, Sharqiyah packs in a varied range of attractions, from the wind-blown dunes of the Sharqiya Sands (formerly known as the Wahibah Desert) through to the craggy heights of the Eastern Hajar mountains and long stretches of unspoilt coastline, many of them visited regularly by nesting turtles. Cultural attractions include the handsome old port of Sur, home to Oman's only surviving dhow-building yard, through to the great mudbrick castles and fortified houses of the Interior, best seen in Ibra and Jalan Bani Bu Ali. This is also where you're most likely to see traditional Bedu going about their daily life, especially in the traditional souks of Ibra and Sinaw.

It is possible to make a rewarding loop through the region, travelling down the coast through Qurayyat to Sur and then on to Ras al Jinz, before heading back inland via Jalan Bani Bu Hassan and Ibra, with a detour into the Sharqiya Sands en route – an enjoyable three- or four-day excursion.

Qurayyat to Qalhat

Qurayyat ❶ (87km/54 miles) on the first, tarmacked stretch of Route 17 from Muscat, is a quiet coastal town of little interest beyond its old

fort, which was recently renovated. Qurayyat is most animated when the fishing boats return and lay their catch out on the beach. At the eastern end of the beach is a rocky outcrop crowned by a watchtower which you can wade out to at low tide. A creek, today silted up, before the turn-off to Sur was in all probability Qurayyat's old port.

South of Qurayyat on the coast lies the **Bimmah Sinkhole** ❷, now enclosed within (and signed as) the Hawiyat Najm Park. One of numerous similar sinkholes in Oman, it is

Main Attractions
Wadi Shab
Sur
Ras al Jinz
Jalan Bani Bu Ali
Sharqiya Sands
Ibra
Masirah island

The view across to Al Ayjah from Sur.

The Mausoleum of Bibi Maryam in ancient Qalhat.

A view across the lagoon to Al Ayjah.

around 100 metres (330ft) in circumference and about 20 metres (66ft) deep. Marine life including sponges and small fish indicate a connection with the sea. Filled with blue-green water, it is a lovely place to clamber down for a swim.

Further south along the coast lie two of the country's most beautiful wadis. The first is **Wadi Shab** ③ (76km/47 miles from Qurayyat), a narrow, palm-fringed ravine hemmed in by spectacular cliffs – the wadi is so narrow that it remains in shadow until midday. It's possible to drive (in a 4x4) a kilometre or so into the wadi over loose gravel, but after that, progress is on foot only, following the narrow footpath which winds up the gorge, past huge boulders, rock pools and the ruins of a couple of abandoned villages. A few kilometres further down the coast lies the **Wadi Tiwi**, almost identical to Wadi Shab save for the presence of a road which winds its way up the wadi through a series of tiny traditional villages.

A little further down the coast lie the remains of the ancient city of Qalhat ④, once one of the leading ports in the southern Gulf and visited by both Marco Polo and Ibn Battuta. The city is believed to have been founded by the Persians around the 2nd century, reaching the height of prosperity under rule from Hormuz in the 13th and 14th centuries. The extensive remains of collapsed walls, towers and assorted other structures cover the area, although it is difficult to make much sense of them. The only notable surviving structure is the **Mausoleum of Bibi Maryam**, last resting place of the saintly woman who, according to Ibn Battuta, had ruled the city until a few years before his visit in 1330. The mausoleum's original dome has now collapsed, though the remains of the delicately moulded arches and doorways survive more or less intact.

Sur

From Qalhat the road descends to **Sur** ⑤ (150km/93 miles from Qurayyat), a major trading port with East Africa until early in the 20th century and still the biggest traditional port in Oman. Sur finally gave in to the better

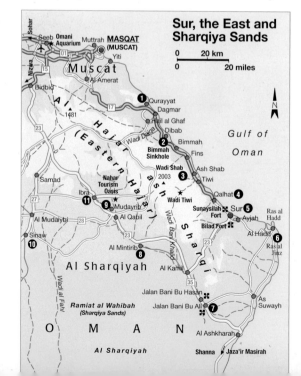

Sur, the East and Sharqiya Sands

shipping facilities of Muscat, although its economic fortunes have been revived by the construction of a huge industrial zone on the north side of town. Old Sur and the small suburb of Al Ayjah continue to provide visitors with a pastel-coloured cameo of the past.

Sur's most interesting sights are the traditional **dhow-building yards**, the only surviving example in Oman (although there are several in the UAE). The yards lie on the edge of the creek, some 4km (2.5 miles) east of the town centre. Access to the yards is free, and the workers, mainly Indian, do not mind being photographed. You can learn more about the town's maritime heritage at the Maritime Museum, located in the Wilayat of Sur.

Old merchant-style houses line the creek in **Al Ayjah**, a short drive over the bridge near the dhow yards. The little whitewashed community was founded in 1928 by rebellious sheikhs from the dissident Bani bu Ali, who established an independent customs post and ran up their own flag which took the Sultan, aided by the British Resident in the Gulf, two years to remove. At low tide the view of Al Ayjah from Sur crosses extensive mudflats and beached bumboats, which in the evening are bathed in rose-coloured sunlight; at high tide this is one of the most charming corners of Oman.

Two forts guard Sur. The main one, **As Sunaysilah Castle** (Sun–Thu 8am–5pm; free), with its four distinctive towers, is built on a hill overlooking the sea approaches to Sur. Inside the courtyard are a mosque and a small prison, while to the far left a wooden door gives access to the water cistern. A second fort, **Bilad Sur**, lies 6km (4 miles) south from the town centre.

Ras al Haddand Ras al Jinz

The jutting headland known as **Ras al Hadd** is the first point in Arabia touched by the rising sun. The tiny village is dwarfed by its massive fort (Sun–Thu 8.30am–2.30pm; free), whose high walls tower over the surrounding houses, although most of the interior is simply a huge empty courtyard.

Significant numbers of green turtles come to nest along the coast around Ras al Hadd, although the biggest

A landscape of palm trees and river at Wadi Shab.

DHOWS OF OMAN

The word "dhow" is habitually used in English as a cover-all term to describe traditional wooden Arabian boats. Locals, however, distinguish between a variety of designs. Traditional Arabian dhows were curved at both ends – such as the large-scale *boom*, used for long-distance ocean crossings. Other types of vessel – such as the *sambuq* and *ghanjah* – sported high, square sterns, thought to be inspired by Portuguese galleons. Traditional dhows were also notable for their so-called "stitched" construction, whereby the planks of the boat were sewn together using coconut rope, and propelled by distinctive triangular *lateen* sails, although conventional nails have long since replaced traditional coconut rope, and virtually all modern vessels are powered by diesel engines rather than by sail.

Dhow detail.

The dhow yard in Sur.

nesting sight lies further south, at **Ras al Jinz ⬤**, 23km (14 miles) along the coast. This is one of Oman's most memorable natural spectacles, as dozens of turtles come ashore nightly to dig a hole in the sand and lay their eggs, covering them carefully before returning exhausted to the sea. The eggs, which may number up to 100 per turtle, take about 60 days to hatch, after which the tiny turtles must burrow their way to the surface and head as quickly as they can for the safety of the sea.

Turtle-watching tours depart from the modern visitor centre (tel: 9655 0606; www.rasaljinz-turtlereserve.com; daily 9am–8pm) in the morning and in the evening and last around 60 to 90 minutes There is a maximum of 100 visitors per evening and another 100 visitors per morning session; bookings either by phone or email are essential; three weeks or more in advance is recommended since places are usually booked up early.

Continuing along the coastal road past Ras al Jinz, the next sizeable settlement is the sleepy fishing town of **Al Ashkharah**. There is a choice of routes here: either south along the tarmac road to Shanna (departure point for boats to Masirah Island) or north, heading back inland to Muscat via Jalan Bani Bu Ali and Ibra.

North from Al Ashkharah

Some 30km (19 miles) inland from Al Ashkharah the little-visited town of **Jalan Bani Bu Ali ⬤** offers an absorbing taste of traditional small-town life in provincial Oman. This is the home town of the Bani bu Ali (who also installed themselves in Al Ayjah in Sur; see page 153). The Bani bu Ali were the only tribe in Oman to subscribe to the conservative Wahhabism sect of Islam followed in Saudi Arabia; the town retains a certain reputation for extreme religious conservatism, and women visitors are advised to dress very modestly – although foreign visitors are also sufficiently rare to elicit an unusual measure of generally good-natured curiosity.

The main sight in town is the vast **fort**, probably the single largest unrestored mudbrick structure in the entire country: a huge, slowly disintegrating edifice whose towers and battlements still rise high above the surrounding streets, although considerable sections of wall have now collapsed. Inside, the labyrinthine remains of various buildings survive, decorated in places with fine arches and arcading. There is also a small mosque, topped by a pair of flattened domes, strikingly similar to the famous old 15th-century mosque at Bidiyah (see page 229) in the eastern UAE.

Close to the fort stands the quaint **Al Hamooda Mosque**, an eye-catching structure topped by 52 tiny domes and with a *falaj* running in front of the main façade. Non-Muslims are prohibited from entering, although they may be able to look through the door for a glimpse of the unusual interior, filled with a dense cluster of stumpy columns.

Heading north from Jalan Bani Bu Ali, is another 10km (6 miles) to the twin town of **Jalan Bani Bu Hassan**.

There's another sizeable **fort** here (Sun–Wed 7am–6pm; free), although this one has been comprehensively restored, as well as some impressively tall and large traditional houses scattered around the surrounding area, looking a bit like medieval mudbrick skyscrapers poking up above the palms.

The roadside town of **Al Kamil** lies 75km (46 miles) north of Al Ashkharah – a mainly modern affair, though a few fine old two- and three-storey mudbrick mansions can still be seen. Heading north again, it's 42km (26 miles) from Al Kamil to the turn-off east to the side road to **Wadi Bani Khalid**, one of Oman's most spectacular wadis.

Al Mintirib ❽ on the northern edge of the Sharqiya Sands is about 45 minutes' drive from Al Kamil. A market depot for local Bedu, it sells everything from male stamens for pollinating female date palms to mobile phones, and is also home to the inevitable fort (Sun–Thu 8.30am–2.30pm; free). Tracks lead off from here into the Sharqiya Sands, including the access routes for a couple of the sands' remote desert camps. Alternatively, **Al Qabil** has a comfortable hotel which can also be used as a base for visiting the Sharqiya Sands.

The Sharqiya Sands and around

Sunset and sunrise provide spectacular photo opportunities of this unique desert covering 10,000 sq km (3,860 sq miles) of the eastern Sharqiyah, described by Nigel de Winser, the project director of a British Royal Geographic Society (RGS) expedition to the Sharqiya Sands in 1985, as "a perfect specimen of sand sea".

The 35 scientists in the expedition spent four months studying the ecosystem of the Sharqiya Sands (formerly known as the Wahibah Desert) and discovered 150 species of plants, including woodlands of native ghaf inland from Al Ashkharah. Among the desert's most valuable trees is the *Proposis cinera*, which helps stabilise the shifting sands as well as provide fuel, shade and food for livestock. A hardy tree, it sends down an immensely long tap root to the water table, but most desert plants are sustained on dew.

Beach at Ras al Jinz.

A rare dew-drinking beetle was among 16,000 invertebrates collected by the RGS team. Two hundred species of mammals, birds, amphibians and reptiles were also logged. Early-risers here may see patterns made by nocturnal creatures in the sand – the swishing trail of a side-winding viper, the hip-hop footprints of a hare and the pad marks of a Rüpell's sand fox to name a few. During the day the desert is devoid of life as the creatures burrow away from the intense heat.

The dune systems of the Sharqiya Sands are believed to have existed before the last pluvial period in Arabia around 4,000–6,000 years ago. Aligned mainly east–west and soaring upwards of 60 to 80 metres (200 to 260ft), the dunes commence less than 1km (.6 mile) off the road between Al Qabil and Al Minitrib.

Around 3,000 Bedu live on the fringes of the Sharqiya Sands, mostly herders of sheep, goats and a few camels. Coastal families living south of Al Ashkharah double as fishermen, while men around Al Qabil and Al Mintirib act as guides for tour operators.

The best way to experience the sands is to spend a night or two at one of the increasing number of desert camps hidden away in various parts of the dunes. Access to most camps is via 4x4 only, although most places can arrange pick-up from the highway. The further into the dunes you go, the more pristine the scenery becomes. Most camps offer a range of desert activities, including dune-bashing and more sedate (and much quieter) camel or horse rides, sometimes guided by local Bedu. You might also find sandboarding, trekking and quad-biking trips, as well as cultural visits to local Bedu encampments. Needless to say, you shouldn't attempt to venture off into the sands without the services of a guide – the wide and uninhabited expanses of dune, with daytime temperatures nudging over 40°C (104°F), can bring ill-equipped visitors to grief very quickly.

North of Al Qabil, 1km (0.75 mile) east of the main highway, the village of **Mudayrib** ❾ is one of the prettiest in Sharqiyah, surrounded by a protective necklace of six watchtowers posed on top of the surrounding hills. Down

Camel in the Wahibah Desert.

THE BARON INNERDALE

A small stone monument at the northern end of Masirah Island (now part of the military airbase, and out of bounds to the public) commemorates one of the more gruesome episodes in modern Omani history. In 1904 the *Baron Innerdale* steamship was travelling from Karachi to Liverpool when she ran aground near Masirah. After three days, crew and passengers took to a lifeboat, landing soon afterwards in Masirah. Subsequent events remain unclear. Arriving at Masirah, there appears to have been some misunderstanding, leading to a fight, during which the stranded crew and passengers of the *Innerdale* were massacred. The furious Sultan Faisal had nine of the killers executed, flattened Hilf village and banned the islanders from building permanent houses – a decree which remained in force until 1970.

in the village itself stand a number of imposing old fortified houses built by local merchants who had grown rich through the village's location on one of the main trade routes between Muscat and the coast.

Also north of Al Qabil, a side road strikes west around the top of the sand to reach the small town of **Sinaw** ⑩. The town's Thursday souk is a fascinating melting pot, as Bedu come from miles around to sell their goods and exchange news. Lining the walls around the market are shops filled with items essential to desert life, as well as silver jewellery and pottery. Before 11am is the best time to visit the souk.

Bustling **Ibra** ⑪ is the main town of the region, still north of Al Qabil. There's another colourful souk here, also popular with local Bedu, although even more interesting is the famous women's souk held on a Wednesday from 8am until noon. Run by women, the souk caters to women's needs, with as many as dozens of local Bedu selling bolts of silk and satin brocades, jewellery, *kohl*, sandalwood, kitchen goods, spices and other produce.

Almost uniquely for a settlement of its size, there is no fort in Ibra, although the town preserves rich reminders of its past in the old mud-brick villages of **Al Minzahah** and **Al Kanatar** on the edge of town (and clearly signed from the main highway), two picture-perfect walled villages packed with fine old merchant houses sporting elaborately carved windows and archways. On the edge of Al Kanatar lies the venerable **Al Qablateen Mosque** (very similar to the Al Hamooda mosque in Jalan Bani Bu Ali; see page 154), with a dense cluster of columns inside the solid (though now roofless) rectangular structure.

Masirah Island

Lying 18km (11 miles) off the coast at the far southern end of Sharqiyah province, **Masirah Island** (Jaza'ir Masirah) is one of Oman's most remote tourist attractions and a popular destination for both locals and expatriates – though it still sees few foreign tourists. The island is roughly 80km (50 miles) long by 18km (11

TIP

Most women at Ibra's women's souk do not object to having their picture taken, but always ask first. *"Mumkin sura, min fadlich?"* ("May I take your picture?")

Men gathering on Masirah Island.

Masirah is also popular amongst windsurfers, who consider it one of the best sites in the region thanks to the offshore winds blowing down the coast, particularly during the breezy *khareef* (monsoon) season from June to September.

Customers in Ibra's souk.

miles) wide, with a sand-fringed coast dotted with dozens of unspoilt villages climbing inland to the modest hills of the interior, rising to 274 metres (900ft) at Jabal Hamra.

Hilf, at the northern tip of the island, is Masirah's only real town, with several simple hotels, petrol stations, ATMs and a reasonable selection of shops. If you have a 4x4 and camping equipment, however, you can take your pick from any of the beaches around the coast for a memorable spot of wild camping. Car ferries run between Hilf and Shanna on the mainland; the crossing takes around 90 minutes and costs around OR8 per car (usually more for a 4x4). Ferries leave when full – roughly every one to two hours – and normally run until around 5pm, although it is best to be at the jetty by 3pm, just in case. Note also that ferries occasionally stop running in bad weather. There is a project to build a causeway bridge spanning the 25km (15.5 miles) between Masirah Island and the mainland.

Away from Hilf, Masirah remains largely untouched by the modern world. Wild camping aside, wildlife is the main attraction here, particularly the island's turtles. Four of the five main species of marine turtle nest here, and Masirah is believed to host the world's largest population of loggerhead turtles, while hundreds of green, hawksbill and olive ridley also visit the island. Note that turtles nest only on the east and far southwestern coasts of the island; loggerheads usually stick to the northeastern coast, while other species can be seen further south. Ask locally to find the best places to turtle-spot – the nesting site on the beach right next to the Mesirah Island Resort (http://masiraislandresort. com), 10km (6 miles) from Hilf, is a good bet at certain times of year. The hotel also offers seasonal turtle watches. Dolphins and whales are also frequently seen off this coast.

Turtles aside, Masirah is also particularly rich in birdlife, with around 328 species recorded here. Additionally, the island is known for its remarkable seashells and other marine relics, including the island's celebrated endemic cowry shell (*Cypraea teulerej*).

THE BIRDLIFE ALONG DHOFAR'S COAST

The special climate of coastal Dhofar in southern Oman has made its wadis, hills and creeks particularly rich in birdlife.

Dhofar's geographical location and unique monsoonal microclimate makes it one of the most rewarding birdwatching destinations in the Arabian peninsula, thanks to the presence of a wide range of indigenous and migratory species that visit the region, and which are unknown elsewhere in Oman. In spring or autumn you can expect to find many Eurasian migrants dropping in to rest and feed on their way between winter quarters in Africa and their breeding grounds to the northeast.

There are numerous rewarding birding spots throughout the regions. The coastal khawrs around Salalah, and ocean-side locations further afield including Mughsayl, Mirbat and Hasik, all offer rich ornithological pickings. In addition, the spectacular Tawi Atayr (the aptly named Well of Birds) is another rewarding destination, as are the various springs (ayn) which dot the region (such as Ayn Hamran and Ain Razat) and the dramatic Wadi Darbat. The uplands of the Jabal Samhan are also worth a visit, the haunt of majestic raptors including Egyptian vultures, the Arabian Scops owl and Verraux's eagle.

Elsewhere, commonly spotted residents include Rüppell's Weaver, Abyssinian Sunbird, African Silverbill, as well as the more mundane Graceful Warbler and Yellow-vented Bulbul. You may also see Black Kite and Fan-tailed Raven, the former perhaps nesting here in winter, the raven foraging from its cliff roosts and nests.

A regular sight amidst Salalah's coastal woodlands, Rüppell's Weaver is one of the region's most distinctive bird species, instantly recognisable thanks to its colourful yellow plumage and famous for its intricately woven nests.

One of the three kingfisher species regularly sighted in Oman (along with the Common and Collared varieties), the Grey-headed Kingfisher is usually seen posed motionless on branches or overhead cables, scanning the ground for insects.

A glossy ibis. These quaint migratory waders, with their long and hugely curved beaks, can often be seen foraging for food amongst the coastal mudflats of Oman.

...e delicate Yellow wagtail is one of the sixteen wagtails found ...Oman and the UAE, typically spotted foraging for insects ...idst coastal grasslands and scrub.

...ne of the region's most iconic birds of prey, the Egyptian ...lture can often be seen riding the thermals above the mountains of Oman, instantly recognisable thanks to its distinctive black-and-white wings, sometimes approaching two metres in length.

One of two species of kite found in Oman, the Black Kite (although it's brownish in colour, rather than black) can often be spotted hovering overhead above the Salalah mountains and lagoons.

ALONG DHOFAR'S CREEKS

Good views of waterbirds are to be had at most of the khawrs (creeks) which dot the coastline around Salalah. Khawr Salalah, right on the edge of the city, is usually thronged with resting or feeding birds, as is Khawr Rawri, a particularly magical location below the ruins of ancient Sumhuran.

Common species include visiting Greater Flamingo, egrets and herons, Glossy Ibis feeding on the grassy banks with resident moorhens and coots, gulls and terns, as well various ducks in autumn including Cotton Teal (Indian Pygmy Goose), Pheasant-tailed Jacana, occasional lapwings, various species of snipe, roosting Yellow Wagtails, and a variety of waterbirds from the large visiting Eurasian Curlew and Black-tailed Godwit to the diminutive spring-nesting Kentish Plover.

Don't neglect the surrounds of the creeks, where Little Pratincole may roost unseen, and a flock of Alpine Swift may mill over your head, or (early on a May morning) you may find the bushes bursting with fat Marsh Warblers, dawn arrivals from wintering in Africa and now on their way to nest in Europe.

Flocks of nesting Greater and Lesser Flamingos add an incongruously African touch to parts of coastal Salalah, often seen splashing about the coastal khawrs (creeks) which fringe this part of the southern Oman coast.

DHOFAR

The only part of the Gulf that is visited by the southwest monsoon, Dhofar is a lush summer retreat for northern Omanis, with a rich history rooted in the ancient frankincense trade.

D hofar, Oman's southern province, is a ruggedly beautiful region quite different from the rest of Oman. Its mountains attract the *khareef* (southwest monsoon) blowing off the Indian Ocean, resulting in a cool, wet summer (June–September) when the rest of the country is paralysingly hot. Waterfalls pour off the *jabals* into coastal wadis, and low-hanging mists occasionally disrupt air services to the capital, Salalah. Lush woodland is sustained by rainfall of 27 to 150mm (1 to 6 inches) a year, but beyond its limits you can die of thirst. "To the south, grassy downs, green jungles and shadowy gorges fell away to the... Indian Ocean... whereas immediately to the north a landscape of black rocks and yellow sand sloped down to the Empty Quarter. I looked out over the desert. It stretched away unbroken for 1,500 miles to the orchards around Damascus," wrote Wilfred Thesiger in *Arabian Sands*.

Occupying about one-third of the total area of Oman, Dhofar adjoins the Rub al Khali (Empty Quarter), first crossed by Bertram Thomas in 1930 and then by Thesiger in the 1940s (see page 58). The province shares a border with Yemen to the west (Yemen and Oman completed their

demarcation of the border in 1995), and in the northeast melts into the gravel plains of the Jiddat al Harasis.

Salalah

Most people travel to Dhofar by air, a spectacular 90-minute flight from Muscat. On the approach to **Salalah ❶** the brown terrain is flecked with green and the drop down onto the coastal plain is sudden and exciting. Likewise 1,000km (620 miles) after leaving Muscat, the highway sweeps into Salalah, flanked by lines

Main Attractions
Salalah
Jabal Samhan and Wadi Darbat
Tawi Atayr and Taiq Sinkhole
Sumhuram and Khawr Rawri
Mirbat
Jabal Qamar

Pottery incense burners for sale in Al Husn Souk, Salalah.

Sultan Qaboos Palace.

A female goat shepherd near Salalah.

of coconut palms, which here replace the date palm of the north.

Modern Salalah is now a sprawling expanse of whitewashed, low-rise buildings. The commercial centre is around As Salam Street and the parallel 23rd July Street. **As Salam Street** is usually the liveliest in the city, lined with hundreds of shops selling virtually everything under the sun; **23rd July Street** is wider and quieter, home to dozens of banks, airlines and Salalah's best selection of restaurants. The **New Souk**, off the north side of the street, is a pleasant pedestrianised complex with dozens of tea shops and traders selling locally grown tropical fruits such as coconuts, papaws and bananas.

The old town – centred on the district of Al Haffa – lies a couple of kilometres (a mile) south of here, centred on the aromatic **Al Husn Souk** Ⓐ, just inland from the sea. This is undoubtedly the highlight of Salalah, with dozens of shoebox shops selling traditional products – Omani caps, walking sticks, perfumes and, especially, frankincense, of which Al Husn has probably the best selection in the country. The best time

to visit is after dark, when the alleyways between the shops are perfumed with burning incense. Many of the shops are run by local women, veiled but friendly. Bags of frankincense sell for as little as OR1 (about £2/US$3), although top-quality *hojari* silver frankincense costs considerably more.

West of Al Husn Souk stretches the huge **Sultan Qaboos Palace** Ⓑ, an imposing marbled building (not open to the public) which replaced the original fort in which Sultan Qaboos was born in 1940. Qaboos has always had close links with the city, having spent most of his early life here, while his mother is also Dhofari. East of the souk stretches Salalah's attractive **corniche**, with leaning coconut palms shading the beach, a wide and beautiful expanse of white sand stretching for miles down the coast. You will also find a few traditional Dhofari-style houses dotted along the beach (and Ash Sharooq Street, one block inland) with their distinctive carved windows, balconies and battlemented rooftops.

On the east side of the city, beyond Al Haffa, lie the extensive remains of

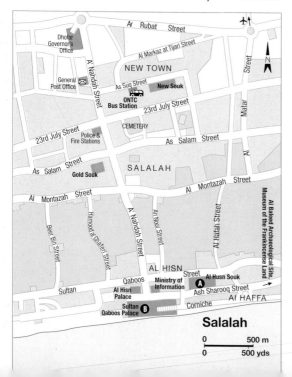

Salalah

0   500 m

0   500 yds

the ancient city of Zafar, the forerunner of modern Salalah (and the origin of the name Dhofar). Zafar's heyday came between the 12th and 16th centuries, when it was one of the leading commercial centres of southern Arabia, its fame attracting many visitors, including both Ibn Battuta and Marco Polo. The extensive ruins of the city are now protected as the **Al Baleed Archaeological Site** (Sat–Wed 8am–2pm and 4–8pm, Thu–Fri 4–8pm), a large area of parkland covered in various fragmentary remains of houses, mosques, gateways, walls and other structures. The best-preserved section is the old Zafar citadel and the Grand Mosque at the western end of the site.

Next to the entrance to the archaeological site, the **Museum of the Frankincense Land** (same opening hours and ticket) offers hit-and-miss coverage of the history of Salalah and Dhofar spread over two large rooms. The Maritime Hall holds exhibits relating to Omani boat-building and maritime traditions, with assorted navigational instruments and intricate wooden models of traditional boats. The adjacent History Hall hosts a random muddle of exhibits, including finds from Al Baleed and nearby Sumhuram.

East of Salalah

The area east of Salalah is particularly rich in attractions, including the ancient ruins of Sumhuram, the scenic heights of Jabal Samhan and the characterful old town of Mirbat.

Heading out of the city, the first point of interest is **Ain Razat**, a lush picnic spot around a spring, rich in birdlife. Past here, it is a further 13km (8 miles) to **Taqah ❷** (36km/22 miles from Salalah), the second-largest town in Dhofar. The majority of its 17,000 population are fishermen netting huge catches of sardines during the winter. When the vegetation dies off, dried sardines become an important food supplement for mountain cattle. There is also a pretty little renovated fort (Sun–Thu 9am–4pm, Fri 8–11am) in the middle of town.

Continue for 6km (4 miles) beyond Taqah to reach the turn-off on the left leading up into **Jabal Samhan**, the

TIP

There is a wide range of attractions scattered around Salalah which can be combined into rewarding excursions from the city. If you don't fancy navigating yourself, a number of local tour agents organise guided tours of the various sights covering either a half-day or full day – full-day trips to the east of the city are particularly rewarding.

Tropical plants, including bananas, flourish.

SOUTHERN TRIBES

About nine mountain tribes known collectively as the *Jebali* live in the coastal ranges – Jabal Qamar, Jabal Samhan and Jabal Qara – rising behind Salalah. Brown-skinned and with rounded heads, in appearance they resemble Ethiopians more than either Omanis or the long-skulled Bedu of the Jiddat al Harasis and Sharqiya Sands. Most are herdsmen running stocky mountain cattle and keeping camels for prestige. During the monsoon, as the weather in the mountains cools down, they move their tents to the coastal plain around Salalah. The Jebali continue to speak a number of local languages closer to Amharic (one of the languages of modern Ethiopia and Eritrea) than Arabic, including Shehri, spoken by the Qara, and Mehri (or Mahri), spoken by the Mahra.

The lush, scenic Ain Razat.

green coastal range which backs this section of the coast. Right next to the turning is the opening of **Wadi Darbat** ③, marked by a huge cliff of pock-marked travertine that transforms into a spectacular waterfall during the *khareef* – probably Dhofar's most photographed sight.

Past the Wadi Darbat waterfall, the road climbs steeply up into the hills. After around 17km (11 miles) there's a signed turn-off on the left to **Tawi Atayr** (Well of Birds) ④, one of the most dramatic of the various sinkholes that dot the porous limestones of the Salalah mountains. This enormous cavity plunges more than 100 metres (330ft). With a local guide, you can scramble down a rugged path to the bottom. A subterranean stream leads out of the sinkhole, but no one has yet managed to follow it to the end.

Some 11km (7 miles) further north lies another, and even more impressive, sinkhole, the vast **Taiq Sinkhole** ⑤ (misleadingly signed as "Taiq Cave") – a vast bowl scooped out of the russet-coloured uplands. According to some estimates this is

the world's third-largest sinkhole, at around 1km (0.75 mile) long, 750 metres (2,460 ft) across and some 200 metres (660ft) deep.

Returning to Tawi Atayr and heading east, the road climbs up to the escarpment of Jabal Samhan, the scenery becoming increasingly barren as you near the top, from where there are jaw-dropping views over the hills and down to Mirbat and the coast way below. Among the botanical wilderness, look out for the curious *Adenium obesum*, whose pink blossoms grow straight out of the trunk. The mountains around here are also said to be home to some of the country's tiny number of surviving Arabian leopards – although no one has seen any for years.

Back on the coastal highway, it's another 2km (1 mile) to the turn-off to the ruins of the town of **Sumhuram** ⑥ (Sat–Fri 8am–7pm), an Unesco World Heritage site. Sumhuram was formerly a major trading point on the Arabian frankincense route, but appears to have been abandoned in the 5th century AD after a sandbar

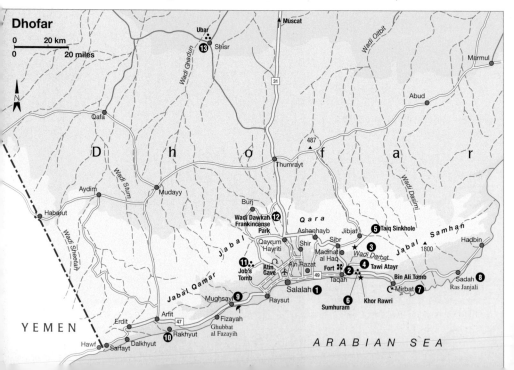

(which can still be seen) formed across the mouth of Khawr Rawri, cutting off the town's access to the sea.

The remains of the town have now been meticulously restored, showing the foundations of houses, temples and streets protected by thick walls, more than 3 metres (10ft) deep in places. Next to the single gateway, through the walls, are two beautifully preserved inscriptions commemorating the foundation of the city, carved in the ancient South Arabic *musnad* alphabet. Inside, the considerable remains of a temple dedicated to the Mesopotamian moon god Sin can still be seen.

Immediately below Sumhuram, the idyllic **Khawr Rawri** is the largest of a dozen creeks between Salalah and Sadah. With a particularly low salt content, it supports freshwater fish from small guppies to ponderous milk fish measuring almost 1 metre/ yd long. Pelican, stork, spoonbill and flamingo are among 186 species of birds recorded in the vicinity.

A right turn off the tarmac road before Mirbat leads to an unusual white double-domed **Mausoleum** of **Ali Bin**, a 14th-century Muslim divine from Yemen. The mausoleum stands in the middle of an extensive cemetery, studded with thousands of headstones. The oldest are clustered around the mausoleum itself, often sporting elaborately carved inscriptions. Inside the mausoleum is a single darkened room, perfumed with incense, with the saint's coffin under an embroidered cloth.

A kilometre (0.75 mile) or so beyond lies **Mirbat** ❼ (74km/46 miles from Salalah), the most picturesque town in Dhofar. Its small fort with cannon emplacements pointing seawards offers good views. Beyond the headland, the old town has some fine old houses, with the distinctive carved wooden shutters that are a particular feature of the region. Anywhere else they would have been bought and restored by Europeans, but here they are falling into disrepair.

It is 64km (40 miles) from Mirbat to **Sadah** ❽. Known as the "Frankincense Highway", the road east crosses the rugged coastal plain with great views of Jabal Samhan. Sheltered

Fishing boats on the beach, Mirbat.

MAGNETIC ATTRACTION

Just inland from the coast near Mirbat lies one of Oman's more eccentric attractions, the enigmatic Magnetic Point (or Anti-Gravity Point, as it is also known). Following a sloping track leading inland down to the beach (you will need to travel with a local tour operator to discover the exact location), you'll find that cars left in neutral will begin magically reversing themselves back up the hill, in apparent defiance of all laws of physics and common sense.

Local guides assert that this is the result of some mysterious magnetic phenomenon, although the more plausible (if prosaic) explanation is that just some kind of weird optical illusion – a local example of the type of "Gravity Hill" (or "Magnetic Hill"), of which many other examples have been recorded worldwide.

Camels in Wadi Darbat.

A local man at Sumhuram.

from the monsoon, a few straggly frankincense trees grow in the wadis. On reaching Sadah, turn left at the Abalone Roundabout and drive down to a tiny harbour where a few boats are usually moored. Local women as well as men work as abalone divers, wearing only goggles and diving to depths of 10 metres (30ft) to prise the shells off the rocks. The season is short (Nov–Dec) to allow regeneration.

Historically, **Hadbin** (170km/105 miles east of Salalah) was linked to the export of frankincense, but today, like Sadh, it relies on fishing and occasional abalone diving. It has several small food stores, but no other facilities. Travel beyond here is strictly by 4x4 with a back-up vehicle.

West of Salalah

Leaving Salalah, the road west heads out past the enormous port and industrial complex at **Raysut**, 10km (6 miles) from Salalah. Past here the road winds inland, just out of sight of the ocean until it sweeps back to the coast and offers spectacular views of the towering sea cliffs above

Mughsayl **❾**, 45km (28 miles) from Salalah. Mughsayl is known for its giant blowholes (follow the signs on the left to Al Marneef Cave), which spurt water up to 30 metres (100ft) high during the *khareef*, although the sprays are less impressive at other times of the year, and may dry up entirely. Walking along the rock shelf, you can hear the eerie sound of the sea rushing beneath your feet. Mughsayl has a good swimming beach, and the creek at the southern end is popular for birdwatching from December to February and April to June.

Past Mughsayl, the road climbs dramatically up into the barren **Jabal Qamar**. The stretch of highway here is known as the Furious Road, blasted out of sheer rock faces and climbing some 400 metres (1,312ft) in just 5km (3 miles), with endless hairpins. Some 6.4 million tonnes of rock and 160,000 tonnes of asphalt went into building the road at a cost of around £75 million (US$120 million).

Around 14km (9 miles) past Mughsayl the road finally reaches the top of the ridge, with spectacular views along the coast and down to the sea way below. On your left, a graded track (a 4x4 is usually required) winds down to the coastal village of **Fizayah**, home to a superb beach hemmed in by spectacular sea cliffs and dramatic limestone formations.

It is possible to continue west from here as far as **Rakhyut** **❿** (148km/92 miles from Salalah), a small village built in the lee of the cliffs with a couple of basic food stores and nothing else, although there is not a great deal to see en route, and you'll have to negotiate a couple of police checkpoints (bring your passport) along the way. The area beyond Rakhyut is currently off-limits due to its proximity to the Yemen border.

Job's Tomb

Job's Tomb **⓫** (open 24 hours) lies to the north of Salalah. Famed in the Old Testament for maintaining his faith in

God in spite of the sufferings sent to test him, Job (Ayoub in Arabic) is revered by Muslims as well as Jews and Christians.

It is about a 30-km (19 miles) drive from Salalah to reach the site held by Muslims to be the patriarch's tomb (Al Nabi Ayoub). Enter the gate beside the mosque and walk down the path to a white shrine with a gold dome. A single long grave, the tomb is covered with a green embroidered shroud, garlands and pages from the Koran left by faithful pilgrims. Non-Muslims are allowed to enter the shrine, but must cover their heads and remove their shoes first.

The Empty Quarter and Ubar

North of Salalah and the Dhofar mountains stretch the endless deserts of the Empty Quarter (Rub al Khali), extending across northern Dhofar and into Saudi Arabia. The tarmac road to Thumrayt part of Highway 31 to Muscat, starts climbing into Jabal Qara 5km (3 miles) outside Salalah, a gradual rise into an increasingly inhospitable landscape. The inland side of the mountains forms a plateau which

dips gradually to the north, eventually giving way to gravel hills dissected by numerous wadis and the desert.

Some 35km (22 miles) north of Salalah lies the **Wadi Dawkah Frankincense Park** ⑫, on the left of the main road (there are no restrictions to visiting: simply park your car and walk over). The arid wadi contains an estimated 2,000 frankincense trees in the 9 sq km (3.5 sq miles) listed by Unesco as a World Heritage Site. Those attaining the maximum height of 5 metres (16ft) are more than 200 years old. The trees are threatened by feral camels tearing off the leaves, as well as visitors making incisions in the trunks to see the sap oozing out, as the trees cannot repair such damage and eventually dry out. The Bait Kathir Bedu, who own hereditary rights to the trees, are still allowed to collect the resin, but the way they cut the trunk does no permanent damage.

The edge of the Empty Quarter is marked by the ramshackle little town of **Thumrayt**, a popular pitstop with passing truck drivers and crammed with cafés and petrol stations. North

The dramatic coastline at Mughsayl.

THE HALLANIYAT ISLANDS

Lying 30km (18 miles) offshore from Hadbin are the four rocky and remote Hallaniyat (or Kuria Muria) Islands. A few fishermen inhabit Hallaniyat, the largest of the islands and location of their only permanent settlement, although there are no regular boat services to the archipelago. The Hallaniyat have an unusual history. In 1854, Sultan Said gifted the islands to the British after they had proposed a scheme for harvesting guano from them (the foreign secretary, Lord Clarendon, it is said, offered the Sultan a snuffbox in return). The guano scheme failed to take off, however, and the islands were soon after attached to the Aden Settlement, in what is now Yemen. They remained a British possession until 1967, when they were returned to Oman.

TIP

There's good diving all along the Dhofar Coast (except during the *khareef*). Trips can be arranged through the well-equipped dive centres at the Hilton and Crowne Plaza hotels in Salalah, or at the Marriott Hotel in Mirbat, which is conveniently close to some of the area's best dive sites.

Mausoleum of Bin Ali, near Mirbat.

of here, the highway sets off on its interminable desert crossing towards Muscat, a long, flat, monotonous and hot drive. The turn-off to Ubar is 40km (25 miles) north of Thumrayt.

Ubar ⑬ or Wubar is the name of the legendary city which T.E. Lawrence dubbed the "Atlantis of the Sands". The site lies close to the village of **Shisr**, 72km (45 miles) northwest of Thumrayt via a featureless gravel road. The historian Al Hamdani, writing in AD 6, described Ubar as "a city lying astride the fabled incense routes with imposing architecture, vast orchards and fabulous wealth". The Qur'an has an account of how the citizens of "Irem" (believed to be Ubar), like the biblical inhabitants of Sodom and Gomorrah, were punished for their excessive lifestyles, and how the city, which was built over the top of a huge limestone cavern, collapsed and then was buried under drifting sand dunes.

In 1992, after a long search, the remains of what were claimed to be the ancient city of Ubar were rediscovered by an expedition led by Ranulph Fiennes and Nicholas Clapp – although

controversy remains over whether or not the ruins they uncovered are really the remnants of Ubar/Irem, or just one of many *caravanserais* dotting the overland frankincense route from southern Arabia. The remains themselves are fairly unimpressive, the fragments of a few walls and towers next to the large sinkhole into which the town suddenly collapsed some time during between AD 300 and 500.

Artefacts discovered at Ubar include a soapstone chess set dating from AD 1000, a glass bangle from AD 700 and a frankincense burner made in around AD 300. At the site itself, there is little to see beyond the ruins of a wall, several towers and the limestone cave pierced by pipes for pumping water across the desert to Thumrayt.

Beyond Ubar, tracks stretch into the increasingly impressive dunes of the Empty Quarter, a marvellous place for an overnight stay out under the stars. Needless to say, you should only venture into the desert with a competent guide and relevant equipment and provisions – a number of tour operators in Salalah can arrange this for you.

THE SEARCH FOR UBAR

The search for the remains of Ubar was one of the great archaeological treasure hunts of recent times. The first hint that there might be more to the legend of Ubar than was previously thought was provided by English explorer Bertram Thomas, the first European to traverse the Empty Quarter in 1930–31. Travelling north of Shisr, Thomas saw a series of "well-worn tracks", described by his Bedu companions as the "Road to Ubar", which they said lay buried under the sands, although no one could say where. Thomas's great rival Harry St John Philby searched for the city without success, while Wilfred Thesiger also appears to have explored the area.

Nothing more was heard until the 1980s, when American filmmaker Nicholas Clapp persuaded NASA to provide radar imaging, carried on board the US Space Shuttle, of the area in which Ubar was thought to lie. A satellite picture of the area was assembled, and in 1990 a team including Clapp, Ranulph Fiennes and archaeologist Juris Zarins set out to follow these leads on the ground. Some 18 months later, they discovered the remains of Ubar. Both Fiennes and Clapp wrote books describing the search (*Atlantis of the Sands: The Search for the Lost City of Ubar* and *The Road to Ubar: Finding the Atlantis of the Sands* respectively) – with each appearing to claim the leading role in the discovery of the site.

Frankincense – the Perfume of the Gods

Few countries in the world have as distinctive an olfactory signature as Oman's, and whether you're in a traditional souk, a mudbrick fort, a modern shopping mall or an office block, the distinctive aroma of burning frankincense is never far away.

Oman has long been famous for frankincense. The frankincense trade brought enormous prosperity to the ancient cities of Dhofar, from where ships laden with the precious perfume would depart to Egypt and the Mediterranean along the Red Sea, or overland by camel via inland settlements such as the legendary Ubar (see page 170).

A wonder resin

Demand has waned somewhat since then, but frankincense remains a key ingredient in traditional Omani life. Frankincense burners are traditionally passed around after a meal to perfume clothes and hair, while the resin is also used as an ingredient in numerous perfumes, including the heady Amouage, Oman's bespoke scent *par excellence*.

The smoke of frankincense also helps to repel mosquitoes, while certain types of frankincense resin are also edible, and continue to be widely used in traditional Arabian and Asian medicines to promote healthy digestion and skin – scientists are also investigating its possible uses in the treatment of chronic inflammatory diseases such as Crohn's disease, osteoarthritis and even cancer.

Collecting the resin

Frankincense (in Arabic, *luban*) is a resin obtained from one of four trees of the Boswellia genus, particularly the *Boswellia sacra*, a distinctively short and rugged species, rarely exceeding 5 metres (16ft) in height. *Boswellia sacra* can survive in the most inhospitable conditions, sometimes appearing to grow straight out of solid rock, and thrives particularly in the semi-arid mountains around Salalah.

Frankincense is collected by cutting small incisions into the bark of the tree, causing it to secrete a resin, which is allowed to dry and harden into so-called "tears". Virtually all frankincense is taken from trees growing in the wild – the difficulty of cultivating the trees means that they're not generally farmed on a commercial scale, in the manner of, say, dates.

Sourcing the finest

Most of the global supply of frankincense is now produced in Somalia, although Omani frankincense – particularly that from Dhofar – is generally considered the finest. There are many different types of frankincense, graded according to colour, purity and aroma. "Silver" (or *hojari*) frankincense is generally considered the best, with whiter and purer tears being favoured over the more yellowish, discoloured resin which is typical of Somali produce.

Aficionados flock to the Al Husn Souk in Salalah, generally reckoned to stock the best frankincense in the country, though you'll find packets of resin for sale in souks and shops around the country – Mutrah Souk in Muscat has a particularly good selection, if you know what you're looking for.

A frankincense tree, near Salalah.

THE MUSANDAM PENINSULA

Separated from the rest of Oman by the UAE, this rugged peninsula offers some of the country's most spectacular scenery, with soaring mountains falling into a series of dramatic fjords.

At the northernmost tip of Oman, separated from the rest of the country by a large swathe of UAE territory, lies the Musandam peninsula, a remote region of dramatic mountains and sheer-sided *khawrs* (fjords), popularly described as the "Norway of Arabia" and widely considered to be the most scenically spectacular in Oman.

Musandam is historically one of Oman's most remote and impoverished areas, home to tribes who had little in common, either culturally or linguistically, with those further south, eking out a difficult existence amidst the region's inhospitable mountain and *khawrs*. The inhabitants of the Musandam interior, the Shehi, until recently lived largely in caves and rock shelters, speaking a form of Arabic largely unintelligible to outsiders and carrying a distinctive two-headed axe, or *jerz*, rather than the traditional Omani *khanjar*. Even more unusually, the inhabitants of Kumzar (see page 175) continue to speak a unique language – Kumzari – based on Iranian blended with elements of Arabic, along with numerous loan-words from Hindi, English, Spanish and French – said to be the result of sailors shipwrecked along the coast who settled in the village. The region has also enjoyed close connections with Iran, just a short boat trip away over the Strait of Hormuz. Until recently a flourishing smuggling trade connected the two, and the influence of Iran continues to be strong to this day.

Development has been slow in coming – the first reliable road link between the peninsula and the outside world wasn't constructed until 1982 – although the area now has a decent infrastructure and basic tourist facilities, mostly found in the bustling town of Khasab, which offers the perfect base for excursions into the *khawrs* and mountains. The region's only other major settlement is the Omani section of the

Main Attractions

Khasab
The coastal road to Bukha
Khawr Sham
Kumzar
Jabal Harim

An Omani girl in Musandam.

Man and daughter in Khasab.

town of Dibba (see page 230) on the UAE border at the southern end of the peninsula, which is also home to a couple of hotels, although it is effectively cut off from the rest of Musandam.

Khasab

The only sizeable settlement in Musandam, the compact but bustling town of **Khasab ❶** lies close to the northern tip of the peninsula at the head of a steep rocky wadi – an ideal base for dhow trips out onto the surrounding fjords or mountain safaris up into the Jabal Harim. The town itself divides into two parts: the New Souk area, the bustling heart of modern Khasab, and, 2km (1 mile) north on the coast, the more ramshackle Old Souk area. The latter is where you'll find the town's fine **fort** (Sat–Thu 9am–4pm, Fri 8–11am), built by the Portuguese in the 17th century with attractively restored rooms and an unusual detached round tower standing in the middle of the courtyard, which now doubles as an interesting miniature museum on Musandam.

Directly in front of the fort stretches Khasab's extensive **harbour**, formerly

Enjoying the scenery along the Khawr Sham.

the epicentre of the town's roaring smuggling trade with Iran. Various changes to customs regulations and other factors have now wiped out these contraband activities, although there are usually still plenty of Iranians in town, who pop over the Straits of Hormuz to buy up cheap household appliances for resale back home.

The coastal road to Bukha

The 28km (17-mile) coastal road from Khasab to Bukha is Musandam's only surfaced connection with the outside world, a spectacular feat of engineering which winds dramatically around the sea cliffs and *khawrs* of the coast. The first few miles out of Khasab are particularly fine, blasted out of the feet of the mountains around Khawr Qida and revealing vivid bands of sedimentary layering. On the far side of the bay, **Wadi Tawi** has petroglyphs featuring camels, sheep and hunters pecked into the rocks. From here the road climbs up to the village of **Al Harf** at the highest point of the ridge, offering spectacular views over the Strait of Hormuz – on a clear day you can see Iran.

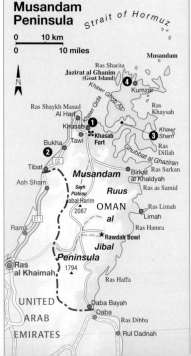

Musandam Peninsula

Strait of Hormuz

0 ——— 10 km
0 ——— 10 miles

N

Musandam

Ras Sharita
Jazirat al Ghanim (Goat Island)
Khawr Ghdiz Zip
Kumzar ❹

Ras Shaykh Masud
Al Harf
Khawr Qida
Khasab ❶
Khasab Fort
Khawr Sham ❸
Ras Khaysah
Ras Dillah

Bukha
Tawi
❷
Ghubbat al Ghaziran
Ras Sarkan

Tibat
02
Birkat al Khaldyah

Ash Sham
Musandam
Sayh Plateau
Ras as Samid

Jabal Harim
2087
Ruus
Ras Limah

Rams
E11
OMAN
al
Limah
Ras Hamra

Rawdah Bowl ★
Jibal
Peninsula
Ras
al Khaimah
1794 ▲
Ras Haffa

UNITED
Daba Bayah
ARAB
Daba
Ras Dibba
EMIRATES
Rul Dadnah

It is another 12km (7 miles) or so from here to the quiet town of **Bukha** ❷, home to an impressive seafront fort (Sat–Thu 9am–4pm, Fri 8–11am; free), surrounded by a moat (formerly flooded with sea water) and an unusual tower, its distinctive tapering shape designed to reduce the impact of cannonballs. The interesting ruins of a large stone mosque stand next door. It is another 15 minutes' drive from Bukha to the UAE border at Tibat.

Khawr Sham and Kumzar

Khasab is the starting point for dhow cruises down the wonderful **Khawr Sham** ❸, the biggest fjord in Musandam, ringed with the craggy red-rock mountains. Half a dozen tiny villages lie dotted around the *khawr*, accessible only by boat and now being steadily depopulated as the inhabitants abandon their difficult *khawr*-side existence to head off to Khasab or beyond, although some locals still spend their summers here fishing in the fjord. You're also likely to see pods of dolphins frolicking around the *khawr*, chasing boats for fun.

Halfway down the *khawr* lies the rocky little **Jazirat Telegraph** (Telegraph Island), named after the telegraph station established here by the British in 1864 along the route of the London-to-Bombay submarine telegraph cable, although the station lasted just four years and was abandoned in 1868. The foundations of the old British buildings can still be seen, and the island is a popular destination on dhow cruises, which often stop here for lunch. Boats can moor next to the island at high tide; at low tide you'll have to swim across.

An even more dramatic boat trip leads out to the famously remote town of **Kumzar** ❹, the most inaccessible in Oman. There are no roads to Kumzar and the only way to reach the place is by boat – around two and a half hours by dhow or 45 minutes to an hour by speedboat. Unfortunately it is no longer possible to visit the town itself – outsiders have been banned since 2010 after locals complained about the intrusive behaviour of visiting tourists, but it is still well worth the trip out for the magnificent marine scenery en route. Trips head out into the

Jabal Harim.

GEOLOGY OF MUSANDAM

Just past the summit of Jabal Harim, look out for the remarkable "fossil wall" right next to the road: an extraordinary layer of sedimentary rock studded with the petrified outlines of hundreds of perfectly preserved ancient submarine creatures. These fossils attest to the remarkable geology of the peninsula, and the fact that the rock from which the towering mountains of Musandam are made up was originally formed deep under the sea. Having been originally thrust up out of the sea, Musandam is now slowly returning whence it came, with the entire peninsula falling back into the sea at the dramatic (for geologists) rate of 5mm a year, a process which has formed the spectacular *khawrs* (actually flooded valleys) which you see today.

open sea around the coast, passing the entrance to Khawr Ghob Ali and then past Jazirat al Ghanim (Goat Island), a former grazing ground for sheep and goats. The journey continues into the Strait of Hormuz, with wonderful sea views of craggy headlands, distant islands and (generally) oil tankers plying up and down the strait, before turning in towards Kumzar itself, a colourful huddle of buildings wedged below sheer cliffs.

The mountains

South of Khasab stretch the rugged Musandam mountains – a jagged massif of dolomite, limestone and shale, rising to the heights of the wild Jabal Harim at 2,087 metres (6,847ft) above sea level, a rewarding half- or full-day excursion from Khasab by 4x4 (count on a half-day to Jabal Harim, or a full day to reach the Rawdah Bowl). The route follows the broad Wadi Khasab behind town before climbing up into the mountains along the dirt-track road which continues all the way through to Dibba (see page 230), with increasingly spectacular views of the mountains en

route. Dozens of little rock dwellings can be seen along the sides of the track, now used as shelters for goats or as temporary refuges, although many were inhabited until less than 15 years ago by the reclusive Shehi.

After around 45 minutes the road reaches the **Sayh Plateau**, a rare flat piece of land in the otherwise convoluted landscape. Past here the road climbs again to reach the top (almost) of **Jabal Harim** (Mountain of the Women – so named because locals used to send their wives and daughters up here for safety in times of trouble). Rocks at the top are dotted with numerous petroglyphs along with an incongruous array of marine fossils, evidence that the entire range formerly lay below the sea.

Past here, the road descends abruptly, through some of the most memorable mountain scenery anywhere in the country to the remote **Rawdah Bowl**, a small plateau, roughly 3km (2 miles) across, encircled by mountains on all sides and home to wandering camels and various old stone buildings and other remnants of traditional life, including an unusual cemetery pre-dating the arrival of Islam.

Arabian leopard.

ARABIAN LEOPARDS

Leopards in Arabia? Indeed it is true – but for how long? Persecuted by humans as a threat to their domestic animals, the Arabian leopard is now critically endangered, with perhaps just a couple of hundred left in the wild. Reports of actual sightings are virtually unknown, and most evidence is the result of finding fresh spoors or reports from villagers of hearing the leopard's distinctive rasping cough. Most of Oman's surviving leopards are thought to live in Jabal Samham in Dhofar, though a few may still survive in the rocky recesses of Musandam – despite a systematic cull of local leopards by villagers protecting their herds back in the 1980s. Fortunately, the killing of a leopard now entails a fine of OR5,000 and up to five years in jail.

AL Ittihad Square, Abu Dhabi.

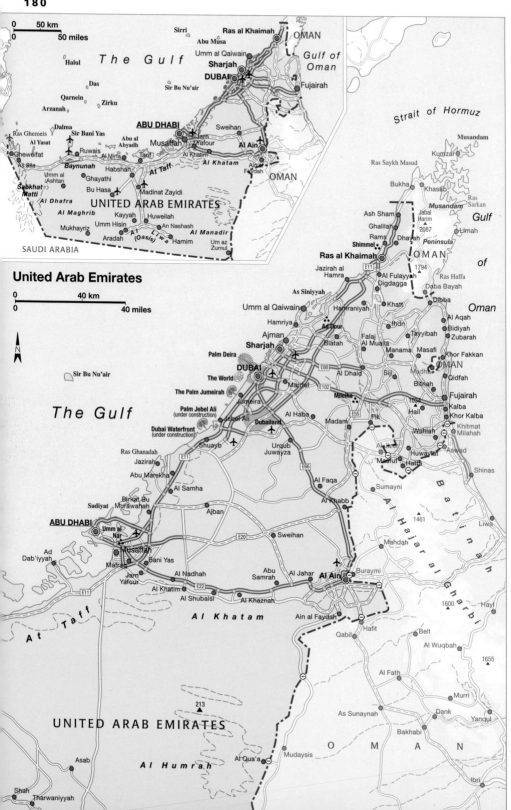

United Arab Emirates

THE UAE

A detailed guide to the entire country, with principal
sites clearly cross-referenced by number to the maps.

Sports fans at Al Rashid Stadium.

The modern UAE is more of a confederation than a country. Squeezed into an area roughly the size of Austria, the contrasts between the seven emirates that comprise the nation could hardly be greater, whether in terms of size, wealth, cultural outlook or general atmosphere.

Most foreign visitors head straight for the bright lights of Dubai, by far the most cosmopolitan and absorbing destination in the UAE, home to a wide range of attractions, from the bustling souks of the old city centre to jaw-dropping modern landmarks such as the gargantuan Burj Khalifa and the iconic Burj al Arab.

Visit only Dubai, however, and you will come away with a very lopsided impression of life in the modern UAE. National political life is dominated by Abu Dhabi, which is the biggest and richest of the seven statelets, covering around 85 percent of the UAE and boasting well over 90 percent of its total oil revenues. The low-key city itself has struggled to emerge from Dubai's shadow, although there are rewarding attractions here such as the majestic Sheikh Zayed Grand Mosque and the upcoming Saadiyat Island Cultural District with five museums all designed by world-famous architects. It is also worth making the trip to the inland city of Al Ain with its rambling oases and traditional forts.

Emirates Towers, Dubai.

Just down the coast from Dubai, conservative Sharjah is the polar opposite of its brash neighbour, home to a string of absorbing museums and heritage attractions, including a superb Islamic Museum and the various traditional buildings of its absorbing Heritage Area.

North of Sharjah, the tiny emirate of Ajman is notable mainly for its fine fort and traditional boat-building yards, whilst Umm al Qaiwain appears to have been largely forgotten by the modern world, with its dusty town and mangrove-fringed coast. Further north, Ras al Khaimah sits in an attractive setting in the lee of the Hajar mountains, with a range of industrial and agricultural developments centred on the bustling RAK City. Over on the east coast, sleepy Fujairah is the most physically attractive of the emirates, with a long sandy coast backed by the craggy ranges of the Hajar mountains – a beguiling natural contrast to the vibrant cities of one of Arabia's most dynamic and multi-faceted countries.

A minaret of the mosque on Al Ittihad Square, Abu Dhabi.

ABU DHABI

The capital of the Emirates has plenty to offer visitors, from inspiring architecture to fabulous beaches. Two hours away by car is the oasis town of Al Ain.

Abu Dhabi
UNITED ARAB
EMIRATES

Main Attractions

Al Hosn Fort
Abu Dhabi corniche
Emirates Palace
Emirates Heritage Village
Sheikh Zayed Grand
 Mosque
Saadiyat Island
Yas Island

I n March 1948 Wilfred Thesiger emerged with four Bedu companions from the great golden dunes of Rub al Khali (the Empty Quarter) at Liwa – a fertile crescent dotted with dozens of oases – and travelled another 240km (150 miles) across "interminable blinding salt flats" to reach the coastal village of Abu Dhabi. Wading across the creek that separated Abu Dhabi from the mainland (now the site of the Maqta Bridge) they eventually arrived "at a large castle that dominated a small dilapidated town along the seashore".

Such was **Abu Dhabi ❶** until the discovery of enormous oil reserves during the late 1960s, since when this erstwhile dusty backwater has transformed into a thriving international city. Today Abu Dhabi is the capital and largest emirate of the UAE, occupying 86 percent of the country's total area.

Abu Dhabi (Father of the Gazelle) takes its name from legend. In the early 1770s, the story goes, a party of hunters from Liwa followed the tracks of a gazelle to one of the numerous coastal islands they knew in the Arabian Gulf. To their good fortune they found a freshwater spring where the animal had stopped to drink and began a settlement there in the 1790s.

The Al Nahyan, of the Al bu Falasah tribe, have ruled Abu Dhabi and the

Dhafra (Liwa) since about 1690. They are a *fakhd* (sub-section) of the Bani Yas, who came originally from the desert oases of the Liwa. They owned camels, some donkeys and goats and lived in rectangular palm-frond houses built into the sand dunes above carefully tended date palm groves. During the summer many of the men would go to Abu Dhabi to join the pearling fleet as divers. In 1800, under Shakbut bin Dhiyab, the Al bu Falah collectively left the Liwa to settle on Abu Dhabi Island.

A banner at the Presidential Palace.

Al Hosn Fort turret.

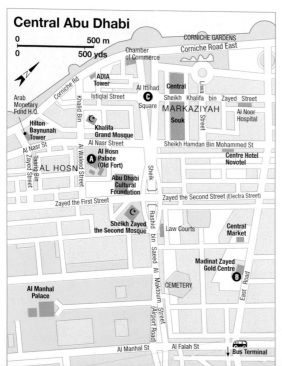

Emirates Palace Hotel.

The country's first president and so-called "father of the UAE", Sheikh Zayed (see page 57), was born in 1918 in eastern Al Ain – a territory fought over for centuries but finally ruled by the Al Nahyan from about 1890. He was named after his illustrious grandfather Sheikh Zayed bin Khalifa Al Nahyan (ruler of Abu Dhabi 1855–1909), known as Zayed the Great. It is these two Zayeds who give their names to Zayed the First Street and Zayed the Second Street (otherwise referred to as Electra Street) which runs from east to west and changes name at the intersection of Sheikh Rashid bin Saeed Al Maktoum Street (Airport Road).

In 1966 Sheikh Zayed succeeded his brother Sheikh Shakhbut bin Sultan Al Nahyan as ruler. The extreme wealth generated by the discovery of oil enabled Sheikh Zayed to build first-rate public facilities for his people, but his benevolence reached beyond the UAE and was appreciated by many international charity programmes and Islamic communities. His son, Sheikh Khalifa, became president following Sheikh Zayed's death in November 2004.

Al Hosn and around

At the very heart of the city lies the old **Al Hosn Fort** Ⓐ. This large white fort was built in about 1763 to protect the town's water source (the outer wall and towers were added later); at one time it was the only noteworthy building along the coast between Dubai and Doha in Qatar. Until 1972, when Sheikh Zayed moved to a new palace, it was also the ruler's residence. The entire complex has been closed for comprehensive redevelopment for years now, and no one seems to know when it will reopen. Next door to Al Hosn, the suave modern **Abu Dhabi Cultural Foundation** was developed under the patronage of Sheikh Zayed to host a range of international and local exhibitions, concerts, plays and film screenings. It is home to a state-of-the-art exhibition on Abu Dhabi's heritage (daily 9am–8pm; free).

Northeast of Al Hosn stretches Abu Dhabi's central commercial district, perhaps best seen from the

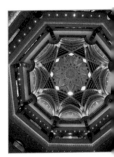

Al Fanar revolving restaurant on top of Le Royal Méridien hotel. There's little in the way of specific things to see here apart from endless identikit glass-fronted buildings lined up along the various streets and a string of small-scale shops and malls at street level below – the most interesting is the **Madinat Zayed Gold Centre ❸** – the local equivalent of Dubai's famous Gold Souk – with two floors of shops stuffed with gold and silver jewellery (www.madinatzayed-mall. com; Sat–Thu 9am–10.30pm, Fri 4pm–11pm).

North of Al Hosn lies the eye-catching **Al Ittihad Square ❸**, dotted with a striking sequence of five quirky oversized sculptures, including an enormous perfume bottle and a gargantuan coffee pot.

North and south of Al Ittihad Square stretches Abu Dhabi's splendid waterfront **corniche**, extending along the top of the island from the Sheraton to the Hilton hotel and lined with an impressive string of high, glass-fronted towers (best seen from the Heritage Village on the Breakwater). Notable landmarks include the elegant blue-glass **Hilton Baynunah Tower** and the folding curves of the ADIA building (opposite the British Embassy). A pleasant swathe of gardens runs alongside the road, busy every evening with joggers and families enjoying the cool sea breeze.

The Emirates Palace and around

At the southern end of the Corniche, about 3km (2 miles) from Al Hosn, rises the vast **Emirates Palace ❹**, one of the city's most eye-catching landmarks, and one of the world's most spectacularly opulent hotels. Constructed in traditional Arabian style, this red-sandstone colossus sprawls for the best part of a kilometre (0.75 mile) down the beach, topped with around 100 domes, while the interior is a riot of Arabian chintz, best appreciated over afternoon tea in the vast foyer or an evening meal in one of the very upmarket restaurants which are scattered around the ground floor.

Beyond the hotel, the road continues south to the enormous gold-domed

Looking up into the grand atrium of the Emirates Palace Hotel.

The chic Central Market.

CENTRAL MARKET

Opened in 2014, the spectacular new Central Market (www.centralmarket.ae/souk; daily 10am–10pm, Fri–Sat until 11pm) – replacing Abu Dhabi's old city souk which was demolished in 2005 –adds a welcome touch of contemporary style to the city centre in a location close to Al Hosn Fort and the Cultural Foundation. Designed by Foster & Partners, the market comprises a magical new souk, blending elements of traditional Arabian architecture with suave modernist decor and an environmentally sensitive design. An emphasis on sustainability means shops in the souk focus on traditional crafts and products, dotted with a range of restaurants and coffee shops and offering what a beguiling taste of traditional Arabia reinvented for the 21st century.

An elegant fountain at the corniche.

Presidential Palace, home to the ruler of Abu Dhabi (who is, of course, also the president of the UAE), although the palace is strictly off-limits to visitors. Alternatively, heading north from the Emirates Palace, a bridge leads across to the Breakwater, an area of reclaimed land which is best known as the home of the glitzy **Marina Mall** ⓔ, one of the city's top shopping destinations, with pretty tented courtyards and fountains (www.marinamall.ae). Rising at the back of the mall, the Burj al Marina tower offers peerless views over the city, either from the Tiara revolving restaurant on the top (42nd) floor or, less expensively, from the coffee shop one floor below.

In front of the mall on the breakwater itself is the pleasant **Heritage Village** ⓕ (Sat–Thu 9am–5pm, Fri 3.30–9pm; free), which commemorates life in Abu Dhabi before oil revenues changed the city for ever. Exhibits include old Bedouin tents, a reconstruction of a *barasti* (palmthatch) house, and a recreation of a traditional souk in which local artisans can sometimes be seen at work. There are also superb views from here to the corniche across the water, with the two distinctive Etisalat towers rising behind – immediately recognisable (like their cousins in Dubai) thanks to the enormous golf balls which sit perched on their summits.

Just past the Heritage Village rises an enormous **flagpole**, visible for miles around. Erected in 2001, this was formerly claimed to be the tallest unsupported flagpole in the world, at 123 metres (404ft) tall, although it's since been surpassed by a number of even taller flagpoles elsewhere.

The suburb of Al Bateen, around 2km (1 mile) east, until recently home to an old-fashioned dhow-building yard, now boasts the **Al Bateen Wharf** development ⓖ, which will include a new fishermen's marina, a walking promenade as well as restaurants and cafés.

From the wharf it is around another 4km (2.5 miles) south to the suburb of Al Mushrif, where you'll find the interesting **Women's Handicraft Centre** ⓗ (Sun–Thu 7am–3pm; free)

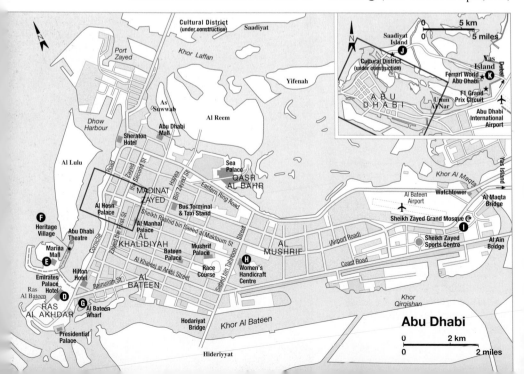

in the Women's Association Complex on Karama Street. Run by the Abu Dhabi Women's Association, this government-funded project aims to help preserve traditional local arts and crafts, including jewellery and dress-making.

South of the centre

Although it is far from obvious, Abu Dhabi is actually built on an island. This stretches for around 10km (6 miles) east from the centre before rejoining the mainland via the Al Maqta Bridge (built in 1968); right next to the bridge you can see the old watchtower, which formerly guarded the entrance to the city.

Close by you can't fail to notice the monumental **Sheikh Zayed Grand Mosque ❶** (www.szgmc.ae; Sat–Thu 9am–10pm, Fri 4.30–11pm; free; free guided tours, several daily), rising imperiously over the southern city. This is undoubtedly Abu Dhabi's single most worthwhile attraction: a spectacular, snow-white mass of domes and minarets visible for miles around – the vast courtyard alone is capable of accommodating some 40,000 worshippers. Completed in 2007, the mosque is one of the world's biggest – and certainly the most expensive, having cost some US$500 million. It is also one of only three mosques in the UAE (along with the Jumeirah Mosque in Dubai; see page 207, and the Al Noor Mosque in Sharjah) open to non-Muslims. If visiting, you will be expected to dress conservatively; female visitors not suitably attired will be offered a black *abbeya* robe to wear.

Saadiyat Island

Foremost amongst Abu Dhabi's planned mega-projects is the massive new **Saadiyat Cultural District ❿** (www.saadiyatculturaldistrict.ae), located on Saadiyat Island, about 3km (2 miles) from the city centre. The centrepiece of the island will be a remarkable cluster of five museums all housed in jaw-dropping neo-futuristic buildings designed by world-famous architects. The attractions are set to start opening from 2015 onwards, although

> **TIP**
>
> For stunning views of the city skyline, an evening dinner cruise aboard a traditional wooden dhow can't be beaten. These are operated by various tour agents and hotels around the city including Al Dhafra, or the swanky Shuja Yacht, run by Le Royal Méridien hotel.

Welcome to Ferrari World.

UMM AN NAR

Just outside Abu Dhabi, the island of Umm an Nar gives its name to one of the major periods of Arabian prehistory, thanks to the treasure trove of prehistoric remains which have been uncovered here. The site was first investigated by a Danish team in 1959, with further excavations being carried out by archaeologists from Iraq and the UAE. Some 50 circular tombs have so far been unearthed, along with a variety of artefacts ranging from necklaces and jewellery to weapons and distinctive red pottery. The location of the archaeological site between a major oil refinery and a military area means that the site is currently out of bounds to the general public, although artefacts discovered here are on display at the Al Ain National Museum (see page 189).

FACT

Until 1953, when a causeway was built across the Maqta, anyone wanting to cross to the other side had to wait for low tide and then wade through the shallow water.

promised completion dates have been constantly pushed back ever since the project was first launched. Scheduled to open later in 2015, the **Louvre Abu Dhabi** (http://louvreabudhabi.ae) by French architect Jean Nouvel has been created in an unprecedented collaboration with the French government and will be home to collections of both Eastern and Western art. Norman Foster's **Zayed National Museum**, which will showcase the life and achievements of the late Zayed bin Sultan Al Nahyan, is due in 2016 (www.zayednationalmuseum.ae), while the following year is to see the opening of **Guggenheim Abu Dhabi** (www.guggenheim.org/abu-dhabi) by Frank Gehry (of Guggenheim Bilbao fame), which will showcase high-profile contemporary art. There are also works under way for the **Performing Arts Centre** by Iraqi-British architect Zaha Hadid and the **Maritime Museum** by Japanese architect Tadao Ando.

Yas Island

Some 20km (12 miles) from the city centre, off the Dubai highway, **Yas**

Island ⓚ is home to the city's new Formula 1 racetrack (which has staged the Abu Dhabi Grand Prix F1 race since 2010). The petrolhead theme is continued with the attached Ferrari Theme Park (www.ferrariworldabudhabi.com; daily 11am–8pm), a state-of-the-art entertainment complex featuring over 20 rides and other attractions, including the world's fastest rollercoaster and F1 racing simulators, plus plenty of more sedate family rides and kids' attractions, a racetrack and a driving school.

Al Ain

The fourth-largest city in the UAE, and the only major inland settlement, **Al Ain ❷** is an easy 90-minute drive from Abu Dhabi down a swift modern highway – a far cry from just 60 years back, when the journey between the towns two took five days by camel. The city grew up around the string of seven oases which still dot the modern city today, making it one of the greenest in the Gulf. For much of its history, Al Ain served as a major stop on overland trading

The curvy Jabal Hafeet road.

routes between Oman and the Gulf, its former strategic importance commemorated by the numerous forts that dot the town and its hinterland, and by the archaeological remains found in the vicinity, which suggest that the area has been continuously settled for over 4,000 years. The city was awarded Unesco World Heritage status in 2011 in recognition of its rich historical significance, with listed sites including the Bronze Age tombs of Hili and Jabal Hafeet and the oases and traditional *falaj* irrigation systems of its various oases. Al Ain is also famous as the birthplace of the emirate's revered ruler, and first president of the UAE, Sheikh Zayed Bin Sultan Al Nahyan, who served as governor of Al Ain during his younger years.

Just over the border from Al Ain is the Omani city of **Buraimi** (see page 148) – now virtually joined up with Al Ain, although to reach it you will have to go through full border formalities (and buy an Omani visa) at the Hili checkpoint on the north side of Al Ain centre. Note that Al Ain can prove incredibly disorienting for first-time visitors, with dozens of seemingly identical roads arranged on a grid plan – fortunately, brown signs point helpfully to many of the town's major attractions.

The old-fashioned **Al Ain National Museum** Ⓐ (Tue–Thu, Sat–Sun 8am–7.30pm, Fri 3–7.30pm) makes a good starting point for tours of the city, with interesting displays covering various aspects of local life and displays of quaint artefacts, ranging from old Qur'ans and antique silver jewellery to farming and cooking equipment, as well as some intriguing photos of Abu Dhabi Emirate in the 1960s.

Next to the museum lies the rustic **Sultan Bin Zayed Fort** (or Eastern Fort; same hours and ticket as museum). One of 20-odd forts scattered around Al Ain and the surrounding desert, this picturesque three-towered structure is best known as the birthplace of Sheikh Zayed Bin Sultan Al Nahyan (see page 57), the much-loved ruler of Abu Dhabi and first president of the UAE, who oversaw the transformation of the emirate

A Heritage Village stallholder.

A decorative window at Sheikh Zayed Grand Mosque.

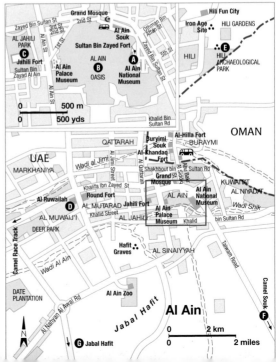

Al Ain Palace Museum.

Hili Archaeological Park, Al Ain.

from impoverished Arabian backwater into today's oil-rich contemporary city-state.

A short walk northwest, the busy **Al Ain Souk** is home to the city's main meat, fruit and vegetable market, attracting a colourful array of local characters including visiting Omanis in big white turbans and local Bedu women in traditional metal face masks.

South of the souk stretches the idyllic **Al Ain Oasis ❸** (daily sunrise–sunset; free), the largest of the seven oases scattered across the city (the name Al Ain, means, literally, The Spring). Various entrances lead into the oasis, with a labyrinthine network of narrow walled lanes running between densely planted thickets of palm trees, dotted with mango, fig, banana and orange trees. The plantations are watered using the traditional *falaj* irrigation method, with mud-walled channels bringing water down from the surrounding mountains.

Follow the road around the north side of the oasis behind the souk to reach the **Al Ain Palace Museum**

(Tue–Thu, Sat–Sun 8.30am–7.30pm; Fri 3–7.30pm; free), an imposing complex owned by the ruling Nahyan family of Abu Dhabi. The sprawling complex is pleasant enough, with rambling, orangey-pink buildings arranged around a sequence of court-yards and small gardens, although there is not much to see.

Close by stands the rather more interesting **Al Jahili Fort ❸** (Tue–Thu, Sat–Sun 9am–5pm, Fri 3–5pm; free), one of the finest traditional buildings in Al Ain, built in 1898, with a much-photographed circular tower on the northern side, consisting of four levels of diminishing size, each surmounted with a line of triangular battlements. The fort is also home to the excellent little "Mubarak bin London" exhibition, showcasing various photographs and personal effects of the legendary explorer Wilfred Thesiger (1910–2003), who stayed at the fort in the late 1940s.

Around Al Ain

There are a number of other forts and watchtowers scattered around Al Ain. The two-storey **Al Ruwailah ❹** fortified house (off Mohammed bin Khalifa Road at the end of a small street) has an intriguing octagonal defensive wall. On the other side of Mohammed bin Khalifa Road, opposite the Al Ruwailah building, is a tower-like fort. Raised on a large mound, this circular fort provided an advanced warning post should intruders approach the palm groves from the desert. There are four more large **fortified houses** in the Qattarah district, south of Hili, set amongst palm groves. One offers good views from its high defensive walls (to find it from Mohammed bin Khalifa Road, pass the football stadium on the right, cross the Dolphin Roundabout and turn right into Third Street: the rear wall faces the road, but the entrance is on the right-hand side).

On the northern side of the city, the **Hili Archaeological Park ❺** (daily

4–11pm) is one of the most important archaeological sites in the UAE (many of the finds unearthed here are displayed in the Al Ain National Museum; see page 189). Pride of place goes to the so-called Great Hili Tomb, dating from the 3rd century BC: a quaint little circular structure decorated with primitive carvings of animals and humans.

Al Ain's old-fashioned **Camel Souk** **F** is also worth a visit, with dozens of dromedaries lined up for sale and a lively crowd of local camel-fanciers haggling over the beast of their choice. The souk is busiest in the mornings around 9–10am, although low-key trading may continue throughout the day. To reach the souk, take the road towards Mazyad from the roundabout in front of the Hilton hotel. After about 3km (2 miles) you'll see the huge new Bawadi mall on your left; the souk is just past here on the left. The Livestock Market, relocated from the centre, is also here.

Further exotic animals can be found at the **Al Ain Zoo** (also known as Al Ain Wildlife Park and Resort; www.

awpr.ae; June–Sept 4–10pm, Oct–May Sat–Wed 9am–8pm, Thu–Fri 9am–9pm, closed during Ramadan) in the southern part of the city, a spacious and well-run place which provides a home to a wide variety of creatures – the bird displays are particularly good.

Beyond the zoo rises the craggy **Jabal Hafeet** **G** (1,180 metres/733ft), the second-highest mountain in the UAE and a breezy retreat from the heat of the plains below. You can drive to the top from the city in under half an hour along the exhilarating modern surfaced road, from where there are huge views over the surrounding mountains. The outdoor terrace at the plush Mercure Grand Hotel, just below the summit, makes a memorable – if surprisingly chilly – spot for a drink. The area is also of particular interest thanks to its remarkable collection of Bronze Age beehive tombs which can be found scattered around the base of the mountain, although you'll need a 4x4 and a local guide if you hope to explore them.

Al Ain local.

Camels for sale in Al Ain.

Reduce your tyre pressure before venturing into the desert.

The Empty Quarter

The western region of Abu Dhabi encompasses the great red-sand massif of the Rub al Khali (the Empty Quarter), the oil fields of Bu Hasa, Shah and Marzuq, and the fertile Liwa oasis. In 1948 Wilfred Thesiger was the first European to explore the Liwa's 80km (50-mile) palm groves and the settlements scattered amidst its huge dunes, rising up to 90 metres (300ft) in places. Thesiger described what he saw in *Arabian Sands*: "The sands were like a garden. There were matted clumps of tribulus, three feet high, their dark green fronds covered with bright yellow flowers, bunches of karia, a species of heliotrope that was rated high as camel-food by the Bedu, and *qasis*, as well as numerous other plants which the camels scorned in the plenty that surrounded them."

Thesiger rode into the Liwa on a camel. Today the journey from Abu Dhabi is made easy with a tarmac road cutting through the desolate limestone ridges, drifts of white sand and stretches of gravel dotted with woody grass. It is a three-hour trip by road from Abu Dhabi to **Liwa** ❸. The Rumaitha oil-field route to Liwa passes an enormous pyramid in the desert, home to the Emirates National Auto Museum (www.enam. ae). Set up by the "rainbow sheikh", a well-known motor enthusiast whose logo is a rainbow, the hangar displays oversized (some six times the original) pick-up trucks and over 30 vintage vehicles.

The Liwa crescent is well served by a four-lane highway. Passing (from west to east) the villages of Aradah, Taraq, Al Hilah, Qatuf, Kayyah, Al Mariyyah, Dhafir, Huweilah, Qumidah, Shah, Tharwaniyyah, Al Nashash, Jarrah, Wedheil, Al Kris and Hamim, it is difficult to imagine how these sparsely populated villages of *barasti* (palm frond) dwellings and carefully tended date palm groves, subsisted here for hundreds of years. The concrete houses, guesthouse and irrigated farms that you see today are a relatively recent addition, developed during the 1980s.

Any visit to the Liwa is a special experience. The effect of the

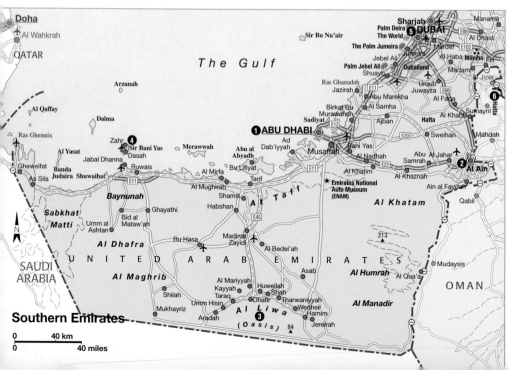

remoteness and beauty of the sands is profound. Every day the dunes change and encroach on the farms nestling below. The scale of the big red dunes is best appreciated in winter, when it is possible to climb to the top of one without the heat burning through the soles of your shoes. Surprisingly, the Liwa has an extensive range of fauna. Hares, foxes, monitor lizards and other animals and reptiles flourish in the harsh, seemingly inhospitable desert environment.

West along the coast

Back on the coast west of Liwa (and some 250km/155 miles west of Abu Dhabi), Ruwais is the site of the country's largest oil refinery, established in 1978, and nearby Jabal Dhanna from where Abu Dhabi's onshore oil is piped to tanker-mooring terminals 5km (3 miles) out to sea.

Lying 9km (6 miles) off the coast roughly opposite Jabal Dhanna, the remote **Sir Bani Yas Island** ❹ is one of the UAE's more unusual attractions (www.sirbaniyasisland.com). Measuring around 16km (10 miles)

long and 8km (5 miles) across, the island was formerly a private retreat of Sheikh Zayed, who established a wildlife reserve here in 1971. The reserve now protects a wide range of wildlife, including important populations of threatened local fauna including hundreds of Arabian oryx, sand gazelles and rock hyraxes – there is also an African section, home to cheetahs, giraffes, Indian blackbuck and other exotic species. Birdwatching is excellent here too, thanks to Sir Bani Yas's position on migratory routes between Europe and Asia; large flocks of flamingos are a common sight. The island is also surprisingly rich in historical remains, including a 7th-century church, the only pre-Islamic Christian site in the country. It's a rewarding destination, although also an expensive one, given that access is usually by seaplane, and the only way to visit at present is to stay overnight at the luxurious Anantara Desert Islands Resort and Spa, Anantara Sir Bani Yas Island Al Yamm Villa Resort or Anantara Sir Bani Yas Island Al Sahel Villa Resort.

Oryx on Sir Bani Yas island.

DUBAI

Past meets future in the Gulf's most absorbing city, with attractions ranging from traditional souks and wooden dhows through to soaring skyscrapers and artificial islands.

Contrary to popular belief, Dubai ⑤ wasn't born yesterday, and although much of the city – and many of its most famous landmarks – have sprung up during the past couple of decades, the city's roots go back far earlier. Archaeological sites in the metropolitan area indicate that Dubai was an important station for caravans travelling between Mesopotamia and Oman as far back as the Bronze Age. A town of sorts has existed here since the early 19th century, while by the early 20th century Dubai had already become one of the most important ports and entrepôts in this part of the Gulf.

Over recent years Dubai has experienced unprecedented urban development and its attractiveness to both visitors and ex-pats has been steadily growing. In 2015 Dubai International Airport overtook Heathrow as the world's busiest international airport and passenger traffic is expected to hit new record highs as Dubai prepares to host the World Expo 2020.

The Creek

At the heart of the old city lies **Al Khor Ⓐ** (The Creek), a wide saltwater inlet which divides the two main city-centre districts of Bur Dubai and Deira and provides a scenic thoroughfare for traditional wooden dhows, *abras* (water taxis) and the occasional ship, as well as a perfect snapshot of Dubai's sometimes startling contrasts between old and new, with traditional coral-and-gypsum houses, wind towers and minarets mixed up amidst the modern development and glassy high-rises.

The best, cheapest and most convenient way of seeing the Creek is to take the five-minute ride across it aboard one of the city's traditional *abras* – one

Main Attractions

Al Khor
Al Fahidi Historical Neighbourhood
Shindagha
Deira souks
Khan Murjan Souk
Emirates Towers and Sheikh Zayed Road
Burj Khalifa and Downtown Dubai
Jumeirah Mosque
Burj al Arab
Madinat Jumeirah

An 'abra', or water-taxi, carries passengers across the creek in modern day Dubai as it has done for many years.

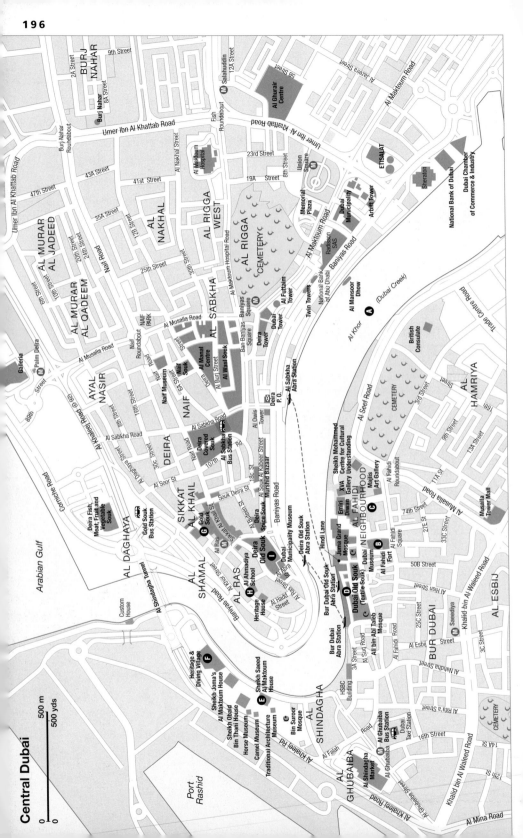

Central Dubai

of the most authentic and inexpensive experiences available in the Emirates. There are two main routes: the first runs between Bur Dubai Abra Station at the west end of the Textile Souk and Deira Old Souk Abra Station, in front of the Spice Souk. The second goes from Bur Dubai Old Souk Abra Station in the middle of the Textile Souk to Al Sabkha Abra Station, a short walk from Baniyas Square. Boats depart every couple of minutes and the fare costs a modest Dhs1.

Alternatively, it is also possible to charter an *abra* for longer tours up and down the Creek. This costs Dhs100 per hour, and boatmen will take you wherever you fancy, either up- or downriver – an hour's cruise will allow you to ride from the city centre down to the Dubai Creek Golf Club and back again.

A more comfortable way of seeing the Creek is to go on one of the ever-popular after-dark dinner cruises – these can be booked through any of the city's myriad tour operators, while many hotels can also arrange trips. Most cruises are aboard traditional old wooden dhows, offering a leisurely overview of the night-time city.

Bur Dubai

South of the Creek lies Bur Dubai, the oldest district in the city, and home to many of its most absorbing historical attractions. A good place to begin is the **Dubai Museum** Ⓑ (Sat–Thu 8.30am–8.30pm, Fri 2–8.30pm), housed in Al Fahidi Fort, the oldest building in the city. Dating from around 1787, the fort was originally built to defend the town against raiders, with large towers at three corners and a spacious central courtyard within, where you will find a traditional *barasti* (palm thatch) hut and a collection of boats formerly used for fishing and pearl diving.

The majority of the museum's exhibits are located in a series of modern underground galleries buried below the fort. These include extensive archaeological finds dating back to the Bronze Age along with wide-ranging displays on just about every aspect of traditional Emirati life, customs and culture, include a colourful

The Dubai Museum is housed in the city's oldest building.

Dubai Wonder Bus.

DUBAI WONDER BUS

For a tour of Dubai with a difference, check out the Dubai Wonder Bus (www.wonderbustours.net), a bizarre-looking vehicle – half bus and half boat. The 60-minute tours depart from the BurJuman centre, from where you'll be driven down to Garhoud Bridge before the bus-cum-boat dives into the water and sails you up the Creek to Shindagha before emerging back onto dry land and taking you back to BurJuman by road. Other offbeat ways of enjoying Dubai include the helicopter tours offered by an increasing number of operators in the city, while adrenalin junkies might consider a tandem skydive above the Palm Jumeirah (see www.skydivedubai.ae for details). More sedate airborne trips over the desert outside the city are available from Balloon Adventures Dubai (www.ballooning.ae).

Colourful fabrics on display in the Textile Souk.

At the Gold Souk.

little replica souk (complete with spooky mannequins), a dhow under construction and a couple of interesting old films.

West of the museum stretches the main section of **Al Fahidi Road**, lined with shops selling a mix of electronic goods, expensive watches and colourful Indian-style fabrics. Turning east, in the opposite direction, brings you after a couple of minutes to the entrance to the historic **Al Fahidi Historical Neighbourhood** (formerly known as Bastakiya quarter) , built in the early 1900s by merchants from Bastak in southern Iran (hence the name). This is the best-preserved traditional quarter in the city: a small but surprisingly disorienting labyrinth of narrow alleyways, flanked with tall coral-and-limestone houses topped with dozens of wind towers *(barjeel)*. These were first introduced to Dubai by Iranian settlers, but have now become synonymous with the UAE. An early form of air-conditioning, these square towers capture cool air and funnel it down into the houses

below, while also allowing hot air to rise and escape. Most of the houses are fairly plain from the outside but surprisingly ornate within, usually with spacious inner courtyards, shaded with trees and surrounded by delicate arches and doorways.

Right next to the entrance to the quarter, the **Majlis Art Gallery** (Sat–Thu 10am–6pm; www.themajlisgallery.com; free) is the oldest in the city, established in 1976 to showcase the work of UAE artists, as well as international ones with UAE ties. The neighbourhood particularly throbs with artistic activity during the annual SIKKA Art Fair in March.

Beyond Al Fahidi Historical Neighbourhood, a promenade continues east alongside the Creek, offering fine views of the high-rises of Deira over the water. A 15-minute walk past the British Consulate brings you opposite the fine cluster of modern buildings in Deira, including the landmark **National Bank of Dubai** with its instantly recognisable curved, glass-and-steel facade – particularly memorable towards dusk, when it

seems to catch fire in the light of the setting sun.

From Al Fahidi, walk back to the Dubai Museum and then head around the back to reach Dubai's **Grand Mosque**. This is one of the oldest mosques in Dubai (dating back to 1900, although it was rebuilt in 1998), and also boasts the city's tallest minaret (70 metres/231ft) and space for 1,200 worshippers. You can take a peek inside from the doorway, but, unless you are a Muslim, don't venture in.

Turn left at the mosque and head down any of the various little alleyways to reach the **Textile Souk** , or Old Souk, as it's sometimes known, the prettiest in Dubai, with dozens of little shops lined up in old coral-and-stone buildings under a high wooden roof; most sell cheap clothes and textiles, while a few offer souvenirs and a few antiques. Here and there the shops open up to reveal glorious views of the Creek, dotted with chuntering *abras* and old wooden dhows, with the wind-towered souks of Deira beyond.

At the southern end of the souk, hidden away behind the Grand Mosque, lies the narrow alleyway popularly known as **Hindi Lane**, stuffed full of shops selling Indian religious paraphernalia – garlands, portraits and horoscopes – and with a tiny Hindu-cum-Sikh temple halfway along. On the southern side of the souk stands the eye-catching **Ali bin Abi Taleb Mosque** (not open to non-Muslims), a Shi'ite mosque built in traditional Iranian style, and covered in a riot of colourful tilework.

Shindagha

Continuing through the Textile Souk and then along the waterfront brings you to Shindagha district. A fine cluster of old Emirati buildings line up along the Creek here, many now converted to small-scale museums, restaurants or cultural attractions.

Easily the most interesting is the **Sheikh Saeed Al Maktoum House** (Sat–Thu 8am–8.30pm; Fri 3–10pm). The former home of the ruling Maktoum family, the house was built in 1896 and offers an impressive example

Wind tower undergoing restoration. This ingenious cooling device was introduced to the region from Persia.

On the way to evening prayers.

DUBAI'S ISLANDS

From a tourist point of view, Dubai's major physical drawback is its lack of coastline – a mere 70km (44 miles) in total. The response to this problem has been typical of Dubai. Since there's not enough beach, they decided to build some more. The Palm Jumeirah has already added 68km (42 miles) to the emirate's coastline, although this is just the first (and smallest) of four proposed offshore developments which are intended to create up to 500km (310 miles) of new waterfront. Two further palm-shaped islands are already under construction: the Palm Jabal Ali, 20km (12 miles) further down the coast, and the Palm Deira, right next to the city centre. Both are stalled due to financial difficulties, although large-scale reclamation works have been finished.

Even more fanciful than the two new palm islands is the World development. Lying a couple of kilometres (around 1 mile) off the coast (accessible by boat only), this vast complex of artificial islands has been constructed in the approximate shape of a map of the world, with many of the world's countries represented by their own islands within the map. As with many other mega-projects in Dubai, however, development work currently remains stalled. Next to the World, there are also plans for a a man-made archipelago in the shape of the solar system, but due to the economic slowdown, the Universe has no planned completion date.

A tradesman at the Gold Souk.

Workers at Deira's Dhow Wharfage.

of traditional Emirati architecture, with elegantly cusped doorways and four fine wind-towers. The house is now home to one of Dubai's most captivating museums, documenting the social, cultural, educational and religious history of the emirate, although the undoubted highlight is the fascinating collection of old photographs from the 1940s to 1960s charting the city's transformation from modest town to modern metropolis.

The **Traditional Architecture Museum** (Sun–Thu 8am–2pm; free), immediately to the south, is also worth a look, occupying another fine old wind-towered house, with interesting displays on architecture in Dubai and the Emirates.

A couple of minutes' walk further along the Creekside (with marvellous views en route) brings you to the so-called **Heritage Village ❻** (Sat–Thu 8am–8pm, Fri 3–10pm; free), a walled compound with traditional buildings arranged around a large sandy courtyard. It's usually fairly deserted during the day, but comes to life after dusk (particularly during the winter

months and local festivals), with souvenir shops, food stalls (often run by local Emirati women) and occasional cultural performances. The **Diving Village** (Sun–Thu 8am–10pm, Fri–Sat 3–10pm) next door is similar but smaller.

Deira

The commercial heart of the old city, life in Deira still largely revolves around the souk. The shops may be largely modern, and jazzy neon signs may have replaced the traditional hand-painted boards, but business here is still conducted more or less as it has been for over a century past, with thousands of shoebox shops wedged into the district's rambling bazaars, retailing everything from cheap toys and textiles to gold and frankincense – a far cry from the modern malls that dominate newer parts of Dubai.

The obvious place to begin any tour of Deira is at the **Gold Souk ❼** (most shops open Sat–Thu 10am–1pm and 4–10pm, Fri 4–10pm). There are a hundred or so shops here, lined up under a wooden roof,

their windows overflowing with vast quantities of gold jewellery ranging from florid Arabian designs to more understated European pieces – the traditional Emirati-style bracelets are particularly nice. Gold here remains amongst the most competitively priced in the world, attracting a colourful array of shoppers from West Africa, Russia, India and elsewhere. Jewellery is sold by weight (despite its intricacy, the quality of the workmanship isn't usually factored into the price), although bargaining is essential. Many shops also sell silver and precious stones, while the area is also a major centre for Dubai's thriving trade in designer fakes – you'll not spend long in the souk without being approached with offers of "cheap copy watch" or similar.

Walk out of the back (western) end of the Gold Souk, turn right onto Old Baladiya Street and follow it around onto Al Ahmadiya Street for a few minutes to reach the pretty **Al Ahmadiya School** ❶ (Sat–Thu 8am–7.30pm, Fri 2.30–7.30pm; free). Established in 1912 by local pearl merchant Ahmad bin Dalmouk (after whom it is named), this was the first semi-formal school in Dubai. Pupils here were taught the Qur'an, Arabic calligraphy and arithmetic, while other subjects including history, literature and astronomy were subsequently added to the curriculum. The school itself closed in 1963, and the building was superbly restored in the 1990s and is now perhaps the most appealing traditional building in the city. The rooms around the courtyard house various low-key exhibits covering the history of the school, along with cute mannequins of pupils in traditional dress (and one rather scary-looking teacher). There are more classrooms upstairs, still equipped with their old wooden desks and chairs.

Next to Al Ahmadiya School stands the **Heritage House** (Sat–Thu 8am–7.30pm, Fri 2.30– 7.30pm; free), dating from the late 19th century and now preserved as it would have been in the 1940s and 1950s, providing an atmospheric snapshot of the social life of Dubai's wealthier inhabitants during that period. Notable features

The elaborate Khan Murjan Souk interior in the Wafi complex.

Statue of an Egyptian pharaoh at the Wafi centre.

include the men's and women's *majlis*, or meeting rooms, where guests would have sat on embroidered pillows, drinking Arabian coffee and discussing the economic, social and political issues of the day.

Turn left out of the Heritage House and follow the road around to reach the Creek, then turn left again along the waterfront, until you reach Deira Old Souk Abra Station after a couple more minutes. Facing the Creek on your left is the warren of lanes and alleyways that make up Deira Old Souk. Ahead of you, stretching down the waterfront, are the old city's **dhow moorings**, with lines of traditional old wooden cargo boats moored up along the edge of the Creek – an unexpectedly old-fashioned sight amongst the modern traffic and office blocks. Huge piles of cargo usually stand stacked up along the road here waiting to be loaded up onto boats and shipped off. Many of the dhows here head off to Iran (and many have Iranian crews), while some head further afield to India, Pakistan and East Africa.

Turning away from the Creek, head into the attractive tangle of covered alleyways making up **Deira Old Souk** ❶, although most of the souk's shops are now devoted to relatively mundane items like cheap toys, textiles and clothing. The most interesting part of the Old Souk is the **Spice Souk**, close to Deira Old Souk Abra Station: a few narrow alleyways lined with huge sacks of frankincense, saffron, crushed rose petals, dried lemons and other local produce. It is one of the prettiest corners of Deira, although unfortunately it is also steadily shrinking due to competition from local hypermarkets like Carrefour, which is where most modern Dubaians now go for their spices.

Oud Metha

South of Bur Dubai, the district of **Oud Metha** is something of a hotchpotch – rather lacking in character or streetlife, but home to some of the inner city's biggest tourist developments, including the glitzy Wafi complex and adjacent Raffles hotel and Khan Murjan Souk.

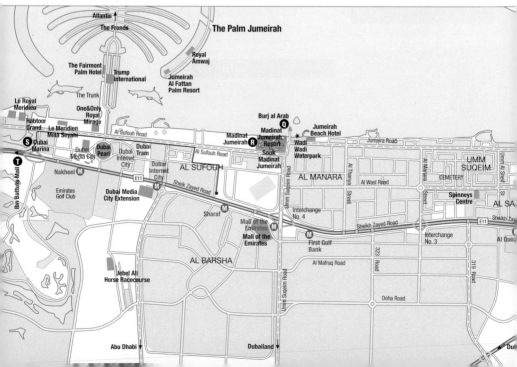

Stretching south of Al Maktoum Bridge, the spacious **Creekside Park**  (Sun–Wed 8am–11pm, Thu–Sat 8am–11.30pm) offers one of the few sizeable open areas in the congested city centre, with fine views over the Creek to the quaint buildings of the Park Hyatt hotel and distinctive Dubai Creek Golf Club clubhouse (inspired by the sails of a dhow and looking like a local remake of the Sydney Opera House) on the far side of the water. The park is also home to the excellent **Children's City** (Sat–Thu 7am–7pm, Fri 2–9pm; www.childrencity.ae) "edu-tainment" centre for kids, with a fun, interactive range of galleries exploring various themes including science, nature, space exploration and cultures of the world. Even without kids, it's worth a peek at the City's striking buildings, painted in bright primary colours and looking a bit like some kind of supersized Lego construction.

A 10-minute walk south of the park is Oud Metha's major attraction, the glitzy **Wafi** complex  (Sat–Wed 10am–10pm, Thu–Fri 10am–midnight; www.

wafi.com), looking like a little slice of Las Vegas dropped into the middle of the Gulf, with a comic-book Egyptian-style design featuring a zany mishmash of huge pharaonic statues, hieroglyphs, spectacular stained-glass windows and half a dozen miniature pyramids dotted across the sprawling roof lines.

Attached to the Wafi complex is the beautiful **Khan Murjan Souk** (Sat–Wed 10am–10pm, Thu–Fri 10am–midnight; www.wafi.com). This is one of Dubai's finest exercises in Orientalist kitsch, with virtually every available surface covered in lavishly detailed Arabian-style design, featuring elaborate Moroccan-style tile work, intricately carved wooden doors and ceilings, and huge hanging lamps. Next to the souk (and continuing Wafi's Egyptian theme) rises the vast postmodern pyramid of the **Raffles** hotel, Oud Metha's most dramatic landmark, visible for miles around and particularly impressive after dusk, when the glass-walled summit of the pyramid is lit up from within, glowing magically in the darkness.

Souvenir t-shirts at Karama Souk.

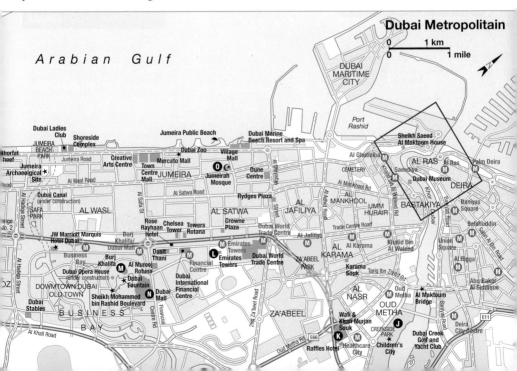

Dubai Metropolitain

There is a huge range of goods on sale, from boxes inlaid with mother-of-pearl to electronics. For many people shopping is a major reason for visiting Dubai.

Emirates Towers.

Karama and Satwa

Home to many of the low-wage Indian and Filipina expats who provide the city with its taxi drivers, waitresses, housemaids and construction workers, **Karama** offers a refreshing insight into life in the city away from the tourist fleshpots and space-age architecture. The district is centred on the low-rent **Karama Souk**, best known as the epicentre for Dubai's roaring trade in designer fakes – imitation bags, watches, sunglasses and other fake-branded items, as well as pirated DVDs – although following government crackdowns these are now kept mainly out of sight in backrooms behind the various shops. The quality of many of the fakes is surprisingly high, although prices can be unexpectedly steep.

It is a short taxi ride from here to the neighbouring suburb of **Satwa**, centred on the attractive **Al Diyafah Street**, Satwa's de facto high street. This is one of the most pleasant afterdark venues in the city, with broad, tree-lined pavements dotted with a long string of cafés and restaurants,

including several excellent Lebanese cafés, and attracting a refreshingly mixed crowd of Indians, Emiratis, expat Arabs and Europeans who come to stroll, and people-watch from the pavement cafés – Dubai on a refreshingly human scale.

Sheikh Zayed Road

Some 3km (2 miles) south of the old city centre – but light years distant in terms of appearance and atmosphere – the futuristic **Sheikh Zayed Road** is one of Dubai's iconic images: a huge, 12-lane highway flanked on either side by rows of densely packed skyscrapers, whose towering facades create an almost unbroken wall of glass and metal, like some kind of architectural Grand Canyon.

Standing proud above the northern end of Sheikh Zayed Road, the twin **Emirates Towers** ❶ were the tallest in the city upon completion in 2000 (while the taller tower was also the highest in the Middle East at 355 metres/1,164ft). They have since been outstripped, most notably, by the gargantuan Burj Khalifa (see page 205)

SKY-HIGH DUBAI

Dubai is now officially the tallest city on the planet – a stupendous achievement for a city which only constructed its first proper skyscraper in 1979. The city now boasts 28 of the world's 200 highest buildings (traditional high-rise centres New York and Hong Kong, by comparison, have just 13 and 11 respectively), with new super-tall structures being constantly added to the city's skyline, despite the financial embarrassments of the past few years. These include iconic structures including the world's tallest building, the Burj Khalifa, and the magnificent Burj al Arab and Emirates Towers, as well as less high-profile landmarks (most of them located in Dubai Marina) such as Princess Tower and 23 Marina, the second- and third-tallest building in the city, both topped out in 2012.

just down the road, but remain two of the most distinctive, and most beautiful, modern buildings in the city, with their unusual triangular summits and huge glass and aluminium facades, which seem to glow magically in the fierce desert light.

Immediately south of the Emirates Towers stretches the **Dubai International Financial Centre** (www.difc.ae), whose focus is the landmark Gate building, an unusual structure resembling a kind of office block-cum-triumphal archway. The building is home to the Dubai Stock Exchange, as well as a number of upmarket art galleries – one of the leading hubs of the city's burgeoning visual arts scene.

Continuing south along Sheikh Zayed Road, the highway is now hemmed in to either side by a long string of elongated skyscrapers packed in shoulder-to-shoulder. The buildings here offer a comprehensive compendium of modern Dubaian design, ranging from the functional to the quirky and the downright bizarre. Notable landmarks include the elegant **Rose Rayhaan** hotel (at

333 metres/1,093ft the second tallest hotel in the world, surpassed in 2012 by the JW Marriott Marquis Dubai), and, opposite, the massive **Chelsea Tower**, its summit adorned with what looks like an enormous toothpick. Further south, at the end of the strip, is perhaps the most distinctive building of them all, the **Dusit Thani** hotel, a bow-legged colossus inspired by the shape of the traditional Thai *wai*, a prayer-like gesture of welcome.

Jumeirah Beach Hotel.

Downtown Dubai

At the southern end of Sheikh Zayed Road lies the massive Downtown Dubai development, built at an estimated cost of a cool US$20 billion. Centrepiece of the development is the staggering **Burj Khalifa** Ⓜ, the world's tallest building, rising close to hand on your right. Opened in early 2010, the Burj Khalifa (828 metres/2,717ft) has obliterated all previous records for the world's previous tallest man-made structures, past and present, smashing the previous record for the world's tallest building (formerly held by Taipei 101 in Taiwan,

Dubai's towering skyline.

An elephant statue at India Court in Ibn Battuta Mall.

Burj Khalifa.

at 509 metres/1,670ft) by a staggering 300 metres (984ft).

The astonishing size of the Burj Khalifa and distinctively tapering outline is hard to grasp close up – the whole thing is best appreciated from a distance, from where you can properly grasp the tower's jaw-dropping size, and the degree to which it dwarfs the surrounding high-rises, many of which are considerable structures in their own right. Expensive visits can be made to the misleadingly named At the Top observation deck (on floor 124, although there are actually 160 floors in total) – see www.burjkhalifa.ae for details.

Lying in the considerable shadow of the Burj Khalifa is the no less monumental **Dubai Mall** Ⓝ (retailers daily 10am–midnight; www.thedubaimall.com). The entire complex covers a total area of 1.08 million sq metres (12 million sq ft), with over 1,200 shops spread across four floors, making it easily the world's largest mall measured by total area (although other malls contain more retail space) – impressively vast, even if the sheer size

of the place can make a shopping trip here feel a bit like a long-distance hike. The mall is also home to the **Dubai Aquarium and Underwater Zoo** (daily 10am–midnight; www.thedubai aquarium.com), whose engaging "viewing panel" can be seen from the mall: a huge, floor-to-ceiling transparent acrylic panel filled with an extraordinary array of marine life, ranging from sand-tiger sharks and stingrays to colourful shoals of tiny tropical fish.

Inserted into the large lake between the Burj Khalifa and Dubai Mall is spectacular **Dubai Fountain**: 275 metres (902ft) long, illuminated with over 6,000 lights and with water cannons capable of shooting jets of water up to 150 metres (492ft) high. The fountain springs into action after dark, shooting choreographed jets of water into the air which "dance" in time to a range of Arabic, Hindi and classical songs. "Performances" are staged every 30 minutes between 6pm and 11pm in the evening, in the afternoon at 1pm and 1.30pm (Sat–Thu) and at 1.30pm and 2pm (Fri), and can be watched for free from anywhere around the lake.

On the far side of the lake stretches the extensive **Old Town** development: a large swathe of low-rise, sand-coloured buildings with traditional Moorish styling – a surreal contrast to the futuristic needle of the Burj Khalifa opposite, best appreciated from the pretty forecourt of the opulent Palace hotel.

In 2016, the area should see the completion of the **Dubai Opera House** (www.dubaiopera.com), designed by world-acclaimed architect Zaha Hadid, whose project styled on traditional Arabian sailing vessels is intended to give the famous Sydney Opera House a run for its money. The multi-purpose venue is also the landmark development of the Dubai new cultural centre, the Opera District, easily accessed from **Sheikh Mohammed bin Rashid Boulevard**, the district's circular thoroughfare lined with restaurants and cafés.

Jumeirah

One of Dubai's wealthiest residential areas, sedate Jumeirah is home to many of the city's rich European expat executives and their tanned and manicured wives (popularly, if rather disparagingly, known as Jumeirah Janes).

At the northern end of the district stands the striking **Jumeirah Mosque ⊙**. Built of stone in the Egyptian Fatimid style in the 1970s, this is one of the city's largest mosques and perhaps the most attractive, with a pair of soaring minarets and intricately filigreed domes. This is also the only mosque in Dubai that non-Muslims can visit, via tours run by the Sheikh Mohammed Centre for Cultural Understanding (tours Sat until Thu 10am; tel: 04-353 6666; www.cultures.ae).

Around 4km (2.5 miles) south of the mosque, **Jumeirah Beach Park** (closed for refurbishment until the end of 2016) is the most attractive public beach in the city. The park is set to re-open with a new look as it will have the **Dubai Canal**, linking the Arabian Gulf with the Dubai Creek, running through it. With its romantic footbridges and neighbouring cafés the canal development

Hatta Heritage Village.

Wild Wadi at sunrise.

is set to breathe new life into the whole neighbourhood.

Continuing south along the Jumeirah Road again, after a further 2km (1 mile) a large brown sign points to the venerable old **Majlis Ghorfat Um Al Sheef** ⓟ (Sat–Thu 7.30am–2.30pm). Originally constructed in 1955, the two-storey *majlis* (meeting room) offers a touching throwback to earlier and simpler times, with its traditional coral-stone walls, shady verandahs and teak doors and window frames. The *majlis* originally served as the summer resort of Dubai's former ruler Sheikh Rashid, serving as the venue for many of the meetings in which the visionary sheikh plotted Dubai's spectacular transformation from Arabian backwater to international super-city.

The Majlis Ghorfat Um Al Sheef marks the southern limits of Jumeirah proper, after which you enter the adjacent suburb of **Umm Suqeim** (although the entire area is usually, if inaccurately, referred to as Jumeirah), home to three of the city's most famous modern landmarks.

The first of the area's trio of super-sized landmarks is the vast **Jumeirah Beach Hotel** (or JBH as it is often known). Opened in 1997, this was the first of the city's mega-hotels, a 100-metre (330ft) high colossus built in the form of a gigantic breaking wave (although from some angles it looks more like a kind of rollercoaster), a design which neatly complements that of the sail-shaped Burj al Arab next door. Immediately behind the hotel is the perennially popular **Wild Wadi** water park (daily Sept–Oct, Mar–May 10am–7pm, Nov–Feb 10am–6pm, Jun–Aug 10am–8pm), a fun place to cool off whilst being shot around waterchutes, twisting through tunnels or plummeting down the hair-raising Jumeirah Sceirah waterslide.

Towering over the coastline just beyond the JBH is the stupendous **Burj al Arab** ⓠ (Tower of the Arabs), opened in 1999. Inspired by the shape of a huge, billowing sail, this marvellous high-rise hotel is far and away Dubai's most memorable modern landmark, its hugely distinctive, instantly recognisable outline

Dubai Marina.

providing the city with a defining landmark to rival the Eiffel Tower, Sydney Opera House or Big Ben.

Located just offshore on its own man-made island, the sheer size of the building is impressive enough: at 321 metres (1,053ft), taller than Paris's Eiffel Tower and a mere 60 metres (200ft) shorter than the Empire State Building in New York, although it is really the elegant simplicity, originality and sheer audacity of the design that captures the imagination. The "sail" itself is constructed from Teflon-coated glass fibre, a dazzling white by day, lit up by spectacular light displays after dark. The building is now home to the city's most exclusive hotel, popularly dubbed the world's first "seven-star" hotel on account of the super-fuelled levels of luxury provided to guests in the hotel's 200-odd suites.

Immediately south of the Burj al Arab rises the mighty **Madinat Jumeirah ❼** complex, opened in 2004. This is one of modern Dubai's most memorable developments: built in a form of a self-contained faux-Arabian city, its huge sand-coloured buildings topped with innumerable wind towers and criss-crossed with miniature canals on which guests at the complex's hotels are ferried around by *abra*. The lovely **Souk Madinat Jumeirah** – a superb mock-Arabian bazaar with winding alleyways lined with upmarket handicraft shops under elaborate wooden roofs and hanging lanterns – is particularly attractive.

A short drive inland from Madinat Jumeirah lies the glitzy **Mall of the Emirates** (retailers: daily 10am–midnight, Thu–Fri until 1am, restaurants: Sun–Wed until 10pm, Thu–Sat until midnight; www.malloftheemirates.com), one of the largest in the city, with an excellent selection of upmarket shops, and the attached **Ski Dubai** indoor ski slope (Sun–Wed 10am–10pm, Thu–Sat 10am–midnight) – one of the city's more bizarre attractions, with its faux-Alpine scenery and huge expanses of (artificial) snow.

Dubai Marina

Bounding the southern end of the city is the vast new **Dubai Marina ❺**

FACT

Ras Al Khor Sanctuary (www.wildlife.ae; hides accessible Sat–Thu 9am–4pm; free) is Dubai's only nature reserve. A tidal lagoon that can host up to 15,000 birds on a single day, it lies at the southern end of the Creek, off Route E66 from Wafi City Mall to Al Ain. Permits are needed for groups of six or more (tel: 04-606 6826).

The magnificent Burj al-Arab hotel.

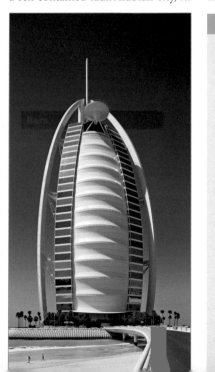

DUBAILAND

Planned in the early noughties as the planet's largest and most spectacular tourist development, with an outlandish medley of theme parks and leisure facilities, Dubailand (www.dubailand.ae) has grown to symbolise the emirate's over-reaching ambition. The sweeping swathe of land on the southern side of the city that it occupies is twice the size of the Walt Disney World Resort in Florida. Due to the financial crisis, work on many parts of the development was stalled, but resumed in mid-2013, and Dubailand is now scheduled for completion by 2020.

However, parts of Dubailand have been consistently operating for some time now, including the Dubai Autodrome (www.dubaiautodrome. com), a Formula One-standard motor-racing circuit, and Dubai Sports City (www.dubaisportscity.ae), complete with international cricket stadium and a golf course.

Situated within the complex is the Global Village (mid-Nov–mid-Apr Sat–Wed 4pm–midnight, Thu–Fri and holidays 4pm–1am; http://globalvillage.ae), a vast entertainment park-cum-shopping centre, with space for concerts, shows and pavilions dedicated to Middle Eastern countries.

Opened in 2013, the Miracle Garden (Sun–Thu 9am–9pm, Fri–Sat 9am–11pm; www.dubaimiraclegarden.com) is the most recent addition. It is full of blooming flowers meticulously arranged in myriad seasonal designs – the epitome of garden kitsch.

development: a swathe of densely packed skyscrapers which have mushroomed out of the desert with magical rapidity over the past decade. Even by Dubai standards, the speed and scale of the development here takes the breath away, especially for those who remember this part of Dubai in its pre-2005 days, when the entire area was little more than untouched desert, bar a modest line of hotels fringing the coast.

At the far southern edge of the city, the **Ibn Battuta Mall** ⊕ (daily 10am–10pm, Thu–Sat 10am–midnight; www.ibnbattutamall.com) is one of the city's most outlandish but engaging attractions, inspired by the travels of the famous Moroccan wanderer Ibn Battuta, with different sections themed after six of the many countries and regions he visited – Morocco, Andalusia, Tunisia, Persia, India and China – all designed with Dubai's characteristic mix of whimsy, extravagance and high kitsch.

Offshore from Dubai Marina lies the vast **Palm Jumeirah**, the world's largest artificial island. As the name suggests, the island is designed in the form of a palm tree. Driving onto the island, the main road runs down the central "trunk" of the tree (adding a whole new dimension to the expression "trunk road"), while a series of sixteen "fronds" radiate away to either side, covered in luxury villas, each with their own little slice of private beach at the end of their gardens.

At the far end of the Palm, the vast **Atlantis** resort (www.atlantisthepalm.com) rears into view above the seafront. The resort is an almost identikit copy of its sister establishment, the Atlantis Paradise Island resort in the Bahamas, with the addition of the few discreet Islamic touches, looking like some enormous Disney palace. Resort attractions include the excellent Aquaventure water park (daily 10am–sunset and Dolphin Bay for swimming with dolphins, plus the kooky Lost Chambers (daily 10am–sunset), a sequence of underwater halls and tunnels running through a huge aquarium dotted with what are claims to be the "ruins" of the legendary city of Atlantis itself.

Madinat Jumeirah.

Hatta

Some 110km (68 miles) from Dubai (around an hour's drive along the fast, modern Highway 44), lies the peaceful enclave of **Hatta ❻**, tucked up close to the border with Oman in the lee of the dramatic Hajar mountains. The road to Hatta passes through Omani territory. No visas are required, though note that if you are driving yourself your insurance won't cover you on the Omani stretch of the road, unless you have arranged additional cover.

Hatta's main attraction is the appealing **Hatta Heritage Village** (Sat–Thu 7.30am–8.30pm, Fri 2.30pm–8.30pm; free). Various styles of mountain dwellings have been rebuilt around carefully restored buildings, including the first fort in the emirate of Dubai, constructed in 1790, which now houses a weaponry museum. Check out the fascinating variety of mud and *barasti* (palm frond) houses, and a restored *falaj* irrigation system that channels water through the village to the neighbourhood's date-palm gardens. At weekends and during public holidays, local women in national dress and

burqa face masks work away at traditional crafts and will pose for photographs (although you should always ask their permission before snapping away). The watchtowers that loom high over the village date back to 1850.

Heritage Village aside, Hatta's main attraction for many are the **Hatta Pools** and the off-road drive that continues beyond the pools through Wadi Qahfi to the Omani village of Rayy. The dirt track that leads to the pools begins several kilometres from Hatta itself. Don't expect idyllic pools, cascading waterfalls and a brimming river at Hatta Pools and you won't be disappointed. The stunning but parched landscape around the pools bears comparison with the surface of Mars. The access track is dusty, the riverbed largely dry, while the spring pools are made up of low-level, slow-moving water. Throughout the year, there is enough water at crossing points to make a splash though.

The Hatta Fort hotel next to the main roundabout in Hatta can provide navigation sheets with directions. Alternatively, you can book a tour in a 4x4 through the hotel.

Al Noor Mosque.

SHARJAH

In the shadow of Dubai, Sharjah is often overlooked by visitors, but it has some fine old architecture and one of the country's best selections of museums and galleries.

Main Attractions
Al Arsa Souk
Bait al Naboodah
Ruler's Fort
Sharjah Art Museum
Sharjah Museum of Islamic Civilisation
Central Souk
Al Majaz waterfront
Sharjah Aquarium

It was Sharjah's good fortune to have been included in Sir Wilfred Thesiger's 1959 book *Arabian Sands*. It's just a shame that Thesiger, respected chronicler of the Arab world, didn't like it.

"We approached a small Arab town on an open beach," he wrote. "It was as drab and tumble-down as Abu Dhabi, but infinitely more squalid, for it was littered with discarded rubbish which had been mass-produced elsewhere."

It's indicative of the amazing pace of change in the UAE that less than 50 years later "drab", "tumble-down", "squalid" Sharjah ❶ is regarded as the UAE's heritage centre, famed for its museums and traditional architecture.

Its ruler, Sheikh Dr Sultan bin Mohammed al Qasimi, instigated the restoration and reconstruction of buildings in the old city centre in the early 1990s. The resulting clusters of coral-stone museums, with their cool, high-sided alleyways and attractive wind towers, offer glimpses of what life was like here 100 years before Thesiger arrived.

Although the city, capital of the country's third-largest emirate, is now overshadowed by Abu Dhabi and Dubai, it is older than both. Recorded references to Sharjah, which means "Eastern" in Arabic, date back to at least 1490, when the Arab navigator Ahmad Ibn Majid wrote that ships

could find it if they followed the stars from the island of Tunb. On a map of 1669, the city is called Quiximi, after the Qasimi family, ancestors of the present ruler. In the 18th century, the Dutch knew Sharjah as Scharge.

By the time British interests developed in the late 18th century, the city was a stronghold from which the seafaring Qasimis, known as the Qawasim, dominated the Arabian Gulf. In 1819 the British, alarmed by the power of the Qawasim, attacked and destroyed its fleet and bases at

At the the American University of Sharjah.

Sharjah and Ras al Khaimah. Sharjah's standing did not diminish, however. Throughout the 19th century it remained the leading city on the Trucial Coast and the second-most important port in the Gulf after Kuwait. The Sheikh of the Qawasim, Sultan Bin Saqr – great-great grandfather of the present ruler – chose Sharjah as his headquarters. From 1823, Britain's resident political agent for the Trucial States and Oman lived here (the political agency didn't move to Dubai until 1954).

The British built the Trucial States' first airport on Sharjah's outskirts in 1932 and maintained a military presence there until independence in 1971. Sharjah was the headquarters of the British-sponsored Trucial Oman Scouts and in 1970 the staging post for Special Air Service (SAS) operations in Oman.

The city's fortunes waned in the 1940s when Khalid Creek silted up and sea trade was diverted to Dubai. Fortunes improved with the discovery of offshore oil in 1972 and the dredging of the creek, but the oil price crash

of 1985 left Sharjah in debt and the emirate was forced to seek a massive bail-out from a Saudi banking consortium. Saudi influence in the emirate has remained strong ever since, leading to the introduction of the emirate's notorious "decency laws" (see page 85) and the total prohibition of alcohol – to the frustration of some locals, who believe that the emirate's conservative regime is stifling the development of Sharjah's business and tourism sectors, already battered by competition from nearby Dubai.

Heritage Area and the Ruler's Fort

Sharjah's reputation for tourism and culture has been steadily growing: the city was the Capital of Arab Tourism in 2015 and the Islamic Culture Capital of the Arab Region in 2014. Back in 1998 Sharjah served as Unesco Cultural Capital of the Arab World, and evidence of this can still be seen in the beautifully restored **Heritage Area** just west of Al Borj Avenue near the corniche, a quaint cluster of traditional mudbrick buildings scattered

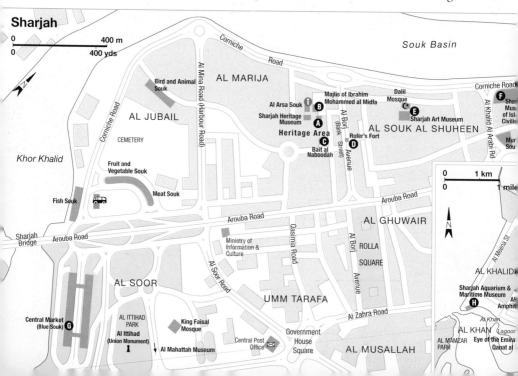

around a sequence of irregular squares and labyrinthine alleyways.

At the centre of the heritage district sits the pretty **Al Arsa Souk** Ⓐ (Sat–Thu 10am–1pm and 4.30–9pm, Fri 4.30–9pm), with rustic coral-stone walls and wooden roof. Inside, the souk's winding alleyways are lined with small antique and bric-a-brac shops selling a range of mainstream souvenirs alongside more unusual curios. In the evening the souk's coffee house is where elderly local men while away the hours between prayers at one of the district's three mosques.

Rooftops across the heritage area are dotted with wind towers, early forms of air-conditioning designed to catch and circulate breezes. The most distinctive tower is the round one above the **Majlis of Ibrahim Mohammed al Midfa** Ⓑ, the only one of its kind in the UAE, tucked away around the back of Al Arsa Souk. In addition to founding the region's first newspaper, Oman, in 1927, Ibrahim Mohammed Al Madfa acted as adviser to the ruling Al Qasimi family. His *majlis*, where he would receive business guests, is now

a small museum (closed until further notice at the time of writing) housing some of his personal effects.

The nearby home of the wealthy Al Naboodah trading family has now been beautifully restored as the **Bait al Naboodah** Ⓒ (tel: 06-568 1738; Sat–Thu 8am–8pm, Fri 4–8pm), an atmospheric two-storey traditional building arranged around a colonnaded courtyard. Rooms have been recreated more or less as they would have been in the early 20th century, with old wooden furniture and assorted knick-knacks. Adjacent to the Bait Al Naboodah is the new **Sharjah Heritage Museum** with six galleries dedicated to the emirate's traditions, customs and culture (Sat–Thu 8am–8pm, Fri 4–8pm).

Close by on Al Borj Avenue stands the venerable **Ruler's Fort** Ⓓ (Tue–Thu, Sat–Sun 9am–1pm and 4–8 pm, Fri 4–8pm), an imposing old structure which formerly served as the residence of the ruling Al Qassimi family, although it is now looking somewhat forlorn in the middle of a small canyon of banks and offices. The interior is home to an interesting museum on

Al Arsa Souk is a good place to browse for antique khanjars (daggers).

An old British cannon at the Ruler's Fort.

Detail of the exterior of the Sharjah Museum of Islamic Civilisation.

the history of the city, due to reopen in 2015 after long-term renovations.

North along the corniche

Continuing west down Al Borj Avenue from the Ruler's Fort brings you to Sharjah's **corniche**, usually busy with dozens of traditional old wooden dhows moored up while their crews load and unload cargo – the wooden masts of the dhows contrasting strangely with the skeletal frames of the oil rigs in Port Khalid beyond.

A couple of minutes' walk north along the corniche brings you to **Al Souk al Shuheen** district, the trading centre of old Sharjah, busy after dark with women shoppers dressed in flowing black robes. A sign here points inland from the corniche to the grand **Sharjah Art Museum ⑤** (Sun–Thu 8am–8pm, Fri 4–8pm; free). The main attraction here is the "Orientalist" collection upstairs, devoted to a fine selection of paintings by 19th-century European artists depicting life in Islamic lands, including some memorable lithographs by Scottish artist David Roberts (1796–1864). The ground floor of the museum

Trader at Al Arsa Souk.

is devoted to temporary exhibitions, usually featuring local and/or Arab artists. The Sharjah Art Museum is also one of the major venues for the prestigious Sharjah Biennial (over two months in alternate years; www.sharjahart.org), a leading fixture on the international contemporary art calendar. The most recent Biennial was in 2015.

Another five minutes' walk north along the corniche brings you to the one of the city's highlights, the superb **Sharjah Museum of Islamic Civilisation ⑥** (Sat–Thu 8am–8pm, Fri 4–8pm), occupying the beautifully restored Souk al Majara, topped with its distinctive golden dome. The ground floor of the museum offers a wide-ranging and excellently presented overview of the various contributions made by Muslim scientists, artists and architects to world knowledge over the past 500 years, including absorbing displays on medieval Islamic chemistry, medicine, astronomy and navigation, backed up with quaint gadgets like armillary spheres, wall quadrants, astrolabes, equatoriums and water-clocks. Upstairs, four

galleries showcase a wide range of superb Islamic arts and crafts, including beautiful historic manuscripts, ceramics, glass, armour, woodwork, textiles and jewellery.

Arouba Road and the lagoons

Return to the Ruler's Fort and continue up Al Borj Avenue to reach Arouba Road, the city's main thoroughfare, which arrows its way purposefully across the centre. At the junction of Al Borj Avenue and Arouba Road stands **Rolla Square**, a popular meeting place for Sharjah's large community of Keralan expats from India. Rolla means "banyan", commemorating a banyan tree which stood here from the early 1800s until 1978, its place now taken by a striking modern sculpture with a hollow centre in the shape of a tree. The entire park underwent major redevelopment in 2014.

About a 1km (0.6 mile) south down Arouba Road stretches the wide open expanse of Al Ittihad Square, once used as a turning circle for aircraft using the original Sharjah airport, although it has now been attractively landscaped with rolling lawns. At the west end of the square rises the soaring **Al Ittihad (Union) Monument**, unveiled in 1989. Close by rises the impressive **King Faisal Mosque**, one of the largest in the UAE, with room for 3,000 worshippers.

The original runway of the old Sharjah airport is now King Abd al Aziz Street, while the former airport rest house, built in 1932 when Sharjah was a stopover on Imperial Airways' London to India and Australia routes, now houses the aviation-themed **Al Mahattah Museum** (Sat–Thu 8am–8pm, Fri 4–8pm; charge). Among the aircraft on display are a World War II-era Avro Anson and a Douglas DC3, which belonged to the Gulf Aviation Co., the forerunner of Gulf Air.

Back on Arouba Street at the lagoon end of Al Ittihad Square is the superb **Central Souk ⓖ** (also known as the Blue Souk, or Souk al Markasi; Sat–Thu 9am–1pm, 4–11pm, Fri 9am–12pm, 4–11pm), a landmark building depicted on the country's Dhs5 banknote. The first-floor antique and carpet

Inside Sharjah Art Museum.

An ornate tile at the Central Souk.

The Sharjah fountain is one of the biggest in the region.

shops are particularly interesting and attract souvenir-hunting visitors staying in other emirates. Persian carpets are a speciality. Nearby, water taxis (abra) offer enjoyable excursions around the lagoon and to the mouth of the creek.

The area stretching north of Arouba Road opposite the Central Souk is home to a sequence of entertaining **wholesale markets**. The fish market is busiest in the early morning, while the nearby fruit and vegetable market is a riot of colour, especially attractive in the evening, when its outdoor stalls are lit by hissing kerosene lamps. The meat market next door is not for the squeamish. A live animal market, selling everything from falcons to cows, is tucked behind shops and restaurants on the south side of nearby Al Mina Road. Most of the falcons are imported from India or Pakistan.

Continuing along Arouba Road, a bridge crosses the **Flag Island**, boasting a giant UAE flag and the expansive **Khalid Lagoon**, now home to one of the world's largest fountains. The 100-metre (330ft) Sharjah fountain can be best enjoyed at sunset from the

lagoon's northeastern shore. At the southwestern shore, in the evening, **Al Majaz waterfront** dazzles spectators with stunning multimedia light-and-sound performances (www.almajaz.ae; Mon–Sat 6.30pm–11pm, Thu–Fri until 12am; free). Colourful water jets moving to the sound of music span some 200 metres (660ft) and are part of the fountain.

Completed in 2005, **Al Noor Mosque** on the eastern shore was the first in the city to open its doors to all visitors (tours: Mon at 10am). Since 2014, the lagoon island facing the mosque has been home to the open-air **Al Majaz Amphitheatre**, which hosts large stage shows.

Southwest of the lagoon, a man-made canal feeds into Al Khan Lagoon at the attractive **Qanat al Qasba** retail and leisure development, with shops lined up along either side of the canal and the imposing **Eye of the Emirates** observation wheel (www.alqasba.ae; summer Sat–Wed 4pm–12am, Thu–Fri 3pm–1am, winter Sat–Wed 10am–12am, Thu 10am–1am, Fri 3pm–1am). At the foot of the wheel the much

smaller **Al Qasba Musical Fountain** has seven to eight light-and-sound shows a day (5–11.30pm, Thu–Fri 8th show at 12.30am; free).

There are a couple of further attractions about 1km (0.75 mile) west of Qanat al Qasba on the edge of Al Khan Lagoon, opposite Al Mamzar Park in Dubai. The state-of-the-art **Sharjah Aquarium** ⊕ (www.sharjahaquarium.ae; Sat–Thu 8am–8pm, Fri 4–10pm) offers an interesting glimpse into the marine life of the Gulf, complete with extensive tanks and walk-through underwater tunnel. The adjacent **Sharjah Maritime Museum** (Sat–Thu 8am–8pm, Fri 4–8pm) is also worth a look, exploring the emirate's former maritime traditions with displays ranging from traditional hand-crafted wooden dhows to traditional fish traps and displays on the local pearling industry.

Out of the centre

Out in the northern suburbs near the Ruler's Office stands the **Sharjah Archaeology Museum** ❶ (Sat, Mon–Thu 8am–8pm, Fri 4–8pm). The purpose-built museum has two storeys of exhibition rooms showcasing objects from Sharjah's past – from finds at the ancient town of Mileiha through to the 1930s and more recent times, as well as Islamic antiquities. The impressive Qur'an monument at the nearby Cultural Roundabout (on the road to the international airport and the town of Dhaid) is also worth a look as is Kuwait Roundabout (east of the museum) with a ship-shaped monument.

Further out of town, next to the airport, the **Sharjah Classic Car Museum** has an exquisite collection of vintage cars (Sat–Thu 8am–8pm, Fri 4–8pm). Even further east, the **Sharjah Desert Park** ❶ (Mon, Wed–Thu, Sun 9am–6pm, Fri 2–6pm, Sat 11am–6pm) lies beyond the airport on the left side of the Sharjah–Dhaid highway. The site houses the **Arabian Wildlife Centre** (www.breedingcentresharjah.com), which is its biggest attraction, and the Children's Farm. The **Natural History Museum**, also located there, has five exhibition halls featuring displays on UAE geology (including a section documenting the story of oil), ecology, flora and fauna and marine life.

Family at Central Souk.

Jewellery for sale at the Central Souk.

THE NORTHERN EMIRATES

Abu Dhabi ●
UNITED ARAB
EMIRATES

The UAE's three northernmost emirates – Ajman, Umm al Qaiwain and Ras al Khaimah – offer a low-key alternative to life further down the coast.

Main Attractions
Ajman Fort
Ajman boat-building yards
Umm al Qaiwain Fort-Museum
Ras al Khaimah National Museum

The fortress housing the Ajman Museum.

The trio of emirates – Ajman, Umm al Qaiwain and Ras al Khaimah – which make up the northern portion of the UAE see only a trickle of foreign visitors and boast few bona fide sights, although all three offer an absorbing glimpse of a very different side of the country – geographically close to Dubai, but surprisingly distant in atmosphere. None of the northern emirates have enjoyed the oil-and-gas bonanzas of their neighbours to the south, and despite significant funding from the government in Abu Dhabi they remain noticeably less wealthy, less populous and less developed than the big cities further south.

Ajman

The smallest of the seven emirates, somnolent **Ajman** ❷ (www.ajmantourism.ae) is now little more than a suburb of nearby Sharjah, strung out along a superb stretch of tranquil beach dotted with a few upmarket hotels – all that you will find here in the way of modern tourist development. Ajman town is best known for its dhow-building heritage. Pearling dhows sailed from its shores from the 3rd century BC until the 1930s, and fishing dhows are still made on Ajman's sheltered creek, though today most are made of fibreglass.

The main attraction in the town itself is the fine old **fort** ❹ (Sat–Thu 8am–8pm), a pretty assortment of sand-plastered round towers, spiky parapets and a superb wind tower which still provides cooling breezes. Built around 1775, the fort served as the ruler's residence until 1970. Inside lies the interesting **Ajman Museum**, showcasing life in the region through the ages, with *barasti* houses and dhows in the courtyard and displays on policing (practised since the days of the Prophet Mohammed in the 7th century), the bedroom of Sheikh Rashid bin Humaid al Nuaimi (1928–81), a market tableau and displays on traditional medicine.

Beyond the fort, off Leewara Street, you'll find Ajman's bustling **souks**, selling bric-a-brac, vegetables, meat and fish alongside a marina where wooden dhows jostle with modern leisure craft.

On the other side of the marina, at the northern end of Arabian Gulf Street, a couple of hotels will let you soak up the sun on their beaches for a fee – the five-star Ajman Kempinski has a particularly attractive beach, along with good restaurants and bars. South of here stretches a long swathe of superb golden sand, remarkably more peaceful when compared to Sharjah and Dubai, with a solitary crumbling **watch-tower** still standing guard over the shore. Most of the UAE's defensive watchtowers are round, but, unusually, this one is square.

From the coast road, Khalid bin al Waleed Street leads to the **Ruler's Palace B**, which stands on the south side of the junction with Kasr az Zahr Street and Sheikh Rashid Street. The palace, home to Sheikh Humaid bin Rashid al Nuaimi, who succeeded his father in 1981, is not open to the public, but it's possible to peer into the leafy compound from its main gate.

On the far side of town lie Ajman's port and **boat-building yards C**, situated on the Creek a short taxi ride from the centre. Ajman's port now houses one of the UAE's largest ship-repair companies, which maintains oil-field supply boats along more than 5km (3 miles) of Creekside wharfs. Two of the most accessible are on **Tareq bin Ziyad Street** in the Mushairef district. Typically, a primitive production line of fishing dhow hulls are propped up on oil drums. Although most boats are made of fibreglass now, the deck rails that rise toward the stern are still made of wood.

Umm al Qaiwain

Umm al Qaiwain 3 (known locally as UAQ) is the second-smallest and least populous of the emirates, with 75,000 residents. In the heat of the day there are usually more animals than people on its streets: a mix of scrawny cats, wandering goats and the occasional grazing cow.

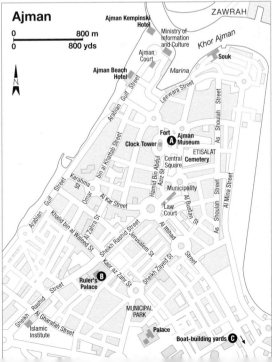

A dhow and a traditional palm-frond canoe at Ajman Museum.

Men in Ajman getting some fish from the catch of the day.

Umm al Qaiwain's name means "Mother of the Powers", reflecting its long seafaring tradition. Fishing remains an important local activity, with lines of boats moored up near the Fish Market on Corniche Road.

The town itself lies on a sandy spit of land north off the main highway that links Ajman, some 20km (12 miles) southwest, with Ras al Khaimah. Approaching from the main highway, you will drive down UAQ's long, straight main shopping street (Al Moalla Road) before reaching the three defensive **watchtowers** off Al Soor Road. Round and of differing sizes, they were once joined together by a sturdy protective wall which has been partially rebuilt.

Beyond here lies the "old" town – occupying a bulge of land at the end of the spit – although there is not much that is old about it apart from the impressive **fort,** now housing the **Umm Al Quwain Museum Ⓐ** (Sat–Thu 8am–2pm and 5–8pm, Fri 5–8pm). The sprucely restored fort itself offers a welcome contrast to the dusty streets outside, with its pretty coral-stone buildings and a neat courtyard studded with trees. The museum is less appealing, with a collection of traditional artefacts, including weapons, and some rather unexciting archaeological finds (pots, mainly) from the nearby site of Ed-Dur.

Umm Al Quwain fishermen.

East of the fort, the low-key **Flamingo Beach Resort Ⓑ** (www.flamingoresort.ae) offers various activities including boat trips, crab-hunting and deep-sea fishing expeditions (advance reservations essential). Boat trips offer a nice way to see As Siniyyah and the various other islands which dot the coast.

Around UAQ

The island of **As Siniyyah Ⓓ**, visible from the old town's Corniche Road, was the site of the original settlement until sweet water supplies ran out. It is now a haven for wildlife, home to herons, cormorants, flamingos and turtles.

Permission is needed to visit As Siniyyah, but the coast either side of the town of **Khor al Beidah** holds further natural attractions, including the country's largest wintering flock of crab plover and numerous other species, while the intertidal mudflats and mangroves are bounded inland by *sabkha* (salt-flats) and dunes that host breeding larks.

Just south lie the fragmentary remains of the archaeological site of **Ed-Dur,** off the coastal highway about

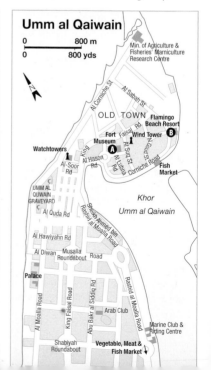

Umm al Qaiwain

0   800 m
0   800 yds

Min. of Agriculture & Fisheries' Mariculture Research Centre

OLD TOWN   Flamingo Beach Resort Ⓑ

Fort   Wind Tower
Museum Ⓐ

Watchtowers

Al Hason Rd

Al-Soor Rd

Fish Market

UMM AL QUWAIN GRAVEYARD

Al Quda Rd

Khor Umm al Qaiwain

Al Hawiyahn Rd

Al Diwan   Musalla Roundabout   Road

Palace

Al Moalla Road

King Faisal Road

Abu Bakr al Siddiq Rd

Arab Club

Rashid al Moalla Road

Marine Club & Riding Centre

Shabiyah Roundabout   Vegetable, Meat & Fish Market

5km (3 miles) north of the turn-off to UAQ town. Extensive artefacts recovered from the site can be seen in the UAQ fort-museum, although there is little to see at the site itself. In 2012, the site was submitted to the Unesco's tentative world heritage list.

About 10km (6 miles) further north along the main highway lies the **Dreamland Aqua Park ❺** (daily 10am–6pm, Fri and weekends often 7/8pm; www.dreamlanduae.com), an unexpectedly large and well-equipped water park in this rather out-of-the-way location. Attractions include a huge wave pool, family raft rides and twister slides – not as state-of-the-art as Wild Wadi and Aquaventure in Dubai, admittedly, but a fair bit cheaper and, during the week, a lot quieter as well.

Ras al Khaimah

The base of the Qawasim "pirates" in the 19th century, **Ras al Khaimah ❻** (or RAK, as it's usually abbreviated) was once a powerful maritime state until being crushed by the British in the early 19th century (www.rasal khaimahtourism.com). Modern RAK is

still something of a backwater, with one of the UAE's most scenic and fertile areas, extensive date palm groves and grazing plains for sheep and cattle, ringed by high mountains and rolling dunes, although it has been slowly catching up with the other emirates in terms of tourism and development.

RAK City

First settled in around 1500, RAK City lies right on the sea, with the oldest part of town next to the mouth of the local *khor* (creek). RAK is notably more built up and livelier than either Ajman or Umm al Qaiwain, although inconsequential compared with Dubai (or even Sharjah). The **central market area**, with gold souk, west of the fort is worth a look for its traditional street life, usually busy with robed Emiratis and their wives, veiled from head to toe in black *abbeyas* – a few still wear the traditional Bedu facemasks which have largely disappeared elsewhere in the country.

The town's main attraction is, once again, its fort, now converted into the **Ras al Khaimah National Museum ❹** (www.rakheritage.rak.ae; Sat–Thu

A western reef heron.

Ras al Khaimah at sunset.

8am–6pm, Fri 3–7.30pm), a rather grand name for a decidedly modest museum showcasing the usual array of local artefacts and archaeological finds. The 19th-century fort itself is more appealing, with a fine wind tower looming over the pleasantly shady courtyard within.

North of the fort is **Al Abrah Market**, a small group of stalls set up on the shore of the creek. On a gravel area opposite this market fish nets are prepared daily by local fishermen, and large rolls of *barasti* (palm fronds) are stored for sale to local farmers. On the same road, under the impressively long Khor Bridge, is Ras al Khaimah's colourful **fruit and vegetable market**, with its extensive range of fresh produce.

Beyond the Old Town, modern Ras al Khaimah expands. Houses and commercial buildings spread from the shore of the creek to the edge of the majestic Hajar mountains, running from here into Musandam in Oman.

Around Ras al Khaimah

South of RAK City, the coastal village of **Jazirah al Hamra** ❼ (The

Red Island) was originally built on a small promontory, which at high tide became an island. The old village and fort still stand but are abandoned, with the new village now on the mainland. This is where you'll find the impressive Al Hamra Fort Resort, designed in the form of a traditional Arabian fortress and occupying a prime slice of beachfront real estate.

A few kilometres north of Al Hamra, the **Iceland Water Park** (daily 10/11am–7/8pm, time varies according to month; www.icelandwaterpark.com) is one of the latest in the UAE's growing chain of state-of-the-art water parks, with an incongruously arctic theme, featuring fake ice-grottoes, penguins and snow-covered mountains towering over a variety of slides, wave-pools and other attractions.

About 10km (6 miles) out of town in the inland village of **Digdagga**, the **Ras al Khaimah Camel Racing Track** offers an entertaining way to spend a Friday morning in winter. Locals enjoy the excitement and thrill of following the camels in 4x4s,

Sunset at Ras al Khaimah.

Modern Ras al Khaimah.

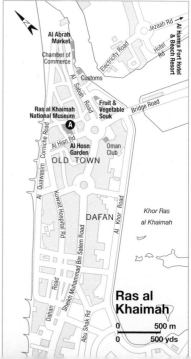

Ras al Khaimah

so watch out for vehicles as well as unwieldly camels.

South of Digdagga, the village of **Khatt** is home to the pleasant **Khatt Hot Springs** (daily 5am–11pm), with segregated enclosures offering private bathing in the pleasantly warm waters – although singularly lacking in atmosphere. The eye-catching Golden Tulip Khatt Springs hotel (www.goldentulip. com) rises impressively from a nearby hill, resembling a kind of modern remake of a traditional Arabian fort.

Excavations during the late 1980s at **Shimmel** (or Shamal) ❽, in the foothills north of Wadi Bih, about 5km (3 miles) north of Ras al Khaimah, have uncovered remnants of a settlement dating from about 3000 BC, including a large circular burial tomb dating to around 2500 BC. Shimmel is also home to **Hisn Shimmel**, popularly known as the Queen of Sheba's Palace. The stony ruins of the "palace" are believed to have been part of a large fortified hill settlement dating from around the 15th century, some 2,500 years after the death of the legendary 10th-century-BC Yemeni queen,

although the view towards Ras al Khaimah and the sea is wonderful.

To reach Hisn Shimmel, head out of RAK on the Oman road heading towards Rams. Turn right after 4.5km (3 miles) at the brown sign and follow this road for 1.5km (1 mile). Turn right at the roundabout and continue for 2.5km (1.5 miles) until you reach a fort-like building. Turn left through the village past a mosque on your left, then turn left past the mosque until a hill surrounded by a broken fence appears straight ahead. You can leave your car at the foot of the hill. Find a convenient break in the fence and climb the hill; you will find the ruins at the top.

The small, quiet villages of **Rams** and **Dhayah**, north of Ras al Khaimah, are also worth a visit, with old watchtowers and other coral and mudbrick buildings (including, in Dhayah, an old fort) nestled amongst palm groves. British forces chose Rams as a strategic landing site for their invasion of the southern Gulf in 1819. The people of Rams fled to Dhayah Fort, where they surrendered after four days of intensive fighting.

A camel ride on the beach in Ajman.

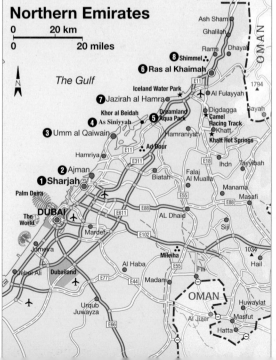

Northern Emirates

Fishermen with their catch on an east-coast beach.

FUJAIRAH AND THE EAST COAST

Straddling the east coast of the UAE is the tranquil emirate of Fujairah, with a largely unspoilt coastline and deserted beaches backdropped by the dramatic Hajar mountains.

Abu Dhabi ●
UNITED ARAB EMIRATES

ugging the eastern coast of the UAE, the beautiful emirate of Fujairah offers a scenic contrast to the rest of the country, its craggy coastline, deserted beaches and dramatic wadis barely touched by tourism. The emirate as a whole remains pleasantly sleepy, bordering on comatose, with a string of low-key towns dotting the coast, backed by the dramatic chain of the rocky Hajar mountains, and with a string of secluded and largely deserted beaches between. The beach resorts of Al Aqah serve as a popular weekend retreat for stressed-out expats from Dubai, but elsewhere modern tourism has made few inroads.

The Arabs of the east coast are Sharqiyyin, who have historically controlled the route through Wadi Ham, which runs from Fujairah past Bitnah and Masafi to link with Wadi Siji where it continues out onto desert plains. Wadi Ham has been the site of many battles down the centuries. Apart from the trade route from Ras al Khaimah to Dibba, it was the only means of access to the Gulf of Oman from the western regions.

Although the Persians, Portuguese and Dutch had a presence on the east coast, the remoteness of the mountains has enabled the people of Fujairah to protect themselves against foreign rule and outside tribal influences. Even so, the emirate's rulers struggled to gain recognition of Fujairah's independence from the British, who maintained that Fujairah was part of Sharjah. In a clash with the British Royal Navy on 20 April 1925, the ruler refused to comply with the terms of the ultimatum from the Political Resident, Lt Colonel Prideaux, and British ships were ordered to bombard Fujairah castle for 90 minutes. It was not until 1952 that Fujairah was acknowledged by Britain as the seventh Trucial State.

Main Attractions
Fujairah Fort
Bidiyah Mosque
Al Aqah Beach

A dramatic sunset.

Fujairah City

The little city of **Fujairah ❶** is modest compared with Dubai and Abu Dhabi, but has enjoyed something of a boom in recent years thanks to the huge new oil-transhipment port on the edge of town, with a cluster of glass-faced high-rises now shooting up out of the neat town centre.

For visitors, the main attraction is the recently restored **fort Ⓐ** (tel: 09-222 9085; Sun–Thu 8.30am–5pm, Fri 2–5pm). Dating back 500 years in places, this is the oldest fort in the UAE and perhaps the most impressive, set against a stunning mountain backdrop. To reach the fort, turn inland from the corniche down Al Nakheel Road at the Coffeepot Roundabout.

Many of the mudbrick village houses that surrounded the fort still stand. Some have been reduced to low walls, but others show signs of being inhabited – air-conditioners protrude from windows and old cars are parked in makeshift carports. A mosque below the fort has been well maintained. It has small, decorative wooden windows and doors typical of the area.

Fujairah Fort.

A five-minute walk south of the fort at the intersection of Al Nakheel and Sheikh Zayed bin Sultan roads lies the old-fashioned **Fujairah Museum Ⓑ** (Sun–Thu 9am–1.30pm and 4.30–6pm, Fri 2–6.30pm), occupying a low-walled building. The museum houses archaeological and ethnographic exhibits from the area, mostly from local sites such as Bitnah, Qidfah and Bidiyah, presenting 4,500 years of local history.

Just south of Fujairah City (and now virtually a suburb of it) is the former fishing village of **Kalba ❷** (part of Sharjah emirate), home to a colourful fish and vegetable souk and the neatly renovated Al Ghail Fort and **Bait Sheikh Said bin Hamad al Qassimi** (Mon 9am–1pm, Sat–Thu 8am–1pm and 5–8pm, Fri 5–8pm), comprising the old village fort and the imposing beachside residence of Sheikh Said bin Hamad. South of the village, it is worth continuing down to the adjacent village of **Khor Kalba** to see the attractive mangrove groves fringing the entrance to the *khor* (creek). At sunset the blue water of

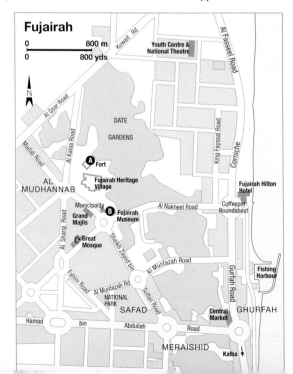

the Gulf highlights their rich green, emphasising the natural beauty of this region.

North along the coast

Heading north along the main coastal highway from Fujairah City, it is 20km (12 miles) to the town of **Khor Fakkan** ❸ (actually a part of Sharjah emirate), protected by a spur of the Hajar mountains. The attractive horse-shoe-shaped harbour is constantly busy with tankers and other ships, while colourful tiers of containers lie stacked up on the quayside. Further north lies the town's breezy corniche and fine beach, along with the quirky Oceanic hotel (http://oceanichotel.com), the town's major landmark with its distinctive round windows styled after a ship's portholes.

Heading inland just south of Khor Fakkan lies the curious little territory of **Madha**, a tiny enclave of Omani territory completely enclosed by the UAE. The main road leads to the modern village of Madha, beyond which lies the smaller village of Nahwa – which,

bizarrely enough, belongs to Sharjah. All of this creates a kind of Russian doll effect whereby a fragment of UAE territory sits within an island of Omani territory, which is itself enclosed by the UAE – a good example of the convoluted borders drawn up in an attempt to follow local tribal allegiances during the settling of modern boundaries.

Moving sands are a driving hazard.

A bullfight in Fujairah.

BULLFIGHTING

Traditional Arab sports such as falconry and camel racing are not suited to the terrain of the east coast. As a result, the large Brahmin bull, which has worked for centuries in the area, is bred to compete in a contest of strength. Two pampered bulls, each weighing a tonne or more and fed on milk, honey and meal, try to force each other to the ground. The sport was possibly introduced in the 16th century by the Portuguese, or may have its source in Persia, where the bull was once worshipped. The Fujairah contests are held on Friday in winter from roughly 4–5.30pm, on the southern edge of town, just inland from the corniche south of the Central Market roundabout (where Hamad bin Abdullah Road heads off towards Sharjah).

coastal views from the watchtower at the summit.

A few minutes' drive north of Bidiyah lies the sweeping **Al Aqah Beach** ❺, one of the most attractive in the UAE and a magnet for residents of Dubai, Abu Dhabi and Al Ain at weekends, although things are very peaceful during the week. The beach is home to a trio of upmarket hotels including the towering Le Méridien al Aqah resort (www.lemeridien-alaqah. com), an incongruously grand structure which looks like it has been airlifted straight from Dubai, the equally vast Fujairah Rotana (www. rotana.com) and, a short distance further on, the more homely Sandy Beach motel (http://sandybeachhotel. ae). All three offer an appealing spot to hole up for a night or two, enjoying the fine wide sands and swimming and snorkelling in the unspoilt coastal waters. Just off the shore from the Sandy Beach motel lies "Snoopy Island", named after the well-known cartoon character lying on his kennel, and now a popular snorkelling and diving site.

Al Aqah Beach.

Further north along the coast, the village of **Bidiyah** ❹ is home to the the oldest mosque in the UAE, dating back to the 15th century – a rustic little structure with two flattened domes supported by a single internal pillar but no minaret. Visitors may be allowed to enter outside prayer time. It is also worth making the five-minute walk up the hill behind the mosque, with superb mountain and

Visitors at Al Bidiyah Mosque, the oldest and smallest mosque in the UAE.

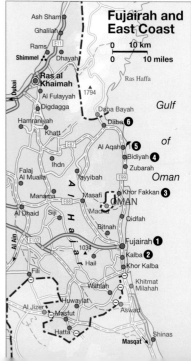

Fujairah and East Coast

From Al Aqah, it's another 15 minutes' drive north to the Oman border and the town of **Dibba** (or Daba) ❻, nestled in the shadow of the mountains at the southern end of the Musandam peninsula. Dibba is actually three towns in one. The largest part of town, known as Dibba Muhallab, belongs to the emirate of Fujairah. Next to this is the smaller area known as Dibba al Hisn, administered by the emirate of Sharjah, and the even sleepier Dibba al Bayah, over the border in Oman.

Dibba Muhallab itself is one of the most pleasant towns in the UAE, although there is not much to see apart from a couple of huge mosques, each sporting a quartet of minarets, on the seafront corniche, and the quirky sequence of oversized sculptures that adorn the town's various roundabouts, including a monster coffee pot, oil lamp and a pile of earthenware pottery.

From here, it is possible to make a pleasant side trip over the border to Dibba Bayah and dip your toe into Oman. The town itself is pleasantly sleepy, fringed with a fine swathe of sand and dotted with fishing boats, often with considerable quantities of fish laid out to dry on the sand. Just inland (signed "Dibba Castle") lies the town's impressive fort – a fine example of traditional Omani architecture, though it isn't open to the public.

Inland from Fujairah City

Heading inland from Fujairah along the main Sharjah highway, it is about12km (7 miles) to Bitnah, home to the atmospheric old Bitnah Fort (not open to the public) off on the right of the highway as it twists and turns through the mountains above the village's sprawling oasis.

Some 30km (19 miles) further down the road is the small town of **Masafi**, perhaps best known as the source of the popular brand of UAE mineral water. Masafi is also home to a lively Friday Market (open all week, despite the name) comprising a long string of shops lining the main road through town selling various souvenirs and handicrafts, including ornamental pots and huge quantities of carpets, although most are machine-made, and of rather low quality.

A modern building in Fujairah City.

KALBA'S HISTORY

Sharjah emirate is unique in having territory on both coasts of the UAE, including the east-coast enclaves of Khor Fakkan, north of Fujairah City, and Kalba, to the south. Kalba itself boasts an unusually long history, dating back to the Umm an Nar period (remains from which have been discovered). The area fell under the control of the Portuguese during the 16th century when it was also visited by the Venetian jeweller Gasparo Balbi, who mentions Kalba ("Chelb") in his *Viaggio dell'Indie Orientali* of 1590 – also the first Western source to mention Dubai. In 1936 Britain recognised Kalba as independent from Sharjah in an attempt to persuade the local sheikh, Said bin Hamad, to grant landing rights for British planes, although Kalba subsequently rejoined the state of Sharjah in 1952.

The lobby at the Burj al Arab.

TRAVEL TIPS

OMAN AND THE UAE

OMAN

THE UAE

LANGUAGE

TRANSPORT

GETTING THERE AND GETTING AROUND

GETTING THERE

By Air

Many major airlines operate direct flights to Oman; for some, it is used as a stopover on flights to and from the Far East. The national carrier, Oman Air, is expanding its network.

Major airlines operating in Oman

Air Arabia, tel: 2470 0828; www.air arabia.com
Air India, tel: 2476 2141; www.air india.in
British Airways, www.british airways.com
Emirates, tel: 2440 4444; www.emirates.com
Etihad, tel: 8007 6423; www.etihad airways.com
Gulf Air, tel; 2477 5000; www.gulf air.com
KLM, tel: 2465 7575; www.klm.com
Lufthansa, tel: 2451 0273; www.lufthansa.com
Oman Air, tel: 2453 1111; www.oman air.com

A taxi sign at night, Muscat.

Qatar Airways, tel: 2416 2700; www.qatarairways.com

By Car

If you are driving from the UAE your passport will be checked at the border crossing in both Oman and the UAE; you'll need to buy additional insurance cover through your car-hire agent if you want to take a UAE hire car into Oman (or vice versa).

By Ship

There are no scheduled passenger services into Oman, but some cruise ships visit Muscat and Salalah.

GETTING AROUND

On Arrival

Muscat International Airport (www.omanairports.co.om) is 30km (19 miles) from the centre of old Muscat. Car hire is available from the airport, and there's also a taxi service

(OR6–15 to most hotels and resorts in Muscat). You can check the fare to your destination at the airport taxi counter, where you can also pre-pay your taxi journey. The drive to Qurum takes about 20 minutes, or around 40 minutes to get to Al Bustan Hotel, depending on traffic. Public buses, run by the Oman National Transport Company (www.ontcoman.com), stop at the Sultan Qaboos Highway outside of the airport complex.
Muscat International Airport
Tel: 2451 9223 or 2451 9456
Salalah International Airport
Tel: 2451 8072

Buses

Reliable bus services operate between the major towns (and between Dubai, Muscat and Salalah), usually two or three times daily. Services are inexpensive and reasonably comfortable, although getting information about timetables and departure points can be remarkably difficult – try asking at your hotel. The Oman National Transport Company has a website (www.ontcoman.com). Micros also run on some inter-city routes, although finding the micro you want is even more difficult than with the buses, and the vehicles themselves are much more cramped and uncomfortable, especially if you've got luggage.

Taxis

When travelling shorter distances within or around cities, the easiest option is generally to pick up a taxi (usually painted a distinctive orange and white). Certain caveats apply, however. Virtually all Omani taxis are

OMAN

unmetered, so you'll have to agree the fee before you set out. Fares generally work out surprisingly high and foreigners are almost always likely to pay significantly over the going rate, whatever their bargaining skills; it is a good idea to check with your hotel to find out what the going rate should be, so you at least have an idea as to what you're aiming for. Be aware that all taxi drivers are Omani (this being a profession reserved for nationals by the government), and outside Muscat may not speak much, or any, English, adding to the difficulties of agreeing a fare and describing your destination. Hiring a taxi directly outside an upmarket hotel or major tourist site is also likely to inflate the cost. It is also a good idea to keep plenty of small notes to hand, as drivers often claim to have no change.

In Muscat, there are a few companies offering metered cab services (Hello Taxi, tel: 2460 7011, and City Taxi, tel: 9510 3152, are two of the more reputable), although you might end up waiting ages for a cab to arrive – or it might simply not turn up at all.

Taxis also commonly operate on a "shared" basis, taking multiple passengers who split the fare between them, although most Omani taxi drivers, seeing a Westerner appear, will assume you want to hire the cab entirely for yourself ("engaged").

Micros

A cheaper alternative to taxis are microbuses, or "micros" (also known as Baisa buses), white minivans which can be seen in towns and cities all over the country. These follow fixed routes, with fixed fares, although finding the vehicle you want can be extremely difficult for casual visitors, given that micros don't carry numbers or signs indicating their route or destination. They can prove useful in Muscat, however. The hub of the network is Ruwi Roundabout, from where micros depart to Fish Roundabout in Mutrah and west along Sultan Qaboos Road as far as the international airport and Seeb. Ask around until you find what you want. Fares are typically 100–500 baisas.

Private Transport

Given the difficulties of using public transport, driving yourself is an attractive option, especially considering the cheapness of car hire and extremely low petrol costs. Most upmarket hotels have car-hire desks.

Outside the major cities, driving is usually quite pleasant, with fast modern roads, usually well signposted in Arabic and English.

Omanis drive on the right-hand side of the road. Driving standards generally are not as good as in the West, so be on your guard for erratic behaviour, particularly taxis and micros stopping or pulling out in front of you unexpectedly, other vehicles tailgating you at speed, dangerous overtaking manoeuvres, vehicles driving at night without lights, and so on. Whatever the provocation, avoid expressing displeasure of any kind – abusive hand gestures or insulting language are both illegal under Omani law and could potentially land you in jail.

Driving in Muscat can be particularly stressful and roads often become very congested, especially during rush hour (roughly 7–9am and 1.30–3.30pm). In Dhofar, in particular, be wary of wandering camels. If an approaching vehicle displays hazard lights, this indicates camels ahead. Adopt the same procedure.

If you have an accident, you must not move the vehicles involved until a policeman arrives, unless it is only a minor accident (in this case, get the other driver's name, vehicle registration number and insurance details; if you do not agree whose fault it is, then go to the police station to report it).

Speed limits go up to 120kph (75mph) on the dual carriageways (in Muscat and between Muscat and Dubai, and Muscat and Nizwa). Other speed limits vary from 40–100kph depending on the type of road and where it is.

Car-hire companies

Avis, tel: 2451 0342, 2476 9392 ; www.avisoman.com
Budget, tel: 2451 0816, 2468 3999; www.budgetoman.com
Europcar, tel: 2452 1369, 2452 1369; www.europcar.com/location/oman
Hertz, tel: 2462 5200; www.nttoman hertz.com
Mark Rent-a-Car, tel: 2478 6885; www.marktoursoman.com
Sixt, tel: 2451 0224; www.sixt.com/car-rental/oman
Thrifty, tel: 2452 1189; www.thrifty. com
Value Plus, tel: 2451 0292; www.valueoman.com

Off-road driving

To appreciate the country fully you need to go off-road in a 4x4, but

A 4x4 at Turtle Beach Resort, Ras Al Hadd.

this is not for the inexperienced, as you will have to navigate steep and dangerous roads.

If you do decide to drive yourself, make sure that you go with another vehicle driven by someone with experience because it is very easy to find yourself in difficulties. You must be properly prepared before you head off into the Interior. Alternatively, tour companies can organise wadi-bashing (driving in riverbeds) trips for you.

Ferry between Muscat and Khasab

A high-speed ferry service operated by the National Ferries Company (www.nfc.com) runs services from Muscat to Khasab on the Musandam peninsula, and from Khasab to Shinas (dispensing with the need for travellers to pass through UAE territory), from Khasab to Lima, from Shannah to Masirah and the Shinas–Dibba–Khasab route. The journey from Muscat to Khasab takes about five hours. All ferries also carry cars, with the exception of the Khasab–Lima line, but this may change in the near future.

Rail

2015 saw the beginning of the construction of a national railway system (www.omanrail.om), which is to total over 2,100km (1,300 miles), connecting Omani major cities and industrial hubs with other countries belonging to the Arab Gulf-Cooperation Council. The completion of the Sohar–Buraimi section is set for 2018, though it is likely that this deadline will be missed.

THE UAE

LANGUAGE

EATING OUT

RECOMMENDED RESTAURANTS AND CAFES

PLACES TO EAT

Compared to the UAE, Oman doesn't have a particularly well-developed dining scene, and outside the capital you'll often struggle to find anywhere to eat beyond the usual down-at-heel coffee shops and cafés which dot the centres of most towns, serving up basic Arab-Indian fare (usually a predictable range of *shwarmas*, biryanis, low-grade curries and maybe some simple seafood). More upmarket dining options can be found almost exclusively in the pricier hotels, although these are often inconveniently located, unless you're actually staying there, and even in these the standards of cooking are often surprisingly poor. The exception to the general rule is Muscat, which now

has a reasonable array of restaurants serving a wide variety of international cuisines – for latest listings, see *The Week* or the quarterly *Time Out Muscat*, on sale in bookstores.

Reservations are usually only necessary in the most upmarket establishments – we've given phone numbers where advance booking is advised. Children are generally made to feel welcome – Omani families usually eat out with kids in tow, who are normally allowed to stay up much later than their counterparts in the West. In more expensive places a 17 percent government tax applies (which includes an 8 percent service charge). This may be factored into the menu price, or may be added afterwards, in which case this should be clear on the menu. If in

doubt, check. Tips of 10 percent are sufficient, although if a service charge has already been added to the bill it's obviously up to you whether you want to make a further contribution – although you may want to bear in mind that the waiters themselves won't necessarily receive any of the 8 percent service charge.

Alcohol is usually only available in hotel restaurants, with a very small number of exceptions, and is typically at Western prices, or sometimes significantly above.

Code to Symbols

L after the price code (eg **££L**) indicates that the restaurant is licensed to sell alcohol; **U** denotes unlicensed premises.

Indian restaurant, Muscat.

MUSCAT

Al Khuwair

Bin Ateeq
Al Khuwair
Tel: 2447 8225
Part of a nationwide chain (there are outlets in Nizwa and Salalah), Bin Ateeq aims to recreate an authentic Omani dining experience, with seating in a string of self-contained, palm-walled individual dining rooms – you eat sitting on cushions on the floor, although the TVs detract somewhat from the traditional ambience, and the rooms themselves are rather stuffy and, unless you're in a large group, not particularly sociable. Food features a decent, but not terribly inspiring range of meat and fish curries plus assorted biryani-style dishes. A nice idea, although it just doesn't quite work. **££U**

Ghubrah

The Beach
The Chedi Hotel
Tel: 2452 4343
One of the most memorable places to eat in the open, located in an open-air pavilion on the beach, with the waves almost lapping against the tables – magical after dark, and with prices to match. Food is seafood fine dining, backed up by an oyster and caviar selection. Open for dinner only, from mid-September until the end of May. **££££L**

The Restaurant
The Chedi Hotel
Tel: 2452 4343
Another of the Chedi's restaurants, not quite as alluring as The Beach but still very fine. There are four separate kitchens here, serving up well-prepared Arabian, Asian, Indian and European/international food, backed up by a huge wine list. Sit either indoors or in the beautiful palm-filled courtyard outside. **££££L**

Madinat Sultan Qaboos

Kargeen
Madinat Sultan Qaboos shopping complex, between Al Noor Plaza and Al Madine Plaza
Tel: 2469 9055
www.kargeencaffe.com
One of Muscat's most unusual and engaging places to eat, occupying a string of small buildings set amid large, shady gardens, with seating either inside or out. The huge menu offers a vast range of crepes, pasta, pizzas, steaks, seafood, sandwiches, grills and shwarmas, as well as some unusual Omani-style mains, including the classic shuwa. **££U**

Mutrah

Al Ahli Coffee Shop
Mutrah Souk
Lively little café tucked away inside the northern end of Mutrah Souk – perfect for a pitstop during an extended shopping trip. The menu features a big range of cheap sandwiches, burgers and shwarmas, plus more substantial dishes, and there is also a good range of juices and other drinks. **£U**

Al Boom
Marina Hotel, Mutrah Corniche
Tel: 2471 3100
Superb views of the Mutrah Corniche are the main draw at this small rooftop restaurant, with a huddle of tables crammed into the tiny outdoor terrace – arrive early to be sure of bagging a seat. Food is an unexceptional mix of Indian, Arabian, Chinese and Continental, plus some decent seafood dishes sourced fresh from the adjacent fish market. **££L**

Haji Ali Juice Centre
Mutrah Corniche, next to the souk entrance
www.hajialijuicecentre.in
Draws in steady crowds of tourists thanks to its prime corniche location, but worth paying the slightly inflated prices for the breezy harbourside views and people-watching opportunities. The menu features a big range of mainstream snacks, burgers, sandwiches and shwarmas along with more substantial grills, fish and pizza, plus juices, shakes and proper coffee. **££U**

Qurm and Shati al Qurm

Al Angham Resturant
Royal Opera House
Tel: 2207 7777
www.alanghamoman.com
Located in the Royal Opera House, this suave Omani restaurant serves exquisite traditional dishes, all artfully presented, in an unforgettable ambience with opulent Arabian decor. Needless to say, such a culinary experience will not come cheap. **££££L**

Al Candle Café
On the beach behind the Grand Hyatt Hotel
Relaxed little beachside café, with sea breezes, coastal views and a very laid-back atmosphere. Popular after dark with local Omanis and other expat Arabs who come for the café's cheap shisha accompanied by Turkish coffee or Moroccan tea, while there's also a small but good menu of burgers, falafel sandwiches and a few grills. **£U**

Come Prima
Crowne Plaza Hotel, Al Qurm Street
Tel: 2466 0660
Cosy little Italian restaurant serving up a range of upmarket pasta and pizza plus more elaborate, modern Italian-style mains using fresh, authentic ingredients. **£££L**

D'Arcy's Kitchen
Jawharat A'Shati Complex
Tel: 2469 9119
Looking rather like an English country teashop, with chintzy decor and waitresses in frilly pinafores, D'Arcy's pulls in a loyal crowd of local expats for its hearty all-day breakfasts, sandwiches and soups alongside burgers, pastas and other mains ranging from fish and chips to stir-fries. **££U**

Japengo
Al Shati Street, Qurm Beach
Tel: 9289 2868
In a prime beach front location midway along the main stretch of Qurm Beach, this attractive modern café serves up a shamelessly eclectic menu featuring everything from salads and sandwiches to sushi, pasta, pizza, stir-fries, Lebanese grills and fish and chips. Nothing outstanding, but reasonable value at the price. **££U**

Left Bank
Off Sultan Qaboos St, below Mumtaz Mahal
Tel: 2469 3699
Chic modern bar-restaurant, with seating on a stunning outdoor terrace overlooking the city below. Food is an eclectic range of international dishes – everything from fish and chips to curries – although prices are on the high side. There's also a good drinks list, including excellent cocktails. Alternatively, eat at the superior Mumtaz Mahal upstairs, then come here for a drink afterwards. **£££L**

Mumtaz Mahal
Near Qurm Natural Park
Tel: 2460 5907
www.mumtazmahal.net

PRICE CATEGORIES

Prices are per meal per person.
£U = under OR6
££U/££L = OR6–12
£££U/£££L = OR12–25
££££L = more than OR25

The best Indian restaurant in Oman, perched on a hilltop overlooking Qurm Natural Park and with an airy dining room offering great views of the city below. The inventive menu features a mix of classic Mughlai and Punjabi dishes alongside some more unusual house specials and South Indian-inspired creations. Good wine list, plus superior live music Sun to Thur. **£££L**

Ruwi

Saravanaa Bhavan
Ruwi Street
www.saravanabhavan.com
One of Ruwi's classic budget Indian no-frills cafés (part of the global chain), offering excellent North and South Indian vegetarian cuisine at give-away prices. Usually crammed with local subcontinental expats – don't be surprised if you have to queue during busy periods. **£U**

Shiraz
Crowne Plaza Hotel
Tel: 2466 0660
This understated restaurant serves some of the best Iranian cuisine in town. Choose from a range of hearty kebabs, tasty *polos* (Iranian-style biryanis – exotic combinations including salmon and saffron, orange-flavoured chicken, and chicken and blackberry) and traditional "stews" (duck and pomegranate, shrimp and tamarind, green hammour). **£££L**

Tuscany
Grand Hyatt Muscat
Tel: 2464 1234
Regularly voted the best Italian in Oman, featuring quality authentic Italian cuisine served up under the direction of its Piedmontese chef using a mix of authentic Italian ingredients alongside local seafood, plus a good selection of superior pasta dishes and wood-fired pizzas. **£££L**

Trader Vic's Restaurant
Intercontinental
Tel: 2468 0000
Part of an international chain, this Polynesian-themed restaurant is notable mainly for its party atmosphere, excellent drinks list

(including killer cocktails) and live music. Food is an eclectic range of international dishes, although prices are a bit steep for what you get. **£££L**

Ubhar
Bareeq al Shati Mall, Shatti Al Qurum
Tel: 2469 9826
http://ubharoman.com
Groundbreaking restaurant specialising in upmarket reworkings of traditional Omani classics, with dishes like camel biryani, fish *machbus*, *harees* (chicken with wheat), date ice cream and *halwa* in puff pastry. There's also a choice of mainstream pastas, burgers and sandwiches. **££U**

Woodlands
Bank al Markazi Street
Tel: 2470 0192
Attractive mid-range restaurant serving up superb South Indian cuisine, specialising in spicy Chettinad cooking from Tamil Nadu alongside a good selection of North and South Indian classics, as well as a reasonable wine list. **£££L**

Southern Muscat

Bait al Bahar
Shangri-La Barr al Jissah Resort
Tel: 2477 6565
Soothing beachside restaurant with wonderful sea views through floor-to-ceiling windows and from the large rooftop terrace. Seafood is the order of the day, focusing on fresh local catch, attractively presented. Open for dinner only. **££££L**

Beach Pavilion
Al Bustan Palace
Tel: 2476 4000
Idyllic terrace restaurant hugging the waves on the superb beach at the Al Bustan Palace Hotel. Seafood is the speciality here, with a range of local and international offerings, although there are also some meat alternatives. Non-guests need to reserve in advance. **££££L**

Blue Marlin
Marina Bandar Al Rawdah
Tel: 2474 0038
In the smart Marina Bandar Al Rawdah, with terrace seating overlooking the posh yachts and

an international menu featuring breakfasts, sandwiches, burgers and pasta dishes along with more elaborate seafood mains using catch sourced fresh from the Mutrah fish market. **££L**

Capri Court
Al Bandar Hotel, Shangri-La Barr al Jissah Resort
Tel: 2477 6565
Competing with Tuscany for the title of the best Italian in Oman, with an intimate dining room or tables on the outside terrace and an upmarket mix of classic and contemporary Italian cuisine, plus excellent wine list. **£££L**

China Mood
Al Bustan Palace
Tel: 2479 9666
Beautiful Chinese restaurant with upmarket food – mainly Cantonese, along with a few Szechuan dishes plus dim sum. **££££L**

Odyssey
Oman Dive Centre
Tel: 2482 4240
http://omandivecentre.com
Attractive beachside restaurant on a sunny outdoor terrace offering well-prepared pastas, salads and sandwiches alongside international meat and fish mains, including lots of daily specials. **££L**

Shahrazad
Al Husn Hotel, Shangri-La Barr al Jissah Resort
Tel: 2477 6565
Very upscale Moroccan restaurant, specialising in indulgent tagines and other North African classics. Dinner only. **££££L**

Sultanah
A1 Husn Hotel, Shangri-La Barr al Jissah Resort
Tel: 2477 6565
One of the top restaurants in the country, with cruise-liner decor themed after the original *Sultanah*, which in 1840 became the first Omani ship to cross the Atlantic. Food is top-notch international fine dining, plus changing specials based on the day's "port of call". Excellent but predictably expensive wine list. Dinner only. **££££L**

OUTSIDE MUSCAT

Buraimi

Tropicana
Buraimi Hotel
Tel: 2565 2010
Pleasant hotel restaurant with seating either in the spacious interior or the gardens outside. Food comprises

a passable range of Continental, Chinese and Indian dishes – the last are probably your best bet. **££L**

Khasab

Al Shamaliah
Khasab New Souk

The best of the various cafés thronging Khasab's new souk, with lively outdoor seating always busy with locals and expats. Food comprises an inexpensive but above-average selection of the usual kebabs, *shwarmas* and fruit juices,

OMAN

Open-air restaurant, Shatti Al Qurm, Muscat.

as well as a decent range of meze, although the Chinese and Indian options are less inspiring. **£U**

Nizwa and Salalah

Al Fanar Restaurant
Falaj Daris Hotel
Tel: 2541 0500
One of Nizwa's best restaurants, with seating either inside the plain modern dining room or, much nicer, on the pretty poolside terrace outside. The menu features a good range of international cuisine, including Lebanese and a mix of well-prepared Indian, Chinese and Continental standards, plus a few Omani specials – try the tasty *kabsa dijaj* (although some nights only buffet food is available if the hotel is full). **£££L**

Al Masharef
Next to the Tanuf Residency on the southern edge of town
Lively Turkish restaurant serving up excellent grills and *shwarmas*, backed up by Lebanese-style pastries and fruit juices. Popular evening hangout with locals – a big screen is often set up for important football matches, drawing an enthusiastic crowd. **£U**

Baalbeck Restaurant
23 July Street, Salalah
Tel: 2329 8834
Excellent and inexpensive Lebanese restaurant, with friendly staff, a sociable atmosphere and tasty meze, grills and *shwarmas* served up in generous portions. There's a handful of outside tables overlooking the street – although the quaintly rustic interior is every bit as nice. **££U**

Bahjat Al Sham
Aldiyar Hotel

Good value for money Middle Eastern fare in the Aldiyar Hotel. Food features the usual grilled meats, fried fish, chicken biryanis and *shwarma*. Thanks to its tasty dishes and reasonable prices the place is also popular with locals. **£U**

Bin Ateeq
Tel: 2541 0466
Nizwa branch of the Oman-wide chain. **££U**

Bin Ateeq, Salalah
23rd July Street, Salalah
The most central of the three Salalah branches of the nationwide chain. **££U**

Chinese Cascade
23rd July Street, Salalah
The best Chinese restaurant in southern Oman, with an attractively spacious dining room and a reliable range of moderately priced Cantonese classics. **££U**

Oasis Club
Port Road, Raysut Industrial Area, Salalah
Tel: 2321 9248
A wonderfully located restaurant with great steaks and other Western favourites. You can drink a beer on the terrace watching the ships come into the harbour, which undoubtedly adds to the place's popularity. **££L**

Palm Grove
Hilton Salalah
Tel: 2321 1234
Attractively rustic open-air beachside restaurant offering a range of Continental, Arabian, Asian and Italian dishes. Alternatively, head indoors to the hotel's Al Maha Restaurant, serving international dinner buffets, or the more formal Sheba's steakhouse, with succulent

cuts of prime US and Australian beef. **£££U**

Udupi
23rd July Street, Salalah
This is a slice of India in Salah. The restaurant serves a great selection of Indian dishes – vegetarian only – but the food is that good that even devoted carnivores will praise it. The midday buffet is exceptionally good value for money. **£U**

Seeb

Keranadu
Al Bahjah Hotel
Tel: 2442 4400
An unexpected haven of authentic Indian cooking in the low-key Al Bahjah Hotel. The restaurant specialises in spicy Keralan cuisine, while there's a good spread of North Indian classic as well, including a good vegetarian selection, plus a few Chinese and Continental options. **££L**

Sohar

Sallan
Sohar Beach Hotel
Tel: 2684 1111
Suave hotel restaurant serving up a well-prepared selection of Continental, Chinese, Indian and Arabian mains, with seating either on the attractive candlelit terrace overlooking the gardens, or inside during hotter months. **£££L**

Sur

Al Rasagh
Sur Beach Hotel
Tel: 2554 2031
Decent range of international food including Continental, Chinese and Indian dishes – the last are probably the best. **££L**

Sur Sea Restaurant
Sur Souk, in the middle of town by the Sur Hotel
Lively little Omani café with tasty, bargain-basement food and a bustling atmosphere – the street-side terrace is great for people-watching. Food features the usual mix of quasi-Indian dishes and *shwarmas*, plus some Chinese and seafood options, all inexpensively priced. **£U**

PRICE CATEGORIES

Prices are per meal per person.
£U = under OR6
££U/££L = OR6–12
£££U/£££L = OR12–25
££££L = more than OR25

THE UAE

LANGUAGE

ACTIVITIES

THE ARTS, NIGHTLIFE, SPORTS, SHOPPING, CHILDREN'S ACTIVITIES AND TOURS

THE ARTS

Dance, Music and Theatre

There never used to be many scheduled cultural activities in Oman – even in Muscat – but that was set to change following the long-awaited opening of the new Opera House in the capital in late 2011.
Royal Opera House Muscat
Shatti Al Qurum
Tel: 2440 3300
www.rohmuscat.org.om
The country's premier venue for music hosts a range of opera and other musical, theatrical and cultural events. The country's leading musical institution – Royal Oman Symphony Orchestra, which formerly performed mainly in the auditorium of the Al Bustan Palace – now also performs here.

Art Galleries

Bait Muzna Gallery
Tel: 2473 9204
www.baitmuznagallery.com
Saidiya Street, Way 8662, House 234, opposite Bait al Zubair
Located in a traditional Omani house, hosting exhibitions of artworks in a variety of media, mainly by local artists, or works by international artists with a local theme.
Al Madina Art Gallery
145/6 Al Inshirah Street, Madinat Qaboos
Tel: 2469 1380
www.almadinaartgallery.com
More of a shop than a gallery, selling furniture, gift items and paintings.
MuscArt
18th November Street, Ghubra Plaza, 3rd Floor, Al-Ghubrah Al-Shamaliya

Tel: 2449 3912
www.muscart.net
Painting and photography exhibitions of local and international (often expatriate) artists.

Cinemas

Cinema information lines do not usually open until after 2pm. Children under 3 years of age are not permitted, and credit card purchases must be over RO5 (US$13). A mix of English, Arabic and Hindi films are shown. For current listings see the cinema website or a local newspaper.

Muscat area
Al Bahja Cinema
Seeb, Markaz Al Bahji Mall
www.albahjacinemaoman.com
City Cinema (Al Shatti Plaza)
Shati al Qurm (near Ramada Hotel)
Tel: 2460 7360
http://citycinemaoman.net
City Cinema (Ruwi)
Building 6060, Way 4381, Block 183, Ruwi
Tel: 2456 7668

A Muscat coffee shop at night.

http://citycinemaoman.net
Star Cinema
Ruwi
Tel: 2479 1641

Sur
City Cinema
Buidling 134, Way 176, Sur Commercial Centre
Tel: 2456 7668
http://citycinemaoman.net

Sohar
City Cinema
Buidling 100, Way 2248, near Al Waqaibah Roundabout
Tel: 2456 7668
http://citycinemaoman.net

Festivals

For details of Islamic festivals, see page 87.
Muscat Festival
Month-long festival, held from late January to late February, celebrating Oman's culture and history. It includes a wide range of shopping opportunities, and activities such as

OMAN

dance, magic shows, music and craft demonstrations. For more details, visit www.muscat-festival.com.

Salalah Tourism Festival (formerly the Khareef Festival)
This festival (mid-July to Aug) celebrates the monsoon season when the southernmost tip of Oman transforms from a dry desert to a lush green carpet. Events include sport, dance, music and handicrafts sale.

National Day Celebration
National Day is officially 18 November, Sultan Qaboos's birthday (although the actual date is often shifted by a few days for practical reasons). Various events are held around Muscat and coloured lights are strung along the main highway for the celebrations.

NIGHTLIFE

Western-style nightlife in Oman is extremely limited – even in Muscat. Drinking options tend to be restricted to hotel bars and restaurants. Bars come in three forms: English-style pubs, "sports bars" (often with live sport on TV and pool tables), and live-music bars, usually featuring Indian or Arabian live music (usually at absolutely deafening volumes) and nubile young ladies dancing around on stage in (by Omani standards) decidedly risqué costumes. In Muscat there are also a few fine (and very expensive) hotel bars, often with beautiful decor and accomplished live music.

For a taste of real Omani nightlife, head for the nearest souk and make like a native, cruising the shops and coffee shops, which usually stay busy until around 10pm.

Bars

As well as the places listed below, a few of the restaurants listed in Eating Out (see page 236) are also good places for a drink, including Left Bank, Trader Vic's and Al Boom.

Al Ghazal
InterContinental, Shati al Qurm. Quintessential Muscat-style British pub (despite the very Arabian name), with wood-panelled interior, pool tables and live sport on TV. Live music nightly except Monday, plus quiz nights, pool and darts competitions and karaoke.

Copacabana
Grand Hyatt, Shatti Al Qurm
The city's top nightspot, hosting resident and visiting international DJs playing an eclectic range of music

Kayaking at the Khawr Sham fjord in Musandam.

from Arabian and Bollywood tunes through to rhythm and blues and hip-hop. Closed Sat and Sun.

John Barry Bar
Grand Hyatt, Shatti Al Qurm
Gorgeously chic little bar (and prices to match), with nautically themed decor complete with ersatz portholes, a ceiling covered in ships' rigging and bar staff in sailors' uniforms. Live background music is provided by a jazz duo most evenings from around 9pm.

Long Bar
Al Bandar Hotel, Shangri La's Barr al Jissah Resort & Spa
Cool bar with contemporary Arabian decor and a good range of signature cocktails, plus the usual beer and spirits. Rarely crowded.

Piano Lounge
Al Bandar Hotel, Shangri-La's Barr al Jissah Resort & Spa
Very cool little bar, with svelte modern decor and resident cocktail pianist. Alternatively, head outside to the long outdoor terrace, with beautiful sea views.

Rock Bottom Café
Ramee Guestline Hotel, Qurm Heights
Downmarket but hugely popular pub-cum-nightspot, with a noisy crowd of under-dressed teenage drinkers and a testosterone-charged atmosphere, although the band (three days a week) is usually pretty good.

Safari Pub
Grand Hyatt, Shatti Al Qurm
This poky African-themed bar isn't particularly good for a drink but is one of the best places in the city for live music, provided by a regularly changing roster of international bands.

Serai Pool Bar
The Chedi, Ghubrah
Very chic outdoor bar next to The Chedi's beautiful canopied pool – you can also order a selection of food from neighbouring The Restaurant.

SPORTS

Participant Sports

Diving, snorkelling and watersports
The relatively untouched waters off Oman offer some of the best diving in the Middle East, with warm, clear water and excellent underwater flora and fauna – the main centres are at Muscat, the nearby Daminiyat Islands, Dhofar (particularly around Mirbat) and, especially, Musandam. The long coastline also offers excellent opportunities for watersports – a number of the dive operators listed below also offer watersports.

PADI-accredited dive schools (many of which also run snorkelling and boat trips) include:

Muscat
Euro Divers
Bandar Al Rowdha
www.euro-divers.com
Swiss-owned company, running diving, snorkelling and dolphin-watching trips.

Lua Lua Diving & Adventure
Tel: 9691 7330, http://lualuadiving.com
One of the best diving companies in Muscat offering PADI courses and diving excursions.

Oman Dive Centre
Bandar al Jissah
Tel: 2482 4240, http://omandive centre.com
A leisure resort that organises excursions to 20 dive spots and also runs snorkelling and dolphin-watching trips.

Omanta Scuba
Wave Marina, Shati al Qurm
Tel: 9977 7045, www.omantascuba.com
Recently opened dive centre boasting a fast catamaran that can get you to the

THE UAE

LANGUAGE

Decorated pottery, Bahla.

Daminiyats in just one hour. Also runs boat trips, including dolphin-watching tours with snorkelling and lunch.

Al Sawadi
Euro Divers
Al Sawadi Beach Resort
www.euro-divers.com
Well-run diving and watersports centre, and the closest dive school to the superb Daminiyat Islands.

Musandam
Extra Divers
Golden Tulip Hotel, Khasab
www.extradivers-worldwide.com
Musandam's top dive centre, running trips (diving and snorkelling) all around the nearby coast and *khawrs*.

Dhofar
Extra Divers
Marriott hotel, Mirbat
www.extradivers-worldwide.com
Close to some of Dhofar's prime dive sites.
Sub Aqua
Hilton Salalah Resort
Tel: 9989 4032, www.subaqua-divecenter.com
Diving and snorkelling trips, mainly around Mirbat, and also Mughsayl. Also runs fishing and dolphin-watching tours.

Golf

Muscat area
Almouj Golf
Tel: 2200 5990, www.almoujgolf.com
Superb new 18-hole links-style course designed by Greg Norman – plus golf academy.
Muscat Hills Golf & Country Club
Seeb, close to the airport
Tel: 2451 4080, www.muscathills.com
Championship-standard 18-hole course – and the first green course in Oman.

Spectator Sports

Although Oman has a number of sports stadia, there are few high-profile events. The national football team normally plays at the stadium in Wattayeh. Powerboat racing takes place at the marina.

Traditional spectator sports are horse racing and, on the southern Batinah Coast, bullfighting (bloodless, bull-versus-bull contests of strength). Matches start around 4pm during the winter in Barka and Seeb and are free.
Camel Racing
Held at tracks in Seeb, Salalah, the Interior and Batinal regions. Usually take place during public holidays and National Day celebrations. Free.
Oman International Rally
http://rally-oman.com
Oman's biggest motorsport event, held in March.
Tour of Oman
www.tourofoman.om
First held in 2010, this cycling event draws a strong field of international riders. Held over six days in February at various locations around Muscat and the Western Hajar.

SHOPPING

Shopping in Oman still revolves around the traditional souks that can be found in every town in the country – most famously at Mutrah in Muscat, Salalah and Nizwa, which serve as showcases of traditional Omani craftsmanship and produce ranging from antique *khanjars* and Bedu jewellery to *halwa*, rose-water and frankincense. Muscat also boasts a number of modern malls, although these are rare elsewhere in the country.

Frankincense and Bukhoor

Available in many different grades, depending on its place of origin. The best place to buy frankincense is Al Husn Souk in Salalah, although it can be found in souks all over the country. Frankincense is also used in traditional perfumes and *bukhoor*, a characteristic Omani creation made from fine wood chips doused in various oils and spices, and available in many different "flavours" – it looks a bit like tea. It's usually sold in distinctive little golden tubs and can be burnt in a frankincense burner.

Carpets and Handicrafts

Expensive Persian carpets are available from the large shopping centres. In the same shops you'll see chests and tables with brass detail from Pakistan and India.

Gold

Oman is one of the cheapest places to buy gold. The price is determined by the weight of the article. Mutrah Souk has a huge section of gold outlets and all the shopping centres contain specialist gold stores.

Khanjars

These are the curved daggers worn by Omani men. They have intricate designs, and the handles can be made from a variety of materials. The scabbard is made of silver. Styles vary, depending on the region in which they are made. The best places to get these are Mutrah or Nizwa souks.

Pottery

Bahla is the best place to buy typical Omani pots. If you're travelling on the road to Nizwa you will see pottery for sale at the roadside in Fanja.

Silver

Oman is famous for its silver, and you can find both old and new items in the shopping malls and Mutrah Souk. But buying antique silverware is not for the inexperienced, and you may be taken for a ride by the vendor.

Shops

Omani Craftsmen's House
Opposite Sabco Centre, Qurm, Muscat
Similar to the well-known Omani Heritage Gallery, selling good-quality

traditional artefacts including pottery, incense burners and rugs.

Omani Heritage Gallery
Jawaharat A'Shati Complex, Shati al Qurm, Muscat
Tel: 2469 6974
www.omaniheritage.com
Traditional Omani handicrafts including Bahla pottery, Dhofari frankincense burners, woollen rugs, caps, coffee pots and modern jewellery.

Sabco Centre
Qurm, Muscat
This low-key mall (and shops in the surrounding streets) has one of the country's best collections of carpet and handicrafts shops, as well as a branch of nationwide Al Haramain Perfumes chain and an outlet for the opulent Amouage perfumerie.

Tahani
Jawaharat A'Shati Complex, Shati al Qurm, Muscat
Next door to the Omani Heritage Gallery and full of an intriguing range of quality antique Bedu jewellery, khanjars, coffee pots and mandoos (traditional Omani wooden chests), plus assorted Western antiques ranging from old box cameras to wind-up telephones.

CHILDREN'S ACTIVITIES

Unlike the UAE, Oman has few attractions specifically aimed at children (although the Children's Museum in Muscat is worth a visit). The beach is likely to be the main attraction, although older kids will probably enjoy adventure activities like dune- and wadi-bashing, boat trips around Muscat and Musandam, dolphin- and turtle-spotting trips, and the chance to explore some of the country's fairy-tale forts and the spooky Al Hoota Cave – guaranteed to fire young imaginations.

Mutrah Souk, Muscat.

SPECIALIST TOURS

Oman offers a wide variety of tours, ranging from gentle excursions by car to challenging hiking, climbing and caving. Many places in the country can be reached as day trips from Muscat, although it's strongly recommended to leave the capital for at least a night or two at some point to get a sense of how the rest of the country lives.

Mainstream tours generally feature a predictable mix of forts, museums, easily accessible wadis and other major tourist sights. There are also other operators offering more original and challenging activities which might include any selection from a range of activities including dune- and wadi-bashing, camel safaris, turtle-watching, dolphin-spotting, dhow cruises, hiking, climbing, caving and so on.

Al Sansool
Tel: 9274 8669
www.alsansool.net
Fishing, snorkelling and dolphin-watching private cruises.

Desert Discovery Tours
Tel: 9462 2725
www.desertdiscovery.com
Range of standard and more adventurous tours, specialising in the Sharqiya Sands area.

Gulf Leisure
www.gulfleisure.com
Adventure travel specialist, particularly good for game-fishing trips but also offering a range of wadi- and dune-bashing trips, mountain-biking, climbing, trekking and canyoning.

Holiday-In-Oman (Muscat Diving and Adventure Centre)
Tel: 2454 3022
www.holiday-in-oman.com
Oman's leading adventure tour company, run by the Muscat Diving and Adventure Centre and offering

a huge range of activities including mountain-biking, climbing, trekking, diving, canyoning and caving, along with more mainstream cultural tours and self-drive itineraries.

Khasab Travel and Tours
Khasab, Musandam
Tel: 2673 0464
www.khasabtours.com
The top tour operator in the Musandam peninsula, professionally run and with excellent guides for either dhow trips along the khawrs or 4x4 mountain safaris, as well as city tours of Khasab itself.

Mark Tours
Al Iskan Street, Ruwi
Tel: 2478 2727
www.marktoursoman.com
Wide choice of tours includes dhow cruises, dolphin- and turtle-watching trips, city tours, safaris, wadi-bashing and self-drive tours.

Musandam Sea Adventure Tourism
Khasab
Tel: 2673 0424
www.msaoman.com
Dhow cruises, mountain safaris and other excursions around the Musandam peninsula.

Oman Last Minute
Tel: 9771 0486
www.omanlastminute.com
This popular companies runs a wide range of day and package tours, catering to various needs and interests.

Oman World Tourism
Tel: 2456 5288
www.omanworldtourism.com
Hotel packages in Muscat plus various day tours and more adventurous camping trips.

Sidab Sea Tours
Tel: 9946 1834
www.sidabseatours.com
Marina Bandar Al Rowdha-based company offering various sea tours, from glass-bottom boat cruises to dolphin-watching and snorkelling trips.

Sun & Sand Tours
Tel: 9937 3928
www.sunsandtour.com
Range of 1–11-day tours covering every part of the country, including challenging hikes through Snake Gorge and around Jabal Shams, camel safaris in the Sharqiya Sands and an adventurous tour overland down the coast to Salalah.

Zahara Tours
Tel: 2440 0844
www.zaharatours.com
Large and reputable company offering a range of shorts tours in the vicinity of Muscat, plus a 10-day itinerary 'Discover Oman'.

A – Z

A HANDY SUMMARY
OF PRACTICAL INFORMATION

A

Admission Charges

Museums and fort admission prices range from 500 baisa to OR3 (US$1.30–7.80), but some attractions can cost up to OR10; galleries are free. Al Hoota Cave is OR5.500 (US$14) for adults and OR3 (US$8) for children aged 6–12; free for the under-6s. Public beaches are free to use. In general, hotels do not allow non-guests to use their beaches and pools.

B

Budgeting for Your Trip

Oman is not a cheap destination, and certainly not promoted to budget travellers. Tours are fairly expensive (between OR35/US$90 for a half-day

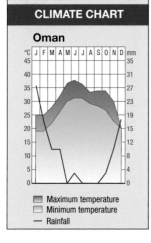

CLIMATE CHART

Oman

- Maximum temperature
- Minimum temperature
- — Rainfall

city tour to over OR100/US$260 for a full-day wadi tour). Be sure to establish whether the charge you are quoted is per person or per vehicle. Hotels are also fairly expensive. Expect to pay OR30–70 (US$80–180) for a double room per night in a three- or four-star hotel. A good dinner at a mid-range restaurant is likely to cost OR7–15 (US$18–40) per person without wine.

Car-rental costs range from OR12 to 15 (US$31–40) per day and from OR25 to 65 (US$65–170) per day for a 4x4. Most car-rental companies include insurance, but do double-check exclusions.

C

Children

Most of the five-star hotels offer babysitting services and many have separate children's areas, although some limit the number of children staying at any one time. Most can provide cribs or children's beds but these should be requested when booking.

Major supermarkets carry baby and children's products, although you may not always be able to find Western brands – bring anything essential with you.

Climate

The best time to visit Oman is from October to March. The coolest months in Muscat are December and January when nights are cool and daytime temperatures rarely go above 30°C (86°F). May to September is the "off season", when it is hot and humid except in Dhofar, where it rains during the monsoon. July and August are the

hottest months, with temperatures sometimes hitting 50°C (122°F). Rainfall is rare (except during the Dhofar monsoon), but torrential when it does occur, often causing flash floods.

What to wear

For most of the year loose-fitting cotton or linen clothes are ideal to cope with the heat. From November to March a light jacket or jumper may be needed in the evening. Swimwear or revealing clothing should only be worn on the beach. Err on the conservative side for swimwear.

Visitors are expected to cover upper arms and legs. Capri pants, shirts and skirts or shorts below the knee are all acceptable. Sunglasses, sun cream and a hat are essential, as are boots if you want to explore the mountains.

Crime and Safety

Oman is one of the safest tourist destinations in the world. Crime is rare and rape is largely unknown. That said, theft is not unknown and it is sensible to observe the same sort of precautions as you would at home; in particular, lock your vehicle and never leave valuables in view of passers-by.

For up-to-date advice on security in the region, see www.fco.gov.uk or call: 0845 850 2829 (UK); US citizens see http://travel.state.gov.

Traffic laws in Oman are strictly upheld, and the legal blood-alcohol level for driving is zero.

Customs Regulations

Oman is a Muslim state, and Islamic customs are strictly observed. Non-Muslims can import alcohol, to a maximum of 2 litres per person.

OMAN

Do not bring narcotics or obscene materials into Oman. There are severe penalties even for so-called soft drugs. Possession of cannabis, even in very small quantities, will incur a minimum 12-month prison sentence followed by deportation. It's also required that travellers carrying prescription drugs take a letter from their doctor explaining that the drugs are required for health reasons.

D

Disabled Travellers

Unfortunately, Oman is poorly set up for disabled travellers. Outside the top-end hotels in Muscat, few places have accessible rooms, and getting around also presents considerable challenges – none of the country's taxis or buses are equipped for disabled travellers. It is best to contact a reputable travel agent to discuss your requirements before travelling. Muscat Diving and Adventure Centre (www.holiday-in-oman.com) and Oman Travel (www.omantravel.uk.com) are two recommended operators for travellers with disabilities.

E

Electricity

220/240 volts AC, using UK-style plugs with three square pins. UK appliances will work directly off the mains; appliances with two-pin and/ or round-pin plugs will require an adaptor (widely available from any supermarket), while US appliances may also require a transformer.

Embassies and Consulates

In the event of an emergency, contact your embassy or consulate in Muscat; most are located in the suburb of Hayy as Saruj near the Grand Hyatt Hotel.
Consulate of Canada
Tel: 2479 4928; www.canadainternational.gc.ca
Consulate of Ireland
Tel: 2470 1282
Embassy of United Arab Emirates
Tel: 2440 0000
Embassy of the UK
Tel: 2460 9000; www.ukinoman.fco.gov.uk
Embassy of USA
Tel: 2464 3400; http://oman.usembassy.gov

Emergency Services

Ambulance, fire and police, tel: 9999
Muscat Royal Oman Police, tel: 2456 0021 or 2456 2030
Salalah Royal Oman Police, tel: 2329 0099 or 2329 0103
Royal Oman Police www.rop.gov.om

Etiquette

Generally, Oman remains very traditional. It's fine to wear shorts on the beach, but not in the shops. Women should wear garments that cover their upper arms and their legs down to the knee. Displaying the soles of the feet is seen as insulting.

When taking photographs of local people, especially women, always ask permission first. Taking photographs of military establishments and ministry and government buildings is not allowed.

Non-Muslims are not allowed to enter mosques (with the exception of the Sultan Qaboos Mosque in Muscat). During Ramadan do not eat, smoke or drink in public.

G

Gay and Lesbian Travellers

Homosexuality is illegal. Although there is a large underground gay community, nobody discusses it or even admits it exists. Any display of public affection, such as hand-holding, is frowned upon, even between heterosexual couples.

H

Health and Medical Care

Make sure you have full medical insurance. No specific vaccinations are required for Oman except a compulsory certificate against yellow fever if coming from an infected area. However, typhoid and hepatitis A vaccinations are recommended, and you should ensure your tetanus and polio injections are up to date. It is advisable to seek medical advice, as requirements do change. Tap water is safe to drink in urban areas; mineral water is available everywhere.

Medical services

There are numerous pharmacies across the UAE, all of which should be able to produce at least one

English-speaking pharmacist. Major cities have at least one 24-hour pharmacy. There is a 24-hour pharmacy in Muscat in Ruwi (tel: 2479 4186; www.muscatpharmacy. net). Note that some medicines which are available over the counter in the West may not be available in Oman, while it also helps to know the generic name of any drug you might require, in case the particular brand you're used to purchasing at home isn't available. There are good hospitals in major towns and clinics elsewhere. Pharmacies are mainly open 9am–1pm and 4–9pm, and some open 24 hours. All the following hospitals have English-speaking staff; for a complete list of hospitals in Oman as well as duty pharmacies see the Ministry of Health website www.moh.gov.om.

Hospitals in Muscat

The Royal Hospital, tel: 2459 9457
Al Nahdha Hospital, tel: 2483 1255
Muscat Private Hospital, tel: 2458 3600, www.muscatprivatehospital.com
Aster Hospital, tel: 4400 500, www.asterhospital.com

Outside Muscat

Nizwa Hospital, tel: 2521 1111
Sur Hospital, tel: 2556 1100
Sohar Hospital, tel: 2684 0166
Sultan Qaboos Hospital, Salalah, tel: 2321 6000

I

Internet

There are plenty of internet cafés in Muscat, especially in Mutrah and Ruwi, and in Salalah. Regular cafés and restaurants in Muscat are increasingly offering free Wi-Fi internet. Elsewhere, however, you might struggle to get

A shop sign at Bahla Fort.

THE UAE

LANGUAGE

online unless you're staying in more upmarket hotels, all of which have internet access.

M

Media

Print

All media is government-controlled and censored, as are books and magazines entering the country. There are four daily English-language newspapers – the *Oman Observer* (http://omanobserver. om), the *Times of Oman* (www. timesofoman.com), the *Oman Tribune* (www.omantribune.com) and the *Muscat Daily* (www.muscatdaily.com). They contain good local news and sports results and their international news coverage has improved, too. UAE papers are also available, including *The National*, published in Abu Dhabi and easily the best local news source for the region (although still subject to censorship).

The Week (www.theweek.co.om) comes out every Wednesday with lifestyle information and listings. *Black and White* is a free fortnightly magazine covering the arts, lifestyle and current affairs (www.blackandwhiteoman.com). The quarterly *Time Out Muscat* is also worth checking out.

Broadcast media

All hotel rooms in Oman have TVs, often offering literally hundreds of satellite channels from across the world, almost always including BBC World and CNN for latest news plus a variety of entertainment and film channels.

The country's only English-language radio station is Hi Fm (95.9

Magazines on sale in Nizwa.

FM; www.hifmradio.com), broadcasting mainstream Western pop and limp chat, although you can't usually pick it up outside Muscat.

Money

Credit cards are accepted in the major hotels, but in smaller hotels and restaurants it is advisable to check first. The best rates are from foreign exchange dealers.

Currency: Rial (omr/or) divided into 1,000 baisas. The Omani rial is pegged to the US dollar at an exchange rate of US$1 = OR0.385 (meaning that OR1 = US$ 2.60).

Tipping

A tip of 10 percent is considered the norm in restaurants, although some places add a service charge of 10 percent to the bill, in which case tipping is not strictly necessary. It is not usual to tip custodians of museums, forts and suchlike, who are usually Omani citizens rather than immigrant workers. Fares for taxis should be agreed before you get into the car – always haggle, it's expected.

O

Opening Hours

Oman runs on an Islamic rather than a Western schedule, with the working week running from Saturday to Wednesday (although some businesses also open on Thursday mornings). Friday is the Islamic holy day, equivalent to the Christian Sunday.

Bear in mind there are no standard opening times and that the following are offered as a guideline only. Government offices are open

8am–2.30pm Sat–Wed. Hours of private-sector businesses vary widely. Most open 8am–1pm and 4–7pm, though not all open in the afternoon. The majority of businesses are closed on Friday. Most large malls open 10am–10pm Sat–Thu and 2–10pm Fri. Smaller shops and supermarkets are open 8am–1pm and 4–7pm.

Souks are usually open 8am–1pm and 4–9pm.

Banks usually open 8am–2pm Sat–Wed and 8–11am Thu.

P

Photography

You should always ask permission before taking photographs of people, especially women ("*mumkin sura, min fadlak?*" to a man or "*mumkin sura, min fadlik?*" to a woman) – but don't be surprised if women say no. Digital imaging services are available at photo shops around the country.

Postal Services

There are post offices in larger towns all over the country, usually opening Sun–Thu 8am–1.30pm. In Muscat, the most convenient branch is the main post office in Ruwi, at the northern end of Markaz Mutrah al Tijari Street.

Public Holidays

There are eight public holidays in Oman. Three of these fall on fixed dates: New Year's Day (1 Jan), Renaissance Day (23 July) and National Day (18 Nov). The other five are all religious festivals with dates fixed according to the lunar calendar (falling approximately 11 days earlier year on year). These are: the Islamic New Year, the Prophet Mohammed's birthday (Mouloud), Ascension of the Prophet (Leilat al Meiraj), Eid al Fitr (end of Ramadan) and Eid al Adha (Feast of the Sacrifice). Christian expatriates are usually allowed Christmas Day off.

R

Religious Services

Catholic Church of St Peter and St Paul, Darsait, tel: 2470 1893, www. ruwichurch.org
The Protestant Church in Oman, Darsait, tel: 2479 9475, www. churchinoman.com

A postbox in Muscat.

T

Taxes

Hotels and restaurants charge a 17 percent tax rate, which consists of municipality and tourism tax and service charge. Most prices are quoted inclusive of taxes, although not always – if in doubt, check. There is no VAT or sales tax in Oman.

Telephones

Calling from your hotel room is likely to be expensive. It is considerably cheaper to make calls home from public phone booths, although these can be hard to find (and noisy, too). Phone cards are available from supermarkets for both local and international calls. A good alternative is to bring your own mobile phone and buy a local SIM card – the telecoms operators, Ooredoo (www.ooredoo.om), Omantel (www. omantel.om) and Friendi Mobile (www.friendimobile.com), have shops nationwide.

The country code for Oman is 968. Oman telephone numbers are all eight digits, with no area codes. Muscat numbers begin with 24, Salalah with 23. Mobile numbers are also eight digits long, beginning with a 9. To phone overseas from Oman, dial 00 followed by the national code of the country you are calling. For directory assistance in Oman call 1318.

Time Zone

GMT + 4 hours, BST + 3 hours, EST + 9 hours, PST + 12 hours.

Toilets

Public toilets are scarce. More upmarket shopping malls usually have facilities, as do the majority of museums, forts and other tourist attractions. Otherwise your best bet is to head for the nearest hotel.

Tourist Information

Official tourist information is found at www.omantourism.gov. om; tourist information call centre tel: 8007 7799. A small tourist desk sometimes supplies maps and brochures in the arrivals hall at Muscat International Airport. In the UK, tourist enquiries are handled by PR company Representation Plus in London (tel: 020-8877 0554, www. representationplus.co.uk).

Tour Operators

A number of companies operating from the UK arrange holidays, tours and activities.
Abercrombie & Kent, UK tel: 012-42 855 801, www.abercrombiekent. co.uk; USA tel: 800 554 7016, www. abercrombiekent.com.
Destination Oman, tel: 0844-482 1672; www.destinationoman.co.uk
Gane & Marshall, tel: 01822-600 600; www.ganeandmarshall.co.uk
Gateways, tel: 0161-437 4371; www. gateways.co.uk
Kuoni, tel: 01304-855092, 0800 092 4444; www.kuoni.co.uk
Odyssey World, tel: 01453-767790; www.odyssey-world.co.uk
Responsible Travel, tel: 01273-823 700; www.responsibletravel.com/ holidays/oman
Shaw Travel, tel: 01635-47055; www. shawtravel.co.uk
Steppes East Travel, tel: 01285-601 625; www.steppestravel.co.uk
Tropical Sky, tel: 01342-886971; www.tropicalsky.co.uk
The Ultimate Travel Company, tel: 020-3582 9235; www. theultimatetravelcompany.co.uk
Voyages Jules Verne, tel: 0845-166 7033; www.vjv.com.

V

Visas and Passports

A valid passport is required to enter Oman, plus a visa. The type of visa issued depends, in part, on your nationality, as does its cost.

Visitors from the UK, USA, Ireland, Australia and New Zealand

arriving at Muscat International Airport can obtain a tourist visa upon arrival. This can be purchased at the Travelex Foreign Exchange bureau in the immigration arrivals hall. The desk is directly in front of you as you enter the terminal. Most currencies are accepted for payment, or you can pay by credit card. Once you have paid the OR20 an automatic receipt will be issued; this must be presented at the immigration desk. A 10-day tourist visa costs OR10, a 30-day visa OR20, and both are single-entry visas. Your passport must have a validity period of not less than six months after your arrival.

Residents and their families

Most people residing in a GCC (Gulf Cooperation Council) country, relatives and those travelling with them, do not need to obtain a visa to enter Oman. However, if you have members of your family travelling at a separate time, written authorisation and identification documents must be submitted.

Arriving from Dubai

Oman, Dubai and Qatar operate a common visa facility. This means visitors who already have a valid visa for Dubai or Qatar do not need to get a separate visa for Oman.

W

Weights and Measures

Oman employs the metric system.
1 inch = 2.54 centimetres (cm)
1 foot = 0.30 metres (m)
1 mile = 1.61 kilometres (km)
1 pound = 0.45 kilograms (kg)
1 American gallon = 3.79 litres (l)
1 British gallon = 4.5 litres

Women Travellers

Oman is a pretty safe place for women travelling alone, but you should still observe normal precautions. Have your shoulders and knees covered at all times. This is not law but it shows respect, and as women are stared at all the time, it makes sense to avoid unwanted attention by leaving tight-fitting or revealing clothing behind. Women do wear sleeveless tops in bars and clubs, but wear a pashmina or shawl around your shoulders until you are inside. Women get honked at when walking around, which should just be ignored.

OMAN

THE UAE

LANGUAGE

TRANSPORT

GETTING THERE AND GETTING AROUND

GETTING THERE

By Air

Dubai is now the Middle East's major air hub and **Dubai International Airport (**otherwise known as DXB) is one of the busiest airports in the world, served by most of the big international carriers and with non-stop connections to cities through Europe and Asia (as well as a few places in North America). Another Dubai airport, Al Maktoum International (known as DWC), which opened for passenger services in 2013 with WizzAir as the launch carrier, still lags behind in popularity compared to its older brother. Abu Dhabi is also increasingly well connected. Sharjah also has a sizeable airport, serving mainly other destinations around the Gulf or in the Indian subcontinent.
Abu Dhabi, tel: 02-505 5555, www.abudhabiairport.ae
Dubai, tel: 04-216 2525, www.dubai airport.com
Sharjah, tel: 06-558 1000, www.sharjahairport.ae

A cruise ship in Abu Dhabi.

There are smaller airports at:
Al Ain, tel: 02-505 5000
Fujairah, tel: 09-222 6222, www.fujairah-airport.com
Ras al Khaimah, tel: 07-207 5200, www.rakairport.com
Major airlines in the UAE:
Air India, tel: 02-263 22300(Abu Dhabi), 04-221 6789, 06-597 0444 (Dubai); www.airindia.in
British Airways, tel: 02-611 8600 (Abu Dhabi), 8000 441 3322 (Dubai); www.britishairways.com
Emirates, tel: 600 55 55 55; www.emirates.com
Etihad Airways, tel: 02-599 0000; www.etihadairways.com
Gulf Air, tel: 02-651 6888; www.gulfair.com

By Ship

Arrival by ship is far less common than by plane, although a fair number of cruises stop at Dubai on their way around the Gulf.

By Train or Bus

There are no trains in the UAE apart from the Dubai metro. There are

daily bus services from Muscat and Salalah in Oman.

By Car

The city and inter-emirate roads are well planned and well maintained, and are mainly dual carriageways. Visas are issued to citizens of many nationalities (including most Western countries) on the spot – if in doubt, check with your nearest UAE Consulate or Embassy (see page 262).
To Oman You can fly to Muscat, or go by bus or car from Dubai, but note that if driving a UAE hire car into Oman you'll need to take out additional insurance from your rental agency. Visitors from Western countries can obtain a visa on arrival at Muscat Airport or at the various border crossings from the UAE. If in doubt, contact the Omani Consulate in Bur Dubai, Dubai (behind the Indian Consulate, tel: 04-397 1000).

GETTING AROUND

On Arrival

There are buses and taxis available from the airports, or you can hire a car. If you are with a tour group or being met by a hotel, they will provide a free bus to your accommodation.
Abu Dhabi Bus A1 runs between the airport and the city, stops include the bus station and the Old Fish Market on Al Nasr Street, 24 hours, costs Dhs4. Airport and ordinary taxis are also available. Check the fare in advance. The airport is located on the mainland, approximately 40 minutes' drive from the city centre.
Al Ain The airport is on the Abu Dhabi Road, approximately 20km (12.5 miles)

Catching a bus at night.

from the centre. Bus No. 490 connects both airport terminals with the Al Ain bus station. Airport taxis are more expensive than ordinary metered taxis.
Dubai Dubai International Airport is approximately 20 minutes from the city centre. Buses No. F55 runs between the airport and the Ibn Battuta Metro Station during the metro running hours. When there is no metro service, bus No. F55A runs to the Satwa bus station. Airport taxis are more expensive than ordinary metered taxis, and taxi fares are higher to Bur Dubai across the Creek.
Sharjah The airport is approximately 15km (9 miles) from the centre. There are no buses, so get a metered taxi to the town centre or to nearby Dubai.
Ras al Khaimah The airport is 23km (14 miles) from the centre. Take a taxi.
Fujairah The airport is located south of the city. Metered taxis only.

On Departure

There is no airport departure tax and the UAE's duty-free shops are some of the best in the world, so it's worth getting to the airport early. The UAE is an excellent point of transit for other destinations. Many airlines and tour operators transit through Dubai.

Public Transport

Public transport in the UAE is mainly by taxi or bus (except in Dubai, which now has its own metro system and a brand new tram line). Getting around the country's various cities is usually easiest by taxi. These are generally cheap and now metered in most emirates, and can either be called for by phone or (more usually) flagged down on the street. Women should always sit in the back of a taxi. Buses connect the various emirates.

Abu Dhabi

Bus The main bus terminal is on Al Sharqi Street, about 3km (2 miles) east of the city centre, with regular services to Dubai, Al Ain and Sharjah. Taxis are much more convenient for short trips, as bus routes cater for those living in outer suburbs and workers' camps outside the city. For more information about the bus services in the Abu Dhabi region check http://dot.abudhabi.ae.
Metro 2017 should see the completion of 60km (37 miles) of lines. The entire network will be 131km (81 miles) long.
Taxi All taxis should now have meters, but make sure the driver turns it on when you start the journey. You can call a cab from various companies, including Al Ghazal Taxi Service, tel: 02-635 6060, www.alghazaltransport. ae; Cars Taxi, tel: 02-551 6164, www.carstaxi.ae; or National Taxi, tel: 02-554 2231, www.nationaltaxi.ae. The initial fare is Dhs3.50, with Dhs2 added for every kilometre.

Al Ain

Bus Buses run regularly to Abu Dhabi and Dubai from the bus station behind the Al Ain souk.
Taxi All taxis should have meters, but, as ever, make sure the driver turns it on as you leave. Radio cabs can be summoned from Emirates Cab, tel: 03-782 5741, www.emiratescab.ae.

Dubai

Almost all public transport in Dubai – metro, tram, buses and waterbuses (but not *abras*) is covered by the Nol integrated ticket system (www.nol.ae). You'll need to get a prepaid Nol card before you can use any of these forms of transport. Cards can be bought (or topped up) at any metro station, at numerous bus stops, or at branches of Carrefour, Spinneys, Waitrose and the Emirates NBD Bank. There are four different types of card/ticket. The Red Ticket has been specially designed for visitors, costing just Dhs2, although this has to be topped up with 10 single fares for one mode of transport ; you might prefer to invest in a more flexible

Silver Card (Dhs25, including Dhs19 credit), which stores up to Dhs500 of credit and lasts five years.
Metro Dubai's state-of-the-art metro system (www.rta.ae/dubai_metro) has revolutionised travel within the city since opening in 2009, making getting around large parts of the city far easier – and cheaper – than before. The system comprises a mix of overground and underground lines, with bright modern stations, although the popularity of the system means that it's often surprisingly difficult to get a seat. There are two lines currently open. The Red Line runs from Rashidiya via the airport and old city and then down through Karama and along Sheikh Zayed Road all the way to Jebel Ali, at the far southern edge of the city. The Green Line loops around the old city centre through Deira and Bur Dubai. By 2020, there will be an extension to the Red Line running to the Expo site. The metro system will be gradually developed as there are plans for new extensions and lines. Trains run approximately every 10 minutes from 6am to 11pm Saturday to Thursday, 2am to midnight on Fridays. Fares start at around Dhs2 up to Dhs7 in standard class, or from around Dhs4 to Dhs13 in the superior Gold Class, which offers slightly plusher carriages.
Bus Dubai's bus service isn't generally very useful for visitor trips within the city (for routes see http://dubai-buses.com). For trips to other emirates, there are regular and reliable services from Al Ghubaibah Bus Station in Bur Dubai to Abu Dhabi, Al Ain, Sharjah and (less frequently) Hatta.
Taxi This remains the best way of getting around parts of the city that the metro has not yet reached. Cabs are metered, air-conditioned, mostly reliable and can be flagged down on the street or pre-booked. Taxis from the airport start with the meter at Dhs20, though in the city, meters start at Dhs10. The main operators are Dubai Taxi (tel: 04-208 0000), Cars Taxis (tel: 04-269 3344; www.carstaxi. ae) and National Taxis (tel: 04-208 0808; www.nationaltaxi.ae).
Waterbus or Abra Dubai is split in two by the Creek, which can be crossed (most memorably) by *abra*, or waterbus. Air-conditioned waterbuses serve various points on the Creek, costing Dhs4 per return journey, payable only with a Nol card. They're much less enjoyable than the city's *abras*, however, and at double the price have little to recommend them.
Tram Launched in November 2014, the Dubai Tram operates between Al Sufouh

OMAN

THE UAE

LANGUAGE

Taxis in Abu Dhabi.

and Jumeirah Lakes Towers, with stops including the Dubai Marina and Palm Jumeirah. It takes 36 minutes to ride the entire line. A single fare is Dhs3, and Nol cards can be used. For more information see http://dubaitram.rta.ae.

Sharjah

Bus Regular services to Dubai leave from the bus stand on Al Arouba Street, not far from the Blue Souk. For more information on buses in Sharjah see www.st.gov.ae/en/transport-services-public-routes.php.
Taxi Most Sharjah taxis are now metered; it's probably best to avoid unmetered taxis – if not, make sure you agree the fare in advance. Metered taxi companies are Emirates Cab, tel: 06-539 6666, www.emiratescab.ae; Citi Taxis, tel: 06-533 4444, Sharjah Taxi, tel: 06-568 8444, and Union Taxi, tel: 06-532 5555.

Ajman

There is no bus service or taxi stand, although you should have little problem flagging down a taxi on the street to take you to Sharjah.

Umm al Qaiwain

Taxis only, from the stand on King Faisal Street across from Al Salam Hotel.

Ras al Khaimah

Bus Sporadic bus services connect RAK City with Ajman, Sharjah and Dubai.
Taxi Metred taxis (flag fare Dhs3; Dhs2.50 per km) can be flagged down on the street. Shared taxis leave from the stand near the Cove Rotana Resort, some 7km (4 miles) from the town centre, travelling to Umm al Qaiwain, Ajman, Sharjah and Dubai.

Fujairah

Bus Occasional buses connect Fujairah City with Dubai.
Taxi Metered taxis (flag-fare Dhs3; Dhs1 per 750 metres). Shared taxis leave from the stand on the Dubai/Sharjah road some 5km from the centre, for Sharjah and Dubai.

Private Transport

The UAE has a very modern road system, but the general standard of driving is poor and characterised by impatience and carelessness. Lane discipline is bad and reckless driving common. Once out on the main highways cars travel fast. Roads are mainly dual carriageway (two-lane), well signposted and in good condition. Authorities are trying to improve road safety through the use of traffic cameras monitoring speed offences.

Be aware that the penalty for drink-driving is a month in jail and the country has a zero-tolerance policy. It is illegal to use a mobile phone when driving, and seat belts are compulsory for drivers and front-seat passengers. Any accident, however minor, must be reported to the police. In most of the emirates you must not move the car until the police arrive. In Dubai, cars can be moved to the side of the road if they are blocking traffic and if the accident is not serious. Always wait with the car for the police.

Inter-Emirate Travel

This is unrestricted and easy by road. It is advisable to carry your papers on you while travelling in the UAE: there are no checkpoints or passport controls to go through between emirates, but occasionally the police do spot checks on the road for illegal immigrants or alcohol, although this is rare. Inter-emirate buses provide another option.

Car Hire

Hiring a car makes travelling around much easier. Most car-hire companies will accept foreign licences. Hire costs are relatively low, and there is fierce competition between companies, so a good bargain can usually be found. For insurance reasons, visitors can only drive rental cars; a temporary licence from the police is needed if you wish to drive a privately owned vehicle.

Car-hire companies

Avis
Abu Dhabi, International Airport, Royal Jet Terminal next to terminal 2, tel: 02-575 9555
Dubai, International Airport, arrivals terminal 1, tel: 04-224 5219
Fujairah, tel: 06-559 5925
Sharjah, International Airport, arrivals, tel: 06-558 0655; www.avis.com

Budget
Abu Dhabi, International Airport, terminal 3, tel: 02-599 8969
Dubai, International Airport, arrivals terminal 1, tel: 04-224 5192
Sharjah, International Airport, tel: 06-558 0366; www.budget.com

Europcar
Abu Dhabi, International Airport, terminal 3, tel: 02-599 8959
Dubai, International Airport, terminal 1, tel: 04-224 5240; www.europcar.com

Hertz
Abu Dhabi, International Airport, Sky Plaza Park, tel: 02-599 8939
Dubai, International Airport, terminal 1, tel: 04-224 5222; www.hertz.com

Sixt
Abu Dhabi, International Airport, tel: 02-550 3723
Dubai, International Airport, terminal 1, tel: 04-220 0777; www.sixt.com

Thrifty
Abu Dhabi, International Airport, tel: 02-599 8989
Dubai, International Airport, tel: 04-224 5404; www.thrifty.com

Rules of the road

Drive on the right-hand side of the road.
No right turns at lights.
Speed limits are normally 60kph (37mph) in town and 120kph (75mph) on highways.
Speeding tickets are often issued automatically by camera, without the driver knowing. Car-rental agencies claim these from you.
Always carry your driving licence and car registration card with you.

There are now some toll roads in Dubai: Sheikh Zayed Road between Garhoud Bridge and Interchange 4, Maktoum Bridge and the Airport Road. There are no toll booths, you will need to use a pre-paid Salik Card (Dhs100). Each time you pass a toll gate, Dhs4 will be deducted from the card. For more information visit www.salik.gov.ae.

EATING OUT

RECOMMENDED RESTAURANTS AND CAFES

WHAT TO EAT

Dubai has established itself as the Middle East's leading culinary destination, attracting a string of top international chefs, while Abu Dhabi's dining scene is also developing by leaps and bounds. Both cities offer plenty of top-notch international dining, with cuisines from around the world, often in memorable settings (and with prices to match). Arabian food is, of course, particularly excellent and well represented, and you might

The chef at Bord Eau.

occasionally come across some local Gulf specialities (see page 90). Elsewhere in the country, things are a lot less developed, and you'll often be struggling to find anything more than basic cafés serving up simple *shwarmas* or biryanis except in the few upmarket hotels.

Not that you have to spend a fortune to eat well. Streetside *shwarma* stands can be found all over the place, turning out tasty meals for less than a couple of dollars, while there are also hundreds of good and usually

extremely cheap curry houses aimed at expat Indians and Pakistanis, particularly in places like Bur Dubai and Karama in Dubai.

Alcohol is generally only served in hotel restaurants (and is banned entirely in Sharjah). It usually pays to reserve in advance at more upmarket places – we've provided phone numbers where reservations are advised. Major credit cards are accepted in all upmarket hotels.

Code to Symbols

L after the price code (eg **£££L**) indicates that the restaurant is licensed to sell alcohol; **U** denotes unlicensed premises.

A Note on Drinking

You cannot buy alcohol for home consumption in the UAE unless you hold an alcohol licence, which are only issued to non-Muslims with residence visas. However, alcohol is served in hotel bars and restaurants in most of the emirates, apart from Sharjah. There are many excellent pubs, bars and clubs (see page 256).

ABU DHABI

Al Mayass
Sheraton Hotel & Resort, Corniche Road
Tel: 02-644 0440
http://almayassnyc.com
A branch of a Beirut-based chain, serving hearty and flavoursome Lebanese and Armenian fare. On a hot summer evening book a table on the outdoor terrace. **£££L**

BiCE
Jumeirah at Etihad Towers,
West Corniche Road
Tel: 02-811 5666
Abu Dhabi branch of the much-loved Dubai restaurant, serving up fresh and inventive classic and modern Italian fare, including pastas, pizzas, risottos, plus meat and seafood mains. **£££L**

Bord Eau
Shangri-La Hotel
Tel: 02-509 8511
One of the best restaurants in town, serving up top-notch modern French haute cuisine, beautifully presented, in a rather stately European-style dining room. Open lunch (Sat–Thu) and dinner (daily). **££££L**

OMAN

THE UAE

LANGUAGE

Emirates Palace Café
Emirates Palace Hotel, Ras al Akhdar
Tel: 02-690 7999
The magnificent lobby of the
landmark Emirates Palace provides a
suitably memorable setting for superb
high teas, served either in traditional
English or Arabian styles. **£££L**

Finz
Beach Rotana Hotel, Tourist Club Area
Tel: 02-697 9011
Often voted the best seafood
restaurant in town, with a range of
fresh fish and seafood served up in
an eclectic variety of international
styles. Seating either inside or on the
pleasant waterside terrace. **£££L**

Hakkasan
Emirates Palace Hotel
Tel: 02-690 7999
Super-swanky restaurant with opulent
decor and the city's best Chinese
cuisine, ranging from classics like tofu
claypot to more contemporary creations
like black pepper wagyu beef. **£££££L**

Hanoi
Khalifa Sreet, Al Markaziyah
Tel: 02-626 1112
Excellent Vietnamese establishment,
more of a café than a restaurant, but
with superbly spicy and authentic
cooking – vermicelli salads, chilli-
salted squid and so on – at extremely
modest prices. **££U**

India Palace
Al Salam St, Tourist Club Area
Tel: 02-644 8777

www.indiapalace.ae
Abu Dhabi institution, always lively,
and serving up a decent range of
North Indian meat and veg curries
and tandooris. **££U**

Indigo
Beach Rotana Hotel, Tourist Club Area
Tel: 02-697 9011
Suave Indian restaurant, with
superior decor and a nice selection
of North Indian classics, along with
a few seafood options and assorted
vegetarian dishes. **£££L**

Lebanese Flower
Off 26th Street, Al Khalidiya
One of the city's most popular
Lebanese restaurants, with a
pleasantly rustic interior and a good
selection of tasty grilled meat and fish
dishes, plus assorted *meze*. **£U**

Mezzaluna
Emirates Palace
Tel: 02-690 7999
Suave restaurant specialising
in contemporary Italian and
Mediterranean cuisine – and one of
the more affordable of the Emirates
Palace's many bespoke eating venues
(though still far from inexpensive).
£££££L

Rodeo Grill
Beach Rotana Hotel, Tourist Club Area
Tel: 02-697 9011
One of the best steakhouses in Abu
Dhabi, with prime cuts of US Angus
and Australian wagyu along with other
meat dishes and some seafood. **£££L**

Rosewater
Jumeirah at Etihad Towers, West Corniche
Road
Tel: 02-811 5666
A popular and classy buffet restaurant
with extensive international menu,
including seafood, sushi, steaks,
curries and salads. There is even
a chocolate fountain. Open for
breakfast, lunch and dinner. **££L**

Royal Orchid
Hilton Hotel, West Corniche Road
Tel: 02-681 1900
An old Abu Dhabi favourite, offering a
wide range of well-prepared and very
reasonably priced Thai and Chinese
food. **££L**

Stratos
Le Royal Méridien, Al Markaziyah
Tel: 800 101 101
www.stratosabudhabi.com
Balanced atop the roof of Le Royal
Méridien hotel, Stratos Revolving
Lounge Bar and Grill offers unrivalled
views of the city below, backed up
with well-prepared modern European
meat and seafood creations. **£££L**

Talay
Le Méridien, Tourist Club Area
Tel: 02-644 6666
www.talayabudhabi.com
Fine Thai cooking, with the emphasis
on seafood backed up by a decent
selection of meat and a few
vegetarian options. Seating either in
the stylish interior or on the breezy
terrace outside. **£££L**

AL AIN

Arabesque
Danat Al Ain Resort
Tel: 03-768 6686
Amazing selection of international
dishes, from salads, burgers, pizza
and steaks to Arabic stuffed vine
leaves and Indian dhal curry. **££U**

Al Mallah
Near Globe Roundabout

Excellent little Lebanese café serving
up hearty *shwarma*, kebabs and good
juices. **£U**

Min Zaman
Al Ain Rotana Hotel
Tel: 03-703 1071
Stylish Lebanese restaurant, with a
good selection of authentic *meze* and
grills, plus *shisha*. **££L**

Trader Vic's
Al Ain Rotana
Tel: 03-754 5111
http://tradervics.com
Local branch of the worldwide
chain serving up reasonable
international food, potent
cocktails and a lively atmosphere.
£££L

DUBAI

Armani/Amal
Armani Hotel, Downtown Dubai
Tel: 04 888 3888
Old-time traditional Indian favourites,
including tasty curries and tandooris.
A great dining experience, and though
a bit pricey, it includes spectacular
views of the Dubai Fountain (ask for a
terrace table). **£££L**

Al Dawaar
Hyatt Regency Hotel, Deira
Tel: 04-317 2222

On the 25th floor of the huge Hyatt
Regency, Dubai's only revolving restaurant offers stunning city views com-
plemented by an upmarket (if rather
expensive) international buffet. **£££L**

Al Mahara
Burj al Arab, Umm Suqeim
Tel: 04-301 7600
Centred on an enormous fish
tank, this spectacularly designed
subterranean seafood restaurant
is one of Dubai's most expensive

restaurants, with sumptuous
international seafood. **££££L**

Al Makan
Souk Madinat Jumeirah
Tel: 04-368 6593
http://alkoufa.com
Located in atmospheric Souk Madinat
Jumeirah, Al Makan offers a rare
chance to sample authentic Emirati
cuisine in a restaurant setting,
along with a good selection of more
mainstream Lebanese food and grills.

Outdoor terrace seating overlooks Burj al Arab Hotel. **£££U**

Al Mallah
Al Diyafah Street, Satwa
One of several lively Lebanese cafés along Al Diyafah Street, with a good range of inexpensive Middle Eastern *meze*, snacks and meals (including good grills and *shwarmas*) and plenty of seating on the pavement outside – a great place to watch the nightlife of Satwa roll past. **£U**

Al Muntaha
Burj al Arab, Umm Suqeim
Tel: 04-301 7600
Next to the Skyview Bar at the very top of the Burj al Arab, 200 metres/yds above the Arabian Gulf, with fantastic views and excellent (and inevitably expensive) modern European cuisine. **£££££L**

Al Nafoorah
Jumeirah Emirates Towers, Sheikh Zayed Rd
Tel: 04-366 5866
The best Lebanese restaurant in town, with an extensive range of beautifully prepared hot and cold *meze*, grills and a good wine list, including Lebanese vintages. **£££L**

Alta Badia
Jumeirah Emirates Towers Hotel, Sheikh Zayed Road
Tel: 04 366 5866
This new Italian restaurant at Jumeirah Emirates Towers mixes classic Italian flavours with creative culinary inventions, plus stunning views. A wide selection of vegetarian dishes. **£££££L**

At.mosphere
Burj Khalifa
Tel: 04-888 3828
www.atmosphereburjkhalifa.com
On the 122nd floor of the Burj Khalifa, At.mosphere is the world's highest bar and restaurant, located almost half a kilometre above ground level. Choose between The Lounge for a drink, light meal or a pricey afternoon tea, or splash out on a meal at The Restaurant, serving upmarket international fare in its svelte dining room. **£££££L**

Bastakiah Nights
Bastakiya, Bur Dubai
Tel: 04-353 7772
Located in a historic courtyard house in Bastakiya, this is one of the city's most atmospheric and romantic restaurants. The menu features a mix of Arabian and Iranian dishes – relatively expensive and pedestrian compared to other places in the city, but it's the setting that really seals the deal. **£££U**

Blue Elephant
Al Bustan Rotana Hotel, Garhoud
Tel: 04-282 0000
www.blueelephant.com/dubai

A candidate for best Thai restaurant in Dubai, located in a quaint little tropical-style "village" with a consistently good, and quite reasonably priced, selection of classic Thai fare. **£££L**

The Boardwalk
Dubai Creek Yacht Club
Tel: 04-295 6000
The mainstream menu of international food is reliable enough, but it's the terrific Creek and city views from the outdoor seating on the restaurant's eponymous boardwalk that really steal the show. **£££L**

Buddha Bar
Grosvenor House, Al Sufouh Road, Dubai Marina
Tel: 04-317 6000
One of the best-looking restaurants in Dubai, modelled after its famous Parisian namesake, and with a fine array of Japanese, Thai and Chinese mains. Always buzzing. **£££L**

Elements
Wafi, Oud Metha
www.elements-cafe.com
Funky little venue in the Wafi complex serving a wide selection of reasonably priced café fare ranging from sandwiches, salads and pizzas to dim sum and sushi, plus more substantial meat and fish mains. **££U**

The Exchange Grill
Fairmont Hotel, Sheikh Zayed Road
Tel: 04-311 8316
The city's most exclusive steakhouse, this small and very upmarket establishment serves up choice Gold Angus and wagyu cuts, backed up by one of the city's most extensive wine lists. **£££££L**

Indego by Vineet
Grosvenor House Hotel, Al Sufouh Road, Dubai Marina; Tel: 04-399 8888
Overseen by Vineet Bhatia, India's first Michelin-starred chef, this stylish restaurant showcases Bhatia's outstanding "contemporary Indian" cooking, with a seductive blend of subcontinental and international ingredients and techniques. **£££L**

Japengo Café
Mall of the Emirates, Sheikh Zayed Road
Tel: 04-341 1671
Chic modern café-restaurant, with a shamelessly eclectic menu featuring everything from sushi and sashimi to stir-fries, pizzas, pastas, *meze* and good old-fashioned lamb chops, plus sandwiches and salads. There are other branches, including one overlooking the canal in the Souk Madinat Jumeirah, another in Mirdif City Centre and one in the DIFC district. **££U**

Kan Zaman
Creekside, Shindagha
Tel: 04-393 9913

In a fine location near the mouth of the Creek, Kanzaman ("once upon a time") has breezy outdoor and waterside seating and a good selection of Lebanese *meze*, Turkish coffee and shisha (hubbly bubbly pipes). **££U**

Khan Murjan Restaurant
Khan Murjan Souk, Oud Metha
Beautiful courtyard restaurant at the heart of the Souk Khan Murjan. The menu features an unusually wide range of Middle Eastern dishes, from mainstream Lebanese grills and *meze* to traditional Gulf dishes like *fouga* and *goboli*. **££U**

Lime Tree Café
Near Spinneys, Jumeirah Road
Tel: 04-349 8498
www.thelimetreecafe.com
Set in an attractive modern villa, this neat little café offers a classic slice of expat Jumeirah life. Healthy specialities include outstanding carrot cake, tasty wraps and delicious smoothies. **£U**

More
D71, near Financial Center Road, Al Murooj
Tel: 04-343 3779
www.morecafe.co
A funky Dutch-owned bistro with a wide range of superior international café fare. A difficult place to beat for its combination of excellent atmosphere, quality, value and service. There are branches in the Mall of the Emirates and DIFC. **££U**

Nina
Arabian Courtyard, One&Only Royal Mirage
Tel: 04-399 9999
Innovative modern Indian restaurant, combining subcontinental flavours with international ingredients and cooking techniques – anything from traditional butter chicken to frogs' legs and rambutan. **£££L**

Noodle House
Emirates Towers Boulevard, Jumeirah Emirates Towers, Sheikh Zayed Road
www.thenoodlehouse.com
Something of a local institution, this cheerful noodle bar chain is a kind of Dubai Wagamama, with good, reasonably priced Thai, Chinese, Malay, Singaporean, Indonesian and Japanese dishes served up at long communal tables. You might have to queue at busy times. There are six other branches within the city including Souk Madinat Jumeirah and the Dubai Mall. **££L**

PRICE CATEGORIES

Prices are per meal per person.
£U = under Dhs60
££U/££L = Dhs60–120
£££U/£££L = Dhs120–230
££££L = more than Dhs230
L = licensed, U = unlicensed

OMAN

THE UAE

LANGUAGE

Pars Iranian Kitchen
Al Dhiyafa Road, Satwa Roundabout
Pleasant garden restaurant next
to Satwa Roundabout serving up
excellent and authentic Iranian fare –
grills, *polos* (biryanis) and the like – at
very competitive prices. **££U**

Pierchic
Al Qasr Hotel, Madinat Jumeirah
Tel: 04-366 5866
Fabulous, very romantic international
seafood restaurant at the end of
its own wooden pier with stunning
views of Burj al Arab and the Madinat
Jumeirah resort. **££££L**

Ravi Restaurant
Al Dhiyafa Road, just off Satwa Roundabout,
Satwa
This legendary little café remains
enduringly popular with locals, expats
and tourists alike for its cheap and
tasty Pakistani-style chicken, mutton
and vegetable curries, while the
outdoor seating offers a good (if
noisy) perch from which to enjoy the
passing streetlife. **£U**

Rhodes W1
Grosvenor House Hotel
Tel: 04-317 6000
www.rw1-dubai.com
Dubai outpost of UK celebrity chef
Gary Rhodes, with a short but inventive menu showcasing Rhodes's
distinctive brand of modern European
cuisine, accompanied by classic British puddings like jam roly-poly and
steamed steak and kidney pudding.
££££L

Shakespeare & Co
Al Saqr Business Tower, Sheikh Zayed Road
www.shakespeare-and-co.com
Chintzy little European-style café
tucked away halfway down Sheikh

Zayed Road and a nice place for a
coffee or light lunch, with soups,
salads, sandwiches and crepes along
with substantial mains. **££U**

Shu
Jumeirah Road,
opposite Jumeirah Beach Park
Tel: 04-349 1303
http://shucafe.com
Chic Lebanese café with seating
either in the cool interior or on the
relaxed outside terrace. If you're
feeling adventurous, try the house
speciality: fried sparrow with
pomegranate syrup. **££U**

Table 9
Hilton Creek, Deira
Tel: 04-212 7551
www.table9dubai.com
This former Dubai outpost of the
UK celebrity chef Gordon Ramsay is
now run by another talented British,
Darren Velvick. The suave restaurant
is still one of the best in the city and
the food is top-notch. **££££L**

Tagine
One&Only Royal Mirage, Al Sufouh Road
Tel: 04-399 9999
This exquisitely decorated little
Moroccan restaurant is one of the
most appealing in the city, with *Arabian
Nights* decor and a fine array of
traditional Moroccan cuisine, including
a delicious selection of tagines and
traditional dishes like spicy *harira* soup,
lamb's brain and pigeon pie. **£££L**

Teatro
Towers Rotana, Sheikh Zayed Road
Tel: 04-312 2202
This long-established restaurant
is usually one of the liveliest along
Sheikh Zayed Road, with theatrically
themed decor and an eclectic menu

featuring Italian, Indian, Chinese and
Thai, plus a bit of sushi – generally
well-cooked and reasonably priced.
££L

The Thai Kitchen
Park Hyatt, Garhoud
Tel: 04-317 2222
One of the best and most romantic
Thai restaurants in town, set on the
Park Hyatt's idyllic Creekside terrace
and offering a sumptuous range of
unusual regional specialities served
in tapas-size portions. **£££L**

XVA Café
Bastakiya, Bur Dubai
Tel: 04-353 5383; www.xvagallery.com
Delightful courtyard café in a historic
house that is now an art gallery and
boutique hotel. The menu offers fresh
and healthy vegetarian fare including
salads, soups and sandwiches. **£U**

Zengo
Le Royal Meredien Beach Resort & Spa,
Al Sufouh Road
Tel: 04-316 5550
http://www.zengo-dubai.com
This first-class Asian restaurant
serves innovative tasty dishes
created by celebrity chefs Richard
Sandoval and Akmal Anuar. A skilful
blend of Japanese and Chinese
cuisines plus a fantastic ambience
make for a great dining experience.
£££L

Zaatar W Zeit
The Walk, Dubai Marina
http://www.orderzwz.com
Cheery Lebanese-style fast-food
joint, with salads, wraps and pizzas
alongside various kinds of *manakish*
(a kind of Middle Eastern-style pizza)
and other Lebanese snacks. Online
ordering. **£U**

SHARJAH

Canton Chinese Restaurant
Radisson Blu Hotel, Corniche Street
Tel: 06-565 7777
Cantonese Chinese classics in an
attractive dining room in Sharjah's
top hotel. **£££U**

Danial
Crystal Plaza, King Faisal Street
Tel: 06-574 4668
www.danialrestaurant.com
Chintzy Iranian restaurant, in a

convenient location just behind the
Central Souk, serving a reasonable
buffet spread at lunchtime along with
a selection of Middle Eastern and
Iranian dishes. **££U**

Sanobar
Al Khan Street
Tel: 06-528 3501
www.sanobar-restaurant.com
Lebanese restaurant specialising in
seafood, freshly grilled, plus assorted

meze, with seating either in the
quaint interior or on the sea-facing
terrace. **££U**

Souk al Arsah Coffee Shop
Souk al Arsah, Heritage Area
Cute little café next to the pretty
courtyard at the heart of the Souk al
Arsah – a good place to grab a tea
or coffee or to try one of the café's
spicy chicken, mutton and fish
biryanis. **£U**

EAST COAST

Sadaf
Corniche Road, Fujairah; Tel: 09-222 8577
A recommended Fujairah restaurant
with local food and typical Arab

atmosphere. No frills, but good value
for money. **££U**

The Views
Le Méridien Al Aqah Beach Resort, Al Aqah

Tel: 09-244 9000
Fine sea views and international
food from the brasserie-style menu.
£££L

OMAN

ACTIVITIES

THE ARTS, NIGHTLIFE, SPORTS, SHOPPING, CHILDREN'S ACTIVITIES AND TOURS

THE ARTS

Dance, Music and Theatre

Although the UAE has few concert and dance performances, big-name rock and pop acts do visit now and then, usually in Dubai. The Amphitheatre in Dubai Media City is the usual venue for big-name events (www.dubaimediacity.com). Otherwise, the venues below sometimes host performances.

Al Majaz Amphitheatre
Sharjah, Khalid Lagoon
A new open-air venue, which hosts large-stage productions and spectacular music shows.

Dubai Community and Arts Centre (DUCTAC)
Mall of the Emirates, Sheikh Zayed Road, tel: 04-341 4777; www.ductac.org
Home to a trio of lively little venues: the Centrepoint Theatre, Kilachand Studio Theatre and Manu Chhabria Arts Centre, which host a wide range of productions, including film, music and theatre, with the emphasis on local and community-based projects.

Dubai Opera
Downtown Dubai, close to Sheikh Mohammed bin Rashid Boulevard
A 2,000-seat venue for the performing arts due to open in 2016 in a state-of-the-art building designed by Zaha Hadid.

Madinat Theatre
Madinat Jumeirah, Dubai, tel: 04-366 6546; www.madinattheatre.com
Dubai's first proper theatre when it opened in the mid-noughties, although don't expect much beyond a fairly predictable range of mainstream musicals, children's shows and other stereotypical crowd-pleasers.

The Palladium Dubai
Media City, tel: 04-363 6897; www.thepalladiumdubai.com
State-of-the-art new entertainment venue hosting a very mixed range of events, including regular stand-up comedy and live-music shows through to international seminars and awards ceremonies.

Art Galleries

Abu Dhabi

Ghaf Gallery
Al Khaleej al Arabi St, near Khalidiya Gardens, off the corniche, tel: 02-665 5332
Solo shows and mixed exhibitions featuring work by local and international artists.

Qibab Gallery
26th Street, Al Bateen, tel: 02-665 2350
Specialises in Iraqi art, but also exhibits works by a wide range of other international artists.

Salwa Zeidan Gallery
Al Khaleej al Arabi St, near Khalidiya Gardens, off the corniche, tel: 02-666 9656; www.salwazeidangallery.com

Madinat Theatre.

Works by leading Middle Eastern artists and emerging local talent in a range of media.

Dubai

Artspace
The Gate Village Building 3, Level 2, DIFC, Sheikh Zayed Road, tel: 04-323 0820; www.artspace-dubai.com
Upmarket gallery specialising in established Middle Eastern artists.

Courtyard Gallery
Al Quoz, Street 6A, off Sheikh Zayed Road, tel: 04-347 9090; www.courtyardgallerydubai.com
One of Dubai's oldest galleries, in an entertainingly quirky development off Sheikh Zayed Road and showcasing the work of leading regional and international artists.

Gallery Isabelle van den Eynde
(formerly the B21 Gallery)
Street 8, Alserkal Avenue, Unit 17, Al Quoz Industrial 1, tel: 04-323 5052; www.ivde.net
Showcases work by up-and-coming Arab artists.

Green Art Gallery
Street 8, Alserkal Avenue, Unit 28, Al Quoz Industrial 1, tel: 04-346 9305; www.gagallery.com
Exhibits and sells quality paintings.

THE UAE

LANGUAGE

There are great views from the restaurant at the top of Marina Mall in Abu Dhabi.

Majlis Gallery
Al Fahidi Neighbourhood,
Bur Dubai, tel: 04-353 6233;
www.themajlisgallery.com
The UAE's oldest gallery, showing
original art by well-known artists for
sale in old wind-towered house.

thejamjar
RKM Properties, Street 17a, Comm
368, Al Quoz 3, tel: 04-341 7303;
www.thejamjardubai.com
Exhibits work by local and
international artists and also runs
assorted community projects and art
classes.

The Third Line
Street 6, Al Quoz 3, next to The
Courtyard, tel: 04-341 1367;
www.thethirdline.com
Displays work by contemporary
Middle Eastern artists.

XVA Gallery
Al Fahidi Neighbourhood, Bur Dubai,
tel: 04-353 5383; www.xvagallery.com
Long-established gallery-café in fine
traditional building.

Sharjah
Sharjah Art Museum
Tel: 06-568 8222, www.sharjah
museums.ae
Exhibitions of cutting-edge new
Middle Eastern art.

Cinema
Note that films are commonly
censored, with anything of a remotely
sexual nature (or featuring anything
approaching nudity) removed.

Abu Dhabi
Cine Royal
Khalidiya Mall, tel: 02-681 9444;
www.cineroyal.ae
Novo Cinemas
https://novocinemas.com
Locations include Abu Dhabi Mall,
BAS Mall – Baniyas and WTC Mall.
Vox Cinema
Marina Mall, tel: 02-681 8484;
www.voxcinemas.com

Dubai
Novo Cinemas
Tel: 04 232 85 23; https://novo
cinemas.com.
The city's largest cinema chain, with
a range of multiplexes, including the
Cineplex at Wafi, in the Galleria Mall
in Jumeirah, Cinecity at Al Ghurair
City, the Megaplex at Ibn Battuta Mall
and the Dubai Festival City Mall.
Movies Under the Stars
Rooftop Gardens, Wafi, Oud Metha;
tel: 04-324 4100; www.wafi.com
Free open-air movie screening on
Sunday evenings from October to
May (starting at 8pm), with seating on
beanbags.
Vox Cinemas
www.voxcinemas.com. Two large
modern mulitplexes, at Deira City
Centre and the Mall of the Emirates.

Sharjah
Sahara
Buhairah Centre, Mega Mall and
Sahara Mall Centre; https://novo
cinemas.com

NIGHTLIFE

The UAE boasts a fair selection of
Western-style nightlife, mainly in
Dubai, while Abu Dhabi is gradually
catching up, based around a mix of
British-style pubs, elegant bars and a
small number of clubs.

Pubs and Bars

Abu Dhabi
Belgian Café
InterContinental Hotel, Al Bateen
Convivial Belgian style café-bar, with
speciality beers and good food.
Brauhaus
Beach Rotana Hotel, Tourist Club Area
Lively German-style pub-cum-
restaurant, with speciality beers
on tap or by the bottle, plus a good
selection of German-style food.

Captain's Arms
Le Méridien Hotel, Tourist Club Area,
www.captainsarms-abudhabi.com
Popular British-style pub with good
array of draught beers and outdoor
seating overlooking the hotel gardens.
Jazzbar
Hilton Hotel, Corniche
Long-established nightspot with good
live jazz (nightly), candlelit tables and
cocktails. Usually fairly chilled-out,
although can get lively later on.
Left Bank
Souk Qaryat al Beri
This chic bar-restaurant is a bit of a
hike from the centre, although worth
it for the superb views, cool decor
and good music, with nightly DJ and
dance floor.
P.J. O'Reillys
Le Royal Méridien, Al Markaziyah,
www.pjspubabudhabi.com
Perennially popular Irish pub, often
with the best – or at least noisiest –
atmosphere in town, with regular DJs
or live bands and a bit of a dance floor.
Sax Club
Le Royal Méridien, Al Markaziyah
One of the city's more glamorous
drinking venues, with moody lighting,
swanky cocktails and one of Abu
Dhabi's more fashionable crowds.
Live band and DJ nightly.
Yacht Club
InterContinental Hotel, Al Bateen
Smooth modern bar and terrace
overlooking the marina with a fancy
drinks lists and good food.

Dubai
360°
Jumeirah Beach Hotel
Dubai's ultimate chill-out bar, on a
breakwater amidst the waves facing
the Burj al Arab with a very cool crowd
and regular DJs.
Alta Badia Bar
Emirates Towers
Cool chrome-and-glass bar at the
summit of the Emirates Tower with
huge views and an almost equally big
drinks list.
The Agency
Emirates Towers Boulevard, Sheikh
Zayed Road
The city's top wine bar, with a huge list
of international tipples.
Bahri Bar
Mina A'Salam Hotel, Madinat
Jumeirah
Seductive little bar with Moroccan-
style decor and peerless views of the
Burj al Arab from the outside terrace.
Bar 44
Grosvenor House, Dubai Marina,
www.bar44-dubai.com
Cool cocktail bar atop the soaring
Grosvenor House hotel, with

unrivalled Marina views, fancy drinks and a dressy crowd.

Barasti Bar
Le Méridien Mina Sehayi, Dubai Marina, http://barastibeach.com
Enduringly popular nightspot on the beach, with a lively pub-style deck upstairs and a cooler chill-out area on the beach below. Regular live DJs.

Belgium Beer Café
Crowne Plaza Hotel, Festival City, www.belgianbeercafe.com
Surprisingly authentic Belgian-style pub-cum-restaurant, with an excellent range of speciality beers and good traditional Belgian cuisine. Two more locations in Dubai.

Blue Bar
Novotel, World Trade Centre, Sheikh Zayed Road
Cool bar with a good selection of speciality Belgian beers and live music (mainly blues and soul) later on.

Cin Cin
Fairmont Hotel, Sheikh Zayed Road
Very exclusive bar boasting soothing decor, a huge list of wines, vodkas and whiskies, plus cigar bar. Live DJ some nights.

Eclipse
InterContinental Hotel, Festival City
Smooth modern bar at the top of the Festival City InterContinental, with a good drinks list and sweeping city views.

Long's Bar
Towers Rotana Hotel, Sheikh Zayed Road
Lively pub with probably the longest bar in the Middle East.

Neos
The Address, Downtown Dubai
One of the highest bars in Dubai, with vertiginous views over the surrounding Downtown Dubai and Burj Khalifa.

Rooftop Terrace & Sports Lounge
Arabian Courtyard, One&Only Royal Mirage, Dubai Marina
Opulent Arabian-style rooftop bar.

Skyview Bar
Burj al Arab
At the top of the Burj al Arab, with psychedelic decor and vast sea and city views. Minimum spend of Dhs350 per person, and you'll need to reserve in advance on tel: 04-301 7600 or BAArestaurants@jumeirah.com.

Sho-Cho
Dubai Marine Beach Resort, Jumeirah, www.sho-cho.com
Chic and very posey little bar-cum-Japanese restaurant, eternally popular amongst the city's Lebanese and Bollywood party crowd. Live DJ most nights.

The Terrace
Park Hyatt, Garhoud

Alluring, upmarket Creekside terrace-bar, with lovely waterside views and a very chilled-out atmosphere.

Viceroy Bar
Four Points Sheraton, Khalid Bin al Waleed Road, Bur Dubai, www.the viceroypub.com
One of the nicest English-style pubs in town, with cosy wood-panelled interior and decent drinks and food.

Clubs

Abu Dhabi

Luce
Danat Al Ain Resort
Al Ain's most stylish venue mixes upmarket Italian restaurant with stylish lounge bar which kicks on into the small hours, ably assisted by live Latin band.

Rock Bottom Café
Al Diar Capital Hotel, Al Markaziyah
Unashamedly downmarket venue, always lively, with nightly DJ and/or live band.

Dubai

Boudoir
Dubai Marine Beach Resort, Jumeirah, http://clubboudoirdubai.com
Chintzy bar-cum-nightclub – it looks a bit like a 19th-century French brothel – attracting a cashed-up selection of expats and the city's Lebanese party crowd drowning in cocktails and champagne. Live DJs nightly.

Chi@The Lodge
Oud Metha, next to Al Nasr Leisureland
The biggest club in the Middle East, with room for 3,500 revellers. Hosts regular big-name international DJs and occasional bands.

Zinc
Crowne Plaza Hotel, Sheikh Zayed Road, www.facebook.com/zinc nightclub
The longest-running club in Dubai, kept afloat by its relatively attitude-free atmosphere, eclectic soundtrack and general reputation for unpretentious dancing and partying.

SPORTS

The UAE offers numerous choices for summer sports: there are long, deserted beaches open to the public, desert and mountains to explore, and pools, sports facilities and clubs in the cities. Many independent sports clubs and hotels have gymnasiums, swimming pools and tennis courts where daily entrance rates are usually available.

Other sports available include abseiling, aqua-biking, deep-sea fishing, dune-buggy driving, fishing, golf, polo, ice-skating, go-karting, sailing, sand-skiing, skiing, water sports of all kinds and more. Horse and camel races usually take place on Thursday and Friday during the cooler winter months, and are open to everyone. Dhow sailing and racing are memorable sights – see press for details.

Major tournaments that attract world-class players, including golf, tennis, powerboat racing and horse racing, are also held throughout the winter – see the Sports and Outdoor Activities chapter on page 103 for more information.

Diving and Watersports

In Dubai, the beachfront resort hotels are the easiest places to arrange watersports. All the marina beach hotels (apart from the Ritz-Carlton) have their own watersports centres, with activities including windsurfing, sailing, kayaking, water-skiing, wakeboarding and parasailing. Local operators include **Sky & Sea Adventure** (tel: 04-399 9005, www.watersportsdubai.com), who can be found at the Hilton Jumeirah Resort.

Watersports can also be arranged in Abu Dhabi through **Sea Hawk** (tel: 02-673 6688; www.sea-hawk.ae), in Al Ain through **Wadi Adventure** (tel: 03-781 8422; www.wadiadventure. ae) and in Fujairah through the **Sandy Beach Hotel** (tel: 09-244 5555, http://sandybeachhotel.ae).

The best diving in the UAE is off the east coast; alternatively, the superb dive sites of the Musandam peninsula in Oman are also within easy striking distance.

Al Boom Diving
Tel: 04-342 2993, www.alboomdiving. com
Runs dive centres at the Atlantis The Palm, the Aqua Centre Jumeirah in Dubai, and at the Al Aqah Méridien hotel in Fujairah, offering a range of PADI courses and dives, plus Musandam excursions.

Pavilion Dive Centre
Jumeirah Beach Hotel, Dubai, tel: 04-406 8828, www.jumeirah.com
PADI courses and introductory dives, plus trips to nearby wrecks and to Musandam.

Sandy Beach Hotel
Al Aqah Beach, Fujairah, tel: 09-244 5555, http://sandybeachhotel.ae
Excellent base for east-coast dive sites.

OMAN

THE UAE

LANGUAGE

Golf Courses

Abu Dhabi

AD City Golf Club
Al Mushrif, tel: 02-445 9600,
www.adcitygolf.ae
Verdant nine-hole course close to city
centre.
AD Golf Club
Umm an Nar, tel: 02-558 8990,
www.adgolfclub.com
Championship-standard course
and home to the Abu Dhabi Golf
Championship.
Al Ghazal Golf Club
Near Airport, tel: 02-575 8044,
www.alghazalgolf.ae
One of the world's finest sand
courses.
Yas Links
Yas Island, tel: 02-810 7710,
www.yaslinks.com
Superb new 18-hole course (plus
floodlit 9-hole par-3 course).

Dubai

Al Badia Golf Course
Festival City, tel: 04-601 0101,
www.albadiagolfclub.ae
Attractive Creekside course designed
by Robert Trent Jones II with
numerous water features.
Arabian Ranches Golf Club
Arabian Ranches, Dubailand, tel:
04-366 4700, www.arabianranches
golfdubai.com
Links-style grass course set in the
middle of natural desert.
Dubai Creek Golf Club
Garhoud, tel: 04-380 1234,
www.dubaigolf.com
Superb Creekside course (designed
by Thomas Bjorn). Also has a floodlit
9-hole par-3 course.
The Els Club
Dubai Sports City, Dubailand, tel:
04-425 1000, www.elsclubdubai.com
"Desert links" course with greens and
fairways surrounded by rolling dunes
and untouched desert.
Emirates Golf Club
Dubai Marina, tel: 04-380 1234,
www.dubaigolf.com
The oldest all-grass championship
course in the Gulf, and current home
of the Dubai Desert Classic.
Jumeirah Golf Estates
Dubai Marina, tel: 04-375 9999,
www.jumeirahgolfestates.com
Four separate state-of-the-art courses
– "Fire", "Earth", "Water" and "Wind"
(designed by Greg Norman, Vijay
Singh, Sergio Garcia and Pete Dye) –
set amidst dramatic desert scenery.
The Montgomerie Dubai
Dubai Marina, tel: 04-390 5600,
www.themontgomerie.com

Links-style course designed by Colin
Montgomerie.

Skiing

Ski Dubai
Mall of the Emirates, www.skidxb.com
The first indoor ski resort in the
Middle East, with real snow and five
runs.

Sports Clubs

Abu Dhabi

AD Chess Club
Tel: 02-633 1110, www.abudhabi
chess.com
AD Country Club
Tel: 02-657 7777, www.adcountryclub.
com
Gym, fitness classes, tennis, squash
and other sports.
AD Equestrian Club
Tel: 02-445 5500, www.adec-web.com.
AD Harlequins Rugby Club
www.abudhabiquins.com
The Club
Tel: 02-673 1111, www.the-club.com
Wide range of sports including
tennis, squash, sailing, kayaking and
climbing.

Dubai

Dubai Archers
www.dubaiarchers.com
Dubai Exiles RFC (rugby)
Tel: 055-997 4948, www.dubaiexiles.
com
**Dubai International Marine Club
(sailing)**
Tel: 04-399 5777, www.dimc.ae
Dubai Polo and Equestrian Club
Tel: 04-361 8111, www.poloclubdubai.
com
Dubai Roadsters (cycling)
www.dubairoadsters.com
Jebel Ali Equestrian Club
Tel: 04-884 5101, www.facebook.
com/JebelAliEquestrianClub
Jebel Ali Shooting Club
Tel: 04-883 0828

SHOPPING

Shopping in the UAE is an intriguing
blend of the contemporary and
traditional, and although the country
has been taken over by vast modern
shopping malls, traditional souks
survive in many places. Dubai is far
and away the best place to shop
(and even has its own shopping
festival; www.mydsf.ae), with a string
of landmark shopping complexes,
including the vast Dubai Mall, as
well fascinating souks of Deira and

Bur Dubai. Abu Dhabi is less well
equipped, although there are a
couple of good malls and some other
interesting shops, while Sharjah
boasts a pair of wonderful souks.
Elsewhere, shopping opportunities
are rather limited.
   Goods on offer are similarly
diverse, ranging from top-fashion
designer-label fashion and cutting-
edge electronics to traditional
jewellery, perfumes, dates and spices.
Bargaining is expected in the souks,
but in the shopping malls prices are
usually fixed.

What to Buy

Good buys in the country include
gold and other **precious stones**
(particularly diamonds), which sell
here for considerably less than in the
West. Antique Bedu **silver jewellery**
can also be found, at a price. **Carpets**
can be a good buy, too – the cheapest
are at the Blue Souk in Sharjah, and
there is also a reasonable selection
in Deira Tower on Baniyas Square.
Spices of all kinds are notably
cheaper here than in the West. It
is also fun to buy some **perfume** –
most shops will help you mix up your
own personalised bespoke scent if
you don't like any of the brands on
offer. Colourful souvenirs range from
traditional Arabian **coffee pots** to
kitsch Burj al Arab **paperweights**.

Abu Dhabi

Souks

The central souk (at Khalifa Street)
was demolished in 2005 and
replaced as the stunning new **Central
Market** (www.centralmarket.ae/souk)
by Foster + Partners, housing a range
of upmarket boutiques and smaller
crafts shops.
   Madinat Zayed (on East Road,
near the Post Office) is where
you'll find Abu Dhabi's **Gold Souk**,
with two storeys of shops inside a
modern mall.
   A string of low-key markets can be
found dotted around **Al Mina district**
– Abu Dhabi's nearest equivalent to
a traditional souk. The Carpet Souk
is a square of shops selling a mix
of low-grade factory rugs and more
collectable items, while the nearby
Food Souk boasts a good selection
of little date shops. Past here the
Iranian Souk – despite its colourful
name – is mainly devoted to the sale
of household goods and plants.
   At the **Heritage Village**, you can
see craftsmen making glassware,

leather goods and silverware, all of which are for sale.

At the far western end of the city, between Maqta and Musaffah bridges (not far from the Sheikh Zayed Grand Mosque), the new waterside **Souk Qaryat al Beri** (http://soukqaryatalberi.com) features attractive modern Arabian decor and a small but select array of upmarket boutiques, jewellers and other outlets.

Shopping malls
Abu Dhabi Mall
Near the Beach Rotana Hotel, Tourist Club Area, www.abudhabi-mall.com
Abu Dhabi's ritziest mall, with a wide range of designer outlets plus more workaday shops.
Marina Mall
On the Breakwater, near Emirates Palace, www.marinamall.ae
Attractive modern mall arranged around a couple of large courtyards under tent-like roofs. The soaring Burj al Marina (Marina Tower) at the back offers great city views from its top-floor restaurant and coffee shop.

Dubai

Dubai is famous for its shopping – things are particularly lively during the annual Dubai Shopping Festival (Jan–late Feb, www.mydsf.ae), when stores across the city slash prices and the malls are engulfed in crazed consumers.

Souks
Gold Souk, Sikkat al Khail Street
Deira. The region's most famous gold souk, selling a vast range of gold jewellery in Arabian and European designs, very competitively priced, as well as other precious stones.
Karama Souk, Karama. Infamous for its designer fakes – although prices are higher than you might expect.
Khan Murjan Souk, Wafi, Oud Metha.
Gorgeous modern recreation of legendary Baghdad market, hosting well over 100 upmarket craft shops.
Souk Madinat Jumeirah, Madinat Jumeirah. Lovely modern souk in traditional quasi-Moroccan style.
Good, though relatively expensive, handicrafts.
Spice Souk, Deira. A couple of alleyways piled up with huge sacks of spices and other regional produce – frankincense, saffron, dried lemons, rose petals and so on.

Shopping malls
BurJuman
Khalid Bin al Waleed Roads, Bur Dubai, www.burjuman.com

Shoppers at the Gold Souk.

The biggest mall in the old city centre; the glitzy southern extension is good for designer fashion.
Dubai Festival City Mall
Festival City, www.festivalcentre.com
Large, colourfully designed mall at heart of Festival City development in an attractive Creekside location.
Dubai Mall
Downtown Dubai, www.thedubaimall.com
The world's biggest mall, with a staggering 1,200-odd shops.
"Fashion Avenue" is home to the biggest array of designer labels in Dubai, while the in-house "Gold Souk" houses a further 120 shops selling gold, jewellery and Arabian perfumes and artefacts.
Emirates Towers Boulevard
Emirates Towers, Sheikh Zayed Road
Small but very exclusive mall stuffed with high-end fashion and jewellery shops.
Ibn Battuta Mall
Between interchanges 5 and 6, Sheikh Zayed Road, www.ibnbattutamall.com
Dubai's quirkiest mall.
Mall of the Emirates
Interchange 4, Sheikh Zayed Road, www.malloftheemirates.com
Second-largest mall in the city, full of excellent, largely upmarket shops – particularly good for fashion.
Mercato
Jumeirah Beach Road, Jumeirah, www.mercatoshoppingmall.com
Quirky Italian-themed mall hosts a small but well-chosen range of shops.
Good for clothes.
The Village Mall, Jumeirah Beach Road, www.thevillagedubai.com
Small mall, home to a clutch of interesting independent boutiques.
Wafi
Oud Metha, www.wafi.com

This zany Egyptian-themed mall has a good range of shops, and is usually a lot more peaceful than many other places in the city.

Sharjah

Central Souk (also known as the Blue Souk)
Next to Sharjah Creek. Two huge blue-domed buildings full of mainly ordinary shops on the ground floor, but a treasure trove of antique furniture, carpets and Gulf mementoes awaits upstairs – particularly good for carpets.
Al Arsa Souk (Old Souk)
Behind Borj Avenue. Lovely little traditional souk full of handicrafts shops, and with an excellent coffee house.

CHILDREN'S ACTIVITIES

Abu Dhabi

Abu Dhabi Ice Rink
Tel: 02-403 4333; www.zsc.ae
Off Airport Road near Zayed Sports City Stadium. Olympic-size rink with teachers on hand plus ice hockey lessons at the weekend.
Ferrari World
Yas Island, tel: 02-496 8000; www.ferrariworldabudhabi.com
Huge new theme park featuring all manner of rides, including the world's fastest rollercoaster.

Al Ain

Al Ain Zoo
South of town, tel: 03-799 2000; www.awpr.ae
Spacious, well-run wildlife park.

OMAN

THE UAE

LANGUAGE

Dubai

Many of the beachside hotels have dedicated kids' clubs, while most of the larger malls also have children's play areas catering for all ages – these include **Fun City** (Arabian Centre, Century Mall, Ibn Battuta Mall, Lamcy Plaza, Mercato, Oasis Centre, Reef Mall; http://funcity.ae), **Magic Planet** (Mall of the Emirates and Deira City Centre) and the **Wafi Encounter Zone** at the Wafi mall.

Aquaventure
Atlantis, The Palm Jumeirah, tel: 04-426 2000; www.atlantisthepalm.com
Superb water park, centred on stunning Ziggurat and the stomach-churning "Leap of Faith".

Dolphin Bay
Atlantis, The Palm Jumeirah, tel: 04-426 2000; www.atlantisthepalm.com
Swim with dolphins.

Children's City
Creekside Park, Oud Metha; www.childrencity.ae
Fun "edu-tainment" complex with displays and interactive exhibits on a variety of themes.

Dubai Aquarium and Underwater Zoo
Dubai Mall, tel: 04-448 5200; www.thedubaiaquarium.com
Spectacular aquarium.

Dubai Dolphinarium
Next to Gate #1 at Creekside Park, tel: 04-336 9773; www.dubaidolphinarium.ae
Twice-daily dolphin shows plus interactive swimming sessions.

Dubai Ice Rink
Dubai Mall, tel: 04-448 5111; www.dubaiicerink.com
Olympic-size rink.

Dubai Zoo
Beach Road, Jumeirah, tel: 04-349 6444
Old-fashioned zoo.

KidZania
Dubai Mall, tel: 04-448 5222; www.kidzania.com
Innovative attraction based on an imaginary city where kids can dress up and role-play a variety of adult characters, from airline pilot to archaeologist.

Lost Chambers
Atlantis, The Palm Jumeirah, tel: 04-426 2000; www.atlantisthepalm.com
Stunning subterranean aquarium dotted with kooky "ancient ruins".

Sega Republic
Dubai Mall, tel: 04-448 8484; www.segarepublic.com
State-of-the-art indoor theme park featuring a range of adrenalin-

You can even learn to ski in Dubai, as shown here at Ski Dubai.

pumping rides and other amusements.

Ski Dubai
Mall of the Emirates, www.skidxb.com
Go skiing, build snowmen or chuck snowballs at the Gulf's first ski-slope.

Wild Wadi
Next to Jumeirah Beach Hotel, tel: 04-348 4444; www.jumeirah.com/en/hotels-resorts/dubai/wild-wadi
Brilliant water park with rides and slides to suit all ages.

Wonderland
Oud Metha, next to Garhoud Bridge; www.wonderlanduae.com
Old-fashioned theme park with a variety of rides and the modest Splashland water park.

Umm al Qaiwain

Dreamland Aqua Park
Ras al Khaimah Road, 17km (10.5 miles) past Umm al Qaiwain, tel: 06-768 1888; www.dreamlanduae.com
Large, well-equipped water park.

TOUR OPERATORS

There are numerous tour operators in Dubai (along with a smaller number in Abu Dhabi and elsewhere), all offering largely the same trips: city tours, trips to neighbouring emirates, desert safaris and dhow cruises. Arabian Adventures is the biggest and best run, although the following are all reliable. It's easiest to book by phone at most places, as offices are often inconveniently located and tricky to find (with the exception of Arabian Adventures, which has a travel desk in a number of leading hotels in Dubai and at Le Méridien in

Fujairah). All operators will pick you up from your hotel.

Abu Dhabi

Desert Adventures, Al Raha Beach Hotel, tel: 02-556 6155, www.desertadventures.com
Net Tours, Khalifa Street, near Sheraton Hotel, tel: 02-679 4656, http://nettoursuae.ae **Orient Tours**, tel: 02-667 5609, www.orienttours.ae
Sunshine Tours, tel: 02-444 9914, www.adnh.com

Dubai

Alpha Tours, tel: 04-701 9111, www.alphatoursdubai.com
Arabian Adventures, tel: 04-214 4888, www.arabian-adventures.com
Branches in a number of hotels across the city.
Balloon Adventures Dubai, tel: 04-285 4949, www.ballooning.ae
Hot-air ballooning over the desert.
The Big Bus Company, tel: 04-340 7709, www.bigbustours.com
Double-decker bus tours of the major sights in hop-on, hop-off open-top buses.
Desert Adventures, tel: 04-450 4450, www.desertadventures.com
Net Tours, tel: 04-376 2333, www.netgroupdubai.com
Orient Tours, tel: 04-282 8238, www.orienttours.ae
Wonder Bus Tours, tel: 04-359 5656, www.wonderbustours.net
Bur Juman Centre, Bur Dubai. Tours of city and Creek aboard an amphibious vehicle – half bus, half boat.

Sharjah

Orient Tours, Al Aruba Street, tel: 06-568 2323, www.orienttours.ae

A – Z

A HANDY SUMMARY
OF PRACTICAL INFORMATION

A

Admission Charges

Admission charges to government-run heritage sites, museums and parks are extremely modest, sometimes free, never more than Dhs5. Conversely, entrance fees to privately run attractions can be stratospheric, particularly for families – excursions to attractions like Ski Dubai, either of the Dubai water parks, the observation deck at the Burj Khalifa or Ferrari World in Abu Dhabi can put a significant dent in your finances, often pushing north of US$100 for two adults and a couple of kids.

Age Restrictions

Car-rental agencies require drivers to be at least 21, rising to 25 and 30 for 4x4, although this is sometimes waived upon payment of a "young driver" surcharge. Children under 10 are not allowed to sit in the front passenger seat of cars, while the minimum age for entry to bars and nightclubs varies between 18 and 21. On the water and in some theme parks, the minimum age for activities is seven or eight, but it also depends on the child's height (often with a minimum of 1.1 metres/3ft 6ins). For diving lessons, the minimum age for junior open-water training is 10, but children can begin learning in a pool from the age of eight.

B

Budgeting for Your Trip

The cost for a standard double room ranges from around Dhs350 per night in a one-star city-centre hotel to Dhs575–1,000 at a four-star hotel and Dhs1,000-3,500 at a five-star hotel. Sandwiches and curries from street-level restaurants can be bought for as little as Dhs5–10. Main courses in most decent Western-style, non-hotel restaurants are between Dhs25–45. For fine dining, allow upwards of Dhs55 per person for mains. Soft drinks start at Dhs1 in shops but are heavily marked up in restaurants. Imported alcoholic drinks tend to be more expensive than in the West.

Generally taxis are significantly cheaper than those in Western cities (although the fare from Dubai Airport comes with a Dhs20 mark-up). Bus tickets offer good value, costing around Dh3, while a creek crossing on a traditional *abra* is just Dhs1.

Package deals arranged from your home country are likely to be cheaper than separately arranged air travel and accommodation. The best prices occur in low season (July–Sep), when the UAE is at its hottest.

C

Children

Childcare facilities are on a par with those in the West. Most malls have changing facilities in the women's public toilets; many also have supervised indoor play areas. Many of the more upmarket beach resorts also have kids' club and babysitting services.

Climate

Summers are very hot. From **May to September** daytime temperatures are rarely below 40°C (104°F), with humidity up to 90 percent.

From **October to April** there is very good weather (sunny and warm), with temperatures ranging from as low as 10°C (50°F) inland to 30°C (mid-80s°F), with little or no humidity. However, strong winds sometimes bring sandstorms, and it occasionally rains very heavily. The rain usually comes sometime from January to March, and can result in large areas of flooding. The desert inland gets much colder than the coastal regions at night and during the winter months.

What to bring

In the summer months it is extremely hot, so bring a sun hat, sunblock and wear cool cotton clothes. A jumper or jacket is needed at night in the cooler winter months. Women are advised to wear modest clothes in the streets, particularly in the souks, so avoid short shorts and skirts

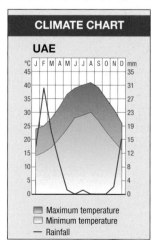

CLIMATE CHART

UAE

Legend:
- ☐ Maximum temperature
- ☐ Minimum temperature
- — Rainfall

Sand dunes at Liwa, Abu Dhabi.

and keep your shoulders covered to avoid unwanted attention and risk offending anyone. Men should not bare their torsos for the same reason. On the beaches swimsuits, shorts or bikinis are fine. In Sharjah, women are only allowed to wear swimwear on private beaches. For business a light suit is useful.

Crime and Safety

The UAE is generally a safe country for both men and women. The crime rate is low: major crimes are relatively rare, and even petty theft is less common than in most other countries. The level of personal security is also high: for women to avoid personal harassment not walking around alone at night is recommended, but there is no real physical danger.

Taxis are safe to take during the day, or at night within towns as long as a woman is wearing demure clothing and knows her route so that she can avoid being taken on a "detour". Fares, except in metered taxis, should be agreed in advance, to avoid arguments at the end of the journey. Inter-emirate registered taxis are fine, and taxi shares are safe for women in the day. At night, lone women are advised not to get a taxi out of town into desert areas, or for a long inter-emirate drive.

Customs Regulations

Duty-free goods can be brought into the country:
400 cigarettes or 0.5kg loose tobacco.
Non-Muslims can bring in 4 litres of alcohol (or 12 cans of beer), unless you are arriving in Sharjah where

alcohol is prohibited. You are not allowed to bring in alcohol if arriving overland. Check these allowances have not changed when you travel.

Books and magazines are expensive, so it's wise to bring some paperbacks to read, avoiding any that may cause offence. The same applies to DVDs and videos. There are also severe penalties if you are found carrying drugs. This applies not only to carrying drugs but also, potentially, if you have drugs in your bloodstream or any other evidence of being in possession of illegal substances – one man was jailed on account of microscopic quantities of cannabis found in a piece of gum stuck to the sole of his shoe. Prescription medicines can also get you into trouble – either carry a letter from your doctor explaining that these are needed for health reasons or, if at all possible, leave them at home.

D

Disabled Travellers

Many of the country's better hotels now have specially adapted rooms for disabled travellers, while some modern malls also have disabled parking spaces and specially equipped toilets. Dubai is particularly accessible. Dubai Taxi (tel: 04-208 0000; www.dubaitaxi.ae) has specially designed vehicles equipped with ramps and lifts, while the metro features tactile guide paths, lifts and ramps to assist visually and mobility-impaired visitors, as well as wheelchair spaces in all compartments. The city's water buses

can also be used by mobility-impaired visitors, and staff will assist you in boarding and disembarking, while there are also dedicated facilities for passengers with special needs at the airport. Sadly, but not surprisingly, most of the country's older heritage buildings are not accessible.

E

Electricity

220/240 volts. The majority of sockets accept three square-pin 13-amp British-style plugs. Adaptors for two-pin appliances can be bought in supermarkets.

Embassies and Consulates

As Abu Dhabi, not Dubai, is the federal capital of the UAE, Dubai tends to have foreign consulates rather than embassies. Embassies are usually open 8.30am–1.30pm, with all closing on Friday and some closing on Saturday.

Abu Dhabi

Australia, Al Muhairy Centre, Sheikh Zayed the First Street, tel: 02-401 7500; www.uae.embassy.gov.au
Canada, Abu Dhabi Trade Towers (Abu Dhabi Mall), West Tower, tel: 02-694 0300; www.canadainternational.gc.ca/uae-eau
Ireland: 2 Khalifa Al Suwaidi Development,Road 19 off 32nd Street, Al Bateen, tel: 02-495 8200; www.embassyofireland.ae
UK, Khalid Bin al Waleed Street (Street 22), tel: 02-610 1100, http://ukinuae.fco.gov.uk/en
US, off Airport Road, tel: 02-414 2200; http://abudhabi.usembassy.gov

Dubai (Consulates)

Australia: Bur Juman Business Tower, Khalifa bin Zayed Road; tel: 04-508 7100; www.uae.embassy.gov.au
Canada: 19th Floor, Jumeirah Emirates Towers (Business Tower), Sheikh Zayed Road; tel: 04-404 8444; www.canadainternational.gc.ca/uae-eau
New Zealand: Jumeirah Emirates Towers (Business Tower), Sheikh Zayed Road; tel: 04-331 7500; www.nzte.govt.nz
South Africa: 3rd Floor, New Sharaf Building, Khalid Bin Al Waleed Street, Bur Dubai ; tel: 04-397 5222; www.dirco.gov.za/dubai
UK: Al Seef Road, Bur Dubai; tel: 04-309 4444; http://ukinuae.fco.gov.uk/en

Emergency Numbers

Police and ambulance, tel: 999
Fire, tel: 997
**Dubai Police Headquarters,
tel:** 901 (contact centre, non-
emergency enquiries); www.dubai
police.gov.ae
**Dubai Police Tourist Security
Department, tel:** 800 243

US: at the corner of Al Seef Road
and Sheikh Khalifa bin Zayed Road;
tel: 04-309 4000; http://dubai.
usconsulate.gov

UAE Embassies

UAE Embassy in London
30 Princes Gate, London SW7
1PT, tel: 020-7581 1281 (Mon–Fri
9am–4pm); www.uaeembassyuk.net
UAE Embassy in Washington
3522 International Court, NW
Washington DC 20008, tel: 202-243
2400; www.uae-embassy.org

Etiquette

Although the UAE is a very liberal
country compared with other
states in the Gulf region, it is still a
conservative Muslim country, and
visitors should respect this. Women
especially should remember that
clothing that is acceptable in a
nightclub or on the beach is not
appropriate to wear on the street
during the day.
    Outside the cities, dress more
conservatively. Everyone should cover
their upper arms and women should
wear longer skirts or trousers. Men
should not wear shorts in a business
situation.
    During the holy month of Ramadan
don't eat, smoke or drink in public.
Never drink and drive as you could
end up in jail for a month, and don't
offer alcohol to Muslims.
    If visiting the home of a UAE citizen
it is customary to remove shoes
before venturing on the carpets,
though increasingly many local
families no longer follow this custom.
Avoid showing the soles of your feet
when sitting down. If you wish to
take a present, a box of pastries or
sweetmeats is a safe option.

G

Gay and Lesbian Travellers

Homosexuality is not tolerated in
the UAE and is officially illegal, so
discretion is strongly advised.

H

Health and Medical Care

Travel insurance is advisable as
healthcare can be expensive,
although there are good government
hospitals as well as numerous private
clinics.
    No special injections are required
for the UAE. Cholera and yellow
fever certificates are only necessary
if you arrive from an infected area.
It is wise to drink bottled water.
The drinking water is safe, but
your system may not have time to
acclimatise.
    You can buy most items in the UAE,
but if you're taking certain medicines
then you should bring a supply with
you. Just make sure you can also
produce a prescription if asked, as
certain drugs that are readily available
in the West are prohibited in the UAE
without one.

Medical services

There are good government hospitals
where treatment is free to health-card
holders (only available with residence
visas).
    Emergency treatment is available
to everyone but it is often easier for
visitors to visit a private clinic and
make a health insurance claim rather
than spend time queuing in the
government hospitals.

Hospitals

Abu Dhabi
Al Noor Hospital, Khalifa Street,
tel: 02-626 5265, 800 26422,
www.alnoorhospital.com.

Kids on the beach in Ajman.

Dubai
Dubai Hospital, between the
Corniche and Baraha Street, Deira,
tel: 04-219 5000, http://web.dohms.
gov.ae/dh.
Rashid Hospital, off Oud Metha
Road, near Maktoum Bridge, Oud
Metha, tel: 04-219 1000
Latifa Hospital (formerly Wasl), Oud
Metha Road (just west of Wafi), Oud
Metha, tel: 04-324 1111.

Private clinics

Abu Dhabi
Gulf Diagnostic Centre, 30th Street
(Khaleej Al Arabi Street), tel: 02-417
7222, www.gdc-hospital.com.
New National Medical Centre,
several locations, tel: 02-633 2255,
www.nmc.ae.
Dubai
Al Borj Medical Centre, Al-mazaya
centre,Sheikh Zayed Road, tel:
04-321 2220; www.alborjclinic.com.
**Dubai London Clinic and Speciality
Hospital**, several locations, tel: 800
352, www.dubailondonclinic.com.
General Medical Centre, Magrudy's
Centre, Jumeirah Road; tel: 04-349
4880, www.gmcclinics.com.
Manchester Clinic, each,
Jumeirah Road, tel: 04-344 0300,
www.manchester-clinic.com.
Sharjah
Al Zahra Private Hospital, Al Zahra
Square (Clocktower Roundabout), tel:
06-561 9999, www.alzahra.com.

Dentists

Abu Dhabi
Advanced American Dental Centre,
behind BMW showroom, Al Bateen,
tel: 02-681 2921.

OMAN

THE UAE

LANGUAGE

Dubai

American Dental Clinic, Villa 54, next to Dubai Zoo, Beach Road, Jumeirah, tel: 04-344 0668; www.americandentalclinic.com.
British Dental Clinic, Al Wasl Road, Jumeirah, tel: 04-342 1318, www.britishdentalclinic.com.

I

Internet

Internet access is provided by the two national telecoms providers, Etisalat (www.etisalat.ae) and Du (www.du.ae), although access to certain websites may be blocked due to political, religious or sexual content. Internet connectivity is available in the guest rooms and business centres of larger hotels, although often at exorbitant rates. Internet cafés are surprisingly thin on the ground. In Dubai, the easiest place to get online is Bur Dubai (where internet cafés can be found in small roads and alleyways off Al Fahidi Street).

However, many restaurants, cafés and shopping malls now offer free Wi-Fi, so things are a lot easier if you have your own Wi-Fi-enabled laptop, tablet or phone. The whole of the Dubai Mall is a free Wi-Fi hotspot and you can also get online for free on the Dubai Metro, at the Dubai airport (up to 30 minutes), along Mohammed Bin Rashid Boulevard and in the DIFC. Look for free Wi-Fi and charging points in major Dubai parks and beaches. You can also surf the internet for free at the Abu Dhabi airport and in many cafés, including Costa and Starbucks. Various Wi-Fi hotspots are also operated by Etisalat and Du, which offer access at numerous places around the main cities, including many malls, numerous coffee shops and selected hotels, with various pay-as-you-go packages. See the websites for full details of charges and hotspot locations.

L

Lost Property

If you lose your property, call the relevant authority or organisation in the general area where you believe you lost your belongings. This might be the local police station, mall management office, taxi company, hotel or bar. The

An Abu Dhabi camel farm.

number for lost property (Baggage Services) at Dubai International Airport is 04-224 5555, or email them via the lost and found form at www.dubaiairport.com. If you leave something in a taxi or on the metro, call the RTA on 800 9090.

M

Maps

Ongoing developments mean that maps of the UAE, Dubai in particular, are often out of date even before they're printed. The best local maps are published by Explorer, which produces a wide range of maps, regularly updated, covering the entire country and all its various cities and which are generally available in bookshops around the country. Good country maps include *Dubai Insight Flexi Map*.

Media

Print

The press in the UAE is not officially censored, although local journalists usually steer well clear of expressing negative or controversial opinions about local matters, making for a rather dull media. Local English-language newspapers are the broadsheet *Gulf News* (http://gulfnews.com), *Khaleej Times* (www.khaleejtimes.com), *The Gulf Today* (http://gulftoday.ae), and the tabloid *Emirates Today* (www.emirates247.com) and *7 Days* (http://7daysindubai.com), although easily the best local paper is *The*

National (www.thenational.ae), published in Abu Dhabi. If you want to read foreign newspapers, it is easiest to do so online.

The main sources of information on events, concerts and hotel functions in the UAE are *What's On* (http://whatson.ae), *Time Out Abu Dhabi* (monthly; www.timeout abudhabi.com) and *Time Out Dubai* (weekly; www.timeoutdubai.com), available at most bookshops and hotel newsagents.

Note that imported magazines are routinely censored, with any pictures showing nude or incompletely dressed women (or any other material which the authorities deem offensive) struck through with a black marker.

Broadcast media

The main English-language TV stations are Dubai's One (www.dcn. ae/dubaione) and Ajman TV (www. ajmantv.com). These show imported serials and English-language films, and most have news in English.

International satellite TV stations including CNN and BBC World News are almost always available on hotel TVs, which usually offer a vast range of satellite channels from across Arabia and Asia.

Dubai has a number of local English-language radio stations, including Virgin Radio Dubai (104.4FM; www.virginradiodubai.com) and Dubai 92 (92FM; www.dubai92. com), churning out mainstream Western pop and inane chat. In Abu Dhabi, Abu Dhabi Classic FM (www.adradio.ae/abudhabiclassicfm) broadcasts light classics, easy listening and world music at 87.9FM.

The BBC and Voice of America are also available on short- and medium-wave radio, as well as online.

Money

There are ATMs all over the UAE, most of which accept foreign Visa and MasterCard credit and debit cards. Any currency can be exchanged at one of the many banks or at money exchanges in all major malls. Money changers offer varying rates and are sometimes better value than banks.

Travellers' cheques are sometimes accepted in major shops and are easily exchanged at banks. It is best to have the purchase receipt with you. Credit cards are accepted in major hotels but anywhere else, check first. Smaller shops may add 5 percent to your bill if you pay by credit card. If you plan to bargain, you'll need cash.
Currency 1 UAE Dirham (abbreviated variously as dh, Dhs or AED) = 100 fils. The value of the dirham is linked to the US dollar at the rate of $1=Dhs3.6725.

Tipping

A tip of 10 percent is usually sufficient in restaurants, although note that many places automatically add a 10 percent "service charge" to your bill, in which case you might feel that a tip is not necessary. Supermarket employees who carry bags to your car are usually tipped, as are petrol attendants who wash your windscreens.

O

Opening Hours

The UAE runs on an Islamic calendar, with the weekend falling on Friday and Saturday. Government offices usually work from 7/7.30am–1.30pm Sun–Thu. International companies keep the hours of 9am–5pm Sun–Thu. Local companies and shops in souks typically open 9/10am–1/1.30pm and 4/4.30–9/10pm Sat–Thu. Generally, banks are open 8am–1pm Sat–Thu; some also open Fri 8am–noon. Larger shopping malls open from 10am–10pm Sat–Thu and on Fri from around 2pm–late evening. Most shops operate limited opening hours during religious holidays, if they open at all.

P

Photography

Don't photograph men or, especially, women without asking permission first. The best place to photograph local people is at the Heritage and Diving Village in Dubai or Hatta Heritage Village where they are more used to the attentions of camera-toting tourists.

Postal Services

Poste restante facilities are not available in the UAE. Mail is usually delivered to a PO Box number, not directly to a residence. The main **Abu Dhabi Post Office** is located on Al Sharqi Street. The main **Dubai Post Office** is located on Zabeel Road, Al Karama.

Public Holidays

Religious holidays follow the Islamic calendar and vary annually, usually falling 11 days earlier year on year. The main holidays are the Eid Al Fitr (the end of Ramadan), Eid Al Adha (during the month of the Hajj, or pilgrimage to Mecca), the Islamic New Year, the Prophet's Birthday, and the Ascension of the Prophet. Other holidays with fixed dates include New Year's Day (1 January) and National Day (2 December). Some emirates honour their rulers, as in Abu Dhabi where 6 August is a holiday to mark the accession of former president HH Sheikh Zayed.

R

Religious Services

Islam is the official religion of the UAE, with nationals being mostly Sunni Muslims; however, there is freedom of worship for Christians in church compounds. The main services are held on Friday – the local weekend.

Abu Dhabi

St Andrew's Church
Tel: 02-446 1631, www.standrewauh. org. Between Al Khubairat School and Sheikh Mohammed Bin Zayed Mosque, off Airport Road.
St Joseph's Catholic Cathedral
Tel: 02-446 1929, www.stjosephs abudhabi.org. Between Karamah Street and Airport Road, close to Al Khubairat school.

Al Ain

St Mary's Catholic Church
Tel: 03-721 4417, www.stmarysalain. com.

Dubai

A Hindu temple is located in the souk area of Bur Dubai, near the Abra station. The Christian churches are in two main areas, along Oud Metha Road in Bur Dubai, and in a compound near Jabal Ali village.
Holy Trinity Church
Tel: 04-337 0247, www.holytrinity churchdubai.org.
United Christian Church of Dubai (UCCD)
Tel: 04-884 6623, http://uccdubai. com.
St Mary's Church (Roman Catholic)
Tel: 04-337 0087, www.saintmarys dubai.com.

Sharjah

St Martin's Church
Tel: 06-566 3388, http://stmartins harjah.org.
St Michael's Catholic Church
Tel: 06-566 2424, www. stmichaelssharjah.org.

S

Smoking

In general, the attitude to smoking is similar to that in Western nations. Smoking is banned in all indoor public venues, including restaurants, malls and offices, although you can still smoke in bars and pubs, in most outdoor eating venues, and in most hotel rooms (although a few hotels are now entirely smoke-free). Tougher smoke-free regulations announced in 2015 will gradually come into force. These include a total ban on indoor smoking unless there is a special smoking room provided. During Ramadan, smoking in public anywhere is forbidden during daylight hours.

T

Telephones

Direct international telephone dialling is available from all phones. Local calls within the same city are free from a subscriber's phone. There are coin- and card-operated public phones on the streets and in shopping malls. Prepaid phone cards can be purchased from local

OMAN

THE UAE

LANGUAGE

shops and supermarkets. Some phones also use credit cards, and in many hotels you can make a call and pay for it at the reception desk. Cheap rates for international calls exist between 9pm–7am and all day on Friday.

As charges for international mobile roaming are high, for longer stays consider buying a local prepaid card. Emirati mobile network operators include Etisalat (www.etisalat.ae) and Du (www.du.ae). Mobile phone numbers are identified by the prefix 050 or 055.

Useful numbers

Calling the UAE from abroad: dial 00 971 followed by city code (minus the initial zero) and number.
City Codes Abu Dhabi: 02; Al Ain: 03; Dubai: 04; Fujairah: 09; Ras Al Khaimah: 07; Sharjah, Ajman and Umm al Quwain: 06. There is no need to use the access code when dialling within an emirate. To phone overseas from Oman, dial 00 followed by the national code of the country you are calling.
Directory enquiries 181.

Time Zone

GMT + 4 hours, BST + 3 hours.

Toilets

The majority of places have Western-style toilets, although you may occasionally find Asian-style squat toilets. Your best bet is to

Public telephones.

head for the nearest reputable hotel, while there are also toilets in all shopping malls.

Tourist Information

Local tourist authorities run useful websites with extensive information in English. These include: www.ajmantourism.ae, www.fujairahtourism.ae, www.rasalkhaimahtourism.com, http://sharjahmydestination.ae, www.visitabudhabi.ae, www.visitdubai.com and www.uaetourism.ae.

The Abu Dhabi tourist authority runs a toll-free number (tel: 800 555) and it also has office overseas, including in the UK (1, Knightsbridge, London SW1X 7LY, tel: 20-7201 6400) and in the USA (Trump Tower, 22nd Floor, 725 Fifth Avenue, New York, NY 10022; tel: 212-338 0101). The Department of Tourism and Commerce Marketing in Dubai also has an office in London (4th floor, Nuffield House, 41-46 Piccadilly, London W1J 0DS; tel: 20-7321 6110) and in New York (10th Floor, 215 Park Avenue South, NY10003; tel: 212-575 2262).

V

Visas and Passports

Visas are required by all nationalities except Gulf Co-operation Council members. Citizens of Australia, Canada, New Zealand, the US, all EU countries

and some Asian countries including Singapore, Malaysia and Japan, get an automatic free single-visit visa upon entry –valid for up to 30 days, although it may be extended for extra 30 days for a charge. If you're planning on staying for over 30 days, check with your nearest embassy or consulate in advance, or when you arrive in the country.

Other nationalities visiting the UAE need to arrange their 30-day, non-renewable tourist visas before entry to the UAE at the local Emirati embassy or if they are flying with Emirates, they can do it online on www.emirates.com. Visas can be sponsored by the company they are seeing on business, by friends or family resident in the UAE or by the hotel they are staying at in the UAE. If a hotel obtains a tourist visa for you, you enter the country on their sponsorship for the duration of your stay. You generally have to stay with them for a few nights and you can then travel freely within the UAE for the rest of your stay. It is very important to keep copies of all paperwork, and of your visa, and useful to carry a photocopy of your passport with you. Entry regulations change from time to time so check before your trip.

W

Weights and Meaures

The metric system is used.
1 inch = 2.54 centimetres (cm)
1 foot = 0.30 metres (m)
1 mile = 1.61 kilometres (km)
1 pound = 0.45 kilograms (kg)
1 American gallon = 3.79 litres (l)
1 British gallon = 4.5 litres

Women Travellers

Unlike in neighbouring Saudi Arabia, in the UAE women are not expected to cover up in public (except when visiting mosques), and they are allowed to drive. Dubai in particular is one of the easiest places in the Middle East for lone women to travel around, and many feel comfortable on their own in the evening.

In terms of personal security, women are generally safe; instances of rape are extremely rare, although not unheard of. Exercise standard precautions and never accept lifts from men met in bars and nightclubs. Dressing modestly will help women avoid unwanted attention.

LANGUAGE

UNDERSTANDING THE LANGUAGE

GREETINGS

Hello or **Welcome** *Márhaba, ahlan*
(reply) *áhlayn*
Greetings *As-salám aláykum* (peace be with you)
(reply) *Waláykum as-salám* (and to you peace)
Good morning *Sabáh al-kháyr*
(reply) *Sabáh an-núr* (a morning of light)
Good evening *Misá al-kháyr*
(reply) *Misá an núr*
Goodnight *Tisbáh al-kháyr* (wake up well)
(reply) *Wa ínta min áhlu* (and you are from His people)
Goodbye *Máa Saláma*
How are you? *Káyf hálak?* (to a man)/ *Káyf hálik?* (to a woman)
Fine, thank you *Zayn, al-hámdu, li-la*
Please *Min fádlak* (to a man)/*Min fádlik* (to a woman)
Thank you *Shúkran*
Thanks be to God *Al-hámdu li-llá*

A sign advertising henna hand art in Taqah.

God willing (hopefully) *Inshá allá*
Yes *Náam* or *áiwa*
No *La*

USEFUL PHRASES

What is your name? *Shú ismak?* (to a man)/*Shú ismik?* (to a woman)
My name is... *Ismi...*
Where are you from? *Min wáyn inta?* (for a man)/*Min wáyn inti?* (for a woman)
I am from: England *Ána min Ingíltra*
the United States *Ána min Amérika*
Australia *Ána min Ustrália*
I have 1/2/3 children *Andi walad/ waladun/thalatha awlaad*
How do you say... in Arabic? *Chayf tegool... bil'arabi?*
May I take your photo? *Mumkin sura, min fádlak?* (to a female: *Mumkin sura, min fádlik?*)
Do you speak English? *Btíhki inglízi?/Teh ki ingleezi?*
I speak English *Bíhki inglízi*

I do not speak Arabic *Ma bíhki árabi*
I do not understand *Ma báfham*
Repeat, once more *Kamán márra*
Do you have...? *Ándkum...?*
Is there any...? *Fí...?*
There isn't any... *Ma fí...*
Never mind *Ma'alésh*
It is forbidden... *Mamnú'a*
What is this? *Shú hádha?*
I want *Uríd*
I like *ana bhib*
I don't like *Ana ma bhib*
I do not want *Mauríd*
Hurry up *Yalla/bi súra'a*
Slow down *Shwáyya*
Go away! *Imshi!*
What time is it? *Adáysh as-sáa?/ kam as-sáa?*
How long, how many hours? *Kam sáa?*
You're welcome *Afwan*
OK *Tayib/N'zain/Kwayyis*
Not OK *Mish kwayyis*
Come in/ After you *Tafdal*
Excuse me *Afwan/lau samaht*
Sorry *Afwan/Muta'assif*
Can I...?/It is possible? *Mumkin?*
I don't know *Mabaraf*
No problem *Ma fi mushkila*
Perhaps *Mumkin*
Not possible *Mish mumkin*
What time is it? *Kam as saa?*
How much? *Bikaim?*
How many? *Cham?*
What? *Shu?*
What is this? *Shu hadha?*
I'm ill *Ana mareed*

VOCABULARY

General

embassy *safára*
post office *máktab al-baríd*
stamps *tawábi'a*
bank *bank*
hotel *otél/fúnduq*

OMAN

THE UAE

LANGUAGE

room *ghurfah*
museum *máthaf*
hospital *mustashfa*
doctor *doktor*
chemist *saydaliyeh*
police *shurta/boulees*
ticket *tádhkara*
passport *jiwáz as-sáfar*
good *kuwáys*
not good, bad *mish kuways*
open *maftúh*
closed *musákkar/múghlik*
old *kadeem*
new *jadeed*
big *kabeer*
small *saghir*
beautiful *zayn*
hot *haar*
cold *bareed*
open *maftuh*
shut *mughlag*

Road sign in Arabic.

Eating out/drinking

restaurant *máta'am*
breakfast *futour*
lunch *ghadaa*
dinner *ashaa*
food *ákl*
fish *simich*
meat *láhm*
chicken *dijaj*
mutton *ghanam*
milk *halíb*
cheese *jabne*
butter *zibdeh*
eggs *bayd*
bread *khúbz*
salad *saláta*
honey *'asl*
yoghurt *laban*
jam *murabbeh*
dates *balah*
olives *zatoon*
delicious *ladhidh*
coffee *káhwa*
tea *shay*
beer *beera*
cup *finján*
with sugar *bi súkkar*
without sugar *bidún súkkar*
mineral water *mái ma'adaniya*
glass *gelaas*
bottle *zajaja/botel*
I don't eat meat *Ana ma bakul laham*
I am a vegetarian *Ána nabbáti* (for a man)/*nabbátiya* (for a woman)
Enough, thanks *Bas, shukran*
the bill *al-hisáb*

Getting around

Where...? *Wáyn...?*
How far is it to...? *Kam kiloometre ila...?*
downtown *wást al bálad*
street *shária*
car *sayára*

taxi *táxi*
shared taxi *servís*
bus *bas*
aeroplane *tayára*
airport *matár*
petrol, super *benzín*
diesel *maazout*
to *íla*
from *min*
in *fi*
right *yamín*
left *yassar*
straight *gida*
here *hina*
there *hunak*
near *gareeb*
far *ba'eed*
town *madina*
city *madinat*
north *shimaal*
south *janub*
east *sharq*
west *gharb*

Days and numbers

today *al yoom*
tomorrow *bokhra*
yesterday *ams*
early *mbach'ir/badri*
late *mit'akhir*
day *yoom*
might *layl*
Monday *yoom al ithnayn*
Tuesday *yoom ath thalatha*
Wednesday *yoom al araba'a*
Thursday *yoom al khamees*
Friday *yoom al jum'a*
Saturday *yoom as sabt*
Sunday *yoom al had*
zero *sifir*
one *wáhid*
two *ithnayn*
three *taláta*
four *árba'a*

five *khámsa*
six *sítta*
seven *sába'a*
eight *tamánia*
nine *tísa'a*
ten *áshara*
eleven *hidáshar*
twelve *itnáshar*
twenty *áishreen*
twenty-one *wáhid wa áishreen*
twenty-two *ithnayn wa áishreen*
thirty *thalatheen*
forty *arba'een*
fifty *khamseen*
sixty *sitteen*
seventy *saba'een*
eighty *thimaneen*
ninety *tis'een*
one hundred *maya*
one hundred and fifty *may wa khamseen*
two hundred *mayatayn*
three hundred *thaltamaya*
four hundred *rab'amaya*
five hundred *khamsamaya*
six hundred *sittamaya*
seven hundred *sabamaya*
eight hundred *tamnamaya*
nine hundred *tissamaya*
one thousand *alf*

Shopping

market *souk*
shop *dukkán*
money *fulús*
no money *mish fulús*
cheap *rakhís*
expensive (very) *gháli (jídan)*
too expensive *ktir gháli*
receipt, invoice *fatúra, wásl*
How much does it cost? *Adáysh?/Bikaim?*
I like this *Buhíbb hádha*
I do not like this *Ma buhíbb hádha*

FURTHER READING

HISTORY AND REFERENCE

The Arabs, Peter Mansfield. Broad history of the Middle East, and a look at its recent politics.
A History of the Arab Peoples, A. Hourani. Excellent introduction to the peoples of the region.

The UAE

Beyond Dubai: Seeking Lost Cities in the Emirates, David Millar. An enjoyable travelogue exploring the Emirates and its history.
Dubai Dreams: Inside the Kingdom of Bling, Raymond Barrett. Intermittently entertaining portrait of the 21st-century city, mixing travelogue, history and reportage.
Dubai: Gilded Cage, Syed Ali Dubai. Perceptive look at the role and status of Dubai's massive expat community, from Indian labourers to wealthy Western execs.
Dubai: the Story of the World's Fastest City (published in North America as City of Gold: Dubai and the Dream of Capitalism), Jim Krane. Superbly readable and perceptive portrait of the modern city. Essential reading for anyone interested in the 21st-century Gulf.
Dubai: the Vulnerability of Success, Christopher M. Davidson. Detailed scholarly history of Dubai, accompanied by chapters on the city's social, political and economic workings.
Rashid's Legacy: the Genesis of the Maktoum Family, Graeme Wilson. Depicts the family's history and approach to transforming Dubai.
Sheikh Zayed Life and Times 1918–2004, through the lens of Noor Ali Rashid. The history of a nation personified in its founder.
Telling Tales: an Oral History of Dubai, Julia Wheeler. Photographs accompany insights from some of Dubai's founding citizens. Written by a BBC Gulf correspondent.
This Strange Eventful History: Memoirs of Earlier Days in the UAE

and Oman, Edward Henderson. A good account of how the country evolved.

Oman

Arabian Album: Travels to Oman, Ronald Codrai. Diary extracts and photographs of Oman before the boom.
In the Service of the Sultan, Ian Gardiner. Gripping first-hand account of the Dhofar rebellion told by one of the British combatants involved in it.
Oman and Its Renaissance, Donald Hawley. Portrait of Oman since the 1970 accession of Sultan Qaboos.
Oman: the Islamic Democratic Tradition, Hussein Ghubash. Excellent academic survey of Omani history, seen through the lens of the country's Ibadi traditions.

Send Us Your Thoughts

We do our best to ensure the information in our books is as accurate and up-to-date as possible. The books are updated on a regular basis using local contacts, who painstakingly add, amend and correct as required. However, some details (such as telephone numbers and opening times) are liable to change, and we are ultimately reliant on our readers to put us in the picture.

We welcome your feedback, especially your experience of using the book "on the road". Maybe we recommended a hotel that you liked (or another that you didn't), or you came across a great bar or new attraction we missed.

We will acknowledge all contributions, and we'll offer an Insight Guide to the best letters received.

Please write to us at:
Insight Guides
PO Box 7910
London SE1 1WE
Or email us at:
hello@insightguides.com

PEOPLE AND SOCIETY

Bedouin: Nomads of the Desert, Alan Keohane. Definitive study of traditional Bedu life and their changing role in modern Arabia.
Don't They Know It's Friday? Jeremy Williams, published by Motivate. Comprehensive guide to doing business in the Middle East.
Explorers of Arabia, Zahra Freeth and Victor Winstone. Profiles of important early travellers.
The Merchants, Michael Field. Focusing on nine of the Gulf's prominent families; gives a good impression of how society has changed since oil.
The New Arabians, Peter Mansfield. A wide-ranging look at post-oil Gulf society by one of the most respected writers on the region. Sadly, it stops in the early 1980s.
Oman Before 1970, Ian Skeet. A sympathetic portrait of pre-oil Oman, giving a wealth of social detail which is still relevant today.
Oman: Under Arabian Skies, Rory Patrick Allen. Oman seen through the eyes of a British expat.
Travelling the Sands, Andrew Taylor, published by Motivate. Explorers of the Arabian peninsula.
UAE – Culture Smart! The Essential Guide to Customs and Culture, John Walsh. Useful guide to customs and etiquette.
Understanding Arabs: A Contemporary Guide to Arab Society, Margaret K. Nydell. Accessible guide to the cultures and customs of the Arab world.
Understanding the Arab Culture, Jehad Al-Omari. Guide to developing successful business relationships in the Middle East.

WOMEN

Arab Women: Old Boundaries, New Frontiers, Judith E. Tucker. Collection of women's writing on the changing lives of Arab women.
Behind the Veil in Arabia: Women in Oman, Unni Wikan. Fairly academic,

but a good book on Gulf customs and traditions, and women's role in rural society.

Mother Without a Mask, Patricia Holton. A personal account from a Western woman who lived with a UAE family.

Women of Sand & Myrrh, Hanan al Shaykh. Collection of women's stories.

COFFEE-TABLE BOOKS

Crossing the Sands, Wilfred Thesiger, published by Motivate. Chronicles the five years the writer spent with the Bedu.

Dubai: A City Portrait, Patrick Lichfield. Lavish coffee-table book.

Dubai 24 Hours, by Michael Tobias. The city as experienced by a team of Dubai's leading photographers during the course of a single day.

Dubai: the Arabian Dream, David Saunders. Account of Dubai's rapid development, illustrated with many stunning photographs.

The Emirates by the First Photographers, William Facey and Gillian Grant. Historical photographs of the region.

Images of Women – the Portrayal of Women in Photography of the Middle East 1860–1950, Sarah Graham-Brown.

The UAE Formative Years, 1965–75. A Collection of Historical Photographs, Ramesh Shukla.

The UAE: Visions of Change, Noor Ali Rashid. Photographs from 1958 to 1997.

Visions of a Nomad, Wilfred Thesiger. Thesiger's photographs taken over 50 years cover the Arab world as well as Asia and Africa.

ARCHAEOLOGY AND GEOLOGY

Atlantis of the Sands: The Search for the Lost City of Ubar, Ranulph Fiennes. Account of Fiennes's role in the rediscovery of the legendary city of Ubar.

Field Guide to the Geology of Oman, Samir S. Hanna. Invaluable practical guide to Oman's unique geology, with 17 field trips.

Filling in the Blanks, Peter Hellyer, published by Motivate. Discoveries made in Abu Dhabi and on the island of Umm Al Nar.

Oman's Geological Heritage, Michael Hughes Clarke. Superb coffee-table book full of photographs of Oman's strange landscapes

and geological formations, with informative accompanying text.

The Road to Ubar: Finding the Atlantis of the Sands, Nicholas Clapp. Absorbing account of Clapp's 20-year search for the lost city of Ubar – and far better than Ranulph Fiennes's account of the same quest.

ISLAM

The Caged Virgin – a Muslim Woman's Cry for Reason, Ayaan Hirsi Ali. Controversial attempts to free women from oppressive Islamic practices.

Islam and the West, Bernard Lewis. A view on the East–West relationship by the Professor of Arabic at Edinburgh University.

A New Introduction to Islam, Daniel W. Brown. A clear and well-organised look at Muslim beliefs as well as the development of Islamic studies.

Nine Parts of Desire – the Hidden World of Islamic Women, Geraldine Brooks. Based on the author's personal experiences of talking to women in the Gulf.

TRAVEL WRITING/ NOVELS

Arabia Through the Looking Glass, Jonathan Raban. An excellent and amusing overview of the different Gulf and Middle Eastern countries.

Arabian Destiny, Edward Henderson. Fascinating autobiography covering Henderson's time in Dubai in the late 1940s and early 1950s and his delicate negotiations with the Omani tribes during the exploration for oil.

Arabian Sands, Wilfred Thesiger. Journeys made from 1945–50 in and around the Empty Quarter of Oman, Saudi Arabia and the UAE.

Dubai, Robin Moore. Blockbuster novel by *French Connection* author Robin Moore, set in late 1960s Dubai and with a Hollywood-style cast of arms dealers, gold smugglers, oil-prospectors and other soldiers of fortune.

Dubai Tales, Mohammed al Murr. Short stories set in Dubai and area.

Dubai Wives, Zvezdana Rashkovich. An entertaining novel set in Dubai from an author who is a Dubai wife herself.

The Sand Fish: a Novel from Dubai, Maha Gargash. Dubai and the northern UAE during the 1950s seen through the eyes of a rebellious teenage girl.

Sandstorms – Days and Nights in Arabia, Peter Theroux. Amusing observations of expatriate life.

Sultan in Oman, Jan Morris. Classic account of Morris's journey through 1950s Oman with Sultan Said bin Taimur.

The Sindbad Voyage, Tim Severin. Compelling account of Severin's efforts to build a traditional Omani dhow, and then sail it to China.

The Son of a Duck is a Floater, Primrose Arnander and Ashkhain Skipwith. A collection of Arab proverbs and sayings.

Travels with a Tangerine: a Journey in the Footnotes of Ibn Battutah, Tim Mackintosh-Smith. Beautifully observed account of Mackintosh-Smith's journey through the Middle East following in the footsteps of Ibn Battuta, with two fine chapters on Oman.

The Wink of the Mona Lisa, Mohammed al Murr. Short stories by a leading UAE writer.

ART AND ARCHITECTURE

Architectural Heritage of the Gulf, Shirley Kay and Dariush Zandi. Traditional architectural styles of the UAE.

Forts of Oman, Walter Dinteman, published by Motivate. Pictorial account of the role of the fort in Oman's history.

Omani Silver, Ruth Hawley. A great book for professional and amateur collectors of Gulf silver.

ARABIC LANGUAGE

Berlitz Arabic Guaranteed, an all-audio course comprising simple lessons on four audio CDs. A free downloadable audio script is available.

Berlitz Arabic in 60 Minutes, all-audio course with more than 250 words and phrases. Audio script provided.

Berlitz Arabic Phrase Book & Dictionary, a two-way dictionary of useful words accompanies language on new technologies, business and general conversation.

Very Simple Arabic Script, James Peters. The title says it all.

WILDLIFE AND FLORA

Arabia: Sand, Sea, Sky, Michael McKinnon. Natural history of the peninsula's land and shore.

Beachcombers' Guide to the Gulf, Tony Woodward, published by Motivate. Useful for anyone interested in knowing more about what they see on the Gulf beaches.

The Birds of Oman, M. Gallagher and M. Woodcock. The book's large size makes it impractical as a field guide, but it is an attractive volume.

Birdwatching Guide to Oman, Dave E. Sargeant, Hanne Eriksen, Jens Eriksen. Useful practical guide to birdwatching in the sultanate, with details of top birdwatching sites, bird lists, and photos and maps

Butterflies of Oman, T.B. Larsen. A 1984 reprint of a first edition, with descriptions and colour illustrations of more than 70 species.

Common Birds in Oman, Hanne and Jens Eriksen. Comprehensive background on the country's avifauna, complete with 400 photos.

Mammals of the Southern Gulf, Christian Gross. Photographic account of the amazing variety of sea life.

Seashells of Eastern Arabia, edited by S. Peter Dance. One thousand photographs and drawings, featuring more than 1,270 species.

Snorkelling and Diving in Oman, Robert Baldwin and Rod Salm. Maps and descriptions of the best places to enjoy Oman's ocean life.

OFF-ROAD DRIVING AND TREKKING

Off-Road in the Emirates, Dariush Zandi, published by Motivate. Spiral-bound guide to 15 routes.

The Off-Roader's Manual, Jehanbaz Ali Khan.

Oman Off-Road and UAE Off-Road, published by Explorer Publishing. Excellent guides featuring satellite imaging and GPS co-ordinates for 20 routes.

Oman Trekking, published by Explorer Publishing. In-depth routes and maps covering 12 of the country's top treks.

OTHER INSIGHT GUIDES

With their expert text and stunning images, the classic Insight Guides inspire and motivate, help with advance planning and provide a great souvenir of your trip. Titles in this region include: *Egypt*, *Jordan* and *Morocco*.

Insight **Explore Guides** are a stylish series of self-guided walks and tours, written by local experts and designed to help travellers of every interest and taste get the most out of a destination. Titles include Marrakesh and, new in 2017, Dubai.

OMAN

THE UAE

LANGUAGE

CREDITS

Insight Guide Credits

Distribution
UK
Dorling Kindersley Ltd
A Penguin Group company
80 Strand, London, WC2R 0RL
sales@uk.dk.com

United States
Ingram Publisher Services
1 Ingram Boulevard, PO Box 3006,
La Vergne, TN 37086-1986
ips@ingramcontent.com

Australia and New Zealand
Woodslane
10 Apollo St, Warriewood,
NSW 2102, Australia
info@woodslane.com.au

Worldwide
Apa Publications (Singapore) Pte
7030 Ang Mo Kio Avenue 5
08-65 Northstar @ AMK
Singapore 569880
apasin@singnet.com.sg

Printing
CTPS-China

First Edition 1998
Third Edition 2015

Editor: Carine Tracanelli
Author: Katarzyna Marcinkowska,
Gavin Thomas
Head of Production: Rebeka Davies
Update Production: AM Services
Pictures: Richard Cooke
Cartography: original cartography
Berndtson & Berndtson, updated by
Carte

Legend

City maps

Freeway/Highway/Motorway
Divided Highway
Main Roads
Minor Roads
Pedestrian Roads
Steps
Footpath
Railway
Funicular Railway
Cable Car
Tunnel
City Wall
Important Building
Built Up Area
Other Land
Transport Hub
Park
Pedestrian Area
Bus Station
Tourist Information
Main Post Office
Cathedral/Church
Mosque
Synagogue
Statue/Monument
Beach
Airport

Regional maps

Freeway/Highway/Motorway
(with junction)
Freeway/Highway/Motorway
(under construction)
Divided Highway
Main Road
Secondary Road
Minor Road
Track
Footpath
International Boundary
State/Province Boundary
National Park/Reserve
Marine Park
Ferry Route
Marshland/Swamp
Glacier   Salt Lake
Airport/Airfield
Ancient Site
Border Control
Cable Car
Castle/Castle Ruins
Cave
Chateau/Stately Home
Church/Church Ruins
Crater
Lighthouse
Mountain Peak
Place of Interest
Viewpoint

Contributors

This new edition of *Insight Guide
Oman & the UAE* was updated by
Katarzyna Marcinkowska, an
editor, writer and photographer with
extensive experience in travel
publishing who has worked on
hundreds of travel guides. She is a
keen traveller and enjoys
contemporary art museums as much
as the great outdoors, particularly
hiking and yachting.

The book builds on the
comprehensive work of **Gavin
Thomas**, who thoroughly reworked
the last edition of the book. Gavin
is a travel writer who specialises in
the Gulf and South Asia; he has
written or contributed to several
titles for Insight Guides. This book
was commissioned by **Carine
Tracanelli** and indexed by **Andrea
Bastien**.

About Insight Guides

Insight Guides have more than
40 years' experience of publishing
high-quality, visual travel guides. We
produce 400 full-colour titles, in both
print and digital form, covering more
than 200 destinations across the
globe, in a variety of formats to meet
your different needs.

　　Insight Guides are written by
local authors, whose expertise is
evident in the extensive historical
and cultural background features.

Each destination is carefully
researched by regional experts to
ensure our guides provide the very
latest information. All the reviews
in **Insight Guides** are independent;
we strive to maintain an impartial
view. Our reviews are carefully
selected to guide you to the best
places to eat, go out and shop, so
you can be confident that when
we say a place is special, we really
mean it.

INDEX

Main references are in bold type

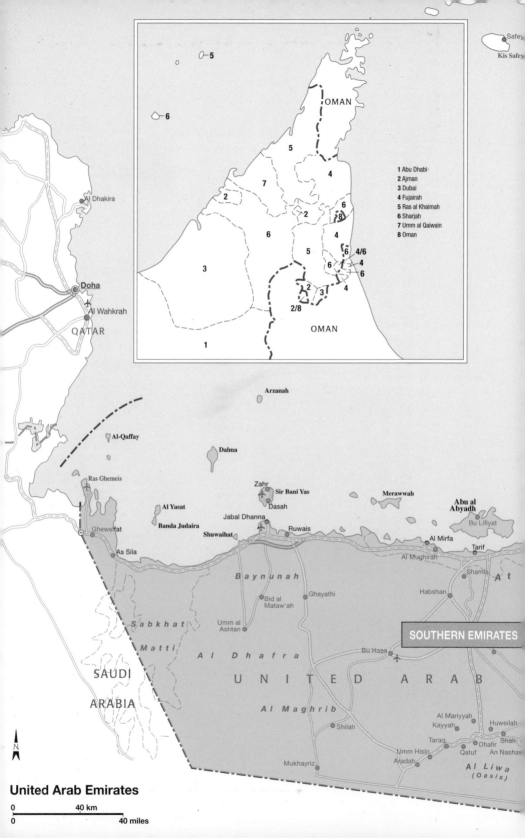

OMAN

1 Abu Dhabi
2 Ajman
3 Dubai
4 Fujairah
5 Ras al Khaimah
6 Sharjah
7 Umm al Qaiwain
8 Oman

OMAN

5

6

5

7

2

6

4

2

6
8

4

6

4/6

5

6

4

6

2

3

4

6

2/8

1

3

Safey
Kis Safey

Al Dhakira

Doha

Al Wahkrah

QATAR

Arzanah

Al-Qaffay

Dalma

Zahr
Sir Bani Yas
Dasah

Merawwah

**Abu al
Abyadh**

Ras Ghemeis

Al Yasat

Jabal Dhanna

Bu Lifiyat

Banda Judaira

Shuwaihat

Ruwais

Al Mirfa

Tarif

Ghewelfat

Al Mughirah

As Sila

B a y n u n a h

Shamis

A t

Bid al
Mataw'ah

Ghayathi

Habshan

S a b k h a t

Umm al
Ashtan

SOUTHERN EMIRATES

M a t t i

Bu Hasa

SAUDI

A l D h a f r a

U N I T E D   A R A B

ARABIA

A l M a g h r i b

Al Mariyyah

Huweilah

Kayyah

Shah

Shilah

Taraq

Dhafir

An Nashas

Umm Hisin

Qatuf

Mukhayriz

Aradah

*A l L i w a
(O a s i s)*

N

United Arab Emirates

0   40 km

0   40 miles